D. H. LAWRENCE: THE CRITICAL HERITAGE

THE CRITICAL HERITAGE SERIES

GENERAL EDITOR: B. C. SOUTHAM, M.A., B.LITT.(OXON)
Formerly Department of English, Westfield College, University of London

---

Volumes in the series include

JANE AUSTEN	B. C. Southam
BROWNING	Boyd Litzinger *St. Bonaventure University* and Donald Smalley *University of Illinois*
BYRON	Andrew Rutherford *University of Aberdeen*
COLERIDGE	J. R. de J. Jackson *Victoria College, Toronto*
DICKENS	Philip Collins *University of Leicester*
THOMAS HARDY	R. G. Cox *University of Manchester*
HENRY JAMES	Roger Gard *Queen Mary College, London*
JAMES JOYCE (2 vols.)	Robert H. Deming *University of Miami*
MILTON	John T. Shawcross *University of Wisconsin*
SCOTT	John O. Hayden *University of California, Davis*
SWIFT	Kathleen Williams *University of California, Riverside*
SWINBURNE	Clyde K. Hyder
TENNYSON	J. D. Jump *University of Manchester*
THACKERAY	Geoffrey Tillotson and Donald Hawes *Birkbeck College, London*
TROLLOPE	Donald Smalley *University of Illinois*

D. H. LAWRENCE

THE CRITICAL HERITAGE

Edited by

R. P. DRAPER

Senior Lecturer in English,
University of Leicester

NEW YORK

BARNES & NOBLE, INC.

First published in Great Britain 1970
Published in the United States of America 1970
by Barnes & Noble Inc., New York, N.Y.
© R. P. Draper 1970

SBN 389 01088 X

Printed in Great Britain

General Editor's Preface

The reception given to a writer by his contemporaries and near-contemporaries is evidence of considerable value to the student of literature. On one side we learn a great deal about the state of criticism at large and in particular about the development of critical attitudes towards a single writer; at the same time, through private comments in letters, journals or marginalia, we gain an insight upon the tastes and literary thought of individual readers of the period. Evidence of this kind helps us to understand the writer's historical situation, the nature of his immediate reading-public, and his response to these pressures.

The separate volumes in the *Critical Heritage Series* present a record of this early criticism. Clearly for many of the highly-productive and lengthily-reviewed nineteenth- and twentieth-century writers, there exists an enormous body of material; and in these cases the volume editors have made a selection of the most important views, significant for their intrinsic critical worth or for their representative quality— perhaps even registering incomprehension!

For earlier writers, notably pre-eighteenth century, the materials are much scarcer and the historical period has been extended, sometimes far beyond the writer's lifetime, in order to show the inception and growth of critical views which were initially slow to appear.

In each volume the documents are headed by an Introduction, discussing the material assembled and relating the early stages of the author's reception to what we have come to identify as the critical tradition. The volumes will make available much material which would otherwise be difficult of access and it is hoped that the modern reader will be thereby helped towards an informed understanding of the ways in which literature has been read and judged.

B.C.S.

Contents

CONTENTS

Birds, Beasts and Flowers (1923)

The Boy in the Bush (1924)

St. Mawr (1925)

Reflections on the Death of a Porcupine (1925)

The Plumed Serpent (1926)

Lady Chatterley's Lover (1928)

CONTENTS

Collected Poems (1928)

The Paintings of D. H. Lawrence (1929)

Pansies (1929)

Pornography and Obscenity (1929)

Obituaries, 1930

I wish to thank the following for permission to reprint copyright extracts or complete items from the sources listed below:

Charles Scribner's Sons for *Critical Woodcuts* by Stuart Sherman: © 1912/1924/1922/1913 by the New York Times Company. Reprinted by permission: Richard Aldington, the *Saturday Review* and Mme. Catherine Guillaume for 'D. H. Lawrence as Poet' by Richard Aldington: Messrs. William Heinemann, the Estate of the late Mrs. Frieda Lawrence, and Lawrence Pollinger Ltd, for *The Complete Short Stories of D. H. Lawrence, Sea and Sardinia, Lady Chatterley's Lover, The Rainbow, Sons and Lovers, Women in Love, The Letters of D. H. Lawrence, A Propos of Lady Chatterley's Lover, The Short Novels of D. H. Lawrence: The Teacher*, for article by H. Yoxall appearing in *Schoolmaster: The Times/Times Literary Supplement* for articles, nos. 2, 31, 40, 55, 60, 62, 77, 83, 85, 89 (all unsigned): Associated Newspapers Ltd. for articles from the *Daily Chronicle*, by Violet Hunt, Harold Massingham, for articles from *Daily News* by Robert Lynd and no. 6 (unsigned); for article from the *Westminster Gazette*, no. 16 (unsigned); for article by James Douglas in *Star*; for articles from the *Guardian* by Allan Monkhouse and Edward Garnett: The society of Authors as the literary representative of the Estate of John Middleton Murry for extracts from his reviews on D. H. Lawrence: The Society of Authors as the literary representative of the Estate of John Galsworthy for his letter to J. B. Pinker: The Society of Authors as the literary representative of the Estate of Katherine Mansfield for her extract from *The Scrapbook*: The Society of Authors as the literary representative of the Estate of Lascelles Abercrombie for his review of *Sons and Lovers*: copyright New York Herald Tribune for reviews by Katherine Anne Porter and Mark Van Doren in New York Herald Tribune Books: Rosemary Manning for Alyse Gregory's review in *Dial*: Myfanwy Thomas for Edward Thomas' review in *Bookman*: Mrs. Valerie Eliot for permission to reprint an excerpt from 'The Contemporary Novel' by T. S. Eliot (original English text of 'Le Roman Anglais Contemporain'), and his review of J. M. Murry's *Son of Woman*: reprinted by permission of *New York Post* © 1923, New

York Post Corporation for Stuart Sherman's review in *New York Evening Post Literary Review*: published by courtesy of the *Daily Telegraph* for reviews in *Morning Post* (Nos. 4 and 10, unsigned); the *New Statesman* for review in *Athenaeum* (unsigned, no. 8); for reviews in *Nation* by Edwin Muir, and unsigned, nos. 14 and 20; for reviews in *New Statesman* by J. C. Squire, John Franklin, Edward Sackville West, T. W. Earp and, unsigned, no. 87; for *Nation and Athenaeum* review by E. M. Forster: reprinted by permission of Ezra Pound and Faber and Faber Ltd., review by Ezra Pound of D. H. Lawrence's *Love Poems and Others* in *New Freewoman*: the *Evening Standard* for articles by Arnold Bennett and nos. 15 and 25 (unsigned): Illustrated Newspapers Ltd. for Clement Shorter's review in the *Sphere*: the *Glasgow Herald* for Catherine Carswell's review and the *Glasgow Herald's* obituary of D. H. Lawrence: Mr. David Garnett for 'Art and the Moralists: Mr. D. H. Lawrence's Work' by Edward Garnett, from *Friday Nights*, published by Jonathan Cape: Conrad Aiken for his review of '*Look! We have Come Through!*' in *Dial*: Signe Toksvig (Mrs. Francis Hackett) for two reviews by the late Francis Hackett: the Editor of *Poetry* for review by John Gould Fletcher, copyright 1919 by the Modern Poetry Association: Mrs. Dorothea M. Shanks for 'Mr. D. H. Lawrence: Some Characteristics', by Edward Shanks: the *Spectator* for articles by L. P. Hartley and no. 57 (unsigned): the Foundation for Economic Education, Inc., for Edwin Muir's review in the *Freewoman*: V. S. Pritchett for his review in *Fortnightly Review*: *Editions Gallimard* for the Preface by André Malraux to the French edition of *Lady Chatterley's Lover*: Mr. Raglan Squire and the Observer for review by J. C. Squire; Mr. E. M. Forster and *The Listener* for text of broadcast talk by Mr. Forster: Curtis Brown Ltd. for *Reputations* by Douglas Goldring: Mr. Louis Untermeyer for his article in *New Republic*.

I have tried to locate the copyright owners for each extract, but I regret that this has not been possible in every instance. My debt to such Lawrence scholars as Harry T. Moore and Warren Roberts, and to the late Edward Nehls, is necessarily extensive, and I gladly acknowledge this. I also owe a particular debt to those scholars who have worked on the history of Lawrence criticism, among whom I am especially grateful to Mr. John Worthen for allowing me to make use of his researches into the critical reception of Lawrence's earlier novels. Miss Lucy Edwards of the Nottingham Public Library and the staff of the University of Leicester Library have given me much help in locating and collecting not only the extracts here reprinted, but also the much larger number that had to be studied before this selection could be made; and I should like to thank the University of Leicester for a research grant which enabled me to make visits to many other libraries.

NOTE ON THE TEXT

The materials printed in this volume follow the original texts in all important respects. Lengthy extracts from the novels and poems of D. H. Lawrence have been omitted whenever they are quoted merely to illustrate the work in question. These omissions are clearly indicated in the text. Typographical errors in the originals have been silently corrected and the form of reference to titles has been regularized.

Bk   *Bookman*

Cr   *Criterion*

CP   *The Complete Poems of D. H. Lawrence*, ed. V. de S. Pinto and Warren Roberts. Heinemann, London, 1964. Two vols.

In   *Independent* (New York)

L   *The Collected Letters of D. H. Lawrence*, ed. Harry T. Moore. Heinemann, London, 1962. Two vols.

LM   *London Mercury*

MG   *Manchester Guardian*

N   *Nation* (London)

NNY   *Nation* (New York)

N&A   *Nation and Athenaeum*

Nehls   *D. H. Lawrence: A Composite Biography*, ed. Edward Nehls. University of Wisconsin Press, Madison, 1957–9. Three vols.

NYTBR   *New York Times Book Review*

NR   *New Republic*

NS   *New Statesman*

Ph   *Phoenix: The Posthumous Papers of D. H. Lawrence*, ed. Edward D. McDonald. Heinemann, London, 1936— reprint of 1961

Ph II   *Phoenix II*, ed. Warren Roberts and Harry T. Moore. Heinemann, London, 1968

SR   *Saturday Review*

ST   *Sunday Times*

T   *Times* (London)

TLS   *T.L.S.* (*Times Literary Supplement*)

WR   *A Bibliography of D. H. Lawrence*, by Warren Roberts. Rupert Hart-Davis, London, 1963.

Introduction

D. H. Lawrence attracted an enormous amount of commentary during his life, of which this selection is a comparatively small part. After the suppression of *The Rainbow* in 1915 he rapidly acquired a certain notoriety to which he responded by being defiant and often contemptuous of his critics. Before then he had been more sensitive to reviews and more willing to modify his work, though he seems always to have had an intense conviction of the importance of his art and a consequent unwillingness to be deflected from his purposes even by such friendly advice as he received from Edward Garnett—and most of his critics were much less friendly. Towards the end of his life he ran into further notoriety through *Lady Chatterley's Lover* and *Pansies*, his paintings met with outright hostility, and at his death the obituarists wrote about him with an animosity rarely displayed on such occasions.

In spite of the heat thus generated some interesting and perceptive criticism was produced; few of his books were actually ignored. And although he was not a favourite among literary circles—after his initial discovery by Ford Madox Ford—most prominent critics commented on some or other of his works. In the present selection I have tried to represent this variety, and to indicate how Lawrence reacted to the critics. Several passages, of limited critical value, have been chosen for their contemporary significance. An author's relationship with his public is in itself a legitimate subject of interest, and I hope this book will do something to satisfy that interest; but I also hope that it will make available some intrinsically useful criticism that would otherwise lie neglected in the dusty files of old newspapers.

The early work

Lawrence's very first publication was *A Prelude*, entered for the *Nottinghamshire Guardian* Christmas competition, 1907, under the name 'Rosalind'. The story won first prize, and two other pieces that Lawrence submitted were also given honourable mention. The judges' comments on these entries were conventional, but encouraging. *A Prelude* had a simple theme 'handled with a freshness and simplicity altogether charming'; and one of the other stories, *Legend*, was praised for its 'vivid realism'.[1]

For the winning entry Lawrence had used the address of his early sweetheart, Jessie Chambers (the Miriam of *Sons and Lovers*), and it was she who helped him to his first appearance in print under his own name by sending some of his poems to the *English Review*. These attracted the attention of the editor, Ford Madox Hueffer, who prided himself on his ability to spot new talent. Hueffer, better known under the name which he later adopted of Ford Madox Ford, became a considerable novelist himself. Four of Lawrence's poems were printed in the November 1909 issue of the *English Review*, where they were noticed by Henry Yoxall, editor of *The Schoolmaster*, who wrote some favourable comments on them in his 'Books and Pictures' column (No. 1). Ford claims that Jessie also sent him *Odour of Chrysanthemums*, but he is not the most reliable of memoirists, and the account he gives in *Portraits from Life* of reading the first paragraph and immediately recognizing its genius may well be a heightened version of the truth. His analysis is nonetheless brilliant, and touches on those things that would be likely to arouse the interest of a professionally minded editor (see Nehls, i, 107-9).

Another reason for Ford's interest was that he saw in Lawrence a spokesman for the working class. 'It is to be remembered', he says, 'that, in the early decades of this century, we enormously wanted authentic projections of that type of life which hitherto had gone quite unvoiced.' Gissing, H. G. Wells, Arnold Bennett and Mark Rutherford had written of the lower middle classes, but 'the completely different class of the artisan, the industrialist, and the unskilled labourer was completely unvoiced and unknown' (Nehls, i, 109). Violet Hunt, who was also on the staff of the *English Review*, and later became the wife of Ford Madox Ford (although their marriage was never properly legalized), found a similar significance in Lawrence's first novel, *The White Peacock* (1911). Her unusual review (No. 5) in the *Daily Chronicle* heralded it as a 'political document developed along the lines of a passionate romance' of great importance to the rulers of Great Britain, for it revealed to them the hitherto unsuspected intellectual capacities of the people, who now had the power to vote them into, or out of, office.

Ford and Violet Hunt both helped to smooth the way for the publication of *The White Peacock*. Heinemann's reader accepted it with alacrity, but some changes had to be made to meet the prudish taste of the time[2]—a foretaste of the greater difficulties which were to come with *Sons and Lovers* and *The Rainbow* (published in England by Duckworth and Methuen respectively). The first English edition, consisting of 1500 copies, came out in January 1911, and must have sold quite rapidly, as it was reprinted in March. A third impression did not, however, appear until 1921. Since then the book has sold steadily, both in Heinemann's hardback edition (amounting at present to some 250,000 copies) and in the various cheap editions, including Penguin, for which the sales must be more numerous still.

Once out *The White Peacock* 'took the town', according to Violet Hunt, and Catherine Carswell, the novelist and later close friend of Lawrence, calls it 'a *succes d'estime*'. These phrases probably refer to its reception in literary society. The reviewers were more cautious. Current ideas about the well-made novel and distaste for French realism made them uneasy about Lawrence's methods and material. The *Athenaeum* (25 February 1911), not the only paper to mistake the author for a woman, found 'her' less crude than Zola, but still 'needlessly frank to a fastidious mind', and the *Nottinghamshire Guardian* (21 February 1911) thought the novel a not very happy attempt 'to write about English rural life and colliery villages in the style of the French naturalists'. The *Scotsman* (9 February 1911), by contrast, praised the presentation of country life, but completely ignored its imaginative qualities. The playwright, Allan Monkhouse (No. 3) found the book promising, but was unhappy with its narrative method, as was the *Morning Post* (No. 4)—though the latter was a sympathetic review which Lawrence himself called 'long and good'. Only the critic of the *Daily News* (No. 6) was completely hostile, and he so extravagantly that Lawrence could take his annoyance as a compliment. Nearly everybody else balanced this negative criticism with some recognition of the new writer's talent, especially for natural description, so that all in all Lawrence could count his first novel a modest success.

In view of what was said about the structure of *The White Peacock* it is interesting to note that as early as 1908 Lawrence himself, though prepared to admit many faults, declared that he would defend its construction throughout (*L* 11 November), and a hint of his method is given in the following remarks recorded by Jessie Chambers:

> The usual plan is to take two couples and develop their relationships, [he said]. Most of George Eliot's are on that plan. Anyhow, I don't want a plot, I should be bored with it. I shall try two couples for a start.[3]

His enthusiasm for *Anna Karenina*, also recorded by Jessie, would further support his belief that the ostensibly loose method of parallelism was well suited to a novel of personal relations. Nevertheless, he worked on his next novel, *The Trespasser*, very carefully, paying special attention to its form. To the author and critic, Edward Garnett, who was at this time acting as publisher's editor to Duckworth's, Lawrence wrote anxiously: 'I hope the thing is knitted firm—I hate those pieces where the stitch is slack and loose' (*L* 21 January 1912). When the book was published several critics again attacked its lack of construction, but the *Morning Post* reviewer (No. 10), praised its 'unusual artistic unity', thus showing a second time his friendliness and perceptiveness with regard to Lawrence.

The Trespasser, more so than *The White Peacock*, was an erotic book, and according to Ford Madox Ford the unrevised version 'much —oh, but much!—more phallic than is the book as it stands' (Nehls, i, 121). If published, he told Lawrence, it would damage his reputation perhaps permanently. 'Is the book *so* erotic?' Lawrence inquired of Garnett. 'I don't want to be talked about in an *Ann Veronica* fashion' (*L* 18 December 1911). In the event, either because Ford exaggerated, or because Garnett helped to tone it down, *The Trespasser* did not have this effect. The *Outlook* (29 June 1912) wrote caustically that the older artists 'who knew the value of the decent fig-leaf, could have taught Mr. Lawrence much', but the *Westminster Gazette* managed to find a moral lesson in *The Trespasser*: rightly understood it led

the mind to a deeper recognition of the inexorable physical and moral laws which, holding humanity in bondage, work out for every trespasser a certain doom.
(8 June 1912)

More to the point, the critic of the *Manchester Guardian*, Basil de Selincourt, emphasized the book's poetic and psychological treatment of love (No. 9), and the *New York Times* stressed the unusualness of Lawrence's focus upon 'the woman of dreams' rather than the traditional *femme fatale* (No. 11).

Lawrence's first volume of poetry, *Love Poems* (1913), met, on the whole, with more judicious response than his earliest novels. Two poets, one English, Edward Thomas (No. 12), and one American, Ezra Pound (No. 13), welcomed him as an ally in the cause of a new kind of expression that should be modern in subject-matter and independent of the jaded poetic diction inherited from late nineteenth-century verse. Pound thought Lawrence had 'learned the proper treatment of modern subjects' before he did himself (letter to Harriet Monroe, March 1913), and in the two reviews which he wrote of *Love Poems* he gave particularly high praise to the dialect poems. (The second of these is included here as it is slightly more detailed than the first.) The *Nation* also placed Lawrence in the ranks of the moderns, and praised his 'vivid, unexpected images' (No. 14). Above all, Lawrence was seen as a poet of strength and individuality—for better or for worse, a force to be reckoned with, and distinctively modern.

Sons and Lovers

It is usually supposed that with *Sons and Lovers* (1913) Lawrence 'arrived' as a major novelist. How many copies of the original edition were printed is unknown, but the book does not seem to have sold as well as Lawrence hoped. It was not reprinted until 1922, but from then onwards new editions were frequent, and sales figures for the early 1930s indicate that it was by that time the most popular of Lawrence's novels (see *WR* 23).

Reviews, however, were plentiful, and Lawrence himself said that he liked them (*L* 21 June). But, if the tone was laudatory, much of the detail was unfavourable, and few critics showed real understanding of the novel's theme. It was, for example, thought *fortunate* for Mrs. Morel that Paul supplied her husband's place (*ST* 1 June 1913), and admiration for 'the heroic little mother' (No. 21) often led critics to miss the significance of her destructive influence on her sons. The complaints made about Lawrence's previous novels were also repeated with regard to *Sons and Lovers*. He was again criticized for neglect of form and his treatment of sex was found even more distressing. Lawrence could not have been surprised at this, for he had already encountered difficulties at the publishing stage. Heinemann's, the firm to which Lawrence first sent the manuscript of *Sons and Lovers*, rejected it, and Lawrence wrote to his friend and former teaching colleague, A. W. McLeod, giving two not altogether consistent reasons which he supposed to account for the rejection: 'Heinemann refused it because he was cross with me for going to Duckworth—refused it on grounds of its indecency, if you please' (*L* ?17 September 1912). In 1925, looking back on this episode, Lawrence seemed to have decided that indecency was the main reason, for he wrote that William Heinemann 'thought *Sons and Lovers* one of the dirtiest books he had ever read. He refused to publish it. I should not have thought the deceased gentleman's reading had been so circumspectly narrow' (*Ph* 233). Duckworth's accepted the novel, and published it in May 1913, but not without making several cuts. Edward Garnett was given a comparatively free hand by Lawrence to make whatever omissions he thought necessary, as Lawrence urgently required money. Most of these cuts seem to have been made on grounds of length, but the correspondence between Lawrence and Garnett suggests that some passages may have been objected to because of their sexual explicitness. (For example, a paragraph was cut describing Paul's kissing Clara's breasts and knees.[4])

The book, however, still remained too erotic for many critics. The well-known essayist and literary critic, Robert Lynd, referred to 'the hot-houses of amorous writing' and said that Lawrence had 'an exaggerated sense of the physical side of love' (*Daily News*, 7 June 1913). The *Academy* critic complained that there was 'no delicacy nor reticence about his work. . . . Evidently he has found life a very bitter, ugly thing, with no joy in it, nor any warmth but the warmth of lust' (28 June 1913). The *Nation* (No. 20) made some criticism on artistic grounds, but what lay behind the reviewer's objections was a reluctance to face Lawrence's meaning. The book was disturbing, as, in a different manner, it was for the *Westminster Gazette*, which saw in Paul an example of that modern phenomenon, the unheroic hero (No. 16). To the *Daily Chronicle* reviewer, Harold Massingham, however, this was an aspect of Lawrence's commendable realism (No. 17), and for the poet, Lascelles Abercrombie (No. 19), his power to disturb the ordinary reader's complacency was something to be applauded. Yet these last two perceptive critics joined in the fairly general condemnation of the book's 'architecture', and just as Lawrence's efforts in *The Trespasser* to shape his novel went unnoticed by all except the *Morning Post*, so only a minority (see Nos. 15 and 18) recognized the formal achievement of *Sons and Lovers*.[5]

Slight as it was, perhaps the most influential comment on *Sons and Lovers* was that made by Henry James in 'The Younger Generation' (*TLS* 19 March and 2 April 1914, reprinted in *Notes on Novelists*, 1914), where Lawrence was said to 'hang in the dusty rear' of Hugh Walpole, Gilbert Cannan and Compton Mackenzie. How carefully James read *Sons and Lovers* is open to doubt. His friend and fellow-novelist, Edith Wharton, reports him as having said, 'I have trifled with the *exordia*,' but according to another friend, Mrs. Belloc Lowndes, he had obstinately refused to read it. James's general theme was the superiority of the selective principle in fiction to the 'slice of life'. Lawrence, he implied, was in the line of those, like Wells and Bennett, whose realism was heavily documented, and a welcome departure from Victorian prudery, but lacked 'a controlling idea and a pointed intention'. In tortuously elusive phrasing James suggested that if *Sons and Lovers* did have a subject, then Lawrence did little to help the reader to see it.

A more carefully considered article, based on the new Freudian psychology, appeared in the next year, 1915. This was the review by the psychologist, Alfred Kuttner, in the *New Republic* (No. 22). (The revised and expanded version published in the *Psychoanalytic Review*, July 1916, is reprinted in *D. H. Lawrence and 'Sons and Lovers'*, 1965, ed. E. W. Tedlock.) Lawrence saw at least the later text, which, he said, carved a half lie out of his poor book, which as art was 'a fairly complete truth' (*L* 16 September 1916). Yet Kuttner's view is not unlike the well-known outline of *Sons and Lovers* that Lawrence gave Edward Garnett (*L* 14 November 1912). Kuttner interpreted the novel as the struggle of a man to free himself from allegiance to his mother and transfer his love to a woman outside the family circle, a struggle which in *Sons and Lovers* ends tragically. Lawrence's account stresses the mother's devotion to her sons, William and Paul, as compensation for the lack of satisfaction in her marriage. As they grow up 'she selects them as lovers—first the eldest, then the second. These sons are *urged* into life by their reciprocal love of their mother—urged on and on. But when they come to manhood, they can't love, because their mother is the strongest power in their lives, and holds them.' Paul's sweetheart (Miriam) tries to fight the mother, says Lawrence, but loses; the affair with Clara is seen, like William's engagement to 'a fribble', as involving sexual 'passion', but not his 'soul', and so a fatal 'split' takes place. Lawrence concludes his outline of the novel by saying that after his mother's death Paul 'is left in the end naked of everything, with the drift towards death'.

It can be argued that both Lawrence's interpretation and Kuttner's are inadequate to the greater complexity of the novel itself, that they over-emphasize the destructive influence of the mother, leaving out of account the grit and determination, the honesty and the capacity for sheer enjoyment of life that Paul also derives from his mother. Nevertheless, both views provide an important corrective to the 'heroic little mother' theme, and since Kuttner's was the only one actually available to the general reading public of the day he must be considered as having made a useful contribution to the understanding of the novel.

What he wrote might well be a half lie, but the corollary is that it also contained a half truth, and one which evidently required to be given prominence in 1915–16.

The Widowing of Mrs. Holroyd, The Prussian Officer and The Rainbow

Lawrence's next major work was *The Rainbow*, but before that appeared *The Widowing of Mrs. Holroyd*, in April, and *The Prussian Officer*, in November 1914. Lawrence's first play was well received in 1914 (cf. *T* 24 April and *NS* 6 June). It was not produced, however, until 1926—by which time it was still admired, but Lawrence's reputation had changed, and the play was thought to show how well he might have written had he stuck to the working-class life he knew, instead of theorizing about relations between the sexes (Ivor Brown, *SR* 18 December 1926). The only other of Lawrence's plays to be produced in his life-time was *David*. As Sean O'Casey says (*NS* 28 July 1934), he never received the sort of encouragement from the theatrical world that would have enabled him to develop his dramatic gifts, and it was not until the revival of his plays at the Royal Court Theatre, London (1965–8) that his achievement as a playwright was fully appreciated.

Some of the short stories collected in *The Prussian Officer* belonged to Lawrence's early period, and these, particularly *Odour of Chrysanthemums* and *Daughters of the Vicar*, were much praised, but the reaction to the more recent tales, *The Prussian Officer* itself and *The Thorn in the Flesh*, was puzzled and even hostile. One reviewer found the killing of the officer by his orderly in the title story 'a very powerful, if at the same time quite horrible, piece of writing' (No. 23); others, disturbed by the atmosphere of passion and violence, wrote of 'the queer dark corners' that Lawrence too much concerned himself with (*NS* 26 December 1914), or spoke of him as 'the Salvator Rosa of modern psychologists' who 'takes the most ordinary human beings and thrusts them into a veritable tempest of emotion' (*Bk* March 1915).

Critics were beginning to find Lawrence's work strange and unnatural. To one reviewer it seemed that his characters were 'almost unconscious of right and wrong' (*MG* 10 December 1914); and the misgivings to which this aspect of *The Prussian Officer* gave rise were greatly increased by the appearance of *The Rainbow* (published 30 September 1915 in an edition of 2,500). The jingoism and moral cant which had begun to afflict war-time England also provided a climate peculiarly ill-suited to the sexual emphases of this novel, producing a note of hysteria in some of the critical reactions. Robert Lynd, for example, denounced *The Rainbow* as 'a monotonous wilderness of phallicism' (No. 26), and to the *New Witness* (18 November 1915) it suggested 'a world of monotonous bestiality in which men and women are chained to a treadmill of vice'. But the two most extravagant outbursts (which may have led the National Purity League to the book, and so to its prosecution and suppression in England)[6] came from James Douglas, literary critic of the *Star*, and Clement Shorter, editor of the *Sphere* (Nos. 27 and 28). Shorter professed not to be an 'opponent of frankness and freedom in literature', but the 'viciousness' of the book was beyond justification, while Douglas saw in it 'a greater menace to our public health than any of the epidemic diseases which we pay our medical officers to fight. . . .' In so far as there was any serious critical argument in Douglas' article it attacked *The Rainbow* for retarding man's progress from sensuality to the life of the spirit. Basically, however, it was a case of what Lawrence, in his Introduction to *Pansies*, was to call 'taboo-insanity', in which 'certain words, certain ideas are taboo, and if they come upon us and we can't drive them away, we die or go mad with a degraded sort of terror'.

Among the few who tried to retain critical sanity were Catherine Carswell (No. 30), the reviewer for the *Standard* (No. 25), and, more doubtfully, H. M. Swanwick (No. 29), but even these were uncertain in their interpretations and assessments. Catherine Carswell, for example, grasped the importance of relationships for Lawrence, but she failed to note the significance of his attack on 'mental consciousness' and the dehumanization of man by industrialism. She praised those scenes which could be understood in realistic terms, but got no nearer Lawrence's ultra-realistic purposes than to deplore some of the stylistic means by which he sought to achieve them.

On 13 November Methuen's were summoned to answer a charge made against *The Rainbow* under the Obscene Publications Act of 1857. As a result of the ensuing court case all copies of the novel were ordered to be destroyed, reported in *The Times* (No. 31). After this judgment no further reviews of *The Rainbow* appeared, although some comments were made on the censorship issue, and the *New Statesman*, in particular, debunked the moral pretensions of Douglas and Shorter. So far as the artistic merit of the book was touched upon it was condemned, both publicly and privately. The novelist, John Galsworthy, was

revolted by its 'perfervid futuristic style' and Lawrence's treatment of
sex left him with the 'painful impression of a man tragically obsessed'
(No. 33). The literary critic, John Middleton Murry, and Katherine
Mansfield, the short story writer, both close friends of the Lawrences
at this time, were doubtful. Katherine, says Murry, 'quite definitely
hated parts of it', and he himself writes of his bewilderment, both then
and later, in *Reminiscences of D. H. Lawrence* (1930):

There were realms of experience which Lawrence knew into which I had not
entered. Nor, even now, can I say that I have ever really entered them. Even
now, I cannot pretend that the fearful struggle between Anna Lensky and Will
Brangwen in *The Rainbow* is a thing I understand; and since it was of such
experience that he was full, and trying to speak, at this time, it is not surprising
to me that I groped in a mist after his meaning.

Arnold Bennett referred to 'Mr. Lawrence's beautiful and maligned
novel, *The Rainbow* . . .' (*Daily News*, 15 December 1915),[7] but, if one
can judge from Lawrence's letter to his literary agent, J. B. Pinker, of
16 December, he was very critical of the novel's construction (see
No. 24 (i)). James and Wells also seem to have been adverse (*L*
23 November). Lawrence, in reply, recognized that the difference
between himself and James went deep: 'subtle conventional design was
his aim', he said of James; but of Wells he could say, 'He admires me
really, at the bottom . . .'.

Lawrence had thus to be supported mainly by his own belief in his
work—which was considerable. He had taken great trouble over the
composition of *The Rainbow*, still submitting his work to Garnett's
scrutiny, although it became increasingly apparent that the older man's
preference for novels of 'character' conflicted with the 'something deep
evolving itself out' in Lawrence, and finally they parted company. The
letters that Lawrence wrote during this period (1913–15) are full of
comments on the themes and methods that were running in his head
(see No. 24), and there is a fundamental self-confidence in them. This
was not destroyed by his novel's reception. What was destroyed, however, was his hope that any accommodation might be reached with
'the world which controls press, publication and all'. In his own words
he 'put away any idea of "success", of succeeding with the British
bourgeois public, and stayed apart' (*Ph II*, 302).

Poetry (1916–19)

Although he was working on *Women in Love*, Lawrence published no further novels during the war. Apart from *Twilight in Italy* (1916), his books were all verse: *Amores* (1916), *Look! We Have Come Through!* (1917), *New Poems* (1918), and *Bay* (1919). It was the second of these which reviewers found hardest to accept, partly because of the nature of its contents, described by the *Athenaeum* as consisting of 'dialogues of the passionate, but not always harmonious pair, self-communings, morbid ecstasies, repulsions, and ravings' (February 1918), but also because of its seemingly loose, undisciplined free verse. The *New Statesman* (26 January 1918) accused Lawrence of resorting to this kind of verse because it was easy, which possibly provoked him to deny, in his Preface to the American edition of *New Poems* (1920—Preface dated 1919), that breaking 'the lovely form of metrical verse' and dishing up the fragments as *vers libre* was, in fact, any way to compose free verse. His point was that free verse had its own nature and its own law, which, however, 'must come new each time from within'.

Already in private correspondence with Edward Marsh, the editor of *Georgian Poetry*, Lawrence had argued his case for more flexible rhythms even in traditional verse forms, emphasizing instinct rather than the mechanical rules of scansion dictated by 'craftsmanship' (*L* 18 August 1913), and 'the hidden *emotional* pattern' rather than 'the obvious form' (*L* 19 November 1913); and these views led on quite naturally to the defence of free verse as the appropriate medium for poetry of the 'immediate present', as expounded by Lawrence in his 1920 Preface. But the poet, Conrad Aiken, as well as the *New Statesman*, may have had something to do with the particular shape that the Preface took, for he, too, had attacked the kind of poetry Lawrence wrote in *Look! We Have Come Through!* (see No. 37). Aiken's criterion for judging poetry was what he called 'the melodic line'. His definition of this was vague, but his Arnoldian touchstones seemed to indicate that it was a grace achieved primarily by traditional methods and dependent on that crystallizing of emotion in durable verbal form which Lawrence called 'exquisite finality'. Incidental dissonance might be allowed, but 'the melodic line' was a norm to which the poet must return. Lawrence, however, rejected the imposition of such a norm, and for him discord was a natural accompaniment of reality:

There is some confusion, some discord. But the confusion and the discord only belong to the reality, as noise belongs to the plunge of water. It is no use inventing fancy laws for free verse, no use drawing a melodic line which all the feet must toe. Free verse toes no melodic line, no matter what drill-sergeant . . . (*CP*, i, 184.)

Among more favourable critics of Lawrence's verse were the American poets, Amy Lowell, Babette Deutsch and Louis Untermeyer. Amy Lowell had tried to recruit him to the Imagist movement, of which she was a leader, but in her review of *Look! We Have Come Through!* (*NYTBR* 20 April 1919) she admitted that 'Mr. Lawrence, in spite of his inclusion in the Imagist Anthologies, cannot be confined within the boundaries of any school.' Untermeyer singled him out as the most notable of a group of poets, including Hardy and Rupert Brooke, who spoke of love with a new frankness (*The New Adam*— quoted by Deutsch in the *Dial*, January 1920). The English critic, Francis Bickley, in a review of *Amores* (No. 34), similarly linked him with 'the militant honesty of some contemporary poets'; but it was another American poet, John Gould Fletcher, who, in possibly the most intelligent appreciation of Lawrence's poetry at this time, explained why this 'fine, intolerant fanatic' was to be regarded as a major figure (No. 36).

General comments

From about 1914 comments began to appear taking account of Lawrence, not only as a subject for reviews, but also as a recognized modern author with a number of works to his credit. Among these Edward Garnett's 'Art and the Moralists: Mr. D. H. Lawrence's Work' (No. 35), first printed in 1916, attempted a discussion of what had become the most frequent topic with regard to Lawrence—the question of the artist's right to go outside the bounds of the publicly accepted 'idealistic' morality. Garnett made some sensible observations, and his distinction between 'the morality of nature and the morality of man' has affinities with Lawrence's *Study of Thomas Hardy* (written 1914, but at that time unpublished). But Garnett's critical comments tend to be along more familiar lines, with highest praise reserved for the working-class verisimilitude of *Sons and Lovers*. Similarly conventional judgments were made by two academic writers, J. W. Cunliffe and Abel Chevalley. In *English Literature During the Last Half Century* (1919) Cunliffe stated that *The Rainbow* had 'nothing like the grip the novelist had shown of the more familiar material in the colliery village'. Abel Chevalley's comments on Lawrence, in *Le Roman Anglais de Notre Temps* (1921—No. 45) are interesting chiefly as a first example of French critical response. The novelist, Arthur Waugh (*Tradition and Change*, 1919), Louis Untermeyer (No. 38) and the novelist and playwright, Douglas Goldring (No. 39), tended to emphasize Lawrence as poet—which, paradoxically, led Untermeyer at least to a higher estimate of *The Rainbow* than most novel critics were prepared to make. In his view it was 'possibly the most poetic and poignant novel of this decade'. Goldring, on the other hand, in spite of his friendly enthusiasm for Lawrence, thought it one of the least artistically successful of Lawrence's books; his chief interest was in *Look! We Have Come Through!*

Such surveys were a tribute to Lawrence's growing reputation. He had become a writer whose complete works had to be taken into account. But it cannot be said that these critics, who presumably had leisure to consider his books with care, showed a much better understanding of his purposes and achievement than the reviewers who had to write more hastily for weekly or monthly publications.

The Lost Girl and *Women in Love*

The Lost Girl and *Women in Love*, both published in November 1920, were partly the work of an earlier Lawrence (though reviewers did not know this), *Women in Love* having been written in 1916, and the first half of *The Lost Girl* in 1913. After the affair of *The Rainbow* none of the regular publishers was willing to run the risk of printing its sequel, and so *Women in Love* had to be privately printed in New York (1,250 copies, 50 of which were issued in England). The first trade edition, of 1,500 copies, was published by Secker in London, 1921, and the American firm of Seltzer issued an edition of 15,000 copies in 1922, since when it has been quite steadily reprinted (*WR* 45). *The Lost Girl* was published in the usual way, by Secker, to whom Lawrence confessed some uneasiness about the public's likely reaction to it: '. . . I find it good—a bit wonderful, really. But when I get a sort of "other people" mood on me, I don't know at all. I feel I don't know at all what it will be like to other people' (*L* 12 June 1920). He hoped at least that it might make some money, which he still badly needed. But by the beginning of 1921 no more than 2,300 out of an exceptionally large edition of 4,000 copies[8] had been sold (*L* 12 February 1921), and 841 out of the 1,500 copies that Secker reprinted in 1925 were remaindered in 1930 (*WR* 47). Only the award of the James Tait Black memorial prize in 1921 made the novel financially rewarding for Lawrence.

Reviewers were split in their opinion of *The Lost Girl*. It was generally recognized to be indebted to 'the Bennett manner' (*N* 22 January 1921), and Garnett compared it to the tales of the *Five Towns* (No. 42). In a letter to Pinker (16 December 1920) Bennett himself praised it highly. But to some critics this was a change for the better—a welcome sign of recovery after the deplorable aberrations of *The Rainbow*—while to others, including Virginia Woolf (No. 40) and Edward Shanks, assistant editor of the *London Mercury* (December 1920), it seemed that Lawrence had surrendered his distinctive originality to produce a book that any of his contemporaries might have written. Katherine Mansfield and Middleton Murry (Nos. 41 and 43) were gloomier still. To them it seemed that the 'decay' of imaginative power since the earlier work was accompanied by a perverse misrepresentation of life as 'mysteriously degraded by a corrupt mysticism'. A notable exception to both schools of thought was the associate editor of the *New Republic*, Francis Hackett (No. 44). He was not happy about Lawrence's work in general, but the emotional honesty of *The Lost Girl* deeply impressed him. Lawrence, he said, 'flings this case of Alvina in the face of an England full of surplus women, and he finds extraordinary and wonderful the woman who can support the insupportable . . .' This remark suggests that of all the reviewers of *The Lost Girl* Hackett was the one who came nearest to appreciating that the novel was a rejection of that false sense of tragedy which Lawrence in 1912 (shortly before writing the first part of *The Lost Girl*) had associated with 'England and its hopelessness' and 'Bennett's resignation' (*L* 6 October 1912).

The smaller number of reviews of *Women in Love* may be due, as Martin Green suggests,[9] partly to its being at first privately printed, and partly to an attempt by the New York Society for the Suppression of Vice to get it banned. Two other books were prosecuted along with *Women in Love*, but Magistrate George W. Simpson, who presided over the case, declared that he could find no obscenity in any of the three books: 'On the contrary, I find that each of them is a distinct contribution to the literature of the present day' (Nehls, ii, 469). Most of the critics, however, were hostile, as Lawrence seems to have expected them to be. In his Foreword to the novel (intended for the first edition, but not actually printed till 1936) he had already replied in advance to attacks on his eroticism, subjectivity and repetitive style (*Ph II* 275-6). Of these critics W. Charles Pilley, assistant editor of *John Bull*, was the most extreme; he called the book 'dirt' and hinted at homosexual horrors (17 September 1921, reprinted Nehls, ii, 89–91). In a different vein was the bantering review of the *Saturday Westminster Gazette* (No. 48). The *T.L.S.* (9 June 1921) performed the curious feat of citing the rabbit episode in Chapter XVIII as an example of Lawrence's 'unconvincing pencraft' (cf. also No. 58), similar distortions came from Murry (No. 49), who quoted from Birkin's meditation on the process of sensual dissolution without referring to the specific rejection of that process in favour of 'the way of freedom' (Penguin ed., 287), and from Rebecca West, whose apparently well-intentioned review (*NS* 9 July 1921) still managed to give the impression that *Women in Love* was an abnormality to be read only as a series of 'desperately devised symbols'.

The best of the reviews were those written by the American critic, John Macy, and the American novelist, Evelyn Scott (Nos. 46 and 47). Macy, the more conventional of the two, saw affinities between Lawrence and the earlier generation of poetic novelists such as Meredith and Hardy; surprisingly, he thought that *Women in Love* lacked the social context given to sexual relations in *The Rainbow*.[10] Evelyn Scott, with more originality, but with greater obscurity, developed the thesis that Lawrence was a type of the affirmative artist whose convictions were too urgent for his art. Scott was also one of the first of Lawrence's critics to see the importance, and paradox, of his anti-intellectualism, calling him 'the priest of an age almost intolerably self-aware'.

Lawrence in the early twenties

In the early 1920s Lawrence's output was prolific. He had no less than twelve books published in the three years from 1921–3. These included two collections of short stories, *England, My England* and *The Ladybird* (published in America as *The Captain's Doll*) which attracted some of the most complimentary reviews to be published in Lawrence's lifetime (Nos. 54–7). In general the shorter form was thought more suitable to Lawrence's genius than the novel, and was judged to act as a brake on his theorizing. Thus the reviewer for the *Nation and Athenaeum* was able to write 'When at his top pitch of creative excitement, and therefore beyond fumbling and philosophizing Mr. Lawrence is a writer of the first rank' (23 February 1924).

By the same law the theoretical works were damned. The pseudo-technical terms used in *Psycho-analysis and the Unconscious* and *Fantasia of the Unconscious* provoked reviewers either to laughter or disgust. Even a reasonably sympathetic critic, such as George Soule (he is the one referred to in the Foreword to *Fantasia*), who felt that there was some sense beneath this 'terrifying exterior', could only regret that Lawrence had not used 'the imagery of fiction or poetry instead of the intellectual terms which he distrusts' (*NNY* 27 July 1921). Middleton Murry (Nos. 51 and 53), however, came out, as he had done for *Aaron's Rod* the year before, in favour of *Fantasia*, professing to find in it a new gaiety and assurance that marked Lawrence's re-ascent to the light after his harrowing of hell in *Women in Love*. The critical grounds for this remarkable change of opinion are obscure; the reviews probably have more to do with the history of the personal relationship between Murry and Lawrence than with the objective qualities of the books themselves.

Critics of the novels (*Aaron's Rod*, 1922; *Kangaroo*, 1923; and *The Boy in the Bush*, 1924) were equally unwilling to take Lawrence seriously as a thinker. H. W. Boynton, reviewer for the *Independent*, described *Aaron's Rod* as an attempt 'to knock up a nice new world for us on the spur of the moment' (27 May 1922), and with regard to *Kangaroo* Raymond Mortimer of the *New Statesman* (29 September 1923) considered that the philosophy had stifled the more worthwhile poetry. Lawrence's mistake, according to the novelist, Alyse Gregory (No. 61), was in trying to turn himself into a socio-political commentator like H. G. Wells. His views on the relations which ought to exist between the sexes were found particularly unacceptable. His insistence on male domination, wrote the American critic, Louise Maunsell Field, was rooted 'in the well-known complex of male sex-fear—the man's fear of the woman and of her power' (*NYTBR* 30 April 1922). Even Lawrence's travel writing was deplored when it betrayed this note (see, for example, No. 50, Francis Hackett's review of *Sea and Sardinia*). Though there were exceptions, such as the *T.L.S.* reviewer of *Kangaroo* (No. 60), most critics felt that the intrusion of Lawrence's half-baked ideas spoilt his work unnecessarily. Why did he not simply leave them out? The answer was given by Edward Shanks (No. 58) who was able to see that Lawrence's convictions— including those with which Shanks could not agree—were inseparable from the art which embodied them:

It is possible to say that the solutions he offers of the great problem oppressing him are empty and false. . . . He may be wrong on looking at this life as a pit. But, if so, out of his error comes a flame of poetry, smoky, strange and disconcerting as it may be, which is at least genuine and which is hardly paralleled by any of the novelists of his generation.

Lawrence's own venture into literary criticism with *Studies in Classic American Literature* (1923) was received as a partly stimulating, partly presumptuous and annoying, but essentially amateur effort, in which the subjectivity and eccentricity sometimes deplored in the novels were seen to be magnified. The breezy, colloquial style was much disliked. 'Here is Mr. Lawrence,' said one reviewer, 'writing in the staccato style developed by Mr. Hearst's newspapers and getting badly mixed now and then in his American slang' (*New York Evening Post*, 13 October 1923). The American critic and editor, Stuart P. Sherman (No. 59), also commented ironically on the style of the book, but his main attention was given to what he called the 'cave-man philosophy' that Lawrence found latent in American literature, and the question of its relevance to contemporary America. This he doubted; but not so Herbert J. Seligmann, author of the first book on Lawrence (*D. H. Lawrence: An American Interpretation*, 1924), for whom *Studies*, and the whole of Lawrence's work to date, was a highly relevant challenge to an America that lived 'off the top, thinly'. Seligmann's, however, was an exceptionally favourable opinion. Other critics praised Lawrence's particular insights, but with serious reservations. Indeed, at least two reviews of *Studies* opened with statements which suggest that critics made reservations before they even began to read. 'The authorship of this book', wrote an English reviewer, H. C. Minchin, 'is a sufficient indication of its queerness' (*ST* 6 July 1924); and Conrad Aiken began: 'Mr. Lawrence's book on American literature is perhaps even more singular than one now expects a book by Mr. Lawrence to be' (*N & A* 12 July 1924). Such comments illustrate not only the critical reaction to *Studies*, but the very state of Lawrence's reputation at this time.

1925-7

This was the period of Lawrence's Mexican writings, in which he carried to the furthest extreme his rejection of conventional Western values and almost completely alienated his critics. *The Plumed Serpent* (1926) especially seemed devoid of normal human interest—Katherine Anne Porter (No. 72), the novelist and short story writer, called it a 'catastrophe'—but the reviewer for the *Manchester Guardian* (29 May 1925) also found *St. Mawr* disturbingly indifferent to the world of 'decent folk who do a considerable amount of honest work, enjoy their lives, and try to behave themselves', and the Scottish poet and critic, Edwin Muir, in a general article (No. 67) on Lawrence printed early in 1925, was already arguing that his marvellous ability to penetrate the instinctive life was achieved at the cost of his sympathy with 'the conscious life of mankind'. Lawrence seemed set irretrievably on a downward path, and critics found him increasingly provocative and perverse.

Lawrence, however, took little heed. His books were meant to disturb. 'Do you think', he wrote to his friend, Carlo Linati,

that books should be sort of toys, nicely built up of observations and sensations, all finished and complete?—I don't. . . . A book should be either a bandit or a rebel or a man in a crowd. People should either run for their lives, or come under the colours, or say *how do you do?*

(*L* 22 January 1925)

He was grateful if a critic seemed to 'care about the deeper implication in a novel' (*L* 11 July 1925), as he felt Sherman did in his long review article for the *Herald Tribune* (No. 68), but he was impatient with adverse criticism, and especially with criticism like Muir's which adopted a lofty tone and spoke of his gifts as 'splendid in their imperfection'. 'Ugh, Mr. Muir,' he wrote, 'think how horrible for us all, if I were perfect! or even if I had "perfect" gifts!—Isn't splendour enough for you, Mr. Muir? . . . For "perfection" is only one of the attributes of "the normal" and "the average" in modern thought' (*Ph* 803).

Lawrence was led by his own consuming purpose, and this in the Mexican books was to try to express the uniqueness of the religious experience which he had encountered among the Indians. Yet almost the only critic to read him in this spirit was the *Manchester Guardian* reviewer of *The Plumed Serpent*, for whom it was 'an intensely religious book' (No. 70). Katherine Anne Porter declared that, fascinated as he was by the Indian experience, Lawrence could not penetrate it, and other critics echoed this judgment in their remarks on Lawrence's treatment of the Indians in *Mornings in Mexico*. According to the English novelist and controversialist, Wyndham Lewis, Lawrence merely attributed to the Indians qualities which derived from the 'evolutionist, *organic* philosophy' of Bergson, Spengler and Whitehead, who were foolish enemies of the white man's superior intelligence. Lewis' ideas, first published in *The Enemy*, September 1927, and reprinted in *Paleface* (1929), were superficial, and the style in which they were expressed was crude and bluff, but several later critics treated them with great respect, and quoted them approvingly.

More thoughtful critics nevertheless recognized that the religious question was very relevant to Lawrence's work. Murry, for example, comparing Lawrence with Proust, James Joyce and E. M. Forster, concluded that Lawrence was the most significant because he possessed the quality of 'religiousness' and was 'in permanent rebellion against a society and an age that has it not' (*Adelphi*, September 1926). From another point of view the Cambridge University lecturer, I. A. Richards (whose article probably influenced Sackville West's review of *Reflections on the Death of a Porcupine*, No. 69), criticized Lawrence, along with Yeats, for failing to face the problem of maintaining attitudes without the support of the traditional beliefs which had been eroded by scientific truth. Lawrence, said Richards, seemed to be reverting to a primitive world-picture 'similar to that described in *The Golden Bough*'. Yet the refusal of Lawrence and Yeats to envisage poetry without beliefs was also for Richards evidence of their seriousness, since 'the temptation to introduce beliefs is a sign and measure of the importance of the attitudes involved' ('A Background for Contemporary Poetry', *Cr* July 1925).

In 1927 E. M. Forster and T. S. Eliot made the first of their various comments on Lawrence. In *Aspects of the Novel* Forster grouped him with Dostoevski, Melville and Emily Brontë as a novelist of 'prophecy' —meaning, rather vaguely, 'a tone of voice', something residing in the rapt quality of untranslatable symbolic scenes. After Lawrence's death Forster also became involved in an exchange of letters with Eliot and Clive Bell, who disputed his claim that Lawrence was 'the greatest imaginative novelist of our generation' (*N&A* 23 and 30 March, 12 and 26 April 1930), and in April of that year Forster gave an obituary talk on Lawrence for the B.B.C. (No. 95).

Eliot, in an article for *La Nouvelle Revue Francaise* (No. 74), used Lawrence as an example of the false seriousness and limited sense of reality produced in the English novel by the fashionable preoccupation with Freudian psychology. Like Wyndham Lewis, Eliot represented Lawrence's interest in the primitive as a betrayal of civilization:

When his characters make love—or perform Mr. Lawrence's equivalent for love-making—and they do nothing else—they not only lose all the amenities, refinements and graces which many centuries have built up in order to make love-making tolerable; they seem to reascend the metamorphoses of evolution, passing backward beyond ape and fish to some hideous coition of protoplasm.

This theme was further developed in *After Strange Gods* (1934), 'a primer of modern heresy' in which Lawrence was made to play a part as one of the principal heretics. There was an obvious clash of temperament between Eliot and Lawrence—the former's academic and orthodox attitudes made him particularly unsuited to be a critic of Lawrence's work. Perhaps, too, like Henry James, he was not very fully conversant with Lawrence's work. Certainly, it is hard to account on any other basis for the astonishing statement in 'The Contemporary Novel' that 'No line of humour, mirth or flippancy ever invades Mr. Lawrence's work; no distraction of politics, theology or art is allowed to entertain us.'

In 1961, however, Eliot remarked (in 'To Criticize the Critic'): 'I find myself constantly irritated by having my words, perhaps written thirty or forty years ago, quoted as if I had uttered them yesterday.' And he added that whenever he allowed an essay to be re-published he made a point of indicating the original date of publication. With this in mind, it should be stated that Eliot's views on Lawrence were modified in later years, and that, despite some slighting references to *Lady Chatterley's Lover* in *After Strange Gods*, in the 1960 obscenity trial he expressed his readiness to appear as a witness for the defence.[11] In the same passage of 'To Criticize the Critic' where he made this fact public Eliot also stated that even in 1931 he was 'wagging [his] finger rather pompously at the bishops who had assembled at the Lambeth Conference, and reproaching them for "missing an opportunity for dissociating themselves from the condemnation of two very serious and improving writers"—namely, Mr. James Joyce and Mr. D. H. Lawrence.' Yet Eliot also confessed that Lawrence was a figure about whom his mind would 'always waver between dislike, exasperation, boredom and admiration', and that his antipathy to Lawrence remained, on the ground of what seemed to him 'egotism, a strain of cruelty, and a failing in common with Thomas Hardy—the lack of a sense of humour'.

Lady Chatterley's Lover

Lady Chatterley's Lover, the most celebrated, or notorious, but neither the best nor the worst, of Lawrence's novels, was first published privately at Florence in July 1928. As trouble was expected from the English police, this edition, of 1,000 copies priced at £2 each, was distributed mainly through Lawrence's personal friends; by December, however, all copies had been sold, and a cheaper edition of 200 copies was printed in November 1928. The book soon appeared in several pirated editions, and in an attempt to compete with these Lawrence issued the Paris edition of 3,000 copies in May 1929, which was also sold out by August 1929 (WR 91–2). The expurgated editions published in 1932, after Lawrence's death, consisted of 3,440 (English ed.) and 2,000 (American ed.). Not until 1959 was an unexpurgated trade edition available in America (15,000), and in England it was thanks to Penguin Books, who in 1960 deliberately tested the revised obscenity law by publishing the complete text of *Lady Chatterley* (200,000), that the novel became generally available.

With the publication of this novel Lawrence brought down on himself the fury of British public outrage, exemplified in the fulminations of *John Bull* under the sensational headline, 'Famous Novelist's Shameful Book' (No. 75). An attack also appeared in the *Sunday Chronicle*, the background to which is interestingly discussed by James Drawbell, former editor of that paper, in *The Sun Within Us* (1963). It was Drawbell who made the decision to denounce Lawrence, even though he was an admirer of his work. 'He had given me countless hours of enchantment,' he says, 'enlarged my experience of life. But in *Lady Chatterley's Lover* he had delivered himself to us in our newspaper office; and in a newspaper office there is little mercy' (p. 281).

Lawrence's purpose was taken as being merely pornographic, but in several letters written during the composition of the book, and, more fully, in 'A Propos of *Lady Chatterley's Lover*' (1929), he stated that he was fighting on behalf of 'the phallic reality, as against the non-phallic cerebration unrealities' (*L* 13 March 1928). In writing a description of 'the whole act' (which Edward Garnett had originally suggested to him (*L* 24 August 1928)) he was doing something which he felt had to be done in order to counter the essentially barbaric view of sex as 'nothing but a functional act and a certain fumbling with clothes' (*Ph II* 497); and he maintained the so-called 'four-letter words' were equally necessary. For the sake of his English and American publishers he attempted an expurgated edition (though always intending to print the complete text as well), but found it impossible: 'I might as well try to clip my own nose into shape with scissors. The book bleeds' (*Ph II* 489). And when, in 1932, Frieda Lawrence authorized the expurgated text, most reviewers endorsed Lawrence's view (see Nos. 77–9). Most interestingly of all, W. B. Yeats, in a letter to a friend (No. 81), wrote that the coarse language of Mellors, accepted by Connie 'becomes a forlorn poetry uniting their solitudes, something ancient, humble and terrible'.

Reviews of the 1928 edition of *Lady Chatterley* were, of course, few. The most distinguished was by the American critic, Edmund Wilson, whose comments on the language were eminently sane, and who recognized that, despite certain excesses and absurdities, the characters had an 'heroic dignity' and 'symbolical importance'.[12] Murry (No. 76) also welcomed the novel, calling it 'a cleansing book', but for him it represented only a half-truth. A third review, by H. J. Seligmann, was printed in the New York *Sun* (1 September 1928), which then remade its literary page to get rid of this 'contaminating essay' from its later editions (Seligmann, quoted Moore, *The Intelligent Heart*, Penguin ed. 478).

One other discussion of *Lady Chatterley* is printed here: that of the distinguished French author and politician, André Malraux (No. 80). In his view, the novel was an attempt to revise the Western myth of sexuality, substituting impersonal passional awareness for the consciousness of personality on which modern love is based. Like Eliot and Lewis, Malraux distrusted the undermining of intellect by instinct, and this distrust led him into some tendentious judgments, but his recognition of the mythical implications in *Lady Chatterley*, and the accompanying concession that myth is extra-rational, marked an important advance in Lawrence criticism.

After *Lady Chatterley*

In 1928 Lawrence's *Collected Poems* were published and in 1929 *Pansies*. The first of these was widely reviewed without adding anything new to the judgments already made on Lawrence's poetry. *Birds, Beasts and Flowers* had appeared in 1923 and was included along with the earlier work in *Collected Poems*, but on both occasions reviewers tended to rate the earlier verse more highly. It was not until after Lawrence's death that justice was done to the importance of *Birds, Beasts and Flowers*. *Pansies*, on the other hand, though condemned by one reviewer as 'the low-water mark' of Lawrence's career (*MG* 27 August 1929), received some discriminating praise in the *T.L.S.* and *Herald Tribune* (Nos. 85-6).

In 1929 there was also an exhibition of Lawrence's paintings at the Warren Gallery which shocked some people, and was raided by the police. From the literary point of view interest centred on Lawrence's

Introduction to the volume of reproductions which accompanied the exhibition (reviewed by the art critic, T. W. Earp, No. 84), and the question of censorship which the subsequent prosecution aroused. The publication of two pamphlets on this topic, *Do We Need A Censor?* by Lord Brentford (Sir William Joynson Hicks), who was British Home Secretary at the time of the seizure of the *Pansies* MS, and *Pornography and Obscenity* by Lawrence, gave an interesting opportunity to compare the arguments for and against censorship, which E. M. Forster and the *New Statesman* did very skilfully (Nos. 87–8).

Obituaries

Lawrence died at Vence, 2 March 1930, and the news was printed in most English papers on 3 March. The image presented by the obituaries was, as Catherine Carswell complained (*Time and Tide*, 14 March), that of 'a man morose, frustrated, tortured, even a sinister failure', and the comments on his literary career emphasized the familiar theme of his decline, as we see, for example, in No. 89. The *Glasgow Herald* varied this by saying that 'while he wrote more splendidly in each succeeding volume, he wrote less truly' (No. 91). Even his positive qualities were presented almost as the liabilities rather than the assets of genius, and the occasion of his death was taken by J. C. Squire, literary critic of the *Observer*, to prophesy that in another generation he might be regarded as 'preposterous and even boring'. A 'precious residuum' of his work would remain, but the rest would 'easily be forgiven and even forgotten'[13] (No. 92). These were the characteristic judgments, by comparison with which the comments of Arnold Bennett and E. M. Forster (Nos. 94–5) have the air of extreme generosity.

The monthlies and quarterlies were more restrained, though not, on balance, more favourable. The English critic, John Heywood Thomas in 'The Perversity of D. H. Lawrence' (*Cr* October 1930) began by saying that Lawrence had died 'before we could tell him how much we admire the profound seriousness of his work', but the main body of the essay was concerned with the derogatory thesis that Lawrence forced himself into sensual contacts as a way of making himself feel his essential spirituality. The appreciation of his work by the American critic, Dayton Kohler, in *Sewanee Review* (January–March 1931), turned out to be a further contribution to the prevalent 'tortured spirit' view, and another American, A. R. Thompson (No.

96), wrote a kind of plain man's retort to the sympathetic account of Lawrence's work given by the young Englishman, Stephen Potter, in *D. H. Lawrence: A First Study* (1930). Against these one may set the warm, if not judicious, tribute of the poet and novelist, Richard Aldington (*Everyman* 13 March 1930), whose enthusiasm for Lawrence was well known from his earlier criticism (here represented, for example, by No. 73), and the intelligently critical survey of Lawrence's work by the American literary and music critic, Paul Rosenfeld (No. 93).

Spread of Lawrence's reputation

No distinction has been made between Lawrence's reputation in Britain and America, since his work from the very first was published in both countries, and, as this selection shows, reviews and critical comments also appeared simultaneously. In other countries, judging by translations, interest in his work began in the 1920s, but did not become considerable until after his death. The first of his novels to be translated into a foreign language was *The Rainbow*, which appeared in German in 1922. This was followed in 1925 by *Jack Im Buschland* (*The Boy in the Bush*), translated by Else Jaffe-Richthofen, the academic elder sister of Frieda Lawrence (née Richthofen), who also translated *The Fox* (1926) and *The Woman Who Rode Away* (1928). Other translators produced German versions of *Sons and Lovers* (1925), *Women in Love* (1927), *Fantasia of the Unconscious* (1929), *Lady Chatterley* (1930), *St Mawr* (1931) and several other works between 1932–9.

Surprisingly, it was the Japanese who next paid attention to Lawrence, translating *Women in Love* (1923), *The Rainbow* (1924), *The Captain's Doll* (1924) and eighteen more items in Warren Roberts' list in the 1930s. Russian interest was also early (*Aaron's Rod* and *The Rainbow* both translated in 1925), but does not seem to have continued. The first French translation was *Le Renard* (*The Fox*), 1928, followed by *England, My England* (1930), *Sons and Lovers* (1931), *The Plumed Serpent* (1931), *Lady Chatterley's Lover* (1932), *St Mawr* (1932), *Women in Love* (1932), and, again, a long list of other works in the 1930s. Italian interest began, like the French, with *The Fox* (1929), and in 1933 five of the novels were also translated: *The Trespasser*, *The White Peacock*, *Sons and Lovers*, *St Mawr* and *The Lost Girl*. Under the editorship of the distinguished Italian biographer of Lawrence, Piero

Nardi, the complete works have now been translated into Italian, including the otherwise unavailable second version of *Lady Chatterley's Lover* (translated by Carlo Izzo).

In other languages the most popular of Lawrence's books have been *Sons and Lovers*, translated into Swedish (1925), Roumanian (before 1930?), Czech (1931), Spanish (1933), Croatian, Finnish and Hebrew (1934), and Danish and Norwegian (1935); and, as might be expected, *Lady Chatterley's Lover*—Czech, Danish, Polish and Spanish (1932), Hungarian (1933), and Hebrew and Portuguese (1938).

Later critical reputation

The subsequent history of Lawrence's reputation can only be sketched very briefly. In the 1930s the pattern of Lawrence criticism was set partly by Middleton Murry's seemingly definitive study, *Son of Woman* (1931), given the influential endorsement of T. S. Eliot in his *Criterion* review (No. 97), and partly by the changing political climate. Murry offered the portrait of an artist whose life-long obsession with his mother distorted his entire treatment of sex and invalidated his art. Aldous Huxley's edition of the *Letters* (1932), which included his own excellent Introduction, did something to counteract this view, but the spate of reminiscences between 1932 and 1938,[14] useful though several of them were in themselves, confirmed rather than changed Murry's emphasis on the biographical–subjective approach to Lawrence. To critics who were increasingly preoccupied with the political and economic problems of the 1930s it was this approach which made Lawrence seem virtually outmoded. 'The world', wrote Horace Gregory (himself the author of a book on Lawrence, *Pilgrim of the Apocalypse*, 1933), 'is moving away from Lawrence's need for personal salvation; his "dark religion" is not a substitute for economic planning . . .' (*NR* 14 December 1932). To specifically socialist critics like John Strachey and Christopher Caudwell the significant thing about Lawrence was that he was a critic of capitalist society who refused to follow through the logic of his own work.[15]

But in 1930 the man who was later to become Lawrence's best advocate and critic, F. R. Leavis, also published his first essay on Lawrence, emphasizing the correctness and relevance of Lawrence's criticism of modern industrial civilization ('D. H. Lawrence', reprinted in *For Continuity* 1933). It was a valuable essay, but immature compared with the later *D. H. Lawrence, Novelist* (1955), in which

Leavis gave his highest praise, not as in 1930 to *The Lost Girl* and *Lady Chatterley's Lover*, but to *The Rainbow* and *Women in Love*. Nevertheless, what Leavis referred to in 1955 as 'the insight, the wisdom, the revived and re-educated feeling for health, that Lawrence brings' he felt also in 1930, and helped to keep alive in the pages of *Scrutiny*, always insisting, however, that 'Lawrence's commentary on experience, his doctrine, must be approached by way of the concrete, the successful art' (*Scrutiny*, May 1932, 26–7).

In 1936 appeared *David Herbert Lawrence et les récentes idéologies allemandes* by the French critic, Ernest Seillère, which made Lawrence sound like a proto-fascist, and in 1939 the American professor, W. Y. Tindall's scholarly, but ironical, *D. H. Lawrence and Susan His Cow*—two books reflecting the attitudes of revulsion or urbane mockery that led to a general neglect of Lawrence during the next decade. In the 1950s, however, Lawrence's reputation revived, and today he is widely read, his tales have been very successfully dramatized for television, and even his plays have begun to receive the attention they deserve. Detailed biographies have been produced, the most notable being H. T. Moore: *The Intelligent Heart* (1955) and Edward Nehls: *D. H. Lawrence, A Composite Biography* (1957–9), and collected editions (not always, unfortunately, complete) have been published of the letters (1962), poems (1964) and plays (1965).

So much criticism has appeared since 1950 that one hears complaints of a 'Lawrence industry'. The most important work is that of F. R. Leavis, whose emphasis on the 'art speech' of Lawrence is followed by such critics as Graham Hough (*The Dark Sun*, 1956), Eliseo Vivas (*D. H. Lawrence, The Failure and the Triumph of Art*, 1960), Julian Moynahan (*The Deed of Life*, 1963) and Keith Sagar (*The Art of D. H. Lawrence*, 1966). The 'religious' Lawrence, though discussed by Father William Tiverton (*D. H. Lawrence and Human Existence*, 1951), Mark Spilka (*The Love Ethic of D. H. Lawrence*, 1955) and George A. Panichas (*Adventure in Consciousness*, 1964), has received less attention, and the 'sexual' Lawrence—surprisingly, in view of the 1960 *Lady Chatterley* trial, and the recent controversy over the question of the supposed homosexuality and forbidden practices in some of his works—has been examined thoroughly by only one critic, H. M. Daleski, in *The Forked Flame* (1965). Another group of critics, including Kingsley Widmer, Eugene Goodheart and George Ford, has emphasized the 'Dionysiac' element in his work, and one of the most recent and interesting variations on this theme is Frank Kermode's 'Lawrence and the Apocalyptic Types' (*Critical Quarterly*, Spring and Summer 1968), which also revives Malraux's theory of Lawrence as a mythologizer.

To some readers Lawrence is now, as Kermode says, 'dated' in the sense that he belongs to what can be recognized as a distinct period in English literature, with its own special flavour and preoccupations, and no doubt the time will soon come when critics will feel obliged to preface their remarks on him with a summary of life and society in the 1910s and 20s. This need not be feared if its purpose is to keep alive a full awareness of the varied and even contradictory aspects of the man and his writings. The one judgment which, if it were to prove true, would be fatal to Lawrence is J. C. Squire's (see above, p. 23). Lawrence's overriding concern with wholeness of being makes his own work something which must be read and enjoyed *in toto*, not in 'residual' parts. It is also to be hoped that the historical view of Lawrence, when it comes, will not disguise those qualities which, as the following extracts show, made him for his own contemporaries a deeply disturbing writer.

NOTES

1. Quoted in P. Beaumont Wadsworth's Foreword to his edition of *A Prelude*. The Merle Press, Thames Ditton, Surrey, 1949, p. 14.

2. According to Warren Roberts (*A Bibliography of D. H. Lawrence*, pp. 16–17), Heinemann's imported plates for *The White Peacock* from the American publishers, Duffield & Co., but asked Lawrence to make certain corrections. One phrase, 'the dirty devil's run her muck over that angel', was changed to 'the miserable brute has dirtied that angel' (see Penguin ed., p. 198), and a passage of six lines on page 230 of the American edition was changed to what is now the standard text (see Penguin ed., pp. 200–1). The American text reads as follows:

> God!—we were a passionate couple—and she would have me in her bedroom while she drew Greek statues of me—her Croton, her Hercules! I never saw her drawings. She had her own way too much—I let her do as she liked with me.
>
> Then gradually she got tired—it took her three years to have a real bellyful of me.
>
> (Quoted Roberts, *op. cit.*, p. 17)

3. *D. H. Lawrence: A Personal Record* by E. T. (Jessie Wood, née Chambers). Second edition, ed. J. D. Chambers, Frank Cass & Co. Ltd., London, 1965, p. 103.

4. See E. W. Tedlock: *D. H. Lawrence and 'Sons and Lovers'*. New York University Press, New York, 1965 (University of London Press, 1966), pp. 66–9. Tedlock, however, wonders 'if this could have been a printer's decision'.

5. Lawrence wrote to Garnett that he had made *Sons and Lovers* 'patiently, out of sweat as well as blood' (*L* 14 November 1912). In a letter to Ernest Collings (24 December 1912) he also wrote: 'They want me to have form: that means, they want me to have *their* pernicious ossiferous skin-and-grief form, and I won't.' 'They' refers to 'old stagers', probably the over-thirties in general, but there is also a reference earlier in the letter to 'the conventionalized literary person' with 'the Radfords and the Rhys' seemingly as examples.

6. Emile Delavenay, in a letter published after this book was prepared for the press (*TLS* 17 April 1969, p. 414), rejects this theory. He suggests that the evidence for regarding the National Purity League as the instigators of the action against the book is hearsay, and that the real motive behind the prosecution may have been the wish of the police to discredit writers 'whose influence on wartime morale was felt to be undesirable'. For further details of the prosecution see the report in *The Times*, 15 November 1915, p. 3 (item No. 31 in this book) and the following: Nehls, i, 328–36; *WR* 27–8; Philip Hobsbaum, letter *TLS* 10 November 1966, p. 1023; T. J. Worthen: *The Reception in England of the Novels of D. H. Lawrence from 'The White Peacock' to 'Women in Love'*. Unpublished thesis, University of Kent, 1967, pp. 273–282; and John Carter: 'The *Rainbow* prosecution', *TLS* 27 February 1969, p. 216. Carter's article contains the texts of Lawrence's letter to the Society of Authors asking them to consider the suppression of his novel, and the replies of Methuen's and of J. B. Pinker, Lawrence's agent at the time, to requests from the Society for details of the seizure of *The Rainbow*.

7. Quoted by T. J. Worthen, *op. cit.*, p. 151. Edward Garnett refers to *The Rainbow* as having 'called forth a weighty testimonial to its merits from Mr. Arnold Bennett' (see No. 35), which suggests a fuller comment, but I have not been able to find one.

8. Unfortunately, first edition and sales figures are unavailable for several of Lawrence's works, especially those published by Duckworth, on account of a fire which during the Second World War destroyed the latter's records. Judging, however, by the figures given in *WR*, 4,000 was an exceptional number for a first edition. 3,000 seems to have been the standard figure for Lawrence's fictional works in the 1920s. (This was the figure for *The Lady-bird*, *Kangaroo*, *The Boy in the Bush*, *St. Mawr*, *The Plumed Serpent* and *The Woman Who Rode Away*, although quick reprints increased the number for *Kangaroo* to 4,000 and for *The Boy in the Bush* and *The Plumed Serpent* to 3,500 each.)

9. Martin Burgess Green: *The Reputation of D. H. Lawrence in America*. University Microfilms, Ann Arbor, Michigan, 1957, p. 39.

10. John Macy also wrote the Introduction to the Modern Library edition of *Sons and Lovers*, 1922.

11. The text of Eliot's deposition, drawn up by the counsel for the defence, but with some handwritten corrections and comments by Eliot himself, is now in the manuscripts section of the Library of Nottingham University.

12. This review (*NR* 3 July 1929) has been reprinted in Edmund Wilson's *The Shores of Light*. New York, Farrar, Straus, and Young, 1952, pp. 403–7, and in *The Achievement of D. H. Lawrence*, ed. F. J. Hoffman and H. T. Moore. Norman, University of Oklahoma Press, 1953, pp. 185–8.

13. Cf. G. K. Chesterton, three years later: 'The life of D. H. Lawrence, for instance, has already become a mere legend, which might be of any antiquity. . . .' ('The End of the Moderns', *LM* January 1933, p. 228.)

14. Ada Lawrence and G. Stuart Gelder: *Young Lorenzo, Early Life of D. H. Lawrence*, 1932; Mabel Dodge Luhan: *Lorenzo in Taos*, 1933; J. M. Murry: *Reminiscences of D. H. Lawrence*, 1933; Dorothy Brett: *Lawrence and Brett, A Friendship*, 1933; Helen Corke: *Lawrence and Apocalypse*, 1933; Earl and Achsah Brewster: *D. H. Lawrence, Reminiscences and Correspondence*, 1934; Frieda Lawrence: *Not I, But the Wind*, 1934; Knut Jaensson: *D. H. Lawrence*, 1934; Jessie Chambers: *op. cit.* (note 3), 1935; Knut Merrild: *A Poet and Two Painters*, 1938.

15. John Strachey: *The Coming Struggle for Power*, 1932; Christopher Caudwell: 'D. H. Lawrence: A Study of the Bourgeois Artist' in *Studies in a Dying Culture*, 1938.

1. Henry Yoxall on four poems in 'Books and Pictures', *Schoolmaster*

25 December 1909, lxxvi, 1242

Henry Yoxall, signed 'Y' (1857–1925). Teacher, author and collector. Editor of *Schoolmaster* from 1909. General Secretary of National Union of Teachers 1892–1924; Liberal M.P. for Nottingham West, 1895–1918. The poems, published in *English Review*, November 1909, iii, pp. 561–5, were 'Dreams Old and Nascent', 'Discipline' and 'Baby-Movements' I and II.

Poems by Mr. D. H. Lawrence, assistant master in the Davidson-road Council School, Croydon, have recently been published in the *English Review*. A monthly of that standing does not admit to its columns the work of mere versifiers, and I congratulate Mr. Lawrence, not only on the prominent publication of some of his poems, but on the fine quality of them.

[Quotes 'Dreams Old and Nascent: I, Old', 1–8. 'I have opened . . . the blue, soft day.' (Unrevised text as in *C.P.*, II, 905.)]

In that there is surely the stuff and artistry of the true poet: metre, rhythm, phrase, picture, melody, atmosphere, and, above all, feeling are there. You hear the clink of the shunting engines, as you read. Perhaps the reference to Lorna Doone is a defect, excusable by the needs of rhyme. Most boys would be thinking of the Doone men. But here and there a boy who had read the book would dream of Lorna, no doubt.

I can only quote passages, and I choose those which relate to school obviously or indirectly. Here, again, is one:

[Quotes 'Discipline', 1–12. 'It is stormy . . . into unbreakable ropes.' (Unrevised text as in *C.P.*, II, 926.)]

That is not so fine, so lucid, or so 'inevitable' as the first I quoted, but it is the real poetic stuff none the less. The difference between the most skilful mere verses and poetry is deep—a gulf that none but the 'real poet' can overstep. The poet writes what he feels, the poetaster what he imagines might be felt on a similar occasion. Thousands of teachers have felt like that before a class, once or twice in their life-times at least, but no other teacher has expressed it. Let me quote again:

[Quotes whole of 'Baby-Movements: I, Running Barefoot.' (Unrevised text as in *C.P.*, II, 912–13.)]

If these comments of mine were not very much of an impertinence I would say that Mr. Lawrence is at present a finer but weaker Walt Whitman, but it may redeem my impertinence if I say I think he can become something higher than Whitman ever attained to.

The second of the two poems, entitled 'Baby Movements' has for sub-title the Wordsworthian phrase 'Trailing Clouds'. It is this:

[Quotes whole of 'Baby-Movements: II, Trailing Clouds.' (Unrevised text as in *C.P.*, II, 913.)]

I hear—not from Mr. Lawrence, who does not know that I know anything about his writings—that a novel of his is soon to appear. Let us welcome him into the rather small band of teachers really *littérateurs*; so far as in me lies to judge, I hail him as a true-born poet. The four considerable poems of his which were published in the *English Review* for November last are really wonderful, coming from a man of hardly twenty-five. It is a delight to mention and applaud and signal them to others. For poets nowadays are as rare as fine, real tenor voices. It is a voice that you hear in these poems, not an echo, not an imitation, not a prose-writer's attempt at the lofty strain. There is nothing strained about this poetry.

THE WHITE PEACOCK

January 1911

2. Unsigned review in
Times Literary Supplement

26 January 1911, 35

The merit of this rather odd book is its feeling for and description of nature on its pathetic side. Perhaps we may add, what is often a merit, its studied neglect of a well-knit plot. But it is not easy to feel much enthusiasm about people of Nethermere—the Beardsalls of the 'Cottage', the Tempests, mineowners in the lone house across the lake, and the farming Saxtons, though George Saxton, who takes to public-house keeping, is a good attempt at character study. But the tale meanders through much that is trivial, and one gets an impression of aimlessness. A good deal of the conversation is quite banal, despite its suggestions of advanced culture; for when such names as Ibsen, Gorki, Schopenhauer, Maupassant, Clausen, Debussy, and others startle the stillness of the woodland, as they frequently do, we have a feeling that it is not the characters but the author who is uttering them. And the reader is annoyed by the unsubstantiality of Cyril Beardsall, in whose mouth the whole story is put. He appears to have poetic thoughts, to sketch from nature, and to work in the fields; but for much of the book he is a wraithlike kind of person who appears to be present without being seen.

3. Allan Monkhouse in *Manchester Guardian*

8 February 1911

Allan Monkhouse, signed 'A.M.' (1858–1936). Novelist and playwright. On the editorial staff of *Manchester Guardian* 1902–32.

There is promise in Mr. D. H. Lawrence's novel *The White Peacock*, but promise of what we are not quite able to define. It is the book of a literary young man with a feeling for nature who is groping his way among the complexities of human character. Yet his strongest impulse seems to be lyrical. We might tell him to shape and build his book better; but he would probably reply that it has all the architecture he cared to give it. It is made after a plan that has some vogue today. Impressions, descriptions, events, conversations are set down with as little selection as possible; and the reader can pick his way among these and make of the whole what his wits and sensibilities allow him. So it is in life. Only, an unedited transcript of life does not make a good novel. Picking our way, however, through the motley company in the book—some of whom seem like a family party talking, not too good-mannerly, a kind of shorthand or coterie slang which leaves the reader out in the cold—we fix our attention on George. The story of George is an ineffective tragedy. It should have been something stronger. George Saxton is a young farmer, handsome, able-bodied, and, outside his own work, wholesomely commonplace—judged by Mr. Lawrence's evidence. But he has for neighbours a cultured family of higher social status who are on friendly terms with the Saxtons. Letty, the daughter, is a full-fledged flirt, fascinating and conscienceless, with just enough passion in her to make her flirtation dangerous. She turns George's head, and makes violent love to him. Even after she has married a rich husband, and he has declined on his humble cousin Meg, she does not leave him alone, but dangles her charms before his eyes, and disturbs an honest life with a vision of what was never meant for him.

The narrator of the story, the flirt's brother Cyril, has a strong liking for George, but unfortunately he takes an interest in the farmer's mental and artistic welfare. From Omar Khayyam George has to go on to George Moore. Aubrey Beardsley and Arthur Melville are spread before his eyes. Letty talks French at him—and even Latin. They talk Strauss and Debussy at him while he and Meg are keeping a public-house! No wonder he takes to drink, and that we leave him doubtfully recovering from delirium tremens. There are other symptoms of ruin. They have stuffed his foolish head with foreign ideas, and he, who should have been a slow, capable, honourable yeoman, maunders that if all had gone well he would have been 'a poet or something, like Burns'. Poor George! Letty, the white peacock, was bad for him. Still worse was the literary and unhumorous Cyril, who sees ordinary English rustics through the morbid eyes of Tchekov or Maupassant—or fain would do so.

But Mr. Lawrence can write. There are some fine rhapsodies in the book inspired by the country round Nottingham and by the impressions of a sensitive young man new to London.

4. Unsigned review in *Morning Post*

9 February 1911, 2

'There's a long and good review in today's *Morning Post*, which is a conservative, very aristocratic paper. They amuse me highly by wondering if I'm a woman.' Lawrence to his sister, Ada, 9 February 1911.

It would be interesting to calculate the number of 'promising' first novels that have been published in the last ten years and to trace the subsequent history of their authors. Someone has said that almost anyone with the power of using a pen at all could write an interesting first novel, but this only means that everyone has something interesting about him, enough at any rate to furnish material for one novel, if he is able or willing to give it expression. It is just this 'if' that is the stumbling-block. Few people are able to express their thoughts, even when they have any, and fewer still can express their selves, which they are bound to have. Still, one does feel when reading a new novel with any gift of expression at all an interest over and above the interest of the actual work, namely, that of making acquaintance with a new human individuality. It is therefore necessary to discount that interest in estimating the value of a new book, and in many cases that is hard to do.

These reflections are caused by reading *The White Peacock*, a book by a new author that we should be inclined to praise inordinately perhaps did we not put ourselves thus on guard. It is a book that piques one's curiosity in many ways. To begin with, what is the sex of 'D. H. Lawrence'? The clever analysis of the wayward Lettie, surely a woman's woman, and the particular way in which physical charm is praised almost convince us that it is the work of a woman; while, if so, we must wonder greatly at the sympathetic understanding of the male point of view as interpreted in the reflections of the supposed narrator of the book—a poetic naturalist—especially in the delicate and restrained treatment of his falling in and out of love with Emily,

36

the school teacher. But even with the question of sex solved, there are further problems to intrigue us. In what *milieu* does the author live? Are these people, who seem so real, pure puppets of his imagination, or do they really discuss Ibsen and Aubrey Beardsley in farmhouses in the Trent Valley? Again, what does our author really mean by these pictures of wasted lives and ill-matched marriages? Is he a new prophet of the old fallacy of 'returning to Nature'? It sometimes looks like it, and yet the apologue which explains the title of *The White Peacock* does not suggest this as a moral, for surely the game-keeper who reverted violently 'to Nature' after freeing himself of his unnatural wife, 'the white peacock', did not make much of his experiment.

Such problems as these concentrate our attention and interest more on the author than on the book; but perhaps the clue to some of them may be found in turning attention more closely to that. It is, in the first place, a book of real distinction, both of style and thought. Many of the descriptive passages, without being in any sense 'purple patches', have an almost lyrical charm about them, and the characterization is, generally speaking, deft and lifelike. There is, however, some quality in the book—something more than a merely immature power of construction—that seems to make it move in a rather unreal atmosphere. It is, we fancy, 'sicklied o'er with the pale caste of thought'; the atmosphere is overcharged intellectually (not an unattractive thing in an age of brainless fiction), and the author has bridged many a gap in the developments of his personages by reason rather than by imagination. For all that, *The White Peacock* is a book not only worth reading but worth reckoning with, for we are inclined to believe that its author has come to stay.

5. Violet Hunt in *Daily Chronicle*

10 February 1911, 6

Violet Hunt (1866?–1942). Daughter of the Pre-Raphaelite painter, Alfred William Hunt; novelist and biographer; prominent member of the *English Review* circle; known as Mrs. Hueffer, but not legally married to Ford Madox Hueffer (Ford).

This novel, by a new writer, is really an important contribution to literature, and we hope that it will meet with some of the attention it deserves. Lord Salisbury wrote, in 1875: 'Power has passed from the hands of statesmen, but I should be very much puzzled to say into whose hands it has passed. It is all pure drifting. As we go down the stream, we can occasionally fend off a collision, but where are we going?' It is into the hands of the persons that Mr. D. H. Lawrence describes that the power, passing from the hands of statesmen, has descended, and because Mr. Lawrence shadows the lives and aspirations of these people with such remarkable vividness *The White Peacock*, in our eyes, seems such an important work.

It should be read by all those superior persons who say that they have no time to read novels because they are engaged in public works. It should certainly be read by those people before all others, because from its pages they will learn something of the mind of the classes, who really returned them to the top of the poll, or turned them down, as the case may be. Of late years we have had two or three works dealing with the real lives and the real aspirations of what it is convenient to call the lower classes. But Mr. Lawrence is supremely unconscious of class. His characters simply do not know that class exists. His scene is laid in a district in the Midlands, partly agricultural, partly mining, and his characters are the sons and daughters partly of miners and partly of quite small farmers. In this remarkable world of his there appears to be no 'county' at all, no great families, no squires, hardly even a parson. And these sons and these daughters of small farmers would do credit to any Hampstead gathering of blue stockings.

They are extraordinarily and bewilderingly 'cultured'. They play Chopin, they analyse the leit-motif of 'Tristan', they quote upon every occasion Browning, Ruskin, the Rossettis, or John Stuart Mill. This would appear incredible. But we happen to be able to supply corroborative detail from outside Mr. Lawrence's book.

As a story, *The White Peacock* is the tale of several families bicentrally revolving round two young men who are full of free passions. The one of them goes up the material scale of life; the other descends it, towards passionate ruin, drink and tragedy. These two characters are well drawn, the subsidiary crowd less well defined.

To say that the book possesses exuberant merits of style and remarkably well shadows a sort of coarse and lusty passion; to say that the book has great merits and the faults that must be found in the work of a young writer; to praise it in any way for its literary qualities would easily find readers for it. But furthermore, let the politician understand that here he will find the voter limned for him. He will find, that is to say, not the mere supine agricultural voter, who is forced to vote as the squire and the parson direct; not the irresponsible voter, who is swayed by the music-hall cry of the moment, but the great body of voters who, swaying, irresistibly now in one direction, now in another, mysteriously decides the fate of Governments. It is a reasoning body, after its lights; it has read John Stuart Mill. The old methods of tub-thumping, and catchwords and sentimental party cries will no longer move it. Any member of it can reason almost as well as any Cabinet Minister. That is why we always find the result of elections nowadays so surprising. But those of us who have read *The White Peacock*—this political document developed along the lines of passionate romance—will be more or less prepared.

6. Unsigned review in *Daily News*

14 February 1911, 3

In a letter to his sister, Ada, 26 April 1911, Lawrence refers to this review: 'Did you see that 'rageous review in the *Daily News*? It amused me. I'd upset *that* man whoever he was, hadn't I? But he acknowledged my power very sincerely.'

The White Peacock stands, apparently, as an image of the soul of a woman: 'all vanity and screech and defilement', says Annable, the game-keeper, whose creed it was to 'be a good animal'. The White Peacock metaphor smears the whole book. Life itself, as well as woman, would appear to be all vanity, screech, and defilement. There is, naturally, as little coherence in life as in the book, and as little humour. Consolation, perhaps, for this muddy existence may be found in outbursts of metaphor and simile (D. H. Lawrence does not seem able to conceive anything without making it 'like' something else), or in lyrical and hectic description of the body of things. 'The swiftness of songs, the triumphant tilt' (should it be lilt? one wonders) 'of the joy of life, the hoarse oboe of privation, the shuddering drums of tragedy, and the eternal scraping of the two deep-toned strings of despair' is an example of the author's style at its worst. At its best it is eloquent—intolerably so—and able to force a mood on the reader whether he resist or not. The writer has a power of arresting attention for a moment, of casting a spell, but it is painful attention, and a blighting spell. As for the people pictured here they are pictures marvellously painted, not people. They are good to look at. We are never allowed to forget their most goodly bodies. They are 'cultured'; insufferably so; and let us know it by quoting Horace or *Tristram Shandy*, and by alluding to Schopenhauer or Bernard Shaw. They had all been to some 'college'. Passingly one wonders what their social status was meant to be. They move easily between public-houses and dinner parties, and among their habits is a trick of messing and caressing and stroking each other's hair or arms.

This is a tale of country life. Immense pains, great cleverness, and a stout resolve to say nothing as an ordinary man would say it, have gone to make it. Its cloying descriptiveness is varied by incidents of the right 'brutality'; D. H. Lawrence is fond of that word. On page 18 a cat is caught in a trap by both fore-feet. George 'smiled, and dropped the writhing cat into the water, saying "Good-bye, Mrs. Nickie Ben" '. On page 75 we have the killing of some rabbits described carefully. Later we have some mice dug out of a hole and their slaying pictured for us. A chicken that falls into the fire and a wood-pigeon that 'lay on the ground on its breast, its eyes bursten and bloody', are other contributions to the 'brutality' of life. These things are so told that they have in them neither pity nor significance. Something of miasma belongs to the book. 'It was midnight, full of sick thoughts,' says the author somewhere. In *The White Peacock* the sick thoughts are always there, though the day be spring and the clouds high. We have said that it is clever; which is, perhaps, all the author wished said.

7. Henry Savage in *Academy*

18 March 1911, lxxx, 328

Henry Savage. Journalist and biographer. Met Lawrence 1913. Lawrence wrote thanking him for this review (see Nehls, i, 209–11).

Hitherto we have only known Mr. D. H. Lawrence as being one of the many interesting poets discovered by the *English Review*. Henceforth we shall certainly know him as the author of *The White Peacock*, for it is beyond all argument an admirable and astonishing piece of work. We use the word 'astonishing' advisedly, for, like most new books of uncommon merit, *The White Peacock* surprises even while it charms. There are pages in it that made the present reviewer, a sophisticated and disillusioned reader of novels, lay down the book and rub his eyes in wonder at the author's individuality and courage. It is no very new story that he has to tell. That a young woman should encourage two young men at once, and should end by marrying the wrong one, is possibly even more frequent in fiction than in life. Again, that the slighted lover should thereon marry beneath him and take to drink is only in accordance with the best traditions of the ingenuous school of novelists. But in the hands of Mr. Lawrence this old theme is quickened with new life. The action takes place in the rural districts of Nottinghamshire, and it would hardly be fanciful to say that Nature is the protagonist of the drama, and that the author has drawn her character with uncommon care. We realize her in all her moods, and she is as interesting as she is convincing.

Nor has the author taken less pains with the drawing of those special manifestations of Nature that are called men and women. The heroine is a delightful picture of a lively, clever girl, who likes excitement of all kinds, and especially the rather dangerous excitement of leading passionate men on to making passionate love. Mr. Lawrence's unravelling of this heedlessness is almost uncanny in its shrewdness. But his greatest success is the character of George, the farmer-lover, whose defeat and degradation supply the book with its motive. This is a really masterly study of passion, now wordless and pitiful, now strung to its utmost intensity of self-expression when the man realizes his weakness, and his own words hurt him like blows. Lettie loves his physical strength and the completeness of his submission, and, wisely enough, according to her lights, marries the other man because his money and social position make him a more suitable match. It is clever of Mr. Lawrence to compel us to sympathize both with George and Lettie. We are made to feel that they are both hard driven by their natures, and are not to be blamed for the inevitable catastrophe. But, in truth, of all the many characters in the book, there is not one who does not move within the bounds of our sympathy; the men are men, the women women, and the children, who appear all too rarely, are such children that we hope the author will be more generous of them in his next work.

Apart from the characterization the book would stand by its vivid pictures of a country life that is new to us, where, side by side with the primitive roughness that lingers wherever men and women till the soil, the new ideas have taken root and are apparently about to flourish. The author treats of the primitive with praiseworthy frankness, and there is no denying the interest of the spectacle of a young farmer looking at Aubrey Beardsley's illustrations for the first time. It is apparent to us that Mr. D. H. Lawrence is one of those rare writers who intends only to tell the truth as he sees it, and nothing but the truth. As a consequence he has given us a book of considerable achievement and infinite promise.

THE TRESPASSER

May 1912

8. Unsigned review in *Athenaeum*

1 June 1912, No. 4414, 613–14

The review is entitled, 'Two Realists: Russian and English', and the first part (omitted here) is concerned with Constance Garnett's translation of Dostoevsky's *The Brothers Karamazov*.

The theme of *The Trespasser* is simple—the passion of the married man Siegmund for the enigmatic girl Helena, its fruition in a few days of union, and then an enforced separation, followed by Siegmund's obsession of suicidal despair and death. Here is a story in which both poet and psychologist watch keenly the lover's feverish elation, his fluctuating moods of joy, and the chill greying of the daylight, as the shadows of morbid impulse steal forward swiftly and envelope him. The theme as treated is curiously individual in tone.

From the opening chapter we are struck by the author's skill in catching shades of social atmosphere. Siegmund, whose vocation is that of a violinist in a London theatre, is bound fast in the squalid cares of a suburban lower-middle-class environment. He has married, young and penniless, with Beatrice, now a disappointed, embittered woman who is dragged down by the weight of family worries, and the threadbare poverty of a struggle to maintain the gentilities she was formerly accustomed to. In his soul Siegmund is free, but he has the sensuous, sensitive nature of the poet, who lives for his imaginative visions, while crushed outwardly by the hostile pressure of unyielding facts.

The story opens with Siegmund's escape from his household, for a few days of happiness with Helena, on a long-projected holiday by the sea. There is not a touch in the narrative of that semi-real superheated passion which, in the middle-class imagination, has usurped the place of passion's pure and simple ecstasy. Siegmund has the poet's capacity of enjoying things; he sees and responds instinctively to the forces and appearances of life, as a child claps its hands and stretches out its arms to anything that pleases it. Helena's is a more egoistic nature. The picture of her relations with her lover suggests deep reservations, as of a woman who cannot lose sense of her own identity even in the supreme intimacy of love. Perhaps this is the secret of the tragedy that now swiftly develops.

With unobtrusive art Mr. Lawrence scatters hints of Siegmund's unstrung nerves, of his brain sick with overwrought tension, of his morbid susceptibility to gloomy ideas. When most full of joy he is accessible to sudden revulsions of disgust at life's blankness. As the hour of enforced separation draws near he is assailed by an accelerating horror. His physical collapse, with a sun-stroke hinted, is manifest in his speech and bearing. He drags himself across London at night to his suburban home, where he is greeted by his wife and children with frigid, insulting silence. The fifty pages that narrate his homecoming, his reception, and the stages of his humiliation, mental agony, and delirium, are clear and strong in their psychological intensity, reminding us of the best Russian school. Siegmund hangs himself, and here again the description of the finding of the body by his wife and a window-cleaner is poetic realism of a Dostöevskian order.

The one artistic blemish of the novel in our judgment is that Siegmund, at the age of thirty-eight, is credited with feeling the ecstatic passions of youth. Certainly *The Trespasser* is not to be classed among 'popular novels', but the discerning reader should treasure it for those temperamental qualities which characterize original work.

Basil de Selincourt, signed 'B.S.' (b. 1876). Author and critic.

Mr. D. H. Lawrence has given us in *The Trespasser* a remarkable study of a tragic theme, enveloping it, however, in an ironical rather than in a tragical atmosphere. The hero of his novel, a man of individuality, a musician and with a musician's temperament, revolting against the petty cares and monotonies of life with the woman he married at seventeen, wrenches himself free from her and from his four children (the eldest already old enough to be critical of their father) and gives himself to five days of bliss with the girl he loves, his pupil Helena, an absorbent, dreamy creature, the personification in his eyes of liberty and romance and of the music of Wagner's operas, so familiar to him from his nightly performances at the theatre. Gifted with a poet's insight and felicity of phrase, but not always maintaining a poet's sensitiveness and discrimination, Mr. Lawrence brings before us in minute detail the processional of their hours of phantom rapture, the fluctuations of their passion, and the effect upon it of that hollowness of foundation which the lovers seldom succeed in banishing for many minutes together from their minds. Human passion, accepted against nature, plucked like some tender flower and planted rootless in soil where it can only wither and perish, is an object of supreme pity, and in his account of those short hours before the withering visibly begins Mr. Lawrence betrays a certain remorselessness; there is something inartistic in the degree of absorption with which he follows the trespassers past every flower and tree and into every nook and cranny of their forbidden wood. Fate drives them forth from it, and the remorseless light which Mr. Lawrence then throws upon their emergence has more of adjusted strength and purpose. The intensity of the poetic medium, too, tells wonderfully here. The hour of dreams was spent in the Isle of Wight; escape and freedom were associated for the lovers with the mists and the sea; and now, when the boat on which they have crossed the Solent brings them into captivity again—'The high old houses stood flat on the right hand. The shore swept round in a sickle, reaping them into the harbour.' Later, in the twilight, from the train windows—'Like sparks, poppies blew along the railway banks, a crimson train. Siegmund waited, through the meadows, for the next wheatfield. It came like the lifting of yellow-hot metal out of the gloom of darkened grass-lands.' The book is full of exquisite perceptions like this, and would be worth reading for these alone. But it has other merits. The style is not only poetical but clear and incisive also; the psychology is penetrative and convincing, and though the author runs some theories he does not let them run away with him. The characters are all individually seen, however small the part they have to play, and the two main actors in the drama become intensely real to us. They become real, and yet, though we share with them every moment of this crisis of life, they do not become dear. Siegmund, affected with sunstroke, returns to his homeless home to hang himself. Helena, after a year of exaggerated listlessness, turns for warmth and comfort to another love. We feel that it is what would have happened, and wonder why we are not more affected by an event so terrible. There is something inhuman in watching such a thing tearlessly. Mr. Lawrence strikes but he has not yet learned to touch us.

10. Unsigned review in the *Morning Post*

17 June 1912, 2

The author of *The White Peacock*, one of the arresting first novels of last year, has given us in *The Trespasser* another interesting and ugly piece of work. This is a morbid tale, evidently written at a white heat of inspiration and with the usual faults of redundancy and the like that come of over-facile writing. It tells of seven days in the life of Siegmund MacNair, a violinist, a man getting on in life, who had married a woman rather older than himself, and had apparently suppressed his *joie de vivre* in a somewhat sordid round of domesticity and duty. Whatever the cause, and D. H. Lawrence (we dare not guess at the prefix) has been at no pains to justify Siegmund's sudden adventure, he yields to the persuasion of a pupil, Helena Verden, to spend an unconventional five days holiday in her company in the Isle of Wight. Every instant of these five days, the joy of the pair, isolated in a paradise of their own making, into which the song of the insistent world occasionally intrudes, seems to be described in full. It is a wonderfully sustained, though a somewhat too unreserved, description of emotion at high pressure.

The terrible sequel is described with the same minuteness and the same vision. Siegmund returns, with a touch of sunstroke, to his family, now all, down to the little girl he loved, taking their cue from his wife and treating him as a moral leper. His sickness makes the pain of his isolation intolerable, and he commits suicide. His wife rises on the stepping-stone of the tragedy, which she has only allowed to affect her to the extent of making her an interesting object of pity, to prosperity as a popular mistress of a boarding-house. Helena, after a year's poignant anguish, allows herself to be given rest and warmth by Cecil Byrne. Siegmund is sacrificed to his women-folk, and especially to Helena, who is revealed in the twice repeated allegory: 'She was no swimmer. Her endless delight was to explore, to discover small treasures. For her the world was still a great wonder-box which hid innumerable sweet toys for surprises in all its crevices.' Siegmund's acquaintance, the musician Hampson, expounds the theme which the author of *The Trespasser* appears to labour. 'She can't live without us, but she destroys us. These deep, interesting women don't want *us*; they want the flowers of the spirit they can gather of us. We, as natural men, are more or less degrading to them and to their love of us; therefore they destroy the natural man in us—that is, us altogether.'

The fact is that *The Trespasser*, like *The White Peacock* before it, deals —in an extremely sincere and interesting way, be it said—with abnormal persons. Neither Helena nor Siegmund reaches to the centre of things, and a sympathetic study of the wife, Beatrice, might make out a good case for her point of view, in spite of the absence from it of the light of any love, save self-love. As it is, the book seems to lack a complete human harmony; the diapason is never once used, and our sympathy is only partially evoked. On the other hand, the beauty of many of the passages of the story, regarded as isolated fragments, is undeniable—there are some fine seascapes and a haunting description of a sunrise—and the story itself has an unusual artistic unity, aided by the effective epic construction which begins it in the middle and keeps the sense of tragedy hovering, as it were, over love scenes and purging them of earthly grossness. *The Trespasser* is, in short, a remarkable book, but it needs to be read by the discriminating and the experienced, who will not take its blemishes for its attractions.

11. Unsigned review in *New York Times Book Review*

17 November 1912, 677

From the beginning of time, from the first story of a Joseph in bondage down to the present-day problem novel, we have been made wearily familiar with a certain type of wicked and ruinous lady who has set, more or less successfully, snares for men's feet. She has been a robust sort of animal, varying with much or little subtlety her natural instinct and her physical pursuit; she has been over-sexed, and she has been entirely bad. But that she was not the only, not perhaps the most, dangerous sort of enchantress we have most of us vaguely guessed. It has remained for an almost unknown author to put the other kind of woman into a book. And *The Trespasser* is not only the frankest of serious contemporary novels; it comes near to being the best.

For the author of *The Trespasser* has, keenly and courageously, analysed the woman of dreams, the seeker after extreme sensations, not physical, but psychic. As one of the characters in the book says, 'These deep, interesting women don't want men; they want the flowers of the spirit they can gather from men; therefore, they destroy the natural man—that is, man altogether.' Helena, in *The Trespasser*, is the sort of woman who for centuries 'has been rejecting the animal in humanity, till now her dreams are abstract, and full of fantasy, and her blood runs in bondage, and her kindness is full of cruelty.' Helena searches for psychic sensation in physical experience, and the search kills.

The Trespasser combines some of the most exquisite imaginative writing in modern fiction with a nakedness of physical detail that is almost morbid in its ugliness. Helena and Siegmund spend their holiday by the sea; and we have little today to equal the author's descriptions of wind and wave and far sea-mist, of shore and moor. The story itself—the narrative of a passion that took a man away from a wretched home, and of his miserable return when holiday time was over—is a revolting tragedy. The commonplace reader will, without doubt, find *The Trespasser* commonplace and hideous; but the commonplace reader ought not to read it at all.

LOVE POEMS AND OTHERS

February 1913

12. Edward Thomas in *Bookman*

April 1913, xliv, 47

Edward Thomas (1878–1917). Poet and critic; friend of, among others, Edward Garnett. Killed in France, 9 April 1917.

The book of the moment in verse is Mr. D. H. Lawrence's. He is remarkable for what he does not do and for what he does. Thus, he does not write smoothly, sweetly and with dignity; nor does he choose subjects, such as blackbirds at sunset, which ask to be so treated. For some time past it has been understood that verse is not best written in jerks of a line in length. Mr. Lawrence goes further, and at times seems bent on insulting rhyme, as in this stanza from 'Dog-tired':

[Quotes 11–15, 'The horses . . . its tired sheen.' (*C.P.*, I, 35—slight textual differences.)]

Correspondingly, he writes of matters which cannot be subdued to conventional rhythm and rhyme—chiefly the intense thoughts, emotions, or gropings of self-conscious men or women set on edge by love or fatigue or solitude. If he trusts to make a general appeal, it is by faithful concentration on the particular—a woman receiving a lover straight from bloodshed, a man repulsed, standing like an 'insect small in the fur of this hill' in the night when

> The night's flood-winds have lifted my last desire from me,
> And my hollow flesh stands up in the night abandonedly.

and saying to the woman:

> And I in the fur of the world, and you a pale fleck from the sky,
> How we hate each other to-night, hate, you and I,
> As the world of activity hates the dream that goes on on high,
> As a man hates the dreaming woman he loves, but who will not reply.

The last comparison would be a flaw were it not that Mr. Lawrence sacrifices everything to intensity, particularly in amorousness. His triumph is, by image and hint and direct statement, to bring before us some mood which overpowers all of a sick, complex man save his self-consciousness. Mr. Lawrence is fearless in treatment as in choice of subject. He will be exact in defining an intuition, a physical state, or an appearance due to the pathetic fallacy—herein resembling the man in 'We have bit no forbidden apple.' He will give us in dialect the plainest outlines of a working-class tragedy, and in careful abstract monologue a schoolmaster's moment of satisfaction when it is sweet in the morning to teach boys who are his slaves:

> Only as swallows are slaves to the eaves
> They build upon, as mice are slaves
> To the man who threshes and sows the sheaves.

Such moods he will sometimes follow with a painful curiosity that makes us rather sharers in a process than witnesses of a result. He does not refuse external things, a gang of labourers at work on timber, a picture by Corot, the Moon. A surprising number of his poems are tributary to the moon, but a moon of his own world, 'divesting herself of her golden shift', or bringing him a pang of reminiscence, or reddening:

[Quotes conclusion of 'End of Another Home Holiday', 'The moon lies back . . . Yet more of me.' (*C.P.*, I, 64.)]

I doubt if much of his effect is due to rhythm. Verse aids him chiefly by allowing him to use a staccato shorthand which would be more uncomfortable in prose. But, whether the verse is always relevant or not, Mr. Lawrence writes in a concentration so absolute that the poetry is less questionable than the verse.

13. Ezra Pound in *New Freewoman*

1 September 1913, i, 113

Ezra Pound (b. 1884). Poet and critic. Born and educated in U.S.A., but lived for many years in Europe. Resident in London 1908–20. Closely associated with *Poetry* (Chicago).

This review is in many ways a repetition of Pound's review of *Love Poems* in *Poetry* (Chicago), July 1913, ii, 149–51. As explained in the Introduction, however, I consider this to be marginally the better of the two.

The disagreeable qualities of Mr. Lawrence's work are apparent to the most casual reader, and may be summed up in the emotion which one gets from the line of parody:

> Her lips still mealy with the last potato.

Love consisteth (at least we presume that it consisteth) not so much in the perception of certain stimuli, certain sensations, whereof many would seem—if we are to believe Mr. Lawrence—rather disagreeable, but in a certain sort of enthusiasm which renders us oblivious, or at least willing to be oblivious, of such sensuous perceptions, as we deem derogatory to the much derided pleasures of romance.

Having registered my personal distastes let me say without further preamble that Mr. Lawrence's book is the most important book of poems of the season. With the appearance of 'Violets' and 'Whether or Not' the Masefield boom may be declared officially and potentially over.

Mr. Lawrence, almost alone among the younger poets, has realized that contemporary poetry must be as good as contemporary prose if it is to justify its publication. In most places Mr. Lawrence's poetry is not quite as good as his own prose, but, despite his (to me) offensive manners of rhyming and of inverting and of choosing half of his words, his verse is considerably better than what we call 'contemporary' verse.

I know of no one else who could have presented the sordid tragedy of 'Whether or Not' with such vigour and economy. 'Violets' at the pen of any of the other younger men would have descended into music-hall sentiment. As it is both poems are great art. The poems are narrative and quotation in fragments is therefore worse than useless. It is for this narrative verse that I think Mr. Lawrence is to be esteemed almost as much as we esteem him for his prose. He is less happy in impressions—I suppose he classifies himself as an 'Impressionist'—and the following composition shows his good as well as his bad:

[Quotes the whole of 'Morning Work', *C.P.*, I, 72.]

To the first five lines one can make little objection beyond stating that they are not particularly musical, but when it comes to 'Morn's crystaline frame of blue,' [Lawrence later altered this to 'high crystalline frame/Of day'] 'ringing cerulean mining' we are back in the ancient kingdom of ornaments and block phrases and ready, quite ready, to forget that Mr. Lawrence is a distinguished writer of prose.

14. Unsigned review in *Nation*

14 November 1914, xvi, 220–1

Here Lawrence's volume is reviewed with two other volumes of poetry: *Immanence* by Evelyn Underhill and *Helen Redeemed and Other Poems* by Maurice Hewlett.

It is not always safe, when contemporary poetry is to be examined, to make too much of that elusive creature the Spirit of the Age. It is a ghost that is too conveniently Protean. One is apt to find it wherever one finds in modern poetry something which is peculiarly likeable; and if it does not immediately appear, there is some temptation to look for it until it does appear. That is one danger; and there is another, complementary to it. For we may be induced to tolerate indifferent work simply because it has somehow captured what seems to be the Spirit of the Age. It is like going to a dull place and finding an old friend there; we do not notice the dulness surrounding our agreeable conversations. What period is there which has not praised poetry merely for some presence there of its own familiar spirit? And yet, after all, poetry is under no obligation to provide this particular kind of entertainment; it may be as clearly the duty of poetry to reject the Spirit of the Age at one time as to accept it at another. And when ought it to be accepted? There is only one possible answer. Poetry is concerned with the Spirit of the Age only as something out of which poetry can be made; only when it is good for poetry need it be accepted. On the whole, then, we should be careful how we slight poetry for not being sufficiently 'modern'; and, conversely, that we do not praise mere modernity, but only modernity when it appears as poetry.

Nevertheless, it has sometimes happened, that when an age has been characterized by some general way of thinking or feeling, and this has proved conspicuously encouraging to poetry, those poets who have neglected this have done so very much at their peril. Contrary to what has often been hastily affirmed, there is something in the spirit of the present time which poetry, both at home and abroad, seems to find decidedly stimulating and enlivening. We possibly may not always approve of what poetry is trying to do nowadays; but it is scarcely to be denied that it is very active, very alert, and sincerely anxious not to be imitative. The mood which is thus beginning to stir poetry into new exertions may be summed up best, perhaps, in some Nietzschean phrase; if we call it, for instance, a mood of determined *yea-saying* to the actualities of existence, we shall get pretty close to it. This kind of realism—realism as impassioned as any idealism could be—is the thing we find common to such poetry of today as contrives to be thoroughly modern without endangering its art; to such poetry as that of Verhaeren abroad or of Mr. Gibson at home. But though this spirit of realism has proved itself to be of extraordinary value to poetry, it does not theoretically follow that poetry which ignores it must suffer. . . .

[The reviewer proceeds to detailed consideration of the volumes by Underhill and Hewlett, concluding his remarks on Hewlett with the comment that 'we scarcely feel that imagination has been through any great or unique experience. Or rather, we feel that well-known experiences have repeated themselves in another form.']

But there is no doubt about the kind of experience we get from Mr. Lawrence's *Love Poems*; it is unique and it is unexpected, and for its intensity of sensuous passion it may, at any rate, be called exciting. And there is no doubt either what all this is due to. Mr. Lawrence's poetry gives us something decidedly new made out of something decidedly familiar. The case here is not one of a recognizable artistic experience in a new form; it is a real transmutation. For this poetry gives us what we have called the characteristic spirit of the age expressing itself in terms of a vigorous individualism. The latter is able to translate the former into a quite novel result; whether Mr. Lawrence's be good poetry or not, it is certainly new. We find in it, and cannot but welcome, an unmistakable and impassioned *yea-saying* to actuality; and this is what we hope for in poetry today. But the precise manner of Mr. Lawrence's assent, on the one hand, to the species of love which is more disturbing and tormenting than delightful, and on the other hand, to the harsh language as well as to the squalor of mean streets— the precise manner of his assent is very much his own. We have, however, already warned ourselves against taking mere modernity for goodness in poetry. As we endeavoured, in order to form a candid judgment, to put away from our consideration the absence of anything noticeably modern in Miss Underhill's and Mr. Hewlett's work, so now we must try to look at Mr. Lawrence's poetry simply as poetry, apart from its very noticeable modernity. The quality in it which must strike a reader first of all will be its fervid intensity, both of sheer passion and of psychological construction. Sometimes it is perfervid; but, whether exaggerated or not, that such quality should be pervading is a good sign. It is that glow of delighted effort which has already been mentioned. The modern spirit does not appoint easy tasks for poetry; and we see at once that Mr. Lawrence has no intention of shirking or scamping these tasks.

But neither the courageous facing of artistic difficulty, nor the glowing intensity which results from such a mood, are enough for poetry. The frank intellectual precision with which passion is set forth, and the keenly penetrating, at times startling, psychological insight—these would certainly be remarkable anyhow. But what makes them into poetry is, first, Mr. Lawrence's power of declaring these things in a series of vivid, unexpected images—imagery which seems remote and appropriate at the same time; and, secondly, as he put this imagery into language, his ability to liberate the stored-up virtue in words. But a quotation will do better than any description:

[Quotes 'Coldness in Love', 1–5 and 21–5, 'And you remember . . . blooms on a crust.' (*C.P.*, I, 98–9.)]

It would be possible to find fault with this: 'The festoon of the sky' is a doubtful phrase. In particular, the metre is uncertain, and seems quite arbitrarily jerky; and throughout Mr. Lawrence's poems the metre, whether some subtle curiosity be intended, or whether it be simply thoughtless, is certainly a difficulty. But, on the whole, the strangeness, and yet the absolute rightness, of such poetry as this (especially of those last three lines) would enable it to carry off much more considerable faults. Indeed, some may think the monotony of Mr. Lawrence's subject *is* a more considerable, and a serious, fault. But, at any rate, it is a subject seized into poetry with extraordinary assurance; and we need not fear that, if we find ourselves strongly attracted by it, we are mistakenly equating poetic value with our pleasure in finding work so conspicuously charged with that 'Amor Fati', that vehemently honest facing of present facts, which we so much desire nowadays.

SONS AND LOVERS

May 1913

15. Unsigned review in *Standard*

30 May 1913, 5

With his third novel Mr. D. H. Lawrence has come to full maturity as a writer; form, which he lacked, he has now mastered, yet he has sacrificed nothing of his vitality. *Sons and Lovers* is so great a book that it needs sharp criticism, but the wish is to dwell in plain pleasure only on the best of it. The author has turned again to Nottinghamshire and Derbyshire for his scenes, and we know from *The White Peacock* how happy he can be in that country. He tells us of colliery, factory, and farm as he records the lives of the Morel family. The picture of the father, a blustering, drunken bully, with the refined, rather shrewish, wife is an admirable beginning. The growing children are always on the side of the mother, yet we know that the father is in many ways a good fellow. He was fond, for instance, of mending boots, 'because of the jolly sound of hammering', and such a man has a charm. We feel that he is simply running to waste, and the wastage of the best in humanity is the keynote of Mr. Lawrence's book. The same process is repeated with variations in the cases of all the sons. Paul, the second boy, takes the chief place in the story. So much of him belongs to his mother that he can never give much of himself but passion to any other woman, and in the end he is left derelict. In description of incident, even more than in revelation of character, Mr. Lawrence shows that he is a master, and in reading his book we feared always to miss a line containing the touch which shows the mark of genius and inspiration as distinct from that of talent and invention. No other English novelist of our time has so great a power to translate passion into words, but that is neither the beginning nor end of his art. His weakness is that he is too often the lyrical poet making his creatures speak his thoughts, and this is a bad fault for a novelist. The dialogue seems at times

58

pompous, and we recall such terms as 'protoplasm', 'despicable', and 'the human form' in the conversation of those who had not the habit of their use. Simple people have complex emotions often enough, but they are plain spoken or they take to silence.

16. Unsigned review in *Westminster Gazette*

14 June 1913, xli, 17

Man as he is rather than man as he ought to be is beyond question the proper theme for the novelist; but there is still something to be said for the old-fashioned prejudice which led all the great novelists, and the great tragedians also, to select man doing his utmost with the circumstances of his case for their central theme, and to relegate to subsidiary positions, for the sake of contrast as well as of truth, the spectacle of circumstances making sport of a perfectly unresisting victim. A central figure, whether in the event triumphant or defeated, had to possess some power of resistance. Nowadays we have done with the hero, and in his place we have the subject. Sensitiveness is the only quality the really modern novelist seeks in the central figure of his tale, and the consequence is that we are in danger of replacing our novels of character by those of mere characterization. This change, which has come to us from France, is likely enough to work its own revenge on the English novelist, and a warning sign of this danger may be found by interested observers in Mr. D. H. Lawrence's third, and in some respects finest, novel, *Sons and Lovers*. The change of view (we will not call it a mistake) which has led Mr. Lawrence, in common with other novelists of great repute or promise, to place more emphasis on feeling than on action has resulted in a draining of interest from the whole of his work. The heroic figure of this novel is not Paul Morel, who occupies the central position of the book, and through whose experience the major part of the story is told, but his grim little mother, who had married beneath her, and was forced to turn to her sons for the satisfaction of her instinct for devotion which had been so cruelly wasted on her husband. Had Mr. Lawrence been able to keep the whole of his story within the bounds of Mrs. Morel's experience he would have sacrificed nothing of its dignity and truth, and would further have been able to spare his readers certain pages of the peculiar heavy morbidity which he mistakes for realism. He would also have escaped an implicit acquiescence in Paul's super-human selfishness in his relations with the two women whom he tries to love, while in no way weakening his record of the struggle which goes on between his devotion to his mother and the clamorous passion of his early manhood. It would, however, be futile to continue a consideration of the book Mr. Lawrence has not written. As it stands, this history of weakness is a remarkable piece of work. Charged with the beauty of atmosphere and observation, of which Mr. Lawrence is so complete a master, and written with a sincerity which can make the reader forgive his worst offences against reticence, *Sons and Lovers* is a book to haunt and waylay the mind long after it has been laid aside. The contrast between the grime and drunkenness of colliery life and the beauty of Derbyshire lanes and farmhouses, the glory of spring, the raptures of childhood, the relief of rest from toil, are all woven into the vacillating tragedy of Paul's youth, and form a part of his mother's life-long effort, so that at no point is the horror unbearable or the joy unsullied. A page from one of the earlier chapters will best show the effect of Mr. Lawrence's very individual methods:

[Quotes from Chap. IV, 'Annie and Paul and Arthur loved the winter evenings . . . the night had swallowed them.' (Penguin ed. 97–8.)]

Sometimes they quarrelled:

[Continues quotation from Chap. IV, 'Paul never forgot . . . and quick, passionate speech.' (Penguin ed. 98–9.)]

We have made no attempt to summarize the story which holds this detailed study of the relation between mother and son and lover together. Definite plot there is none—the book begins with Paul's mother's marriage and ends with her death—but Paul, the unheroic hero, is left still vacillating before his life, and there is no reason why a later book should not continue the record of his aimless way.

17. Harold Massingham in *Daily Chronicle*

17 June 1913, 3

Harold Massingham (1888–1952). Journalist and man of letters.

The wiseacres say that the novel, as literature and as a moral and æsthetic influence, has run its course, that the fiction public has migrated in large numbers to biography and its more serious-minded portion to sociology. The result is that the novelist, having no barricades of taste or criteria to restrain him, runs amok and deluges the remnant with any fashionable and mediocre ideas that may happen to tickle its palate.

There is, of course, truth in this contention, particularly at a time when our standards and values of writing are so haphazard. But it is the vision of one who cannot see the wheat for the chaff. As a matter of fact, there is an ample body of fiction put upon the market each year which, if neither brilliant or finished, is obviously written by sincere and thoughtful people, anxious to express their attitude towards life rather than towards their public and their publishers. And in the company of such is Mr. Lawrence's *Sons and Lovers*, far and away the best book he has yet written.

It has little or no pretensions to plot-architecture, its incident is not external, and in the crisis of psychological evolution it bothers hardly at all about continuity, balance or arrangement. It possesses surprisingly few of the more obvious attractions of the novel. It is simply an objective record of a collier's family in the Midlands, over a period of twenty to thirty years, conveyed without extenuation, without partiality, and with a ruthless fidelity to things as they were in that family which leaves no loophole for special pleading on behalf of the immaculate heroine and the hero without fear or reproach.

Mr. Arnold Bennett, as all the world knows, is the modern specialist in accurate and minute portraiture, using not the scalpel like Zola and Flaubert, but the miscroscope; pursuing the mental and spiritual motions of his creatures with a scientific detachment; examining nothing—not that he does not adorn, but that he does not magnify and throw into significance and relief. And it is plain that Mr. Lawrence, though less of an artist, is in some measure indebted to Mr. Bennett's method. Curiously enough, they employ a similar background, and are vivified by the same genius of locality.

But where Mr. Bennett observes, Mr. Lawrence analyses. Indeed, unity and sharpness of outline are often obscured upon his canvas by a passion for probing the motives and processes of his characters, not as beings, but as thinkers. This introspective fever is peculiarly prominent in his treatment of Paul, the second son of the Morels. We are, of course, on conjectural ground here, but we suspect that Paul is a projection of the writer's own personality. We see him, moreover, never in relation to himself, but to the three women he loved, his mother, the shrinking, mystical Miriam, and the material, defiant Clara Dawes. Within these three he revolves and they determine his destiny. And we feel that Paul can never get far enough away from his creator to solidify into a self-sufficient person.

All this portion of the narrative is more fanciful, more impressionist, and more coloured than the first part, and quite definitely parts company from the Bennett type. It is infinitely more curious and more intense. The 'ego' of the author is, we imagine, more involved. But the earlier pictures of Mrs. Morel and her husband, of her eldest son, William, and his betrothed, Lily Western, are unerringly painted in, without any tragic infusion of the personal element. The irony is in themselves and their circumstances, not in the author's interpretation of them.

But the real triumph of *Sons and Lovers* is William and his fiancée. They are wedged into the smallest possible compass, but the quintessence of their fatal communion is thereby the more poignantly realized. The horror of his entanglement with her has a far more tragic purport than Paul's with Miriam. The one is life, the other an aspect of psychology. We wish we could have seen more of Annie, the only daughter of the household. Her effacement leaves a gap in the structure of the family, and impairs the finish of the perspective.

It is obvious that Mr. Lawrence's latest book is also his most ambitious. Not only are his figures numerous and radically diverse, but in style and treatment he plays upon a many-stringed instrument. It is perhaps its intricate nature that gives to portions of it an abrupt and feverish air. It is at times painfully crowded and intense, and at times a little careless in minor deficiencies.

It was a beauteous evening, calm and pure,
And breathing holy quiet like a nun.

is, for instance, an inexcusably bad misquotation. But as a whole his
work is, in the most vital sense, suggestive and imaginative.

18. Unsigned review in *Saturday Review*

21 June 1913, cxv, 780–1

When were there written novels so strange as these of Mr. Lawrence? Now that he has given us three of them we should be able to make some estimate of his position among writers, yet there is about him something wilful which eludes judgment. Passages in *Sons and Lovers* tempt us to place him in a high class; and it is indeed a good book, even though it has pages where the author's vision is revealed only behind a dense cloud. As a story it is the record of the lives of a miner and his family in the middle counties of England, and from *The White Peacock* we knew how well the Derbyshire and Nottinghamshire country would be pictured. It can now be added that the scene from the towns are little less good. The ruling idea in the book is the pitiful wastage of the best in men and women, and it is first shown in the persons of Morel and his wife. The former is physically a grand specimen of a race which puts its strength into manual labour, but he is ruined by drink, for his will is always weak. Mrs. Morel is a good housewife and a decent woman. Her superior ways mark her to her husband as a lady; yet she shirks none of the duties which his mate should perform for him, the children, and the home. Unhappily there is in her something of the shrew, and the association between the pair serves only to bring out their unpleasant sides. The young family grows up zealous for the mother; but with the touch of skill Mr. Lawrence can show the father as the good fellow whom these others never knew. 'He', we read, 'always sang when he mended boots because of the jolly sound of hammering'; and in that single sentence is revealed the human creature who should have had pure joy of life and an author whose inspiration leaves behind the common artifices of the novelist. There are many other places where the writer quite surprises us by his power to make the narrative pass from fiction into glowing reality, and as an example we cannot do better than quote from the scene where young Paul and his sweetheart are climbing in the ruined tower: 'They continued to mount the winding staircase. A high wind, blowing through the loop-holes, went rushing up the shaft and filled the girl's skirts like a balloon, so that she was ashamed, until he took the hem of her dress and held it down for her. He did it perfectly simply, as he would have picked up her glove.' No man could have invented this piece of description at the factory of the desk; it is a fragment of life, though we cannot know whether it belongs to the world of fact or had its genesis in some glorious flash of imagination. Origin, however, matters nothing. The passage remains as one which not a novelist in a hundred could produce.

Paul Morel, the miner's second son, is the chief person in the book, and his tragedy is his devotion to his mother, for she absorbs almost everything in him but his passions. Miriam, the girl of the tower episode, does battle for him. Despite her fierce purity she gives herself to his desire, but cannot hold him even by her sacrifice, and he drifts into a passionate friendship with a second woman. The idea of waste still rules the story. The mother, who has dreaded the influence of Miriam on his affections, almost welcomes the intrigue with Clara, because the latter is less exacting in her demands. Puritan as she is, Mrs. Morel condones the affair with a married woman in order to keep the greater part of her son for herself. The strife between the generations is admirably suggested, and we know of no active English novelist—today—who has Mr. Lawrence's power to put in words the rise and fall of passion. The death of the mother and Paul's derelict state are the ends to which the story naturally leads, for the author is too good an artist to allow a conclusion which could stultify the force of all that he has built on the characters of his people. What is wrong in the book is the frequent intrusion of the writer. The men and women use words which are his and not their own; their reading is in the literature for which he cares; often they express thoughts which belong to him and not to them. Mr. Lawrence's inability to efface himself is now his most serious weakness, for the faulty construction of his earlier work is in no way evident in *Sons and Lovers*. After reading most of the more 'important' novels of the present year, we can say that we have seen none to excel it in interest and power; the sum of its defects is astonishingly large, but we only note it when they are weighed against the sum of its own qualities.

19. Lascelles Abercrombie in
Manchester Guardian
2 July 1913, 7

Lascelles Abercrombie, signed 'L.A.' (1881–1938). Poet and critic.
In the pre-1914 period Abercrombie was considered as one of the
leading poets of the new generation. After the war, continued to
write poetry and had a distinguished academic career. One of
Rupert Brooke's friends.

'Odi et amo' should have been on the title-page of Mr. D. H.
Lawrence's *Sons and Lovers*. On the whole, the book may be said to
contrast filial and maternal love with the kind of love which is called
amour. A good many amours are described, involving several markedly
diverse persons; but all the affairs and all the persons are unanimous in
one matter—whatever kind of love it may be, some kind of hate is
mixed up in it. A simultaneous passion of love and hatred is, of course,
a well-known psychological fact; and certainly Mr. Lawrence makes
its unfailing appearance in his story curiously credible. But it is not a
very pleasant fact; is it not essentially a weakness of vitality, a kind of
failure—life failing to appreciate itself, hating itself because it cannot
appreciate the splendour of its own fate? Whether or no, it is a fact one
can easily have too much of. If Mr. Lawrence thought to give intensity
to the whole length (the very considerable length) of his story by this
mingling of contrary passions, he miscalculated seriously. The constant
juxtaposition of love and hatred looks like an obsession; and, like all
obsessions, soon becomes tiresome. You begin to look out for the word
'hate' as soon as you have read the word 'love', like a sort of tedious
game. 'Odi et amo' does marvellous well in an epigram; in a novel of
four hundred odd pages it is a bore. The book has other faults. It has
no particular shape and no recognizable plot; themes are casually taken
up, and then as casually dropped, and there seems no reason why they
should have been taken up unless they were to be kept up. Everything

that happens is an extraordinarily long time about it, and sometimes it takes a very long time for nothing at all to happen. Faults like these ought to swamp any virtues the book may possess; set them down in this abstract fashion, and it seems incredible that *Sons and Lovers* can be anything but a dull success of cleverness. So, perhaps, it would be, if Mr. Lawrence were simply a novelist. But he is a poet, one of the most remarkable poets of the day; and these faults of his are actually of no more account than the soot of a brilliant, vehement flame. Indeed, you do not realize how astonishingly interesting the whole book is until you find yourself protesting that this thing or that thing bores you, and eagerly reading on in spite of your protestations. You decide that the old collier, the father, is a dirty brute; and then perceive that he profoundly has your sympathy. The mother is a creature of superb and lovable heroism; and yet there is no doubt that she is sometimes downright disagreeable. You think you are reading through an unimportant scene; and then find that it has burnt itself on your mind. The 'Odi et amo' of the main theme, in fact, is only an exaggerated instance of the quality which runs through the whole book, which may be best described as contrary, in the sense the word has when it rhymes with Mary. Life, for Mr. Lawrence, is a coin which has both obverse and reverse; so it is for most people, but his unusual art consists in his surprising ability to illuminate both sides simultaneously. The scope and variety of the life he describes, his understanding and vivid realizing of circumstance and his insight into character, and chiefly his power of lighting a train of ordinary events to blaze up into singular significance, make *Sons and Lovers* stand out from the fiction of the day as an achievement of the first quality.

20. Unsigned review in *Nation*

12 July 1913, xiii, 577–8

We question if a more strenuous task has ever been set a reviewer of fiction than the appraisal of this book. It is 'difficult' every way—difficult to read (though not for the usual cause, since no obscurity of phrase disfigures it), difficult to appraise, difficult above all to apprehend. Scarce a problem of the fictional art but is set us here, in manner, matter, and design; and so wilful is the author that each close-hugged theory has seemed for us at one moment to be confirmed, at the next disproved, by his practice. One faith, indeed, remains throughout unshaken—the conviction that sincerity is a good, a great good, but not an overmastering good. Sincerity leaps at us here from every page; but while on one it is that of a seer whose vision is well-nigh apocalyptic, on another it seems the mere 'observation' of a helpless realist who cannot separate the All from the everything. The scene of the burnt loaves in Chapter VIII is an example of this. As helplessly as it is given us, we read it—seeking vainly a sufficient reason for its inclusion. In *The White Peacock* there were similar moments, and in it also they were associated (we are nearly sure our recollection is right) with the same type of girl as is the Beatrice of this scene. Mr. Lawrence fails completely in the delineation of this mocking, elfin sort of creature—so completely that her repeated presence in his work is a marvel to us. Directly she appears, all seems to fly apart, and we know not in what fancied world we are, nor whence can come the beings who surround us there. More brutally to express it, we are bored beyond all utterance, and that because the material (whatever its intrinsic worth or worthlessness) is in the hands of one who does not know how to use it. This is what we mean by Mr. Lawrence's 'helpless' sincerity; and this is why we do not regard sincerity as an overmastering good. Rather we regard it as the leaven of the lump, which may or may not do its part in producing the 'bread of life'.

No plot, or as little as may be: here is another faith. And in the earlier chapters of *Sons and Lovers*, it is felt to be triumphantly justified. How would a 'plot' have torn through this fine web of poetry, realism, and shrewd or tender analysis! As every page brings its sheaf of beauties, our confidence and gratitude grow; the Morel family is to us as it were the reflex of the universe—and who can tire of the universe? We'd have Mr. Lawrence do it ever. Scarcely have we turned a dozen pages when we come upon such a splendid thing as this (he is speaking of Mrs. Morel's first meeting with the man whom she marries and learns to scorn):

[Quotes from Chap. I, 'She was a puritan, like her father . . . something wonderful, beyond her.' (Penguin ed. 18.)]

Surely here is 'something wonderful': physiology, psychology, and splendid poetry, so interfused that we can hardly tell which is which! And then the subtlety of this: 'For three months she was perfectly happy; for six months she was very happy'; but she detected him in a lie, and 'something in her proud, honourable soul crystallized out like rock.' . . . The whole story of this marriage is absorbing, and though our sympathy with the sentimental, violent miner-husband is deeper than (we imagine) it was intended to be, we still admire—more intellectually than humanly, it is true; with a drier eye than that which considers the scorned and cast-aside Morel . . . we still admire, we often but not always love, the little, blue-eyed woman, with her crooked, 'winsome' nose, which 'scornfully sniffs' when she is pleased or flattered or moved to tenderness. Her relations with the eldest child, William, are of the normal maternal type, though even here the peculiar 'kink' upon which Mr. Lawrence later so urgently insists, is present: William could not love any other woman well, because he loved his mother well. Both the sons, this William, and the younger Paul, discuss their sweethearts 'endlessly' with Mrs. Morel; for both it results in disenchantment. This is doubtless the fruit of observation, yet life would seem to deny it much of truth—and we cannot accept at all the scenes in which William rails against and 'at' his betrothed to his mother, the unhappy girl being present all the time! That both young men should hate the woman with whom they are sexually occupied is an obsession of the author. 'He hated her'—we could not count the repetitions of those words. One wearies sadly of them, and of the various (or not various) states of feeling to which they have reference. Indeed, to indicate the delight which *Sons and Lovers* will give all who care for the novel in its more developed aspects, we must turn from the relations of any couple but Mr. and Mrs. Morel, and speak of the exquisite nature-pieces—the flower and field pieces above all—where things of piercing beauty are showered like benedictions on our heads. Mr. Lawrence has hardly an equal in these lovelinesses. Nor are they by any means all; there are scenes which no word but the too lightly lavished 'great' can justly characterize—that of the bringing-home of tall William dead, for instance, when up the steps from the street in darkness, to the 'front-room' where the chairs are ranged awaiting them, come the six men climbing, 'bearing the coffin that rode like sorrow on their living flesh'.

Such loveliness, such splendours (the word is not a whit too strong), have kindled our hearts, and all our hearts are warm with gratitude. We read on vividly, our trust now unfaltering, and feel that we are soon to grasp the design in which this high imagination works. But to our amazement and our grief, as the central figure emerges, as we hail the 'hero', as Paul, the second son, develops, and Mr. Lawrence concentrates on him alone, in his relations with his mother and the two women who make up his sexual experience . . . to our grief and our amazement, the book suffers a sea-change, and not into something rich and strange, but into something—the terms must, paradoxically, be used for all this stretch of startling verbal frankness—thin and commonplace. As we feel this more and more decidedly, as we revolt in weariness from the incessant scenes of sexual passion, another and a more far-reaching question than any we have yet considered bristles in our path. Is not all this grown, or growing, obsolete? Do such matters greatly exercise our minds today? . . . Our age, men say, is decadent. If to lean, with such hot-heavy urgence, upon things of sense alone, be the sign-manual of vitality, then, indeed, the judgment is a just one; for we are persuaded that only to the dwellers in back-waters will these scenes prove thrilling, 'shocking', stimulating, or even interesting. Those of us who move amid the true activities, who touch at many points of the electric currents of thought and feeling which light up this time of ours, shall reject these chapters gladly—gladly because with reading of them a sense of our emancipation comes to us more fully than before. Such as we are, we are past this; and if to be so past be decadence, it seems a better thing than we had supposed. But the truth is, of course, that not we, but they, are rightly designated thus. This is the real decadence—this morbid brooding on the flesh, this gross detail of things unspoken, this never-quick, this ever-hot and heavy lustfulness of Paul Morel. Did young man's figure ever more signally fail to move us to interest? We turn from him in fatigued repulsion—so futile he, so garrulous of his lust, so 'decadent' indeed in his relations with Miriam and Clara. 'That's how women are with me,' he says. 'They want me like mad, but they don't want to belong to me.' How should they? There was nothing to belong to. . . . May one say, with no thought of ribaldry, that Paul was 'a mother's son?' But even in the love for his mother there lurks the same unhealthiness. At the end of the book, when she is dead, 'Mother!' he whimpered— 'mother!' In that verb, Mr. Lawrence confesses Paul Morel. Here, in an earlier chapter (named 'The Test on Miriam'), is his creator's apology for him:

[Quotes from Chap. XI, 'A good many of the nicest men he knew . . . they were full of the sense of their mother.' (Penguin ed. 341.)]

Yet Paul, at any rate, did in the event deny himself nothing that he could get, and incur all reproach from 'his' women—who were both far nearer to the sources of life than he was.

What is the outcome—what the star to which this fictional waggon is hitched? Is it the glory of the motherhood of sons? Yet would not one say from reading this that for a young man to be 'full of the sense of his mother' is to destroy him? And since such is the cumulative effect, the book, for all its beauty and power and imagination, is decadent. A man's 'sense of his mother' means one thing, not another which denies the first. . . . But, remembering all that *Sons and Lovers* gives us, we are glad to forget Paul and his 'failures', his 'test on Miriam', his further test (though not this time so labelled) on Clara, his 'question, which was almost a lamentation, "*Why* don't they hold me?"' . . . to forget, in short, that half the book is against the grain, and remember gratefully and glowingly those earlier chapters which keep faith with life.

21. Louise Maunsell Field in
New York Times Book Review

21 September 1913, 479

Louise Maunsell Field. Novelist and reviewer. Reviewed other works by Lawrence, including *The Lost Girl* (*NYTBR* 27 March 1921) and *Aaron's Rod* (*NYTBR* 30 April 1922).

There is probably no phrase much more hackneyed than that of 'human document', yet it is the only one which at all describes this very unusual book. It is hardly a story; rather the first part of a man's life, from his birth until his twenty-fifth year, the conditions surrounding him, his strength and his numerous weaknesses, put before us in a manner which misses no subtlest effect either of emotion or environment. And the heroine of the book is not sweetheart, but mother; the mother with whose marriage the novel begins, with whose pathetic death it reaches its climax. The love for each other of the mother and her son, Paul Morel, is the mainspring of both their lives; it is portrayed tenderly, yet with a truthfulness which slurs nothing even of that friction which is unavoidable between the members of two different generations.

The scene is laid among the collieries of Derbyshire. Paul's father was a miner; his mother, Mrs. Morel, belonged a trifle higher up in the social scale, having made one of those 'romantic' marriages with which the old-fashioned sentimental novel used to end, and with which the modern realistic one so frequently begins. The first chapter, which tells of their early married life before the coming of their second son, Paul, is an admirable account of a mismated couple. Walter Morel could never have amounted to very much, but had he possessed a less noble wife he might, by one of those strange contradictions of which life is full, have been a far better man than he actually was. His gradual degeneration is as pitiful as it is inevitable—the change from the joyous, lovable young man to the drunken, ill-tempered father, whose entrance hushed the children's laughter, the mere thought of whom could cast a shadow over all the house. Mrs. Morel was strong enough to remake for herself the life he had so nearly wrecked—he could only drift helplessly upon the rocks. It is wonderfully real, this daily life of the Morel family and the village wherein they lived as reflected in Mr. Lawrence's pages; the more real because he never flaunts his knowledge of the intimate details of the existence led by these households whose men folk toil underground. They slip from his pen so unobtrusively that it is only when we pause and consider that we recognize how full and complete is the background against which he projects his principal characters—Mr. and Mrs. Morel, Paul, Miriam, and Clara.

Paul himself is a person who awakens interest rather than sympathy; it is difficult not to despise him a little for his weakness, his constant need of that strengthening he sought from two other women, but which only his splendid, indomitable little mother could give him—a fact of which he was constantly aware, though he acknowledged it only at the very end. And it is not easy upon any grounds to excuse his treatment of Miriam, even though it was a spiritual self-defence which urged him to disloyalty. Mr. Lawrence has small regard for what we term conventional morality; nevertheless, though plain spoken to a degree, his book is not in the least offensive.

It is, in fact, fearless; never coarse, although the relations between Paul, Miriam, and Clara are portrayed with absolute frankness. And one must go far to find a better study of an intense woman, so over-spiritualized that she has almost lost touch with ordinary life and ordinary humanity, than he has given us in the person of Miriam. We pity her for her craving, her self-distrust that forbade her to take the thing she most wanted even when it was almost within her grasp; and yet Paul's final recoil is readily comprehensible, his feeling that she was making his very soul her own—would, as his mother said, leave nothing of him. The long, psychic battle between the two, a battle blindly fought, never really understood, is excellent in its revelation of those motives which lie at the very root of character—motives of which the persons they actuate are so often completely ignorant.

Clara is less remarkable than Miriam only because she is necessarily more obvious—a woman in whom the animal predominates, certain after a brief time to weary one like Paul. And better than either, strong of will, rich in love and sympathy, holding her place in her son's heart against even Miriam, who so nearly took him from her, reigning at last supreme over every rival stands the heroic little mother—the best-drawn character in a book which contains many admirable portrayals. From the moment when we first meet her taking her elder children to the 'wakes' and trying to nerve herself to endure a life which appears to be an endless waiting for something that can never come, until at the last she wages her valiant, losing fight against the cancer that is killing her by inches, she is always real, a fine, true woman, mother to the very core. Mr. Lawrence has mercifully spared us the terrible details of her illness; it is only her 'tortured eyes' we see, and her children's grief and horror. Whether or not it was right for Paul to do the thing he did is an open question; only we are sure that in very truth he 'loved her better than his own life'. His impotent resentment of her growing weakness is an excellent bit of analysis; the effect upon him of her death, which he seemed to take so calmly— the blankness, the unreality and emptiness of all things—strikes home. Without her his life was meaningless; yet live he must, and for her sake.

The book is full of short, vivid descriptions:

The steep swoop of highroad lay, in its cool morning dust, splendid with patterns of sunshine and shadow, perfectly still . . . Behind the houses stood on the brim of the dip, black against the sky, like wild beasts glaring curiously with yellow eyes down into the darkness.

Each a picture drawn in a sentence. Although this is a novel of over 500 closely printed pages the style is terse—so terse that at times it produces an effect as of short, sharp hammer strokes. Yet it is flexible, too, as shown by its success in depicting varying shades of mood, in expressing those more intimate emotions which are so very nearly inexpressible. Yet, when all is said, it is the complex character of Miriam, she who was only Paul's 'conscience, not his mate', and the beautiful bond between the restless son and the mother whom 'his soul could not leave' even when she slept and 'dreamed her young dream' which makes this book one of rare excellence.

22. Alfred Kuttner in *New Republic*

10 April 1915, ii, 255-7

This review was expanded into an article for the *Psychoanalytic Review*, iii, No. 3, July 1916. (See Introduction, p. 7.)

Mr. D. H. Lawrence finds himself in agreement with other writers in one important respect. He, too, like the vast majority of fictionists of all time, looks upon the successful mating of his characters as the fundamental problem of his story. And however much we may sometimes tire of the conventional 'and they lived happily ever after', we must admit that novelists are right in focusing attention upon this point. Whether for good or evil, almost every mature fantasy about life probably has an erotic core, so that we are hardly capable of thinking it through without including a marriage idyl by means of which we unconsciously strive to recall that secure haven of love which we dimly associate with our childhood. The melodramatic novelist naïvely looks upon all obstacles to mating as coming entirely from without. More mature writers realize subtler difficulties and put their emphasis almost entirely upon the inner conflicts, but they usually manage to end with a successful mating.

That is just what Mr. Lawrence never really succeeds in doing. With him the inner conflicts, instead of being gradually resolved, luxuriate to inordinate proportions until in the end they prove too much both for the author and his characters. Not that all mating is excluded from his pages. But when marriage does finally overtake some of his characters it usually comes as a kind of dismissal from our attention, or with just that novelistic conventionality to which readers rightly object. The whole creative warmth of the author is automatically withdrawn, and these superficially successful matings, so evidently punished by Mr. Lawrence's neglect, inevitably leave us cold. To the matings which he has most at heart he invariably opposes insuperable obstacles.

Both *The Trespasser* and *The White Peacock* are early studies in mis-mating. These novels already foreshadow the born stylist and reveal Mr. Lawrence as a writer of puzzling importance. But the mis-matings they portray remain obscurely motivated and therefore seem arbitrary; the psychological justification is often inadequate or obscure. We do not understand them, and hesitate to accept them. The same criticism applies to Mr. Lawrence's play, *The Widowing of Mrs. Holroyd*. We see that Mrs. Holroyd hates her husband, but we do not see so clearly why her love for him has died, drunkard though he is. For the author, in spite of himself, has made him lovable notwithstanding his vices, so that his death comes as a sorrow and a rebuke to his wife. The play is more powerful than the novels if only because a livid hate expressed on the stage by an impassioned woman carries its own conviction.

Sons and Lovers marks an astonishing change in its author. If this slow-moving, profound, almost too inevitable study leaves the fascinated reader disturbed and exhausted, it is surely no less exhaustive of the author's true inwardness. Here Mr. Lawrence has found the very core of himself; here he has dipped deep into his own childhood, setting down all that he ever knew or felt. We notice a sudden exquisite refinement of psychological texture, a new, painstaking reverence for the most subtle and intangible details of motivation. The problem of mis-mating is no longer studied in an already established marital relation; here it is not a matter of mis-mating at all but of a radical inability to mate. This inability Mr. Lawrence seeks to explain entirely in terms of his hero's emotional relation to his parents.

That is the really new and contributive thing about *Sons and Lovers*. Paul Morel's childhood unfolds in the vitiated atmosphere of an already unhappy marriage. In the married life of the Morels Mr. Lawrence for the first time gives us a mis-mating which both he and we thoroughly understand. The marriage of this drunken, bullying, morally weak-fibred miner to a woman of superior breeding and a stern, sensitive, puritanically unsensuous temperament, was foredoomed to failure. Her hatred and aversion for him is absorbed by her child almost from the cradle, so that at the age of six Paul prays that his father may be killed. Cut off from companionship with his father— and there can be no doubt that a child learns to love the father largely through imitating its mother—Paul abnormally concentrates all his affection upon one parent.

Under the strain of these relations the boy develops a premature emotional maturity. His childish heart is torn between anguish for his abused mother and a scarcely repressed hatred for his brutal father. Mrs. Morel, her affection for her husband completely atrophied, now turns altogether to her son and deliberately courts his allegiance. He becomes her confidant and her consoler, a quiet, worldly-wise child whose natural initiative is gradually deadened by the burden of this unequal responsibility, while at the same time the too great absorption in his mother effeminizes him. At a time when most children already display the first poetic tentatives of the mating impulse in ideal comradeships with playmates of the opposite sex, Paul dreams only of running away with his mother and living alone with her for the rest of his life.

By the time Paul reaches adolescence the distortion is already complete. He finds himself attracted to Miriam Leivers, a shy, beautiful girl who idealizes him. But the prospect of marrying her fills him only with unhappiness and a strange, paralyzing sense of death. The author now boldly underlines the mutual infatuation of mother and son. A jealous conflict, in which Paul is the helpless pawn, ensues between the two women. Paul gradually becomes persuaded of the unreality of his and Miriam's feelings, and returns to his exultant mother with the tragic conviction that while she is alive no other woman can have place in his affections. There is a final flaring up of his mating impulse towards Clara Dawes, a married woman of strong, sensuous appeal. While under her influence he returns to Miriam and finally possesses both women, hovering for a time between what are for him the sacred and profane loves of his life. His consciousness that with Clara he is merely indulging in a temporary liaison with a married woman makes it easier for him to give himself to her. But in the end Mrs. Morel triumphs again and brings Paul to her death-bed, a confessed and repentant lover. Her death, now desired and even criminally hastened by him as an emancipation from an intolerable situation, makes her triumph only the more complete and leaves Paul standing before us a helpless, tragic, pathetically childish figure. In a final unforgettable chapter Mr. Lawrence pictures him as a human derelict set adrift, with the great nostalgia for death in his heart, and living merely in the memory of a relation which, hallowed only in childhood, has grown utterly ruinous in its perpetuations.

No summary can convey the pathos of *Sons and Lovers*. With all its power and its passion, it remains to a certain extent incomprehensible. We may, for the moment, accept it intuitively. But we hesitate to accept it in its implications. The very idea that an excess of mother love should prove so disastrous to an individual's fate seems monstrous. Instinctively we look upon this as an exceptional case, and fortify ourselves against it by calling the book morbid or perverse. Mr. Lawrence himself has not come to our aid with any supplementary theory, nor, fortunately, does he weaken the natural eloquence of his artistry by any attempt to generalize.

How deeply felt, how little reasoned, the reaction has been with him may be gathered from a reading of his *Love Poems*. These astonishingly self-revealing lyrics repeat, with almost monotonous regularity, Paul's most intimate psychic conflicts. And it would not be at all difficult, going back now, to show that the earlier novels and the play are also, in their essence, nothing more than unclarified and fragmentary expressions of the same personal experience before Mr. Lawrence had arrived at the searching and pitiless insight which in *Sons and Lovers* makes him such a memorable artist. Hatred of the father and too much love of the mother are the *leit-motifs* of everything this author has written.

In order to understand Mr. Lawrence fully we must go beyond his works. Fiction is at best a specialized and limited way of conveying the truth. A novel based upon the truth of the evolutionary theory, poetically visioned by the author at a time when that theory was not yet a part of general knowledge, would, despite all artistic merit, leave a certain margin of incredulity until, let us say, Huxley's lectures had made evolution a household term. In precisely the same way our completer understanding of *Sons and Lovers* depends upon our knowledge of a theory. For without the Freudian psycho-sexual theories *Sons and Lovers* remains an enigma; with it we see that artist and scientist supplement each other, that each in his own way attests to the same truth.

The methods necessarily differ. Where Mr. Lawrence particularizes so passionately Freud generalizes. Freud has proved beyond cavil that the parental influence regularly determines the mating impulse. The child's attachment to the parent of opposite sex becomes the prototype of all later love relations. The feeling is so strong and even fraught with such intense jealousy of the parent of the same sex, that all children seem to entertain conscious and unconscious fantasies in which the rival parent is either killed or removed. In the normal development this first infatuation is gradually obliterated from memory by widening associations and by transference, but the unconscious impress remains, so that every man tends to choose for his mate a woman who has associative connections for him with the early infantile image of his mother, while the woman also makes her choice in relation to her father. As soon as there is any disturbance of the balanced influence of both parents upon the child there follows an abnormal concentration upon the beloved parent. To such distortion of the normal erotic development Freud attaches the greatest importance, seeing in it the major cause of all neurotic disturbances.

Of this *Sons and Lovers* is an eloquent example. A distortion so great that it precludes all mating is not only prejudicial to the individual's true happiness but may lead to an atrophy of all initiative. Paul constantly associates the feeling of death with his inability to mate, and that too is psychologically sound. We recognize the Paul in us. For though we may dislike a happy ending in our novel, we cannot but prefer it in our lives.

THE PRUSSIAN OFFICER
November 1914

23. Unsigned review in *Outlook*
19 December 1914, xxxiv, 795-6

Here are twelve short stories from Mr. D. H. Lawrence's pen—all brilliant, all superhuman, and at the same time *in*human. Of each one read separately we should be able to say that Mr. Lawrence had chanced to light upon an unusual personality and had portrayed it with vigour and force. At the same time we should have realized that many such personalities would burn up the world. All their thoughts are thought at a white heat. Their hates are of the corrosive kind. Their passions are volcanic. In a word they are as unlike the normal folk we know as though they were indeed denizens of another planet.

The first story is of so topically business-like a kind that we are a little astonished to find it in so eminently unpractical a volume. And in a volume so unexpected as this, too, we are amazed to find that it is in so far in accordance with popular feeling as to present the Prussian officer in a distinctly unpleasing light. But, brutal bully as he is, he is by no means the Hunnish individual to whom the war has given his chance of exhibiting himself in his true light. True, the gentleman in question kicks his servant's thighs with the same vigour the German officer has brought to bear on the bombardment of unfortified places, on the massacring of helpless civilians, on the violation of women, and the destruction of those things of beauty which have made the world's holidays. But a subtle savagery is at work in this particular case of bullying that we should find very far to seek in the purely brutish methods which characterize Germany's more collective inhumanities. The Prussian officer of the title dislikes his orderly. The reason of his dislike keeps the reader intrigued to a quite remarkable degree. But the true inwardness of the thing is persistently withheld from us. Once another celebrated criminal, being solicited by an inquiring judge to explain to the court why he had thought it necessary to put a comparatively harmless female out of the way, made reply that he did not like the shape of her nose. In the same way, if hard pressed, the Prussian officer might have answered that he did not like the shape of the limber young fellow's body. There was a sinister quality in his bullying however that we should hardly have expected. There is a subtle quality, too, in the youth's enjoyment in murdering him that gives us pause for thought. This is a very powerful, if at the same time quite horrible, piece of writing:

> The spur of the officer caught in a tree-root, he went down backwards with a crash, the middle of his back thudding sickeningly against a sharp-edged tree-base, the pot flying away. And in a second the orderly, with serious, earnest young face, and underlip between his teeth, had got his knee in the officer's chest and was pressing the chin backwards over the further edge of the tree-stump, pressing with all his heart behind in a passion of relief, the tension of his wrists exquisite with relief. And with the base of his palms he shoved at the chin, with all his might. And it was pleasant, too, to have that chin, that hard jaw already slightly rough with beard, in his hands. He did not relax one hair's-breadth, but, all the force of all his blood exulting in his thrust, he shoved back the head of the other man, till there was a little 'cluck' and a crunching sensation.

Far be it from us to maintain that the killing of that officer was not a right and proper deed. At the same time we do not think so many complicated emotions on both sides would have either led up to it or produced it. It is the same with the killing of the sergeant by the young soldier in the next story, *The Thorn in the Flesh*. It is quite excusable, of course, that a certain impulse should have moved the soldier's fist to give that brutal person 'one for himself', even though the person so maltreated happened to be standing on the edge of a rampart at the moment. It is easy, too, to understand that the young soldier might have felt ashamed of his inability to climb heights without turning giddy. But would he have felt it to the extreme searing depths Mr. Lawrence suggests? And if he had—since the human frame is only capable of a certain amount of emotion—would the same individual be able to conduct his love affairs at the same violent level? It is for the reason that there is a certain moderating level kept in *The Daughters of the Vicar* that we like it best of all the stories here presented to us. But with that one story all moderation, all reasonable restraint, ends. Even the heroine of that quite beautifully written *Shadow in the Rose Garden*, when she feels it necessary for the good of her soul to aggravate her husband, does it with a devastating vigour.

We do not think it would ever be possible for Mr. Lawrence to conceive characters whose blood courses at a normal rate or whose passions are not Gargantuan. But if he should ever be minded to describe them in their tired, or rather their exhausted, moods we should perhaps find their humanity.

THE RAINBOW

September 1915

24. Extracts from Lawrence's letters concerning *The Rainbow*

Between 1913–15 Lawrence wrote four versions of this novel. Its original title was *The Sisters*, which later became *The Wedding Ring*, and then in 1914 *The Rainbow*. The heroine of the third generation, Ursula, was first called Ella, and her relationship with Birkin was included in the one novel. Not until January 1915 was it split into the two works, *The Rainbow* and *Women in Love*. Most of the correspondence is addressed either to Edward Garnett, who was reading the manuscript and suggesting amendments, or to J. B. Pinker, Lawrence's literary agent at this time. The book was completed in March 1915 and published by Methuen's, 30 September 1915, but on 13 November Methuen's were summoned to appear before the London magistrate, Sir John Dickinson, to answer a charge made against *The Rainbow* under the Obscene Publications Act of 1857. As a result all copies of the book were ordered to be destroyed. (See No. 31.) Some of the letters refer to an attempt made to enlist support for the book from various distinguished authors, and give Lawrence's reactions to their comments.

(a) 11 March 1913, to Garnett: 'I am a damned curse unto myself. I've written rather more than half of a most fascinating (to me) novel. But nobody will ever dare to publish it. I feel I could knock my head against the wall. Yet I love and adore this new book. It's all crude as yet, like one of Tony's clumsy prehistorical beasts—most cumbersome and floundering—but I think it's great—so new, so really a stratum deeper than I think anybody has ever gone, in a novel. But there, you see, it's my latest. It is all analytical—quite unlike *Sons and Lovers*, not a bit visualized. But nobody will publish it. I wish I had never been born. But I'm going to stick at it, get it done, and then write another, shorter, absolutely impeccable—as far as morals go—novel'.

(b) ? 18 April 1913, to Garnett: 'I have written 180 pages of my newest novel *The Sisters*. It is a queer novel, which seems to have come by itself. I will send it you. You may dislike it—it hasn't got hard outlines—and of course it's only first draft—but it is pretty neat, for me, in composition. . . . I can only write what I feel pretty strongly about: and that, at present, is the relation between men and women. After all, it is *the* problem of today, the establishment of a new relation, or the readjustment of the old one, between men and women.— In a month *The Sisters* will be finished (D.V.).'

(c) ? May–June 1913, to Garnett: 'I was glad of your letter about *The Sisters*. Don't *schimpf*, I shall make it all right when I rewrite it. I shall put it in the third person. All along I knew what ailed the book. But it did me good to theorize myself out, and to depict Frieda's God Almightiness in all its glory. That was the first crude fermenting of the book. I'll make it into art now. I've done 256 pages, but still can't see the end very clear. But it's coming.'

(d) 30 December 1913, to Garnett: 'In a few days' time I shall send you the first half of *The Sisters*—which I should rather call *The Wedding Ring*—to Duckworth's. It is *very* different from *Sons and Lovers*: written in another language almost. I shall be sorry if you don't like it, but am prepared. I shan't write in the same manner as *Sons and Lovers* again, I think—in that hard, violent style full of sensation and presentation. You must see what you think of the new style.'

(e) 29 January 1914, to Garnett: 'I have no longer the joy in creating vivid scenes, that I had in *Sons and Lovers*. I don't care much more about accumulating objects in the powerful light of emotion, and making a scene of them. I have to write differently. I am most anxious about your criticism of this, the second half of the novel, a hundred and fifty pages of which I send you tomorrow. Tell me *very* frankly what you think of it: and if it pleases you, tell me whether you think Ella would be possible, as she now stands, unless she had some experience of love and of men. I think, impossible. . . .

I am going through a transition stage myself. I am a slow writer, really—I only have great outbursts of work. So that I do not much mind if I put all this novel in the fire, because it is the vaguer result of transition. I write with everything vague—plenty of fire underneath, but, like bulbs in the ground, only shadowy flowers that must be beaten and sustained, for another spring. I feel that this second half of *The Sisters* is very beautiful, but it may not be sufficiently incorporated to please you. I do not try to incorporate it very much—I prefer the permeating beauty. It is my transition stage—but I must write to live, and it must produce its flowers, and if they be frail or shadowy, they will be all right if they are true to their hour.'

(f) 5 June 1914, to Garnett: 'I don't agree with you about *The Wedding Ring*. You will find that in a while you will like the book as a whole. I don't think the psychology is wrong: it is only that I have a different attitude to my characters, and that necessitates a different attitude in you, which you are not prepared to give. As for its being my *cleverness* which would pull the thing through—that sounds odd to me, for I don't think I am so very clever, in that way. I think the book is a bit futuristic—quite unconsciously so. But when I read Marinetti—"the profound intuitions of life added one to the other, word by word, according to their illogical conception, will give us the general lines of an intuitive physiology of matter"—I see something of what I am after. I translate him clumsily, and his Italian is obfuscated—and I don't care about physiology of matter—but somehow—that which is physic—non-human, in humanity, is more interesting to me than the old-fashioned human element—which causes one to conceive a character in a certain moral scheme and make him consistent. The certain moral scheme is what I object to. In Turgenev, and in Tolstoi, and in Dostoievsky, the moral scheme into which all the characters fit—and it is nearly the same scheme—is, whatever the extraordinariness of the characters themselves, dull, old, dead. When Marinetti writes: "It is the solidity of a blade of steel that is interesting by itself, that is, the incomprehending and inhuman alliance of its molecules in resistance to, let us say, a bullet. The heat of a piece of wood or iron is in fact more passionate, for us, than the laughter or tears of a woman"—then I know what he means. He is stupid, as an artist, for contrasting the heat of the iron and the laugh of the woman. Because what is interesting in the laugh of the woman is the same as the binding of the molecules of steel or their action in heat;

it is the inhuman will, call it physiology, or like Marinetti—physiology of matter, that fascinates me. I don't so much care about what the woman *feels*—in the ordinary usage of the word. That presumes an *ego* to feel with. I only care about what the woman *is*—what she is— inhumanly, physiologically, materially—according to the use of the word: but for me, what she *is* as a phenomenon (or as representing some greater, inhuman will), instead of what she feels according to the human conception. That is where the futurists are stupid. Instead of looking for the new human phenomenon, they will only look for the phenomena of the science of physics to be found in human beings. They are crassly stupid. But if anyone would give them eyes, they would pull the right apples off the tree, for their stomachs are true in appetite. You mustn't look in my novel for the old stable *ego*—of the character. There is another *ego*, according to whose action the individual is unrecognizable, and passes through, as it were, allotropic states which it needs a deeper sense than any we've been used to exercise, to discover are states of the same single radically unchanged element. (Like as diamond and coal are the same pure single element of carbon. The ordinary novel would trace the history of the diamond —but I say, "Diamond, what! This is carbon." And my diamond might be coal or soot, and my theme is carbon.) You must not say my novel is shaky—it is not perfect, because I am not expert in what I want to do. But it is the real thing, say what you like. And I shall get my reception, if not now, then before long. Again I say, don't look for the development of the novel to follow the lines of certain char- acters: the characters fall into the form of some other rhythmic form, as when one draws a fiddle-bow across a fine tray delicately sanded, the sand takes lines unknown.'

(g) 18 November 1915, to Pinker: 'I should like to know what Henry James and Bennett say of the book. I know Henry James would hate it. But I should like to know. . . .

I think it would be a *really good* thing to get the public protest from the authors—Bennett, etc. John Drinkwater came in just now—he is anxious to do something. Very many people are in a rage over the occurrence. Will you organize a public protest, do you think?—it would be best.'

(h) 23 November 1915, to Pinker: 'Such many letters come to me about *The Rainbow*—so very many people wanting it. If any man were energetic enough, it would pay him to print it privately, by subscription.

As for Wells and my observation of life—if his own portrayal of life had a tithe of truth in it nowadays, he would be glad. He knows he is making a failure of himself, going to pieces, so he will see a serious piece of work with a yellow eye. He admires me really, at the bottom—too much perhaps.

With Henry James it is different—he was always on a different line—subtle conventional design was his aim.'

(i) 16 December 1915, to Pinker: 'Tell Arnold Bennett that all rules of construction hold good only for novels which are copies of other novels. A book which is not a copy of other books has its own construction, and what he calls faults, he being an old imitator, I call characteristics. I shall repeat till I am grey—when they have as good a work to show, they may make their pronouncements *ex cathedra*. Till then, let them learn decent respect.

Still, I think he is generous.'

(j) 27 July 1917, to Waldo Frank: 'About *The Rainbow*: it was all written before the war, though revised during Sept. and Oct. of 1914. I don't think the war had much to do with it—I don't think the war altered it, from its pre-war statement. I only clarified a little, in revision. I knew I was writing a destructive work, otherwise I couldn't have called it *The Rainbow*—in reference to the Flood. And the book was written and named in Italy, by the Mediterranean, before there was any thought of war. And I knew, as I revised the book, that it was a kind of working up to the dark sensual or Dionysic or Aphrodisic ecstasy, which does actually burst the world, burst the world-consciousness in every individual. What I did through individuals, the world has done through the war. . . .

There is another novel, sequel to *The Rainbow*, called *Women in Love*. I don't know if Huebsch has got the MS. yet. I don't think anybody will publish this, either. This actually does contain the results in one's soul of the war: it is purely destructive, not like *The Rainbow*, destructive-consummating . . .'

25. Unsigned review in *Standard*

1 October 1915, 3

The Rainbow, a book dealing with the history of three generations of a Nottinghamshire family, is by far the most difficult task Mr. D. H. Lawrence has yet attempted, but there is no flaw in its construction. Despite the ramifications of the Brangwen tribe, the multiplication of its members, and the passing of some of them from their farm on the marsh, the characters never escape the writer's grip. The book is a cycle of births, marriages, and deaths. Each new Brangwen slips naturally into his or her place, gradually displaces some one of the older generation, slips out again, perhaps quietly in old age, or it may be is overcome struggling in maturity. Each has a sharply defined personality, though a certain family resemblance is preserved by them all. Mr. Lawrence is a realist to the point of brutality, but he is not of those who are bound by wearisome note-books, nor does he offer a smattering of science as an explanation of life. In fact, he explains nothing. He seems to have excluded himself entirely from his new book, and its readers may well delude themselves that they are watching the Brangwen men, women, and children with their own eyes.

Assuredly *The Rainbow* is not a novel to please all. There are no draperies in it, no asterisks, no reticences, no prettiness. It reveals the latent savage in its characters, though none of the Brangwens is wholly primitive. They are strong as they rise from the soil on which for generations they have been settled, but there are influences of unrest which twist their passions this way and that. Education, the spread of a colliery town, the marriage of one of them with a Polish woman, religion, yet more education, have their necessary effect on the old stock. Something comes into them which may be called degeneracy, but is more likely a painful and tortuous development. It is not a comfortable book. Its very foundation is an agonizing struggle between bodies and minds. Passion brings no satisfaction to these Brangwens, yet without it nothing satisfies. Arrogantly, they would make life fit themselves. In the end one leaves Ursula, the last of them, at rest and in enjoyment of a beatific vision in which Heaven and earth are joined. This kind of tale might be merely morbid, but Mr. Lawrence is a writer of exceptional strength. There is vigour of life and thought in all his people, though they do not always know how to use it. They are imprisoned, and, when they break loose, they rush unsteadily, and the light is painful to them. But not only of human beings can Mr. Lawrence write. Sometimes he can make them seem of secondary importance because of the warm smell of a barn in which cows are stabled. All his senses seem to be very highly developed. Certain scenes in the book leave behind a particularly strong impression, notably the one in which Tom Brangwen, returning 'market-merry' to the farm, is overtaken and overwhelmed by the flood. Not faultless in his choice of language, the author is, however, an artist with words, and he only needs to restrain a slight tendency to too emotional descriptions. Such a book as *The Rainbow* may cause offence and be condemned, for it takes more liberties than English novelists for many years past have claimed, but, whatever its reception, it is an important piece of work. Mr. Lawrence has enough genius to excuse his defiance of all conventions.

26. Robert Lynd in *Daily News*

5 October 1915, 6

Robert Lynd (1879–1949). Essayist and journalist. Joined *Daily News* 1908, became literary editor 1912. Wrote regularly for *New Statesman* under initials 'Y.Y.'

Mr. Lawrence's reputation must suffer from the publication of such a book as this. It is not chiefly that the book will offend the general sense of decency: many an indecent book is none the less fine literature by reason of its humanity, its imaginative intensity, or its humour. *The Rainbow*, though it contains intense pages, lacks these marks of good literature. It is mainly a prolix account of three generations of sexual crises in the Brangwen family. It is the book of a theory, not a book either of life or of art. If Strindberg had tried to write a novel in the manner at once of Pierre Louys and of Miss Victoria Cross, he might have achieved something like *The Rainbow*.

A critic once compared Ibsen in his realistic art to a surgeon. If the author of the present book is like any kind of surgeon, it is a veterinary surgeon. His men and women are cattle who chronically suffer from the staggers. They have both the mental staggers and the moral staggers. If men and women are just this and nothing more, then the imaginative literature of the world is false from Homer down. If Mr. Lawrence had written the *Iliad* there would have been nothing in it but Paris and Helen, and they would have been simply a pair of furious animals.

Here and there is a little break of beauty, but for the most part the book is windy, tedious, and even in its excitements nauseating. It is only in satirical art that one can tolerate the representation of life as a thing without faith, hope, or charity, heart, humour, or variety, considerateness, honour, or self-control. The characters in *The Rainbow* are as lacking in the inhibitions of ordinary civilized life as savages. There are truthful, physiologically truthful, things in the book, but the book itself is not true, either in its representation or in its propaganda. It seems to me largely a monotonous wilderness of phallicism. It is the sort of book which many an artistic schoolboy desires to write, but, on growing to maturity, he refrains. Powers are here—psychological and æsthetic powers—such as belong to no schoolboy, but they are powers wasted. They are wasted because the author has so little curiosity about life except in disproportionately-seen patches. As a result, he is as incapable of the touch of tragedy as he is of the touch of comedy. Ordinary readers would do well to leave the book alone. They would be sure to dislike it intensely, especially those pages which are reminiscent in their subject of Diderot's *La Réligieuse*.

27. James Douglas in *Star*

22 October 1915, 4

James Douglas (1867–1940). Journalist and critic. Literary critic of *Star* and then Editor. Later became Editor of *Sunday Express*.

I think it was Joubert who said that fiction has no right to exist unless it is more beautiful than reality, that in literature the one aim is the beautiful, and that if we once lose sight of that we have the mere frightful reality. *The Rainbow*, a novel by Mr. D. H. Lawrence, reminds me of Joubert's saying. It is certainly not more beautiful than reality. It is, indeed, more hideous than any imaginable reality. The thing is done so coldly, so pompously, so gravely that it is like a savage rite. There is not a gleam of humour in the fog of eloquent lubricity. The thud, thud, thud of the hectic phrases is intolerably wearisome. They pound away like engines, grinding out a dull monotonous tune of spiritless sensuality. The healthy comment is an astonished laugh at the rigid pose of it all—at the hard, stiff, pontifical worship of the gross.

There is no doubt that a book of this kind has no right to exist. It is a deliberate denial of the soul that leavens matter. These people are not human beings. They are creatures who are immeasurably lower than the lowest animal in the Zoo. There is no kindness in them, no tenderness, no softness, no sweetness. They are maladies of the mind, growths upon the brain, diseases more horrible than the good honest diseases known to the pathologist. There is no novel in English so utterly lacking in verbal reticence. The subtlety of phrase is enormous, but it is used to express the unspeakable and to hint at the unutterable. The morbidly perverted ingenuity of style is made the vehicle for saying things that ought to be left unthought, let alone unsaid. It is doubtful whether decadence could further go, for the achievement of mastery in the use of words is deliberately set to serve ignoble ends.

Genius is a trust, a sacred trust. Its magical powers are bestowed upon a man to enable him to purify and not to pollute the sanctuary of the soul. Its imaginative grace is not born to serve as a clue to the deepest haunts of hell. If the divine insight is used to tear open cells of horror and to gloat over unfathomable corruption, what is the retribution? In the silence and secrecy of the stealthy brain it is insanity, the chilly, creeping madness of the sensualist who destroys the godlike mind by wearing out the senses in vain pursuit of all the imps of grossness. But why extend the process to the business of representation? Why thrust its abominations upon the unwary reader who looks to art for some revelation of loveliness and wholesomeness and health and manly ardour? Why take the name of art in vain? Why erect finger-posts upon the primrose path that leads to the everlasting bonfire? Why make the difficult and dreary way of decadence easy to all wayfarers? Why open all the doors that the wisdom of man has shut and bolted and double-locked?

I suppose it may seem priggish to insist upon the responsibility of the artist, upon the duty of reverence, upon the elementary obligation of restraint and selective conscience. But nevertheless I do insist upon these high, old-fashioned sanctities. Art is not anarchy. It is our servant, not our tyrant. Its might and majesty are too august to be abandoned to debasement. The artist is not his own law-giver. He must bow before the will of the generations of man. He must not sell himself into servitude to what Mr. Wells calls 'the wild asses of the devil'. Art is a public thing. It is a dweller in the clean homes and swept streets of life. It must conform to the ordered laws that govern human society. If it refuse to do so, it must pay the penalty. The sanitary inspector of literature must notify it and call for its isolation.

The wind of war is sweeping over our life, and it is demolishing many of the noisome pestilences of peace. A thing like *The Rainbow* has no right to exist in the wind of war. It is a greater menace to our public health than any of the epidemic diseases which we pay our medical officers to fight inch by inch wheresoever they appear. They destroy the body, but it destroys the soul. 'Cant!' cries the cynic. Not at all. It is self-preservation. The poise and balance of the mind are not trivial things. The power to see life as a struggle against putrescence is not a sentimental fad or fancy. Every man and every woman must take sides in that battle, and at their worst they know that they ought to take the side of the angels in their souls against the fiends in their souls. Life can be made very horrible and very hideous, but if literature aids and abets the business of making it horrible and hideous, then literature must perish.

I know it will be said that literature must live at all costs and at any expense of spirit in any waste of shame. Frankly, I do not see the necessity. Life is infinitely more precious than literature. It has got to go on climbing up and up, and if literature strives to drag it down to the nethermost deeps, then literature must be hacked off the limbs of life. It is idle to prate of liberty as a pretext for licence. Where you have unbridled licence you cannot have liberty. The deadliest enemies of literature are the foes in its own household. They forge fetters for it which may not be broken. They make it ashamed to hold up its head before the Philistine. The injury done to letters by men of genius who violate the ancient sanctities is profound and far-reaching. If Mr. Lawrence were not greater than his offence, his offence would not be so rank. But he possesses the heavenly gift of glamour. He can weave veils of shimmering meretriciousness round unnameable and unthinkable ugliness. He can lift the rainbow out of the sunlight and set its arch over the pit from whose murky brink every healthy foot ought to shrink in fear and abhorrence.

The rainbow is the symbol of strange beauty, of transfigured reality, of dreams that transcend the lower nature. It is the romance of God that springs out of earth into heaven. If Mr. Lawrence desires to save his genius from destruction, let me tell him how to do it. He must discover or rediscover the oldest truth in the world—that man is a moral being with a conscience and an aim, with responsibility to himself and to others. If that truth be not true, then life is a tale told by an idiot, full of sound and fury, and signifying nothing. The young men who are dying for liberty are moral beings. They are the living repudiation of such impious denials of life as *The Rainbow*. The life they lay down is a lofty thing. It is not the thing that creeps and crawls in this novel.

28. Clement Shorter, comment in 'A Literary Letter', *Sphere*

23 October 1915, lxiii, 104

Clement Shorter, signed 'C.K.S.' (1857–1926). Journalist and critic. Founded *Sketch* (1893), *Sphere* (1900) and *Tatler* (1903). Editor of *Sphere* 1900–26.

Many years ago Henry Vizetelly, whom I remember very well—I recall one occasion in particular when he lunched with me in order to tell me about his interesting career—was sent to gaol for publishing a translation of one of Zola's more lurid novels. Those were Victorian days. In these times it would not be easy to send a publisher to gaol whatever his enterprise in the direction of lubricity, and I am not in favour of such drastic methods. But Zola's novels are child's food compared with the strong meat contained in an English story that I have just read—*The Rainbow*, by D. H. Lawrence (Methuen).

There is no form of viciousness, of suggestiveness, that is not reflected in these pages. I can only suppose that Mr. Methuen and his two partners for some reason failed to read this book in manuscript and published it upon the strength of the previously well-deserved reputation of the author. Let them turn to the chapter entitled 'Shame', and unless they hold the view that Lesbianism is a fit subject for family fiction I imagine that they will regret this venture. The whole book is an orgie of sexiness. I write thus strongly because I consider that the publishers should protect the public, *not* the circulating libraries, which do it so unintelligently. Moreover, the Budget, I am told, has cruelly affected the circulating libraries. The first things people save upon are books. And so the circulating libraries have something else to think about just now than their futile censorship.

The worst of it is that Mr. Lawrence has written quite a good novel apart from the copious passages marked by what I can only call disease. The figure of the farmer, Brangwen, is very convincing, and his marriage to a Polish woman is true to life. Her daughter, Anna, has reality—more so than her granddaughter, Ursula. There is all the material for a good story, but it is spoilt not only by the crude sex details but by endless repetitions. A girl has eyes 'bright, like shallow water', in one page, and 'pellucid eyes, like shallow water', in the next. We are told of a pair of lovers that a kiss 'knitted them into one fecund nucleus of the fluid darkness' in one sentence, and that 'it was bliss, the nucleolating of the fecund darkness', in the next.

I do not charge Mr. Lawrence with a deliberate attempt to provide nastiness for commercial purposes, as I might charge some writers who were in evidence a few years ago, and of whom we hear little now. Mr. Lawrence is a man of letters, and I believe he has written this book solely from artistic impulses. But they are the impulses of a mind that has decadent tendencies. One sees what Mr. Lawrence set out to do. But the blue pencil of a friend might have made his book a better one as a work of art and a more legitimate one at a time when the circulation of novels must needs be indiscriminate. But I have written too much about a book concerning which it was perhaps a duty to have remained silent. Yet the book will have served one good purpose. The next writer of a piece of frank, free literature who is also an artist will assuredly run no risk of a police prosecution.

I am not an opponent of frankness and freedom in literature. I do not believe that fiction should be written entirely for the school or the home. There have been library committees which have condemned Mrs. Gaskell's *Ruth*, George Eliot's *Adam Bede*, and Mr. Hardy's *Tess* as unsuitable for general reading because they touch certain aspects of sex. I realize that the painter who wishes to depict life must not be handicapped by the restraining influence of people who know nothing of art; but all this does not justify the inartistic intrusion of matter which has no place in the development of a story and adds nothing to the subtle depicting of human beings. In this novel, *The Rainbow*, Mr. Lawrence has ceased to be an artist, and I can find no justification whatever for the perpetration of such a book.

29. H. M. Swanwick in *Manchester Guardian*

28 October 1915, 5

Helena Maria Swanwick, signed 'H.M.S.' (1864–1939). Writer on various political subjects, including women's rights. Speaker and lecturer.

It is not possible to regard such a book as this with indifference. Even the *ennui* with which one reads many of its passages is a very passion of boredom; it is like the horrid *ennui* caused by fixed ideas in delirium; the obsessions of fever clog, and its odd inconsequences dislocate the story and its telling. Yet are there innumerable fine things, and the style has individuality and poignancy, marred, one cannot but feel, utterly, by crazy iteration and benumbing violence.

The characters run into three generations: the original Tom Brangwen, who marries a Pole—a widow with one daughter, Anna; Tom's nephew, Will, who marries Anna; and their child, Ursula. In all these persons, the passion of sex is so manifest as to eclipse all other passion or thought, and it is handled, described, embroidered, glorified, with enormous zest and skill and phantasy. Yet the end is tedium. Not disgust, because, except for a few passages, it is passion that is described and not mere appetite. But a passion so narrowed and exaggerated would grow tiresome in one individual; when it runs through three generations of one family and afflicts even persons outside that family, we cry for relief from such madness and long to turn to a world infinitely varied and bracingly sane.

Some emotions and processes are so vividly and imaginatively and beautifully described that it is difficult to understand an artist such as Mr. Lawrence is not being content to leave them so, just done once. He is like the painter who must have his canvas forcibly wrenched from him lest he go on tormenting the paint till it becomes meaningless. Some of the subjects he chooses, passion of love and child-birth, are great and worthy of great treatment; but it is not great treatment to make them dominate all existence and shove aside all else. Others of which he attempts description are morbid or downright insane developments, and what is disquieting about these is the suggestion that in all the various manias described (erotic, ecclesiastical, alcoholic) there is an approach to truth and insight denied to those who remain sane. One knows very well the dazzling clearness and certainty of illusion, sometimes far transcending any attained by thought or sensation; one knows the ecstasy of revelation, the breaking down of barriers between body and spirit, that comes sometimes through the action of drugs or lesions in the brain; but these illusions and revelations are matter for pathological study. One does not wish to assert that they may not form part of an artist's subject, but the artist should surely be the sane delineator of his insane model. There is all the difference in the world between Shakespeare's attitude towards Lear or Lady Macbeth and this author's attitude towards Anna dancing to God or Ursula in her vampire mood.

30. Catherine Carswell in *Glasgow Herald*

4 November 1915, 4

Catherine Carswell (1879–1946). Novelist and critic. Met Lawrence in 1914. She and her second husband, Donald Carswell, became close friends of Lawrence and Frieda. This review (unsigned) of *The Rainbow* cost Catherine Carswell her job on the *Glasgow Herald*. Her book on Lawrence, *The Savage Pilgrimage*, appeared in 1932.

This is a book so very rich both in emotional beauty and in the distilled essence of profoundly passionate and individual thinking about human life, that one longs to lavish on it one's whole-hearted praise. It betrays, moreover, the hand of a master writer. There are passages here—the accounts of Anna Brangwen's childhood, the narration of Tom Brangwen's wooing, the descriptions of Will Brangwen's home life, and of Ursula Brangwen's bitter baptism as an uncertificated teacher in Ilkeston School—which must take rank with the best work done by great novelists in any age. But for himself Mr. Lawrence is aiming at something quite different and distinct from mere good fiction, and it is this aim of his which principally claims the serious reader's respect and his consideration. The difficulty is to define even to one's self what Mr. Lawrence's aim exactly is, and whether it is in any way constructive. What he certainly does in this finely processional but mostly painful history of the loves of successive generations of the Brangwen family is to make clear his conviction that the modern heart is in a disastrous muddle where love between the sexes is concerned. If *The Rainbow* tells us anything it tells that love in our modern life, instead of being a blessed, joyous, and fruitful thing, is sterile, cruel, poisonous, and accursed. In the marriage of Tom Brangwen with the Polish woman Lydia we are shown a marriage of real passion and tenderness, which would, however, have gone wrong had not Lydia at a critical moment made a movement, a beautiful spiritual movement, of sheer kindness and direct good sense. And so the home at the Marsh is established in well-being. In the marriage of Lydia's daughter Anna with her stepcousin Will, again, we are introduced with what most people will find revolting detail to a passion fruitful in a sense but bitter and terrifying at the core, where the modern poison is at its disintegrating work. Finally, in the loves of Anna's daughter Ursula, which brings us up to the present day, we get merely an intense sexual excitement, without kindness or tenderness, without love or reverence, without humour or gladness or peace, a barren, hateful thing, recognized as such by the so-called lovers themselves. The modern world, according to Mr. Lawrence, is mad and sick and sad because it knows not how to love. Further, in this book at any rate, he does not go. There is no cure offered, nothing but a merciless, almost gloating description of the disease which will be strongly offensive to most readers. It is a pity too that the impassioned declaration is marred by the increasingly mannered idiom which Mr. Lawrence has acquired since the writing of *Sons and Lovers*. The worst manifestations of this at present are a distressing tendency to the repetition of certain words and a curiously vicious rhythm into which he constantly falls in the more emotional passages.

31. Prosecution of *The Rainbow*, *The Times*

15 November 1915, 3

The Times report (entitled '*The Rainbow*. Destruction of a Novel Ordered').

At Bow-street Police Court on Saturday [i.e. 13 November], Messrs. Methuen and Co. (Limited), publishers, Essex-street, Strand, were summoned before Sir John Dickinson to show cause why 1,011 copies of Mr. D. H. Lawrence's novel *The Rainbow* should not be destroyed. The defendants expressed regret that the book should have been published, and the magistrate ordered that the copies should be destroyed and that the defendants should pay £10 10s. costs.

Mr. H. Muskett, for the Commissioner of Police, said that the defendants, who were publishers of old standing and recognized repute, offered no opposition to the summons. The book in question was a mass of obscenity of thought, idea, and action throughout, wrapped up in language which he supposed would be regarded in some quarters as an artistic and intellectual effort, and he was at a loss to understand how Messrs. Methuen had come to lend their name to its publication. Mr. Muskett read extracts from some Press criticisms of the work and continued that upon the matter being brought to the notice of the authorities a search warrant was at once obtained. This was executed by Detective-inspector Draper, who was given every facility by the defendants. He seized a number of copies of the book at their premises and afterwards obtained other copies from the printers, Messrs. Hazell, Watson and Viney.

A representative of Messrs. Methuen said that the agreement to publish the book was dated July 1914. When the MS. was delivered it was returned to the author, who at the defendants' suggestion made a number of alterations. The firm did not receive it back until 4 June last and again they protested against certain passages. Other alterations were then made by the author, after which he refused to do anything more. No doubt the firm acted unwisely in not scrutinizing the book again more carefully, and they regretted having published it.

The magistrate, in making an order as above, said it was greatly to be regretted that a firm of such high repute should have allowed their reputation to be soiled, as it had been, by the publication of this work, and that they did not take steps to suppress it after the criticisms had appeared in the Press.

32. J. C. Squire, discussion of the suppression of *The Rainbow* in the 'Books in General' column, *New Statesman*

20 November 1915, vi, 161

J. C. Squire, writing under the name 'Solomon Eagle', (1884–1958). Poet, critic, journalist. Became literary editor of *New Statesman* 1913, Acting Editor 1917–18. Editor of *London Mercury* 1919–34.

Last Saturday, at Bow Street, Mr. D. H. Lawrence's new novel *The Rainbow* was brought before the bench and sentenced to death. Who lodged an information against the book I don't know. It is conceivable, at a time when the patriotism of our criminals must leave our policemen plenty of leisure, that some cultured constable may have got hold of the work and rushed to his superiors with it. But it is likelier that the prosecution was the work of some Society or individual set upon Mr. Lawrence's track by one of the violent attacks upon the book which appeared in the Press. Two of these attacks figured in court, those of Mr. James Douglas and Mr. Clement Shorter. The prosecution attached much importance to them and the magistrate blamed the publishers for not withdrawing the book as a direct result of these gentlemen's criticisms. And both these critics as well as counsel for the prosecution and the magistrate himself talked a good deal of hyperbolical nonsense.

Some qualification must be made with regard to Mr. Douglas and Mr. Shorter. Mr. Douglas is a man with a genius for invective which I myself heartily appreciate when it is aimed at politicians whom I don't like—and who, incidentally, are never impounded and destroyed by the police as the result of his attacks. It is a weakness of Mr. Douglas to turn sometimes his powers of epigrammatic vituperation against books which he considers obscene. The last time that I remember him doing it the book in question was a volume of boring, erotic, old-fashioned verse (all about breasts, purple lips, etc.) which would have attracted no attention at all had he left it alone. On the present occasion he was irritated by seeing a man like Mr. Lawrence wasting his powers, and fairly let himself go about the obscenity of *The Rainbow*. Mr. Shorter, again, to do him justice, appears to be hostile to censorship, and, in the middle of his abuse, remarked that Mr. Lawrence's book would have 'served one good purpose' in that 'the next writer of a piece of frank, free literature who is an artist will assuredly run no risk of a police prosecution'. All the same both critics carried their language to an indefensible pitch. Mr. Shorter said that 'Zola's novels are child's food compared with the strong meat' in the book. He did not person-ally charge Mr. Lawrence 'with a deliberate attempt to provide nastiness for commercial purposes'; but he had unfortunately said quite enough to put the hounds upon the scent. His reservations were little good in court. The prosecuting counsel, Mr. Muskett, referred to the book as 'this bawdy volume'; and the magistrate, Sir John Dickinson, described it as 'utter filth' and said that he had 'never read anything more disgusting than this book'.

Mr. Muskett we may pass over. Various kinds of lawyers affect various kinds of language. In the case of the magistrate one can only be astonished. I am quite unacquainted with Sir John Dickinson's antecedents. For all I know he may have been Mother-Superior of a Convent before he was translated to the more lucrative but less secluded position that he now graces. But if he has never seen anything more disgusting than *The Rainbow*, all I can say is that he cannot be familiar with many books that are sold in this country and that he must be abysmally ignorant of the literatures of our two Allies, France and Great White Russia. For the critics the excuse of ignorance cannot be advanced. That influential critics, with the interests of literature—not to speak of the livings of authors—in their charge should let loose as Mr. Shorter did is unpardonable. *The Rainbow*, he says, is 'strong meat' compared with Zola. Did he ever read *La Terre?* Of course he did! He must have known that he was talking rubbish. People who dislike censorships should not go miles out of their way to assist censors.

Now, I am not arguing the whole question of censorship. Most people will agree that there is a point at which the police must interfere: we can all imagine things, in our heads, which certainly ought not to be written down and exposed for sale. And I am not maintaining that

The Rainbow is a great work of art. Its author has a strain of genius, but in this novel he is at his worst. It is a dull and monotonous book which broods gloomily over the physical reactions of sex in a way so persistent that one wonders whether the author is under the spell of German psychologists, and so tedious that a perusal of it might send Casanova himself into a monastery, if he did not go to sleep before his revulsion against sex was complete. I think it a bad novel: and it contains opinions unpalatable to me and tendencies that I personally believe to be unhealthy. But in the first place it is very much to be doubted whether, the good faith of the book being evident, censorship in this case was desirable; in the second place if *The Rainbow* is to be interfered with there are scores of other books that demand prior attention; and in the third place it is doing Mr. Lawrence common justice to protest against the way in which his name has been dragged through the mud. How many of those who read the criticisms and gloated over the police court proceedings will realize that he is an uncommercial young writer who, whatever he may write, writes it as he does because of an earnestness which is almost awe-inspiring? It will be no consolation to him that many people, who look on in smug silence whenever a distinguished writer is stigmatized as bawdy, will treasure up his name and rush to buy his next novel when it appears. Critics really should try to keep their sense of proportion.

But on the whole, I suppose, we ought to thank our stars that the censorship in this country is not worse than it is. It is really very seldom that the police act, and when they do they do not act very thoroughly. Once it was Zola: but you can now buy him anywhere. Another time it was Balzac: but the *Contes Drôlatiques* have not, in spite of a horrified bench, disappeared from the booksellers' catalogues. We might be much worse off. If one took the trouble to start prosecutions one could certainly get scores of books condemned each year: there would be not the slightest difficulty about getting judgment, for it is the easiest thing in the world to make a magistrate blush. And the public would be no more excited than it was about the Dramatic Censorship. The larger public gets the kind of literature it wants and is happy. There was a jolly example of it, words and music, in Lord Northcliffe's *Weekly Dispatch* last Sunday. It is a song. It outlines the healing qualities of love. And it has this beautiful, beautiful, beautiful chorus:

> All the time you're living, do a little loving,
> Just a little loving ev'ry day, all the day!

You've not started living, till you've started loving,
So, just start the loving right away.
For life is short;
No one ought
To throw an opportunity away.
Ev'ry day, late or early,
Take an armful of girlie;
When you've found her,
Just cuddle round her,
Do a little loving ev'ry daa-a-a-y.

That is how we really like it put.

33. Galsworthy, letter to J. B. Pinker

Autumn 1915

John Galsworthy (1867–1933). Novelist and playwright. After meeting Lawrence in 1917 Galsworthy referred to him as 'that provincial genius. Interesting, but a type I could not get along with. Obsessed with self.' (*Life and Letters*, ed. H. V. Marrot, London, 1935, p. 433.) Nevertheless, he was apparently willing, along with Arnold Bennett, to help with the publication of *Women in Love*. His reaction to *Sons and Lovers* ('The body's never worthwhile, and the sooner Lawrence recognizes that, the better . . .' though he had 'nothing but praise for all the part that deals with the Mother, the Father and the sons') is given in a letter to Edward Garnett, 13 April 1914 (Marrot p. 724). Lawrence's unfavourable critique of Galsworthy appeared in *Scrutinies*, ed. Edgell Rickword, 1928 (reprinted in *Phoenix*).

'I've read *The Rainbow*, and will send it back to you in a day.

Frankly—I think it's aesthetically detestable. Its perfervid futuristic style revolts me. Its reiterations bore me to death. And—worse than all—at the back of its amazing fecundity—what is there? What real discovery, what of the spirit, what that is touching, or even true? There is a spurious creativeness about it all, as of countless bodies made with tremendous gusto, and not an ounce of soul within them, in spite of incredible assertions and pretence of sounding life to its core. It's a kind of portent; a paean of the undisciplined shallow fervour that passes with the young in these days for art. It has no time-resisting quality whatever. Brittle as glass, and with something of its brilliance.

As to the sexual aspect. The writer forgets—as no great artist does—that by dwelling on the sexual side of life so lovingly he falsifies all the values of his work—for this reason if for no other: the sexual instinct is so strong in all of us that any emphasis upon it drags the whole being of the reader away from seeing life steadily, truly, and whole; drags it away from the rest of the book, stultifies the writer's own efforts at the presentation of human life and character.

I much prefer a frankly pornographic book to one like this. That at all events achieves what it sets out to do; and does not leave on one the painful impression of a man tragically obsessed to the ruin of his gifts.

I am a pagan; but this is not paganism, it is fever. A grievous pity—so much power, and vision (up to a point) run so young to seed. I don't see him getting back now—he will go on, and become more and more perfervid, seeing less and less the wood for the trees. And the worst of it is he will lead away those who think that what glitters must be gold.

I'm sorry, the first part of *Sons and Lovers* was so good.'

AMORES

July 1916

34. Francis Bickley in *Bookman*

October 1916, li, 26–7

Francis Bickley (b. 1885). Editor of historical manuscripts and writer on literary and historical subjects.

There is no particular relationship, in art any more than in daily conversation, between intensity of feeling and frankness of revelation. Certainly he who blurted out

> The expense of spirit in a waste of shame
> Is lust in action

knew the dregs of passion as the author of *Romeo and Juliet* knew its romantic heights; yet we still dispute as to whether he unlocked his heart with the sonnet-key or any other. Donne caged, and all but hid, the fervency of his nature behind the bars of his fantastic and almost incredibly skilful craftsmanship; Rossetti draped his corroding sensuality in daedal tapestries. The desire to strip the soul naked and thus to exhibit it is a characteristic peculiar to an age which combines individualism with a scorn of taboos. One remembers, of course, the 'pungent passionings' of Burns, and Shelley fallen on the rocks of life and crying out in agony; but such cries were, if not involuntary, at any rate unpremeditated. The self-revelations of Byron were to a considerable extent dramatic and conventional, and so were the confessions of Swinburne and the decadents. What one may call the militant honesty of some contemporary poets, an urgency not only to admit their wounds but painfully to probe them, is a new thing. It is exampled most signally in the work of D. H. Lawrence; for he, besides this ardour for complete expression, has an intensity of sense and spirit to express for which it is not easy to find a parallel.

Rupert Brooke was as honest, and in a way as passionate, as Lawrence. But he was far more intellectual; and both his passion and his expression of it were largely the result of a reaction against intellectualism, a reaction which led him to the South Seas and Mamua and then to Lemnos. Lawrence's reactions are personal, within himself; they do not swing him round from one point of view to another—they make him seethe so that his verse comes forth in hot and angry jets.

It is poetry which one might criticize in scientific terminology borrowed from Freud and his like—talking of psychopathology and hyperaesthesia and masochism—were it not so easy for the layman to use the language of specialism foolishly. It is safer perhaps to say merely that it is poetry which shows both in form and subject the signs of an extraordinary sensibility in conjunction with a most restless energy. The poet seems to receive experiences not through one sense only but through all his senses concurrently, as when he writes:

> I will sift the surf that edges the night, with my net, the four
> Strands of my eyes and my lips and my hands and my feet sifting the store
> Of flotsam until my soul is tired or satisfied.

And he has created, or been born with the gift of, a language which is the equivalent of this abnormal receptivity. Actually, sometimes, he seems not to know whether he has seen or heard or felt; and it is natural for him to speak of

> . . . the stealthy, brindled odours
> Prowling about the lush
> And acrid night of autumn.

Such things are the fruit neither of theory nor of caprice. They are obviously the direct rendering of sensations really felt. Lawrence is an impressionist, and a wonderfully successful and vivid one. His effects, though nearly always surprising, are nearly always right. But they are in the nature of lucky shots. For he is impatient of art and, though he sometimes writes almost flawlessly as in 'Brooding Grief' and 'Snapdragon' and the beautifully limpid 'Mystery', he is often violent to metre and rhyme and rhythm, committing cacophonies which irritate the ear.

Yet poetry, rather than prose, is his true medium. He is so subjective and so intensive that, whatever the form his writing takes, he is always essentially a lyric poet. That is why his novels, powerful and beautiful as they are, are difficult to read. For there must always be a core of logical progress in narrative, however deeply it may be wrapped in divagation; and Lawrence's mind, if not illogical, is intensive rather than progressive in relation to its objectives. Nor do the characters of his fiction ever quite disengage themselves from their maker. Even in *Twilight in Italy*, which is not fiction, one is never sure of the objective truth of his portraits: his vision is so personal and so different from that of the ordinary intelligent observer. Not that this is a disadvantage from the point of view of the interest of his book. *Twilight in Italy* is an extremely interesting book. It contains some pages of description of unsurpassable vividness and some pages of philosophy which throw light—not superfluous—on the poems. Lawrence's philosophy is a synthesis of paganism and Christianity, the pagan ideal of absolute being and the Christian ideal of not being.

What is really Absolute [he writes] is the mystic Reason which connects both Infinites, the Holy Ghost that relates both natures of God. If we now wish to make a living State, we must build it up to the idea of the Holy Spirit, the supreme Relationship. We must say, the pagan Infinite is infinite, the Christian Infinite is infinite: these are two Consummations, in both of these we are consummated. But that which relates them alone is absolute . . . a superb bridge, on which one can stand and know the whole world, my world, the two halves of the universe.

In *Amores*—poems of loves which are not all sexual—one may find glimpses of this perfect relation of opposites; but more evident are traces of their secular antagonism.

35. Edward Garnett, 'Art and the Moralists: Mr. D. H. Lawrence's Work', *Dial*

16 November 1916, lxi, 377–81

Edward Garnett (1868–1937). Critic and publisher's reader. Met Lawrence in 1911, advised and encouraged him in his early work, but seems to have found *The Rainbow* too much a departure from traditional novel-writing.

This article was reprinted in Garnett's *Friday Nights*, First Series, London, 1929.

The instinct of men to moralize their actions, and of society to confine in a theoretical network of ethical concepts the whole heaving mass of human activities, is fundamental. The suspicion with which ethics views art—exemplified by Plato's casting of the poets out of the Republic—indicates men's unwillingness to let this framework of moral rules and social conventions (which bulges obligingly this way and that according to particular requirements) be challenged by aesthetic representations which may invalidate it. Both the Governments and the 'average citizen' are never quite easy about the activities of the artists and poets who are likely to be innovating forces. Thus a Byron or a Shelley may suddenly scatter far and wide, in their poems, the seeds of the French Revolution; or an Ibsen may appear whose *Doll's House* may undermine the *bourgeois* conception of marriage; or a Tolstoy may arise, whose interpretation of Christian ethics may threaten the structure of the State. The efforts of the State or Society to stamp as 'immoral' powerful representations of life often as not recoil on the authorities' heads—as in the case of Flaubert's *Madame Bovary*. Since the suppression of Mr. D. H. Lawrence's novel, *The Rainbow*, last year, in unusual circumstances, called forth a weighty testimonial to its merits from Mr. Arnold Bennett, I shall not here comment on the case. Certain books excite the ordinary mind unduly, and it was the unseemly scandal made over *Tess of the D'Urbervilles* and *Jude the Obscure* that brought Thomas Hardy to lay down his magic wand of fiction. In glancing at Mr. Lawrence's two volumes of poems, I should like to indicate why his talent is one of the most interesting and uncompromising literary forces of recent years.

Briefly, he is the poet-psychologist of instincts, emotions, and moods that it is needless to try and moralize. Society's network of ethical concepts is constantly challenged by the spectacle of our passionate human impulses. Take the spectacle of two armies of men struggling to destroy one another. Society moralizes their actions by the single word 'patriotism', and glorifies slaughter by emphasizing their 'heroic' virtues. But other artists, such as Tolstoy and Garshin, arise whose pictures of war show us its crimes against Humanity.

But the more nakedly and vividly does the pure artist of Mr. Lawrence's type depict the slipping of the leash which holds in the animal impulses, and the more he catches the terror of scenes of carnage, the more does the ordinary man look askance at him. Why? Because the artist has torn aside the 'idealistic' veils which conceal the depths of the world of seething passions. But should the artist stamp with a terrible beauty the upheaval of these elemental emotions, what then? The moralists will be very wroth with him. It is difficult to moralize the beauty of passion and the leaping fire of the senses. Accordingly, the moralists try and turn the flank of such an artist by asserting either that his work is without 'high ideals', or that the aesthetic representation of such sensations is not art of 'high rank', or that it has deleterious effects on the reader. But has it deleterious effects on our human consciousness? I believe that the true answer to such objectors—who are, today, legion—is that they do both literature and morals a grave disservice by striving to confine aesthetic representations within too narrow a circle, and that by seeking to fetter and restrain the artist's activities they cripple art's function of deepening our consciousness and widening our recognitions. If the Rev. S. P. Rowe has his place, so also has Boccaccio. We must not forget that the moralists have always special ends in view, and very little would be left us if they had had their will in every age and could today truncate and lop and maim literary and aesthetic classics at their pleasure. Euripides and Aristophanes, Rabelais, Molière, Voltaire, Marlowe, and Shakespeare, Fielding, Byron, Shelley, Keats, and Sterne, Flaubert, Maupassant, Baudelaire, Verlaine, Whitman, Tolstoy himself—all have been condemned and charged with 'immoral' tendencies by the moralists, who

may be answered shortly: 'Your conception of "the good" is too narrow. In your hands aesthetic delineations of the passions would become
tame as domestic fowls.' Thus Art would thereby lend itself to the
propagation of flat untruth. This, indeed, is what frequently happens
in literature. Representations of life are over-idealized or over-
moralized, as the 'heroic' aspects of War by the lyrical poets; and
another class of artists, the realists, have to be called in to redress the
balance and paint the terrible, bestial, heart-rending side, which the
European nations are experiencing today. And as with War so with
Love. Mr. Lawrence, by his psychological penetration into Love's self-
regarding impulses and passionate moods, supplements our 'idealistic'
valuations of its activities and corrects their exaggeration by conventionalized sentiment. The 'idealistic' valuations of Love have their high
abiding place in literature, unassailable as in life; but, under cover of
their virtual monopoly of our Anglo-Saxon attention, we see the
literary field of today covered with brooding swarms of sugary,
sentimental erotics, artificial in feeling, futile and feeble and false as art.
I am not concerned here to stigmatize these cheap sentimental sweets
that cloy and vitiate the public palate, but to point out that their
universal propagation coincides with a veiled hostility to the Beautiful,
and the consequent impoverishment of our spiritual life. The harmful
effects of the over-development of material progress with its code of
utilitarian standards is shown by the artificial and parasitic position in
which poetry and art are thrust in the modern community. Our poets
and artists are kept, so to say, as a sect of *dilettanti*, apart, ministering to
scholarly aestheticism or drawing-room culture, and are disregarded in
the central stir and heat of worldly activities. And our spiritual life,
bound up and entangled in the wheels and mechanism of our worldly,
intellectual, or scientific interests, is conscious of being stunted, of being
cheated of its rightful aesthetic enrichment. And the general abasement
of Art in public eyes, its parasitic and artificial status, runs parallel with
that progressive aspersion cast on 'the life of the senses', that is, of our
sensuous perceptions, with the implication that it is somehow or other
divisible from our 'spiritual' life. Which is absurd.

Mr. Lawrence in his two volumes, *Love Poems, and Others* and
Amores, comes today to redress the balance. As a poet he rehabilitates
and sets before us, as a burning lamp, passion—a word which, in the
sense of ardent and tumultuous desire, has almost shed to the vulgar
mind its original enrooted implication of *suffering*. His love poems
celebrate the cry of spirit to flesh and flesh to spirit, the hunger and

thrill and tumult of love's desires in the whole whirling circle of its impetus from flame to ashes, its swift reaching out to the anguished infinity of warring nature—his love poems, I say, restore to passion the creative rapture that glows in the verse of Keats. And his spiritual synthesis of passion's leaping egoism, its revolt against finite ties and limitations, its shuddering sense of inner disharmonies and external revulsions, its winged delight in its own motion, declare its superior intensity of vital energy to the poetry of his English contemporaries. I do not wish to exaggerate the qualities of Mr. Lawrence's verse. His range of mood is very limited, his technique is hasty, his vision turns inward, self-centred; but in concentration of feeling, in keenness, one might almost say in fierceness of sensation, he seems to issue from those tides of emotional energy which surge in the swaying ocean of life. Shall we say that the source of his power is this quivering fire of intensity, which like a leaping flame at night in a garden throws back the darkness in a chiaroscuro of shapes and colours and movements, from the rustling earth to the starlit sky? So the poet's imagery is steeped in primary emotional hues—moods of pity or cruelty, passionate yearning, sorrow, fear, tenderness, aching desire, remorse, anguish. This imagery springs direct from his sensations and is born of his momentary emotional vision, not of his cultivated, imaginative reflections, unlike that of the majority of our talented *dilettanti* poets. It carries with it to a remarkable degree the feeling, the atmospheric impression, of nature in the passing moment. But we must quote an example:

[Quotes the whole of 'A Baby Asleep After Pain.' (*C.P.*, I, 73-4.)]

This, so simple, so spontaneous, and apparently effortless, holds all the felicity of the moment in the emotional mood. And while psychologically true, the poet's rendering of a sensuous impression is most spiritual in its appeal. But here I must pause, and turn to some consideration of Mr. Lawrence's work in creative fiction.

II

It was evident to a critical eye that with *The White Peacock* (1911) a new artistic force was stirring in fiction. Curiously, those qualities of 'realism' and 'naturalism' both, that had been solemnly exorcised with book, candle, and bell in many professorial admonitions, reappeared here in company with intense poetic susceptibility and with an evident delight in the exuberance of nature. There was nothing here of M.

Zola's 'false naturalism' or of his 'scientific reporting'; on the contrary, the artist's fault lay in the unchastened vivacity of his thronging impressions and rioting emotions. The story, one of country life, traces at length the subtle degeneration of the young farmer, George, who, slow and inexperienced in woman's ways, takes the wrong girl to wife. The book in its frank and unabashed imaginative fecundity and luxuriant colouring, is a baffling one: an extraordinary intimacy with the feminine love instincts is blended with untrammelled psychological interest in the gamut of the passions. But a certain over-bold, lush immaturity, a certain sprawling laxity of taste, confused the outlines. The youthful artist evidently did not know where to be silent, or how to select and concentrate his scenes. These faults were less in evidence in *The Trespasser* (1912), the tale of a sensitive, frail, and ardent man's fleeting amour with a girl, superficial and cold in nature, who is dallying with passion. The same intense susceptibility to physical impressions, the same vibrating joy in sensuous feelings, were repeated here in a solo on erotic strings. The atmosphere is heavy with the odour of meadow-sweet, which is suddenly dissipated by the shock of tragedy. Sigismund's suicide, and the settling down again of his forgetful suburban family into the tame stream of its *bourgeois* commonplaceness, are painted with inflexible sincerity and great psychological acumen. An occasional commonness both of language and tone is, however, at variance with the artist's intensity of perception. But Mr. Lawrence silenced his critics by his third novel, *Sons and Lovers*, an epic of family life in a colliery district, a piece of social history on a large canvas, painted with a patient thoroughness and bold veracity which both Balzac and Flaubert might have envied. The central theme, an unhappy working-class marriage, a woman's struggle to rear her children while sustained by her strong puritanical spirit, develops later into a study of her maternal aversion to surrendering her son to another woman's arms. The theme is dissected in its innermost spiritual fibres with an unflinching and loving exactitude, while the family drama is seen against an impressive background of the harsh, driving realities of life in a colliery district. This novel is really the only one of any breadth of vision in contemporary English fiction that lifts working-class life out of middle-class hands, and restores it to its native atmosphere of hard veracity. The mining people, their mental outlook, ways of life, and habits, and the woof of their domestic joys and cares, are contrasted with some country farming types in a neighbouring village, where the smoky horizon of industrialism merges, to the passionate eyes of a girl and boy in love, in the magic of quiet woods and pastures. The whole treatment is unerringly true and spiritually profound, marred a little by a feeling of photographic accuracy in the narrative and by a lack of restraint in some of the later love scenes. The main theme, a life-conflict between husband and wife, is handled again in a tragedy, *The Widowing of Mrs. Holroyd* (1914), a drama intensely human in its passionate veracity. This is a study, intimately observed, of powerful primitive types, first shown with the hot breath of anger in the nostrils, and then with the starkness, pallor, and rigidity of death. Contrasted with the puerile frivolity and catchy sensationalism of the London stage, this drama stands like one of Meunier's impressive figures of Labour amid the marble inanities of a music-hall *foyer*. In his volume of short stories, *The Prussian Officer* (1914), the intensity of the poet-psychologist's imagination triumphs over the most refractory material. Again it is the triumph of passion thrilling both flesh and spirit, making the material of life subservient to itself, forcing its way from smoky darkness to light through the eager cells of nature. Whether it be the sustained lust of cruelty in the rigid Prussian officer, or the flame of sick misery leaping to revenge in the heart of the young Bavarian orderly; or the cruel suspense and agony of pain in the mutual confession of love of the young miner and the vicar's daughter; or the bitterness of ironic regret of the lovers who have fallen asunder in *The Shades of Spring*; or hate and suffering in a wife's reckless confession of her past in *Shadow in the Rose Garden*; in each of the dozen tales it is the same poetic realization of passion's smouldering force, of its fusion of aching pleasure and pain in the roots of sexual life, the same twinness of senses and soul in the gathering and the breaking waves of surging emotion.

And here is the secret of the individual quality and the definite limitations of Mr. Lawrence's vision. Like a tree on a hot summer noon, his art casts a sharp, fore-shortened shadow. His characters do not pass far outside that enchanted circle of passion in and round which they move. That this circle is narrow compared with the literary field, say, of a Maupassant, is I think due to Mr. Lawrence's poetical intensity restricting his psychological insight. And his emotional intensity, again, is indissolubly one with his sensuous impressionability. And here we may pick up again the dropped thread of our opening remarks about the suspicion with which the moralists always view art. The attack on the literature of passions (and indirectly on sensuous beauty itself which feeds the passions) is generally conducted on the line of argument that such literature is in opposition to the 'higher and more spiritual' instincts of mankind. The reply is that each specimen of such literature can only be judged according to the relation and the equilibrium, established by the artist, between the morality of nature and the morality of man. In the love life the struggle is endless between the fundamental instinct of sexual attraction and the narrowing instincts of worldly prudence and family and social duty. In seeking to cripple or suppress the literature of the passions, the moralists are tipping up the 'idealistic' scale unduly to the detriment of the fundamental human instincts; and this reacts injuriously, just as does the ascetic vilification of the 'body', on the spiritual life. The greater the triumph of materialism and industrial squalor in our commercialized society, the more contempt is poured on the 'world of sensuous delight' and the less regard paid to Art, Poetry, and aesthetic Beauty. So Keats is indicted, as we have seen, of 'selfishly swooning away in a dream of beauty'! And whom would the moralists who cut off the truthful delineation of the passions on the ground that such leads to sensuous indulgence— whom would the moralists put in Keats's place? This is what we ask also in the case of Mr. Lawrence's work, which, as I have said, restores to 'passion' shades of its original meaning of *suffering*. His lovers are not those bright young people of the popular novel whose idea of love seems to be inseparably connected with success and worldly prosperity and having a nice house and being envied by their neighbours. His lovers are shaken, they suffer; to them is revealed the significance of things: they have to pass through much and endure much in attaining or missing their passionate desire. Theirs are spiritual experiences, not merely 'sensuous gratification', as the moralists so glibly phrase it. And therefore Mr. Lawrence's representation of the sensuous and animal strands and instincts in our nature needs, I say, no moralization. These elements exist—they are, in a sense, the foundation on which our moral being has been slowly reared; and the artist who can draw (and few there are who can) a truthful representation of our passionate impulses, kept under or leaping into action, takes an indispensable place in literature. In the literature that explores the relations between the morality of nature, as expressed in the activity of sexual feeling and worldly conduct, Mr. Lawrence's fiction takes a high place. His story, *Daughters of the Vicar*, is an admirable analysis of the frequent clash between the two; and the sketches called *Second Best* and *Shadow in the Rose Garden* re-establish the necessary equilibrium so flagrantly disturbed by the moralists in their exaltation of the 'idealistic' scale. Such studies, to which one may add *The Christening* and *The White*

Stocking, at best make an appeal to our fundamental consciousness that 'the good' as conceived by the moralists confines to too narrow a circle our tides of emotional energies; and this vindication of 'passion' in these stories appears to take its rise in the instinct for racial health. But I have said enough on this head, and will only add that those who challenge the right to existence of such works of art would penetrate to their vulnerable side if they left the road of 'morals' and took the path of 'taste'.

LOOK! WE HAVE COME THROUGH!

December 1917

36. John Gould Fletcher in *Poetry* (Chicago)

August 1918, xii, 269–74

John Gould Fletcher (1886–1950). Poet.

D. H. Lawrence has recently published a third volume of poetry to stand beside his *Love Poems* and *Amores*. This event has, so far as I am aware, passed almost without notice in the English press. The reviewers of the English press know perfectly well that Mr. Lawrence is supposed to be a dangerous man, writing too frankly on certain subjects which are politely considered taboo in good society, and therefore they do their best to prevent Mr. Lawrence from writing at all, by tacitly ignoring him. If they are driven to the admission, these selfsame reviewers are obliged grudgingly to acknowledge that Mr. Lawrence is one of the most interesting of modern writers. Such are the conditions which a modern writer with something new to say is obliged to accept in England today. The Press can make a great to-do about the innocuous, blameless and essentially minor poetry of Edward Thomas (to take but one example); they politely refuse to discuss the questionable, but essentially major effort of a D. H. Lawrence. Is it any wonder that such an attitude drives a man to sheer fanaticism?

For a fine, intolerant fanatic D. H. Lawrence undoubtedly is. That is his value for our present day, so rich in half-measures and compromises. Lawrence does not compromise. In this last collection of poetry he gives us works which are not good poetry, which are scarcely readable prose. He includes them because they are necessary to the complete understanding of his thought and gospel. We, if we are wise, will read them for the same reason. For Lawrence is an original thinker, and his message to our present day is a valuable message.

Briefly, the message is this: that everything which we call spiritual is born and comes to flower out of certain physical needs and reactions, of which the most patent is the reaction of sex, through which life is maintained on this planet. Lawrence therefore stands in sharp contrast to the Christian dogma of the Middle Ages, and to those writers of the present day who still maintain an attitude of respect to the Christian view, which is that we are each endowed with an immortal soul, at strife with our physical needs, which can only be purged by death. Lawrence, like a recent French writer, 'does not desire to spit out the forbidden fruit, and recreate the Eden of the refusal of life'. He is frankly pagan. To him, the flesh is the soil in which the spirit blossoms, and the only immortality possible is the setting free of the blossoming spirit from the satiated flesh. When this is accomplished, then the spirit becomes free, perfect, unique, a habitant of paradise on earth. This is the doctrine of which he is the zealot, the intolerant apostle.

The specific value of this idea need not concern us very greatly. The question is, rather, of its poetical value; and there is no doubt that it is a system of philosophy which is essentially poetical. Poetry is at once highly objective and highly subjective. It is objective in so far as it deals with words, which are in a strong sense objects, and with the external world in its objective aspects. It is subjective, because it also states the poet's subjective reactions to words and to all external phenomena. Lawrence is one of the few poets in England today who keeps this dual rôle of poetry well in mind; and that is why his poetry, though it may often be badly written, is never without energy and a sense of power.

The reason for his failings as a poet must be sought elsewhere than in his attitude to life. We can only understand why he fails if we understand the conditions under which he is forced to write. With a reasonable degree of independence, a public neither openly hostile nor totally indifferent, an intellectual *milieu* capable of finer life and better understanding, Lawrence would become nothing but an artist. He has none of these things; and so he is forced, by destiny itself, to become the thing he probably began by loathing, a propagandist, a preacher, an evangelist.

This brings him into close connection with Walt Whitman, who similarly spent his life in preaching with puritanical fervour a most unpuritan gospel. Indeed, if one examines closely Lawrence's latest technique as shown here in such poems as 'Manifesto' and 'New Heaven and Earth', one is surprised to see how close this comes in many respects to that of the earlier Whitman, the Whitman of 'The Song of Myself'. For example, note the selfsame use of long, rolling, orchestral rhythm in the two following passages:

When I gathered flowers, I knew it was myself plucking my own flowering,
When I went in a train, I knew it was myself travelling by my own invention,
When I heard the cannon of the war, I listened with my own ears to my own destruction.
When I saw the torn dead, I knew it was my own torn dead body.
It was all me, I had done it all in my own flesh.

Every kind for itself and its own, for me, mine, male and female,
For me those that have been boys and that love women,
For me the man that is proud and feels how it stings to be slighted,
For me the sweet-heart and the old maid, for me mothers and the mothers of mothers,
For me lips that have smiled, eyes that have shed tears,
For me children and the begetters of children.

The difference is (and this too is curiously brought out in the technique) that Lawrence is more delicate, more sensitive, more personal. He deliberately narrows his range, to embrace only life and his own life in particular. Unlike Whitman, he has a horror of the infinite, and I am sure that he could never bring himself to 'utter the word Democracy, the word *en-masse*'. He is an aristocrat, an individualist, and indeed, he has only a horror of the collective mass of mankind, which he sees (and in this case, he sees more clearly than Whitman) to have been always conservative, conventional, timid, and persecutors of genius. In fact, the only similarity is, that both he and Whitman are preachers of new gospels, and therefore are obliged to adopt a similar tone of oratory in their work.

For this reason, Lawrence in his best poetry is unquotable, as is the case with all poets who depend rather on the extension of emotion, than on its minute concentration. But now and again he produces something that seems to transform all the poetry now written in English into mere prettiness and feebleness, so strong is the power with which his imagination pierces its subject. Such a poem, for example, is the one called 'The Sea'. I have space for only its last magnificent stanza:

[Quotes 'You who take the moon . . . your shadowing.' (*C.P.*, I, 197.)]

The man who wrote this, and many other passages in this volume, has at last arrived at his maturity—the maturity of the creative artist who is able to grasp a subject through its external aspect and internal meaning simultaneously, and to express both aspects in conjunction, before the subject is laid aside.

37. Conrad Aiken in *Dial*

9 August 1919, lxvii, 97–100

Conrad Aiken (b. 1889). Poet, novelist, critic.
This review was entitled, 'The Melodic Line'. (See Introduction,
pp. 11–12.)

It has been said that all the arts are constantly attempting, within their
respective spheres, to attain to something of the quality of music, to
assume, whether in pigment or pencil or marble or prose, something
of its speed and flash, emotional completeness and well-harmonied
resonance; but of no other single art is that so characteristically or persistently true as it is of poetry. Poetry is indeed in this regard two-
natured; it strikes us, when it is at its best, quite as sharply through our
sense of the musically beautiful as through whatever implications it
has to carry of thought or feeling; it plays on us alternately or simultaneously through sound as well as through content. The writers of
free verse have demonstrated, to be sure, that a poetry sufficiently
effective may be written in almost entire disregard of the values of
pure rhythm. The poetry of H. D. is perhaps the clearest example of
this. Severe concentration upon a damascene sharpness of sense-
impression, a stripping of images to the white clear kernel, both of
which matters can be more meticulously attended to if there are no
bafflements of rhythm or rhyme-pattern to be contended with, have
to a considerable extent a substitutional value. Such a poetry attains a
vitreous lucidity which has its own odd heatless charm. But a part of
its charm lies in its very act of departure from a norm which, like a
background or undertone, is forever present for it in our minds; we
like it in a sense because of its unique perversity as a variation on this
more familiar order of rhythmic and harmonic suspensions and
resolutions; we like it in short for its novelty; and it eventually
leaves us unsatisfied, because this more familiar order is based on
a musical hunger which is as profound and permanent as it is universal.

When we read a poem we are aware of this musical characteristic, or analogy, in several ways. The poem as a whole in this regard will satisfy us or not in accordance with the presence, or partial presence, or absence, of what we might term musical unity. The 'Ode to a Nightingale' is an example of perfect musical unity; the 'Ode to Autumn' is an example of partial musical unity—partial because the resolution comes too soon, the rate of curve is too abruptly altered; many of the poems by contemporary writers of free verse—Fletcher or Aldington or H. D.—illustrate what we mean by lack of musical unity or integration, except on the secondary plane, the plane of what we might call orotundity; and the most complete lack of all may be found in the vast majority of Whitman's poems. This particular sort of musical quality in poetry is however so nearly identifiable with the architectural as to be hardly separable from it. It is usually in the briefer movements of a poem that musical charm is most keenly felt. And this sort of brief and intensely satisfactory musical movement we might well describe as something closely analogous to what is called in musical compositions the melodic line.

By melodic line we shall not mean to limit ourselves to one line of verse merely. Our melodic line may be, indeed, one line of verse, or half a line, or a group of lines, or half a page. What we have in mind is that sort of brief movement when, for whatever psychological reason, there is suddenly a fusion of all the many qualities, which may by themselves constitute charm, into one indivisible magic. Is it possible for this psychological change to take place without entailing an immediate heightening of rhythmic effect? Possible, perhaps, but extremely unlikely. In a free verse poem we shall expect to see at such moments a very much closer approximation to the rhythm of metrical verse: in a metrical poem we shall expect to see a subtilization of metrical effects, a richer or finer employment of vowel and consonantal changes to that end. Isolate such a passage in a free verse poem or metrical poem and it will be seen how true this is. The change is immediately perceptible, like the change from a voice talking to a voice singing. The change is as profound in time as it is in tone, yet it is one which escapes any but the most superficial analysis. All we can say of it is that it at once alters the character of the verse we are reading from that sort which pleases and is forgotten, pleases without disturbing, to that sort which strikes into the subconscious, gleams, and is automatically remembered. For example, in the midst of the rich semi-prose recitative of Fletcher's White Symphony—a recitative which charms and entices, but does not quite enchant or take one's memory—one comes to the following passage:

> Autumn! Golden fountains,
> And the winds neighing
> Amid the monotonous hills;
> Desolation of the old gods,
> Rain that lifts and rain that moves away;
> In the green-black torrent
> Scarlet leaves.

It is an interlude of song, and one remembers it. Is this due to an intensification of rhythm? Partly, no doubt, but not altogether. The emotional heightening is just as clear, and the unity of impression is pronounced; it is a fusion of all these qualities, and it is impossible to say which is the primum mobile. As objective psychologists, all we can conclude is that in what is conspicuously a magical passage in this poem there is a conspicuous increase in the persuasiveness of rhythm.

This is equally true of metrical poetry. It is these passages of iridescent fusion that we recall from among the many thousands of lines we have read. One has but to summon up from one's memory the odds and ends of poems which willy nilly one remembers, precious fragments cherished by the jackdaw of the subconscious:

> A savage spot as holy and enchanted
> As e'er beneath a waning moon was haunted
> By woman wailing for her demon-lover.

> Beauty is momentary in the mind—
> The fitful tracing of a portal:
> But in the flesh it is immortal.

> And shook a most divine dance from their feet,
> That twinkled starlike, moved as swift, and fine,
> And beat the air so thin, they made it shine.

> Part of a moon was falling down the west
> Dragging the whole sky with it to the hills.
> Its light poured softly in her lap. She saw
> And spread her apron to it. She put out her hand
> Among the harp-like morning glory strings,
> Taut with the dew from garden-bed to eaves,
> As if she played unheard the tenderness
> That wrought on him. . . .

Awakening up, he took her hollow lute,—
Tumultuous,—and in chords that tenderest be,
He played an ancient ditty long since mute,
In Provence called, 'La Belle Dame Sans Merci.'

And suddenly there's no meaning in our kiss,
And your lit upward face grows, where we lie,
Lonelier and dreadfuller than sunlight is,
And dumb and mad and eyeless like the sky.

All of these excerpts, mangled as they are by being hewed from their contexts, have in a noticeable degree the quality of the 'melodic line'. They are the moments for which, indeed, we read poetry; just as when, in listening to a modern music however complex and dissonantal, it is after all the occasionally arising brief cry of lyricism which thrills and dissolves us. When the subconscious speaks, the subconscious answers.

It is because in a good deal of contemporary poetry the importance of the melodic line is forgotten that this brief survey has been made. In our preoccupations with the many technical quarrels, and quarrels as to aesthetic purpose, which have latterly embroiled our poets, we have, I think, a little lost sight of the fact that poetry to be poetry must after all rise above a mere efficiency of charmingness, or efficiency of accuracy, to this sort of piercing perfection of beauty or truth, phrased in a piercing perfection of music. It is a wholesome thing for us to study the uses of dissonance and irregularity; we add in that way, whether sensuously or psychologically, many new tones; but there is danger that the habit will grow upon us, that we shall forget the reasons for our adoption of these qualities and use them *passim* and without intelligence, or, as critics, confer a too arbitrary value upon them.

The poetry of Mr. D. H. Lawrence is a case very much in point. His temperament is modern to a degree, morbidly self-conscious, sex-crucified, an affair of stretched and twanging nerves. He belongs of course to the psychological wing of modern poetry. Although we first met him as an Imagist, it is rather with T. S. Eliot, or Masters, or the much gentler Robinson, all of whom are in a sense lineal descendants of the Meredith of Modern Love, that he belongs. But he does not much resemble any of these. His range is extremely narrow—it is nearly always erotic, febrile, and sultry at the lower end, plangently philosophic at the upper. Within this range he is astonishingly various.

No mood is too slight to be seized upon, to be thrust under his myopic lens. Here, in fact, we touch his cardinal weakness; for if as a novelist he often writes like a poet, as a poet he far too often writes like a novelist. One observes that he knows this himself; he asks the reader of *Look! We Have Come Through!* to consider it not as a collection of short poems, but as a sort of novel in verse. No great rearrangement, perhaps, would have been necessary to do the same thing for *New Poems* or *Amores*, though perhaps not so cogently. More than most poets he makes of his poetry a sequential, though somewhat disjointed, autobiography. And more than almost any poet who compares with him for richness of temperament, he is unselective in doing so, both as to material and as to method.

He is, indeed, as striking an example as one could find of the poet who, while appearing to be capable of what we have called the melodic line, none the less seems to be unaware of the value or importance of it, and gives it to us at random, brokenly, half blindly, or intermingled with splintered fragments of obscure sensation and extraneous detail dragged in to fill out a line. A provoking poet! and a fatiguing one: a poet of the demonic type, a man possessed, who is swept helplessly struggling and lashing down the black torrent of his thought, alternately frenzied and resigned. 'A poet', says Santayana, 'who merely swam out into the sea of sensibility, and tried to picture all possible things . . . would bring materials only to the workshop of art; he would not be an artist.' What Santayana had in mind was a poet who undertook this with a deliberateness—but the effect in the case of Mr. Lawrence is much the same. He is seldom wholly an artist, even when he has his medium most under control. It is when he is at his coolest, often—when he tries rhyme-pattern or rhythm-pattern or colour-pattern in an attempt at the sort of icy kaleidoscopics at which Miss Lowell is adept—that he is most tortuously and harshly and artificially and altogether unreadably at his worst. Is he obsessed with dissonance and oddity? It would seem so. His rhymes are cruel, sometimes, to the verge of murder.

Yet, if he is not wholly an artist, he is certainly, in at least a fragmentary sense, a brilliant poet. Even that is hardly fair enough; the two more recent volumes contain more than a handful of uniquely captivating poems. They have a curious quality—tawny, stark, bitter, harshly coloured, salt to the taste. The sadistic element in them is strong. It is usually in the love poems that he is best: in these he is closest to giving us the melodic line that comes out clear and singing. Closest indeed;

but the perfect achievement is seldom. The fusion is not complete. The rhythms do not altogether free themselves—one feels that they are weighted; the impressions are impetuously crowded and huddled; and as concerns the commanding of words Mr. Lawrence is a captain of more force than tact; he is obeyed, but sullenly. Part of this is due, no doubt, to his venturings among moods and sensations which no poet has hitherto attempted, moods secret and obscure, shadowy and suspicious. This is to his credit, and greatly to the credit of poetry. He is among the most original poets of our time, original, that is, as regards sensibility; he has given us sombre and macabre tones, and tones of a cold and sinister clarity, or of a steely passion, which we have not had before. His nerves are raw, his reactions are idiosyncratic; what is clear enough to him has sometimes an unhealthily mottled look to us, esuriently etched none the less. But a great deal of the time he overreaches; he makes frequently the mistake of, precisely, trying too hard. What cannot be captured, in this regard, it is no use killing. Brutality is no substitute for magic. One must take one's mood alive and singing, or not at all.

It is this factor which in the poetry of Mr. Lawrence most persistently operates to prevent the attainment of the perfect melodic line. Again and again he gives us, indeed, a sort of jagged and spangled flame; but the mood does not sing quite with the naturalness or ease one would hope for; it has the air of being dazed by violence, or even seems, in the very act of singing, to bleed a little. It is a trifle too easy to say of a poet of whom this is true that the fault may be due to an obtrusion of the intellect among the emotions. Such terms do not define, are scarcely separable. Perhaps it would more closely indicate the difficulty to say that Mr. Lawrence is not only, as all poets are, a curious blending of the psychoanalyst and the patient, but that he endeavours to carry on both rôles at once, to speak with both voices simultaneously. The soliloquy of the patient—the lyricism of the subconscious—is forever being broken in upon by the too eager inquisitions of the analyst. If Mr. Lawrence could make up his mind to yield the floor unreservedly to either, he would be on the one hand a clearer and more magical poet, on the other hand a more dependable realist.

One wonders, in the upshot, whether the theme of *Look! We Have Come Through!* had better not have been treated in prose. The story, such as it is, emerges, it is true, and with many deliciously clear moments, some of them lyric and piercing; but with a good deal that remains in question. It is the poet writing very much as a novelist, and all too often forgetting that the passage from the novel to the poem is among other things a passage from the cumulative to the selective. Sensations and impressions may be hewed and hauled in prose; but in poetry it is rather the sort of mood which, like a bird, flies out of the tree as soon as the axe rings against it, that one must look for. Mr. Lawrence has, of this sort, his birds, but he appears to pay little heed to them; he goes on chopping. And one has, even so, such a delight in him that not for worlds would one intervene. . . .

38. Louis Untermeyer, 'D. H. Lawrence', *New Republic*

11 August 1920, xxiii, 314–15

Louis Untermeyer (b. 1885). Poet and editor.

The pathos of D. H. Lawrence is the tragedy of immanence at war with impotence; a radiance of white-hot intensity struggling with an agonized frustration. Lawrence's world is a world of lurid landscapes, troubled countrysides pitted with collieries; a world of stumbling, driven men and tortured women drooping beneath an almost unbearable sultriness. Days drag on in an apathy of heat. Nights consume themselves in their own dark fires. There are no winds; the air stifles. Sometimes there come storms. Clouds gather suddenly from nowhere, faint rumblings rise, the atmosphere swells and grows taut; lightnings plunge and fierce rains trample the earth. But nothing clears, nothing is lifted. The rains draw off leaving the sun steaming in a haze with the air heavier than before. When, in the rare extremities of season, the torpor vanishes, a cutting heat stabs and ice burns with an even greater persistence. Nothing is allowed to rest easy or remain casual; self is thrown back upon unhappy self. There is no escape.

Not that Lawrence despairs of finding a haven; his work is a twisted search for a path through, a way out. The novels, the short stories, the poems, even his ruminating notes of travel are a record of seeking and losing and hoping against hope. Examining his work in retrospect, one sees how hard Lawrence tries to rise above his torments, how the body with all its glamour betrays his purpose, and even Beauty, luring him on, arraigns itself against him; a constant promise and a fresh defeat. Defeat is the answer, defeat and the darkness of failure. Frustration is the keynote of all his work; the three major novels, with their mournful cadences unite in a dissonant paean of surrender. *The Trespasser*, an early work, tells the story of an illicit holiday beginning in pain and ending in nothingness. Yet in it is condensed not only Lawrence's baffled eroticism but the whole tragic conflict of love; the elemental clash between that passion which flowers directly from the blood and the deeper, almost opposed desire which is detached from the individual and is abstract, over-exalted and full of impersonal fantasy. *Sons and Lovers* amplifies the theme and adds to it the further tortures of an inhibited and mother-sapped spirit. Finally, in *The Rainbow*, possibly the most poetic and poignant novel of this decade, the dominant strain is given its fullest sweep. Lawrence's need drives him to create richer backgrounds, greater and wider beginnings. Where *The Trespasser* dealt with a fortnight and *Sons and Lovers* with a lifetime, *The Rainbow* covers three generations. Like Lawrence, all his characters are harried seekers, seeking some sort of rainbow behind the storm; plunging with febrile energy and perplexed hunger towards some mystical consummation. Here, as in those tense short stories that twitch and tremble in *The Prussian Officer*, the question returns upon itself. Can there be spiritual exaltation merely in natural beauty? Is there no fulfilment through the flesh?

And so he comes to a baffled aloneness; a thwarted solitary in whom the physical turns metaphysical, a half-liberated protagonist who, torn between a thousand sensual delights and a sudden distrust of the flesh, is tossed from negation to abnegation. Passion offers no way out; religion is a crumbling refuge; art a desperate and futile sublimation. There remains only The Self or the decision not to be. And Lawrence cannot make the choice for himself or his characters. He sees their blundering, and shares their puzzled self-destruction. For it is not merely frustration that poisons him; it is the insistent awareness of this frustration that torments him so. Back to life it drives him, to the gestures of the body with a new bitter-sweetness, a starker self-consciousness. Here in a description of peasants carrying in the hay during a streaming thunder-rain (a fragment from *Twilight in Italy*) is an epitome of this intensification:

[Quotes from 'The Crucifix Across the Mountains': 'The body bent forward . . . to return again with the burden.' (*Twilight in Italy*, Penguin ed., 10–11.)]

It is this continual rousedness of physical sensation which radiates from Lawrence's prose and finds its flushed climax in his poetry. Huge passages in the novels seem like unfinished sketches waiting to be cast in the harder mould of poetic form. The cherry-picking episode in *Sons and Lovers* is perfected and fused in the three quatrains called 'Cherry Robbers'; Miriam and Paul among the flowers take on tremendous

133

proportions when they meet in that triumph of raw neuroticism, 'Snap-dragons.' From *Love Poems* (first published in 1912) to the latest *New Poems*, Lawrence suffers from the same preoccupation and his inability to free himself from it. He is not merely sex-driven, he is self-crucified on a cross of flesh. Far more autobiographical than his prose, his four volumes of verse are almost direct transcripts from the unconscious. Sometimes, as in 'New Heaven and Earth', he no longer tries to control the random current of his thought, and becomes unintelligible. More frequently, in 'Manifesto' and the longer introspective poems, he attempts to act as narrator and interpreter, and the resultant confusion makes one wonder whether he is trying to talk as patient or analyst or both at the same time. The smouldering volume *Look! We Have Come Through!* is a particularly pathetic and illuminating example—even the title is a passionate and despairing wish-fulfilment.

The succeeding *New Poems*, showing how pitifully Lawrence has failed to come through, lack the fusion, the instinctive unity of the preceding collection. But they have a muffled light of their own. If they contain nothing so nakedly brilliant as 'The Ballad of a Wilful Woman', as fiercely knit as 'One Woman to All Women' or as terrible as 'Rabbit Snared in the Night', there is the tearing nostalgia of 'Piano', the shuddering restraint of 'Intime', the grave and magnificent 'Seven Seals'. These solemnly ecstatic lines prove finally that it is not desire itself that sways Lawrence (as so many of his critics have con-tended) but the hunger for complete fulfilment, the ratification and immortality of the body which leaves one free, clear, beyond self. It is this that uplifts him—this shattered dream, this vision of the perfect mating—of two radiantly isolated identities held in the circle of love, moving like two separate stars within a larger orbit; unutterably apart and in inseparable conjunction. Because the dream will not merge into reality, Lawrence loses himself among his own fantasies, wandering from distorted sentimentality to distracted sadism. His lines thicken with pain, grow harsh with passion, rage, bleed, and vanish in a storm of frenzied imagination. How vividly his images rise may be surmised from such scattered snatches as:

[Quotes the following extracts: 'Wedding Morn' 1-2 (*C.P.*, I, 58); 'Noise of Battle' 1-6 (*C.P.*, I, 159); 'Suspense' 1-3 (*C.P.*, I, 99); 'Flat Suburbs, S.W., in the Morning' 13-16 (*C.P.*, I, 51); 'End of Another Home Holiday' 8 and 12-14 (*C.P.*, I, 63); 'Green' 1-3 (*C.P.*, I, 216); 'The Sea' 20-9 (*C.P.*, I, 197).]

It is only when Lawrence turns pamphleteer (*vide* the Preface to *New*

Poems) that he exhibits an erratic and illogical conduct of thought. In his eloquent tribute to free verse as 'the insurgent naked throb of the instant moment', Lawrence loses himself in the rush of his ardour and forgets that no moment of time is unrelated, that the immediate present does not exist by itself. Lawrence writes: 'Free verse has its own *nature*. It has no goal. It has no finish. It is wholly the instant; the quick. . . It is not of the nature of reminiscence. It is not the past which we treasure between our hands.' And every one of Lawrence's backward-turning lines is a cumulative contradiction to his prefatory theorizing. For into every effort to hold the moment in its 'windlike transit', Lawrence— and, for that matter, every poet—must use word-patterns, images, symbols that have associations as old as the race; with every syllable he summons the accretions of his experience, he reanimates his memories and draws upon the very past which has shaped him so he might cope with the rushing present, 'the very plasm of the self'.

It is the effort to find the Self beyond selfhood that makes Lawrence seem another ineffectual angel beating his bruised wings; a darker Shelley of the senses. Sex storms about him. The lightning energizes, the rainbow arches to heal him. But he is not part of them. Plunging beyond bounds into the unfathomable, he seeks assurance if not fulfil-ment of his vision: the final union of swift blood and swifter spirit; the glorious if impossible fusion of lightning and rainbow, sons and lovers, men and women.

39. Douglas Goldring from 'The Later Work of D. H. Lawrence', *Reputations*

London, Chapman & Hall, 1920, 67–78

Douglas Goldring (1887–1960). Author and critic. First met Lawrence 1908. Enthusiastic supporter of his work.

[Goldring begins by saying that it takes time to get to know a man, or a book, worth knowing. During the war many writers cowered before public opinion, but not so Lawrence. (The following extract begins on p. 69.)]

From the occasion of his first appearance on the literary horizon Mr. Lawrence has been a difficult writer. He has never made any advances to the mob; and even his prose style is a kind of barricade to prevent the intrusion of the many into the walled garden of his mind. At one time an additional barricade between his work and those who have subsequently appreciated his individual genius was erected by the 'boosting' of a certain inner circle of the leaders of literary fashion. The very peculiarities of such early books as *The White Peacock* attracted this *clique*, with its flair for the less important phenomena of genius. For a little while they pretended to consider Mr. Lawrence the white hope of English letters; and they succeeded in making his books the vogue among a section of the London intelligentsia. It became the correct thing to admire Mr. Lawrence—until he suddenly applied the acid test of the value of these protestations and of this admiration by publishing *The Rainbow*. Then what a change of front! The deafening silence, broken only by the sound of the white rabbits of criticism scuttling for cover, which formed the sequel to *The Rainbow* prosecution, will not soon be forgotten by those who were in London at the time. Not one of Mr. Lawrence's fervent boosters ventured into print to defend him; not one of his brother authors (save only Mr. Arnold Bennett, to whom all honour is due) took up the cudgels on his behalf. English novelists are proverbially lacking in *esprit de corps*, but surely

they were never so badly shown up as when they tolerated this perse-
cution of a distinguished *confrère* without making a collective protest.
But our intelligentsia has always been more fickle and cowardly than
the man in the street whom it so dearly loves to deride. All this is not
to prove that *The Rainbow* is a satisfactory book. In many ways, irres-
pective of its fate, it is, as a work of art, perhaps one of the least successful novels which Mr. Lawrence has written, as it is the most ambitious.
But if it must be called a failure, it is at all events a splendid and not an
ignoble failure.

The chief effect of *The Rainbow* affair on Mr. Lawrence seems to
have been to cause him to retire more deeply into himself. His work
has become more difficult, his peculiar transcendental philosophy more
obscure. He has sought more and more to discard inessentials, to ignore
the surface of things, until gradually he has released himself even from
the unconscious nationalism of *Sons and Lovers*. In that most beautiful
and perhaps immortal novel, he has shown us the very heart of the real
England, the England which still has a heart. The book is full of the
true English spirit, is fragrant with a love of England, is in the best
sense national, so that it can hardly fail to reveal to the middle-class
Imperialist 'Britisher' who reads it the heart of the 'English' Englishman.

But in his last few volumes, *Twilight in Italy*, *Look! We Have Come
Through!* and *New Poems*, and in a remarkable series of essays which he
contributed to *The English Review*, Mr. Lawrence is concerned with
humanity as a whole. He has transcended nationalism, and views the
agonies inherent in the marriage of man's soul and body from the
standpoint of his mystical philosophy. The argument of *Look! We
Have Come Through!* sets forth a spiritual conflict at once individual
and universal, a conflict of absorbing interest to any human being,
regardless of creed or race, who has reached the stage of development
necessary to its understanding. As a poet, he is concerned only with
what is at the very core of human life, and thus his work—to borrow
the phrase currently applied to pictures and statues of a certain kind—
has always a 'beyond' to it. All great poets, by the divine accident
which we call inspiration, show us at moments, and often quite unconsciously, a glimpse of this beyond. Mr. Lawrence's moments of illumination (and perhaps this proves that in a strict sense he is not a 'great
poet') are, however, never quite unconscious. He seems overwhelmed
by what he has seen, to have seen more than he can possibly express,
perhaps more than is expressible—in words. His quest is for the means

to be articulate. He strives, often with a kind of desperation, to clothe his vision in words, and frequently his poems are battlefields on which he has been defeated. There are times, also, when he is like a man who has been blind, who is just recovering the use of his eyes and is convulsed with the effort to see a little more, a little further into the radiant world which is within an ace of being miraculously restored to his vision. Now he has a sudden glimpse, and in a flash a new heaven and a new earth reveal themselves; but again, in a moment, all is chaos and obscurity, a veil of clouds and a rushing of waters. Thus the poems at the end of *Look! We Have Come Through!* called 'New Heaven and Earth', 'Elysium', 'Manifesto', and 'Craving for Spring', contain alternately passages of great sublimity which do indeed open windows in the mind, and passages of mere bathos and confusion.

Of those who have the patience to read the book through, few, however, will miss the significance of lines such as these:

[Quotes the following extracts: 'New Heaven and Earth', 'When I am trodden quite out . . . yet unaccountably new' (*C.P.*, I, 258) and 'Ha, I was a blaze . . . the unknown unknown' (*C.P.*, I, 259); 'Elysium', 'Delivered helpless . . . of which I come' (*C.P.*, I, 262).]

'Manifesto', an effort to explain the author's sexual philosophy, seems to me to contain more confusion, mingled with commonplace ideas, than the other metaphysical poems, and to have fewer flashes of illumination. But as a statement of some of the cardinal points in Mr. Lawrence's belief, some passages in it have an obvious interest and value:

[Quotes from 'Manifesto', 'Let them praise desire . . . here in the flesh' (*C.P.*, I, 265).]

Many mystics have tried to deny sex altogether, but Mr. Lawrence sees in the bodily union of men and women the central mystery of human life, a mystery indissolubly connected with every real religious impulse of mankind, a symbol of an ultimate spiritual consummation.

Perhaps the most profound and moving poem in this volume is the last one, 'Craving for Spring'. It is a passionate appeal to Life not to forsake the frozen and corrupt world, not to leave it under the dominion of Death.

[Quotes from 'Craving for Spring', 'Come quickly . . . in the world of the heart of man' (*C.P.*, I, 273).]

There are people, perhaps, to whom the passage quoted above, and indeed the whole poem, may sound like the vapourings of a madman.

To others it will sound like a kind of martial music of the soul, filling them with strange fervours and with unspeakable longing.

When Mr. Lawrence drops the cloak of the seer and squeezes his individuality into the confines of more or less 'ordinary' verse, he moves about with a power and confidence which few of his contemporaries can equal. He comes down from metaphysics into the art of poetry, 'trailing clouds of glory', and seems to see all the visible world with freshened eyes, and as if for the first time. Nature reveals her secrets to him as she has done to few poets and those only the most cherished. When he uses more or less conventional metres—as in the 'Hymn to Priapus', in 'A Youth Mowing', 'Giorno dei Morti', 'Sunday Afternoon in Italy', and the wonderful 'Ballad of a Wilful Woman'—he gives them always a personal, unconventional twist, and evolves a new, strange and beautiful music. The following verses from the 'Ballad of a Wilful Woman' will serve to illustrate his use of metre:

[Quotes from 'Ballad of a Wilful Woman', 'While Joseph pitches . . . "Do you catch what they say?"' (C.P., I, 201).]

The whole volume is full of brief, vivid, unforgettable pictures and images, like the following sketch of a type of young woman whom the poet calls 'Frost flowers'—young women who

> dart and flash
> before the shops like wagtails on the edge of a pool.

Or this, from a poem called 'People':

> The great gold apples of night
> Hang from the street's long bough.

And in the piece called 'The Sea', Mr. Lawrence shows once again— as he showed in *The Trespasser* and in several of his other books—that he understands the sea as truly as the greatest of his country's poets, and that he feels for it something which only Englishmen seem to have been able to express.

A good deal of Mr. Lawrence's later work, for reasons which have already been given, leaves the reader with a sense of disappointment. Sometimes ,when he strives hardest to liberate his ideas, he creates only the chaos which he has himself defined:

> What is chaos, my love?
> It is not freedom.
> A disarray of falling stars coming to nought.

But how thankful we should be for the achievement of this lonely genius! Even when his verse is most chaotic, even when he most fails to set free his own thought and his poetry most nearly resembles 'a disarray of falling stars', the sparks from the furnace of his inspiration retain sufficient heat to enable them to set fire to the minds on which they fall.

THE LOST GIRL

November 1920

40. Virginia Woolf in
Times Literary Supplement

2 December 1920, 795

Virginia Woolf, unsigned (1882–1941). Novelist and critic.

Perhaps the verdicts of critics would read less preposterously and their opinions would carry greater weight if, in the first place, they bound themselves to declare the standard which they had in mind, and, in the second, confessed the course, bound, in the case of a book read for the first time, to be erratic, by which they reached their final decision. Our standard for Mr. Lawrence, then, is a high one. Taking into account the fact, which is so constantly forgotten, that never in the course of the world will there be a second Meredith or a second Hardy, for the sufficient reason that there have already been a Meredith and a Hardy, why, we sometimes asked, should there not be a D. H. Lawrence? By that we meant that we might have to allow him the praise, than which there is none higher, of being himself an original; for such of his work as came our way was disquieting, as the original work of a contemporary writer always is.

This was the standard which we had in mind when we opened *The Lost Girl*. We now go on to trace the strayings and stumblings of that mind as it came to the conclusion that *The Lost Girl* is not an original, or a book which touches the high standard which we have named. Together with our belief in Mr. Lawrence's originality went, of course, some sort of forecast as to the direction which that originality was likely to take. We conceived him to be a writer, with an extraordinary sense of the physical world, of the colour and texture and shape of things, for whom the body was alive and the problems of the body insistent and important. It was plain that sex had for him a meaning which it was disquieting to think that we, too, might have to explore. Sex, indeed, was the first red-herring that crossed our path in the new volume. The story is the story of Alvina Houghton, the daughter of a draper in Woodhouse, a mining town in the Midlands. It is all built up of solid fabric. If you want a truthful description of a draper's shop, evident knowledge of his stock, and a faithful and keen yet not satiric or sentimental description of James Houghton, Mrs. Houghton, Miss Frost, and Miss Pinnegar, here you have it. Nor does this summary do any kind of justice to the variety of the cast and the number of events in which they play their parts. But, distracted by our preconception of what Mr. Lawrence was to give us, we turned many pages of very able writing in search for something else which must be there. Alvina seemed the most likely instrument to transmit Mr. Lawrence's electric shock through the calicos, prints, and miners' shirts by which she stood surrounded. We watched for signs of her development nervously, for we always dread originality, yet with the sense that once the shock was received we should rise braced and purified. The signs we looked for were not lacking. For example, 'Married or unmarried, it was the same—the same anguish, realized in all its pain after the age of fifty—the loss in never having been able to relax, to submit.' Again, 'She was returning to Woodhouse virgin as she had left it. In a measure she felt herself beaten. Why? Who knows. . . . Fate had been too strong for her and her desires. Fate which was not an external association of forces, but which was integral in her own nature.' Such phrases taken in conjunction with the fact that Alvina, having refused her first suitor, wilted and pined, and becoming a midwife mysteriously revived in the atmosphere of the Islington-road, confirmed us in our belief that sex was the magnet to which the myriad of separate details would adhere. We were wrong. Details accumulated; the picture of life in Woodhouse was built up; and sex disappeared. This detail, then this realism, must have another meaning than we had given them. Relieved, yet a trifle disappointed, for we want originality as much as we dread it, we adopted a fresh attitude and read Mr. Lawrence as one reads Mr. Bennett—for the facts, and for the story. Mr. Lawrence shows indeed something of Mr. Bennett's power of displaying by means of immense industry and great ability a section of the hive beneath glass. Like all the other insects, Alvina runs in and out of other people's lives, and it is the pattern of the whole that interests us rather than the fate of one of the individuals. And then, as we have long ceased to find in reading Mr. Bennett, suddenly the method seems to justify itself by a single phrase which we may liken to a glow or to a transparency, since to quote one apart from the context would give no idea of our meaning. In other words, Mr. Lawrence occasionally and momentarily achieves that concentration which Tolstoy preserves sometimes for a chapter or more. And then again the laborious process continues of building up a model of life from saying how d'you do, and cutting the loaf, and knocking the cigarette ash into the ash tray, and standing the yellow bicycle against the wall. Little by little Alvina disappears beneath the heap of facts recorded about her, and the only sense in which we feel her to be lost is that we can no longer believe in her existence.

So, though the novel is probably better than any that will appear for the next six months, we are disappointed, and would write Mr. Lawrence off as one of the people who have determined to produce seaworthy books were it not for those momentary phrases and for a strong suspicion that the proper way to look at *The Lost Girl* is as a stepping stone in a writer's progress. It is either a postscript or a prelude.

41. Katherine Mansfield on *The Lost Girl*

December 1920

Katherine Mansfield (1888–1923), short-story writer. Married J. M. Murry in 1919. Close friend of the Lawrences for a period after 1913. In his *Reminiscences of D. H. Lawrence* Murry says that the following notes were sent to him in December 1920 after Katherine Mansfield had been prevented by illness from reviewing *The Lost Girl*.

The text is from *The Scrapbook of Katherine Mansfield*, ed. J. M. Murry. London. Constable, 1939. 156–7.

I made these notes. Read them—will you?

The Lost Girl: It's important. It ought not to be allowed to pass.

The Times [probably *T.L.S.*—see No. 40] gave no inkling of what it was—never even hinted at its dark secret.

Lawrence denies his humanity. He denies the powers of the imagination. He denies life—I mean *human* life. His hero and heroine are non-human. They are animals on the prowl. They do not feel: they scarcely speak. There is not one memorable word. They submit to their physical response and for the rest go veiled, blind—*faceless, mindless*. This is the doctrine of mindlessness.

He says his heroine is extraordinary, and rails against *the ordinary*. Isn't that significant? But look at her. Take her youth—her thriving upon the horse-play with the doctors. They might be beasts butting each other—no more. Take the scene when the hero throws her in the kitchen, possesses her, and she returns singing to the washing-up. It's a *disgrace*. Take the rotten, rubbishy scene of the woman in labour asking the Italian into her bedroom. All false. All a pack of lies!

Take the nature-study at the end. It's no more than the grazing-place for Alvina and her sire. What was the 'green hellebore' to her? Of course, there is a great deal of racy, bright, competent writing in the early part—the 'shop' part. But it doesn't take a writer to tell all that. The whole is false—*ashes*. The preposterous Indian troupe of four young men is—a fake. But how on earth he can keep it up—is the problem. No, it's not. He has 'given way'. Why stop there?

Oh, don't forget where Alvina feels *a trill in her bowels**, and discovers herself with child. A TRILL. What does that mean? And why is it so peculiarly offensive from a man? Because it is *not on this plane* that the emotions of others are conveyed to the imagination. It's a kind of sinning against art.

Earth-closets, too. Do they exist, *qua* earthclosets? No. I might describe the queer noises coming from one when old Grandpa X was there—very strange cries and moans, and how the women who were washing stopped and shook their heads and pitied him, and even the children didn't laugh. Yes, I can imagine that. But that's not the same as to build an earth-closet because the former one was so exposed. No.

Am I prejudiced? Be careful! I feel privately as though L. had possessed an animal and had fallen under a curse. But I can't say that. All I know is: this is bad and ought not to be allowed. I feel a horror of it —a shrinking. But that's not criticism.

But this is life when one has blasphemed against the spirit of reverence.

---

* Penguin text reads: 'And even as he turned to look for her, she felt a strange thrilling in her bowels: a sort of trill strangely within her, yet extraneous to her.' (378)

42. Edward Garnett in *Manchester Guardian*

10 December 1920, 5

Edward Garnett (see No. 35), here signed 'E. G.'.

Mr. D. H. Lawrence's reappearance as a novelist, after five years of silence, is something to be thankful for. His last novel, *The Rainbow*, hastily banned by a censorious magistrate though vindicated by Mr. Arnold Bennett, was not worthy of his remarkable talent. It was jumbled, inconclusive, faulty in planning, overheated in atmosphere, a *réchauffé* of old materials and characters that his fervid imagination could not lay to rest. But *The Lost Girl* is firm in drawing, light and witty in texture, charmingly fresh in style and in atmosphere. The heroine, Alvina, is the daughter of James Houghton, a Midland draper, whose soaring ambitions and refined and elegant taste are quite out of place in the small industrial, vulgar-minded town of Woodbridge, [sic—misprint for 'Woodhouse'], which 'hated any approach to originality or real taste'. All James's schemes for imposing his 'robes et modes' on Woodbridge fall flat, all his later fantastic speculations bring him to grief. His failing business and invalid wife are only sustained by the devotion of two women—the self-sacrificing Miss Frost, the governess, and the practical manageress, Miss Pinnegar. With subtle art Mr. Lawrence exhibits and brands the grubby, ugly industrialism and stodgy, unimaginative bourgeois mediocrity of Woodbridge society through the medium of James's commercial folly and Alvina's unorthodox passion for the wandering Italian, Cicio. Alvina has already sent two suitors about their business, and the sketch of her hesitating aversion for the second, the flat, pale, dry school teacher, Albert Witham, whose persistent gallantry 'that completely missed the individual in the woman' finely illustrates Mr. Lawrence's uncanny skill in analysing the love instincts. People who do not appreciate the analysis of the forces of sensuous passion or the delineation of the feminine surrender to the spells of Eros may be warned that *The Lost Girl* is not for them. But from a continental standpoint the picture of the irruption of the foreign Natcha-Kee-Tawara touring troupe, of Madame and the four young braves, Max, Louis, Geoffrey, and Cicio, into the heavy respectabilities and domesticities of utilitarian Woodbridge is perfectly delicious. Mr. Lawrence has an intimate understanding of the fine shades of the Latin temperament and of the aesthetic basis of its emotional valuations, and the story of Alvina's hypnotized surrender to Cicio's physical charm is quite as fine, and more direct in its psychological truth than Henry James's masterly studies of the clash between French and Anglo-Saxon standards of morals.

The picture is an extremely brilliant one, done with a dexterous lightness of touch that is irresistible. And the aesthetic charm deepens when Alvina, now married to Cicio, is transported to the latter's native village, Pescocalascio, in the Alban mountains. The study in the last fifty pages of the wild, savage beauty of this primitive environment and of its pagan-minded hill peasantry is done with a poet's insight into the elemental forces of incorrigible nature. *The Lost Girl* is indeed the work of a poet who to a Swinburnian intensity of serious emotion curiously joins a democratic irreverence that spares not at all the British Lares and Penates. It is a brilliant book, with a few lapses from good taste that will amaze and perhaps scandalize Woodbridge and all its clan. As a criticism of Midland 'culture' and mentality it invites comparison with Mr. Arnold Bennett's pictures of the *Five Towns*.

43. J. M. Murry in *Athenaeum*

17 December 1920, 836

John Middleton Murry, signed 'M' (1889–1957), editor (*Rhythm, Athenaeum, Adelphi*) and critic. One-time friend and disciple of Lawrence. Wrote biographical study of Lawrence, *Son of Woman* (1931).

There are two ways in which we may approach Mr. Lawrence's new novel: we may regard it either as one among the many, or as marking a phase in the development of one who was by far the most promising, and is still among the most interesting, of the writers of the younger generation. From the former angle it is an interesting book, and there is little more to be said.

But when we consider it as a novel by Mr. D. H. Lawrence, it becomes a different thing, which interests us differently. The very fact that it is a well-constructed, competently written tale of a girl who breaks away from the sterility of middle-class life in a mining district to form a passionate marriage with an Italian, has another importance; for if we compare *The Lost Girl* with *Sons and Lovers*, we remark that the increase of control of a kind is set off by a very obvious loss of imaginative power. Mr. Lawrence is now, as a novelist, commensurable with his contemporaries. *The Lost Girl* is certainly a better novel than most of his coevals could write, but it is largely of the same kind as their novels. *Sons and Lovers* was not; neither was *The Rainbow*. In them there were flashes of psychological intuition, passages of darkly beautiful writing, so remarkable that at times they aroused a sense that the latest flowering on the tree of English literature might be one of the most mysterious.

There is not very much mystery about *The Lost Girl*. Alvina Houghton springs from the same country as Paul Morel; but it is no longer the country of a miraculous birth. Woodhouse is as real, and real in the same way, as Mr. Bennett's *Five Towns*; there is no garment of magical beauty flung over it, like that which gleamed out of the

148

opening pages of *Sons and Lovers*. And in Alvina herself we catch sight of none of the strange potencies that seemed to hover about Paul Morel. We are interested in her; she is perfectly credible; she is even mysterious: but the mystery in her is not that of a revelation of the unknown, but rather of an ignorance in her creator. She is more the idea of a woman than a woman. It is as though Mr. Lawrence had lost some power of immediate contact with human beings that he once possessed; his intuitive knowledge has weakened under the pressure of theory. But whereas the beauties of *The Rainbow* could be held in the mind very separate from the sex-theory which dominated and falsified the book, the texture of *The Lost Girl* is much more closely knit. We can no longer separate the true from the false; the theory impinges on the imaginative reality at every point. We lose our grasp of the central characters just at the moment when it should be firmest. A phrase like 'his dark receptivity overwhelmed her' will intrude at a crisis in the love between Alvina and her Italian lover, Cicio; and the effect is as though the writer's (and therefore the reader's) consciousness had suddenly collapsed. The woman and the man are lost in the dark. What we are told of them may be true; or it may be false: we cannot tell with our waking minds. Mr. Lawrence becomes most esoteric when he should be most precise, for nothing is more esoteric than the language of a theory peculiar to oneself—and, we might add, nothing is uglier.

We are not merely bewildered but repelled when Mr. Lawrence writes in this way of the effect of an actor's imitation of another man upon his heroine:

> Louis was masterful—he mastered her psyche. She laughed till her head lay helpless on the chair, she could not move. Helpless, inert she lay, in her orgasm of laughter. The end of Mr. May. Yet she was hurt.

And it is always through language as vague as this, if less positively ugly, that we are made to grope for the reality of the emotional crises of Mr. Lawrence's story.

Mr. Lawrence's own grasp of the central theme of his story, of the peculiar attraction which held Alvina and Cicio together, despite an amount of ecstatic hatred that would have sufficed to separate a hundred ordinary lovers for ever, may possibly be profound; but he does not convey it to us. He writes of his characters as though they were animals circling round each other; and on this sub-human plane no human destinies can be decided. Alvina and Cicio become for us like grotesque beasts in an aquarium, shut off from our apprehension by the misted glass of an esoteric language, a quack terminology. Life, as Mr. Lawrence shows it to us, is not worth living; it is mysteriously degraded by a corrupt mysticism. Mr. Lawrence would have us back to the slime from which we rose. His crises are all retrogressions.

In short, we are nonplussed by Mr. Lawrence's fifth novel. For a little while we inclined to explain the obvious loss of creative vigour as a paralysis produced by the suppression of *The Rainbow*; but the cause proved to be inadequate. Mr. Lawrence's decline is in himself. Even in the final chapters which describe how Alvina accompanies Cicio to his home in the Italian mountains, we miss some essential magic from the passion of his descriptive writing. We cannot suppose that it was fear of the censor that stayed his hand here.

44. Francis Hackett in *New Republic*

16 March 1921, 77–8

Francis Hackett, signed 'F.H.' (b. 1883). Journalist and critic. Associate editor of *New Republic* 1914–22.

So far as love is concerned, especially sex love, our novelists may be compared to astrologers. They are handling a theme elevated by sentiment and idealism and inwound with egoism, and it seems practically impossible for them to do anything with the theme except to coddle it. They speak of an undifferentiated thing called 'love' as if the word had a clear meaning; and naturally the word soaks up the colour with which each reader is saturated. If there is a profound contradiction between the writer's intention and the reader's susceptibility the reader finds that his own colour won't soak, and he says he 'doesn't like' the writer. But this sort of acceptance or rejection is fortuitous.

We must soon or late see the relativity of this word love, which has millions of meanings, and we must narrow the field of misconception by enlarging our vocabulary. The same word cannot intelligibly be used to cover the relations of Romeo and Juliet, Anthony and Cleopatra, Hamlet's mother and Hamlet's father, Hamlet's mother and Hamlet's uncle. When an enlarged and refined vocabulary is worked out in these matters, and a new word, for example, is found for such an experienced re-arrangement as the union of Hamlet's mother and Hamlet's uncle, the priggishness of a person like Hamlet in holding up the second choice in contrast to the first will be properly revealed. A great part of contemporary social hypocrisy in England and America is due to the implication that marriage, an arrangement largely social, is always or even usually accommodated to the variegations and necessities of love. Whatever kind of insurgence and responsiveness one means by love, it has its own laws regardless of the imperiousness of marriage; and on the far-famed continent of Europe the imperiousness of marriage has gradually been reduced both by males and females to something that suits the human disposition rather better than a straight waistcoat. The well-fed youth of England and America, incidentally, are at the present time experimenting with love in a fashion that the elder astrologers think is terrific. Perhaps it is terrific. But a generation that gave five or six out of the seven million killed in the war cannot be expected to live according to the maxims of Martin Tupper and Queen Victoria. A totally new conception of marriage and love might so be devised that we should lose all our old notions in gaining a definite understanding of what our tolerable cravings and yearnings and aspirings really are.

A novel like *The Lost Girl* is a direct incitement to these observations. For Lawrence, with certain limits, is a peculiarly unsentimental or anti-sentimental artist in the field where sentiment does preclude understanding. I do not really like most of the little I have read of Lawrence. In his report of people and their relations to one another he is extremely intense and sinewy, and he leaves out all the nice, easy, pleasant, inconsequential passages that do relieve the tension and relax the sinews. Lawrence seems to me to be always wrestling inside, and yet to have painful and distressing adhesions. He seems to me to be angular, acrid and heroic. His people always appear to need each other badly, and to miss each other by inches, and to manage life as if they were staggering blindfolded through a crazy Virginia reel. But with this slight accent on Mr. Lawrence's apparent proclivity for unhappiness and his insistence on human aberrance, it must in substance, fascinating in background and powerful in its discernments.[1]

The 'lost girl', Alvina, is plumped down in that sour England of which Clayhanger and The Mummer's Wife have spoken—an England with which D. H. Lawrence is rather impatient. He traces the decline of the Manchester House, owned by Alvinia's father, with a kind of contemptuous resentment, and yet he does not altogether deride the man responsible for it. James Houghton is a thin-spun elegant dreamer who tried to impose 'robes' and fine silks on the barbarous mining town of Woodhouse. In his transition from his grand shop to half a shop remaining from the tailor and haberdasher, and later quarter of a shop remaining from the grocer, he has the presence and aid of a capable forceful woman, Miss Frost, and a deep shock-absorber, Miss Pinnegar, and his fine-grained daughter Alvina. Houghton's wife is simply his emotional pensioner, retired forever to an invalidic room over the shop. On his way down in the world he dreams wilder and

[1] Text thus. Perhaps it should read 'it must be admitted that his work is in substance . . .'

wilder dreams—until he winds up with most of his resources in a cinema theatre, with Alvina playing the piano and a plump little American as manager, especially interested in clinging to the legitimacies of intermittent vaudeville.

Alvina's nature is illustrated both by her surprising excursion to become a maternity nurse in London (where the doctors pinch her haunches, as doctors are always supposed to, in maternity hospitals), and her surprising return to the quiescence and inertia of her home town. In this town, where her father is too elegant and too unsuccessful to be in any given social set, she has practically no chance to meet marriageable men. But in a mild way she dangles an Australian, a returned South African and even the American. The man home from South Africa, with a wooden soul, she almost takes. 'For the fear of being an old maid, the fear of her own virginity, was really gaining on Alvina. There was a terrible sombre futility, nothingness, in Manchester House.' But deadly as her panic is, 'all Alvina's desperate and profligate schemes and ideas fell to nought before the inexorable in her nature. And the inexorable in her nature was highly exclusive and selective, an inevitable negation of looseness or prostitution. Hence men were afraid of her—of her power, once they had committed themselves.'

But Alvina loses herself. To the cinema theatre comes a foreign troupe of interesting youths under a clever Frenchwoman, and one of these youths is an inscrutable Italian with yellow eyes. Mr. Lawrence is old-fashioned in his portrayal of this youth's silent romantic charm. Cicio is perilously near a standardized product of romance with his black-set, tawny eyes, his powerful body, his derisive smile, his heavy mesmeric influence. But Alvina beholds in him 'the sphinx, and she between its paws'. He is a despised foreigner, among these northern industrial people. He is cheap and over-dressed and strange. But she finds him dark and insidious and bewitching. With only a glance from him, and with his peasant muteness to mystify and benumb her, she submits herself to him—'she felt extinguished'.

When it is certain that there is no money, no fortune, with her, Cicio does not want particularly to marry her, and she leaves the troupe abruptly to find a happy security in an appointment as a nurse. But before she consummates her engagement to the resonant benevolent tiresome Scotch doctor, Cicio turns up with his desire to marry her manifested, and her extinction is then completed. She goes with him to the Abruzzi, to his primitive family farm in the fastnesses of the mountains.

This transition has in it a challenging novelty for Lawrence, and he soars to it in a spirit nowhere exhibited in the English part of the book. The icy mountain heights, where the flesh is flayed and exalted, arouses the poet in Lawrence, and he imagines Alvina and Cicio in the barren discomfort of their cold farmhouse with superb command of the scene. There is no conclusion. Alvina is with child when Cicio leaves her to go to the war. Is he leaving her forever? Is he really a stranger to her? A tatter of hope is left with her at the end.

The beauty of this story for D. H. Lawrence is possibly connected with the tragic determinism of love. He flings this case of Alvina in the face of an England full of surplus women, and he finds extraordinary and wonderful the woman who can support the insupportable, can cross oceans and mountains in an answer to her thorough-going self. This is part, certainly, of its eloquence. But Lawrence is no moralist, and this is only one of the answers that Alvina might have made. Apart from the great charm and understanding of his ending chapters, I find *The Lost Girl* mainly affecting not because Alvina is mesmerized, which is unpleasant, but because her escape from virginity is viewed unsentimentally. Others in the story, Miss Frost and Miss Pinnegar, aimed at no such escape, and had full careers. Mrs. Tuke is married and yet trammelled. But Lawrence does vigorously dramatize the situation of the surplus woman to whom sex is urgent.

In bringing all his men from distances Lawrence has a kind of romanticism. There is something in him as well as in his heroine that asks for the indirect and the exotic. But this capriciousness is only one element in the author of *The Lost Girl*. It does not prevent his poignant grasp of the contrast between primitive and complex natures in this searching work of art.

45. Abel Chevalley on Lawrence, from *Le Roman Anglais de Notre Temps*

Oxford University Press, 1921, 229–32

Abel Chevalley (1868–1934). Critic and lexicographer.

(This translation, by Ben Ray Redman, is from the version published as *The Modern English Novel*. Alfred A. Knopf, New York, 1925, 236–8.)

The first literary efforts of D. H. Lawrence were rewarded by the dangerous fame of scandal. A novelist who survives this kind of success doubly merits his renown. But it is not certain that D. H. Lawrence has escaped the consequences of his victory. He is one of those young authors who, during a brief period, were successively awaited and saluted as so many Messiahs. I must confess that in none of them have I been able to discover anything at all Messianic.

D. H. Lawrence is incontestably a poet. He has the temperament of an unequal and volcanic writer. But he emits a deal of ashes with his lava, and all the flashes of his eruptions do not make a steady light.

The son of a northern miner, Lawrence became monitor in a primary school, entered a teachers' normal school, came out of it as a London schoolmaster, and dedicated himself to literature after the success of his first two books: *The White Peacock* (1911) and *The Trespasser* (1912). He was then twenty-five years old.

Nothing could be more naïve, nor more apparently unlikely, than the characters of the young persons who people *The White Peacock*. These English north-countrymen who have read Tchekoff and Maupassant, these little rustics fed on a decadent music, may be discoverable. There is no lack of Swedish and Norwegian farms on which one can find their brothers and their cousins. But, even if they are real, they do not convince us of their reality. The impression created by them is that of speaking marionettes, whom the author, with juvenile pedantry, uses as mouthpieces for what he has retained from his hasty reading.

A feeling for nature that is almost painful in its fierceness, a sensual emotion that is omnipresent and ever burning—this is what strikes one especially in the books of D. H. Lawrence. When he began to write, the experiments and theories of Freud were making a great stir, and the sexual origin of subconscious images, which govern the conscious mind to so great an extent, still had all the freshness of a discovery. The literary verjuice of adolescents was passing readily for genius, provided that their psycho-physiological confidences were coloured by a native poetry and a natural power of expression. All the young English novelists have profited, or suffered, from this orientation, and D. H. Lawrence more than any of them.

His second book, *The Trespasser*, is the story of a tragic episode. Sigmund and Helen spend a week of passion and possession in a solitary house by the edge of the sea. The account of this single week, marked by no other events than the various stages of satiety, fills two-thirds of the volume. It is very long, the story of such a love; it reminds one of the amours of serpents. The final third contains the return of Sigmund to his family; the increasing hostility of children already grown; the feeling of shame, desolation and misery in this household in which the wife, the mother, without revolting, is submerged by her sorrow; the inexorable and furtive approach of the catastrophe; the suicide of Sigmund—all this is of the first order. Helena takes another lover in the same manner, with the same gesture, that she took Sigmund. The woman forgets. The man dies.

Is it because physical love has been, until recently, a forbidden subject in English literature? Do those who deal with it lack simplicity because it requires courage? In any case, these writers always seem like fair-ground Herculeses devoting themselves to feats of strength. With extended arms, they seem to be carrying great cardboard weights. It is an exercise which appears complicated and painful. But the remainder of the story in *The Trespasser* is told with remarkable power and sobriety.

It is more difficult for the French reader to appreciate *Sons and Lovers*, which is considered D. H. Lawrence's best novel, if he is unacquainted with the manners and dialect of the miners in the north of England; and it is impossible, now, for him to read *The Rainbow*, as this book has been suppressed by the censor. It would be regrettable if D. H. Lawrence's literary career should end as it began, in alarms and tumult. His talent deserves a better fate. Noise does not always do good; and the good rarely makes a noise.

WOMEN IN LOVE

November 1920

46. John Macy in *New York* *Evening Post Literary Review*

19 March 1921, 3–4

John Macy (1877–1932). Critic and journalist.

This is a composite review of *Women in Love* and *The Lost Girl*.

In putting out *Women in Love* as 'privately printed', and on larger paper than is customary for a new novel, the publisher may have three purposes: to create curiosity and tickle the taste for something special and limited; to show visible reason, in point of bulk, for charging an excessive price, of which I hope Mr. Lawrence gets a fair share; and to protect the publisher in case anti-vice zealots go sniffing under skirts that enfold a beauty beyond their comprehension. Whatever the publisher's purposes, the reviewer is glad to conspire with him to promote the practical fortunes of Mr. Lawrence. His artistic fortune was made when he was born, and the gods and the muses engaged in an earlier conspiracy than ours.

Yet there is something disquieting in the thought that one of the finest artists using the English language should not have his books published as a matter of course, just as Mr. Galsworthy, or Mr. Bennett, or Mr. Wells has his books published, as fast as he writes them, by Scribner, or Doran, or Seltzer, or Huebsch, or whoever it may be. Why should the work of a man of genius have to be subjected to artificial suffocation or to equally artificial stimulation?

Women in Love is a sequel to *The Rainbow*, in that it carries on the story of Ursula of the family of Brangwen. *The Rainbow* is the stronger book because it has more of the tragic power, the deep social implications of Mr. Lawrence's masterpiece, *Sons and Lovers*. In *Women in Love* we have four young people, two men and two women, whose chief interest, for them and for us, is in amatory relations. This is indicated by the title of the story, one of those obvious titles which only a man of imagination could hit upon, so simple that you wonder why no novelist ever thought of it before. Now the erotic relations of people, though a tremendous part of life, as all the great tragic romances prove, are still only part of life. Nobody knows this better than Mr. Lawrence. The first story of the Brangwen family is richer than the second, not because of the proverbial falling off of sequels, not because Mr. Lawrence's power has declined—far from it!—but because the first novel embraces a larger number of the manifold interests that compose the fever called living. In it there are not only young lovers, but old people, old failures, the land, the town, the succession of the generations, rooted yet restless. Ursula emerges from immemorial centuries of English life, touched with foreign blood out of Poland (when an English novelist wishes to introduce variety and strangeness into the dull solidity of an English town he always imports a Pole, or a Frenchman, somebody not quite English).

Ursula's background is richer than all her emotional experience. Her father, her grandfather, the family, all the tragi-comedy of little affairs and ambitions, the grim, grey colliery district, the entire social situation, are the foundation and walls of the story, and she is the slender spire that surmounts it all—and is struck by lightning. In *The Rainbow* she goes to ashes, and in *Women in Love* she revives, burns again, and finds in her new love a new element of dissatisfaction.

Mr. Lawrence is a tragic poet. He is as dangerous to public morals as Hardy or Meredith. Readers who cannot understand the tragedy of *Richard Feverel* or of *Jude the Obscure*, will not understand Mr. Lawrence or be interested to read a third of the way through one of his books. The stupidity of the multitude is sure protection against his insidious loveliness and essential sadness. He and his admirers will, I hope, regard it as honourable to him that he reminds this reviewer oftener of Meredith and Hardy than of any of his contemporaries. I am not so fatuous as to suggest that his independent and original work is in any unfavourable sense derivative. It must be true that every young novelist learns his lessons from the other novelists; but I cannot see that Mr. Lawrence is clearly the disciple of any one master. I do feel simply that he is of the elder stature of Meredith and Hardy, and I will suggest, in praise of him, some resemblances that have struck me, without trying to analyse or quote chapter and verse in tedious parallels.

Mr. Lawrence is a lyric as well as a tragic poet. In this he is like Meredith and Hardy, and I can think of no other young novelist who is quite worthy of the company. Young people in love, or some other difficulty, become entangled with stars and mountains and seas; they are baffled and lost, seldom consoled, in cosmic immensities. Poets, who happen also to be novelists, are enamoured of those immensities. Towards the end of *Sons and Lovers*: 'Night in which everything was lost went reaching out beyond stars and sun.' The concluding scenes of *Women in Love* are the Alps, 'a silence of dim, unrealized snow, of the invisible intervening between her and the visible, between her and the flashing stars'. I am reminded, by the beauty of the phrasing and by the sense of the pathetic little human being adrift in space, of the flight of the two young people through the Alps, in *The Amazing Marriage*, and of Farmer Gabriel Oak watching the westward flow of the stars.

Sometimes, like Meredith, rather than like Hardy, whose style is colder and more austere, Mr. Lawrence is almost too lyric and his phrases threaten to overflow the rigid dikes of prose. I could pick out a dozen rhapsodical passages which with little change might well appear in his books of verse.

But young people in love cannot spend all their days and nights in ecstatic flights to the clouds. And their flights are followed by pathetic Icarian disasters. From luminous moments they plunge into what Mr. Lawrence calls 'the bitterness of ecstasy', and their pain outweighs their joy many times over, as in Hardy, and as in the more genial Meredith, whose rapturous digression played on a penny whistle is a cruelly beautiful preparation for the agonies that ensue. It may be that the emotional transports of Mr. Lawrence's young people are more frequent and violent than the ordinary human soul can enjoy and endure. The nervous tension is high and would break into hysteria if Mr. Lawrence were not a philosopher as well as a poet, if he did not know so accurately what goes on inside the human head, if he had not an artist's ability to keep his balance at the very moment when a less certain workman would lose it.

There is firm ground under his feet and under the feet of his lovers; it is the everyday life which consists of keeping shop and keeping school and other commonplace activities in street, kitchen, and coal mine. These diurnal details he studies with a fidelity not surpassed by Mr. Bennett or any other of his contemporaries. The talk of his people is always alive, both the dialect of the villagers and the discussions of the more intellectual. Sometimes he puts into the speech of his characters a little more of his own poetic fancy than they might reasonably be supposed to be capable of. But if this is a fault, from a realistic point of view, it is a merit from the point of view of readability, and it makes for vivacity. At times—and is not this like Meredith?—he seems to be less interested in the sheer dramatic value of a situation he has created than in the opportunity it offers of writing beautiful things around it. Not that his situations fail to carry themselves or have not their proper place and proportion. Mr. Lawrence knows how to handle his narrative and he has an abundant invention and dramatic ingenuity. But he is above those elemental things that any competent novelist knows. He has the something else that makes the story teller the first rate literary artist—style may be the word for it, but poetic imagination seems to be the better and more inclusive term. Open *The Lost Girl* at page 57 and read two pages. Without knowing what has preceded or whither the story is bound, anybody who knows what literature is will feel at once that that is it. And the story is worth following. It seems to me more likely to achieve some degree of popularity than Mr. Lawrence's more tragic books. It is pitched in a lighter mood, more in the temper of a story by Leonard Merrick. But in manner it is not like the work of Mr. Merrick or of any other living novelist. No writer of this generation is more singular, more unmistakably individual, than Mr. Lawrence, and none is endowed with his unfairly great variety of gifts.

47. Evelyn Scott in *Dial*

April 1921, lxx, 458–61

Evelyn Scot (b. 1893). Novelist and poet.

This is a composite review of *Women in Love* and *The Lost Girl*.

Michelangelo, El Greco, Cézanne, D. H. Lawrence; so I might begin a classification which would include those who could be called the substitutionists among artists—men who have an individual affirmative to substitute for the interrogation of existence. This would not be a classification according to perfection. D. H. Lawrence has done things which are incredibly bad. However, I do not doubt that the others, when among their contemporaries, have been equally guilty. Waldo Frank, in present-day America, though he is as yet incompletely articulate, belongs to the same artistic type.

The apex of all recorded human experience—the ecstasy of love, art, religious passion—is in its immediate essence the same, a release from the limitation of individuality in a sense of identity with other life. What passes for new in art is merely a readjustment, through technical means, of the pressure which asserts this identity. In the beginning art was confessedly a religious expression. But religion in a group inevitably tends to establish a social rather than an individual interpretation of deity, and so reduce aesthetics to the functional conception called morality. Art distinguished itself from religion that each man might make his own god, individual and unmoral. Hence the purest art is an expression of the most individual experience.

But there is something negative, deathly in this pure art. Being the purest intensive expression of what is, it renounces the extensive expression of a desire to be otherwise. It requires a receptive, negative will. In a facile nature it is a voluptuous verification of sense. In a man like Dostoevsky the will to receive and register human agonies becomes a kind of spiritual masochism. There is in all artists of a certain emotional vigour, the intoxication of self-annihilation balanced against the intoxication of self-assertion: the deathly, intensive expression of pure art, always being tempted to become extensive and romantic.

If an individual is small, his romanticism is merely a short cut to self-assertion. Never having acutely experienced particular values, he grasps the generality of the mob and tries to come into deductive being through it. However, there are persons in whom the particular experience of life is so intense that it grows, through the wholeness of emotion, into the justifiable conviction of an absolute. D. H. Lawrence is one of these. In him the extensive will to live asserts itself from the depths of his sensuous and emotional resolutions.

'*Parturiunt montes, nascetur ridiculus mus.*' So the romantic individual brings forth his realized self. But if the great romantic's creed, finally articulate, is disappointing, the spectacle of the travail in which he gives birth to it is, in cases like that of Lawrence, a magnificently revealing thing.

Women in Love is not pure as an art form, but it is because art is too limited for Lawrence's conviction of reality. Lawrence's poetry seemed out of place in the *Imagist Anthology*. A number of his contemporaries express finely the delicate nostalgic emotions of neo-classicism, the emotions of nuns. The Parnassian muse, though she speaks of orgies, is a virgin. Lawrence is aesthetically unchaste. His genius has consorted with life and has acquired mystical imperfections, nail-prints in the palms.

Women in Love purports to be a novel. In unfolding the love life of Ursula Brangwen and of her sister, Gudrun, Mr. Lawrence has made concessions to the novel form. There are characters in the book—Mrs. Crich, the elder, and Hermione Roddice, particularly—as subtly authentic as any in fiction. There are moments, such as those when Mrs. Crich breaks through her sinister quiescence to speak to her dead husband and when Gerald Crich takes Gudrun, that are intense dramatic revelations. Yet *Women in Love* lacks that quality of the arrested ephemeral which is in the pure art form. Lawrence's moods are taken deep down in an irrevocable substance. There is in him no capacity for the play of relations, for adding notes to an established chord. His resolutions are all absolute. The souls of his characters are unrolled like scrolls.

And so this book falls, as if outside itself, into the category of confessions. Having written it, Lawrence might turn philosopher or priest. It is the last word of his living truth. Anything further in this nature, would necessarily be mere exposition. The book might as well be the last word of an age in revolt against the intellectualism to which it has been betrayed; an after-war world, hectically clutching at immediacy; a world in which Parnassianism has brought forth the dadaists.

To such an age, sex, the most immediate experience of the individual, presents the greatest revelation. The intellectual evaluator is to the first hand revealer of actuality as the anatomist to the observer of physiological processes. Sense and emotion are known in a state of becoming. Intellectual understanding is extraneous to the thing understood, a process, of analysis and classification, of the annihilation of intimate knowledge. Art has carried Bergson to the conclusion from which he was withheld by the timidities of logic. And now Woman, because of her immediate part in the intimate mystery of creation, is revived for worship.

It is an old rôle for her, that of the sacred prostitute. But she accepts it now with the ache of a new awareness. Freedom is hers, if she wills it, but at the price of her own dark importance.

Lawrence rebels half-heartedly against the conclusion of his intuitions. The polarized relations of Ursula Brangwen and Rupert Birkin—less convincing than anything in the book—are obviously tendered as a solution of the erotic problem. Something like this was possibly in Lawrence's mind when he gave to a volume of his poems the title, *Look! We Have Come Through!* But the love of Ursula and Rupert is presented to us with a conjectural uncertainty that makes it pale against the vivid, nameless actuality of the instinctive relationship of Gudrun and Gerald Crich.

Yet even Gudrun rebels at last against 'the stupidity of the phallus', and Hermione Roddice remains for ever withheld in her bitter intellectuality because she dare not understand her own nature too well.

If Mr. Lawrence were a Russian he would take the answer to life as his art gives it, in terms of other-worldliness. The experience of God is an initiation into the soul of chaos. But belonging to the English race of moralists, Mr. Lawrence persists in a search for temporal solutions. In *The Lost Girl*, he doubles on himself, as it were, and begins his quest anew; this time submitting to an objective sequence of which *Women in Love* took little account.

The first half of this story of Alvina Houghton is the cerebral registration of a series of rather boring incidents. Mr. Lawrence, even less French than Russian, has no pure passion of creation. The book means next to nothing until that point where the middle-class English girl eludes her spinsterish fate by eloping with the Italian player. From here on there is a kind of radiance of conviction in the pages. After having threaded a futilely round-about way, we are returned to Mr. Lawrence's old revealed, almost religious certainty. Lawrence, the Englishman, accomplishes a sort of mystical identity with the sense-enwrapped Italian, Francesco Marasco.

Alvina goes to Italy with her husband—to an old, oblivious, rather terrible Italy. The final chapters of this book parallel those of *Women in Love*. In the latter volume, Gudrun, in the rigid ecstasy of the Alps, becomes an unwilling initiate in Nature's impersonal being. Alvina Houghton, lost from her kind in her warmer-coloured wilderness, with aching acquiescence, experiences the same intoxication.

Religions are immediate philosophies. Mr. Lawrence, by accident a novelist, actually is the priest of an age almost intolerably self-aware. Evocative, rather than delineative, he consciously desires what all ritual infers, the release of individuality in the confusion of sense.

48. Unsigned review in
Saturday Westminster Gazette

2 July 1921, lviii, 14–15

Mr. D. H. Lawrence's new and very long novel *Women in Love* is not unlike a serious elaboration of the well-known advertisement, 'Mr. and Mrs. Smith, having cast off clothing of all descriptions, invite inspection. Distance no object.' Not only do all the heroes and all the heroines of this crowded tale cast off clothing whenever there is any excuse (such as seeing a good pond, pool, or stream on a hot day, or in the course of their matutinal and vesperal ablutions); but they do it unexpectedly—at garden parties (Gudrun and Ursula)—after dinner, over their cigarettes (Birkin and Crich), while talking round the fire on a winter morning (ever so many people), for no revealed purpose so far as their consequent actions are recorded, but possibly to give greater ease and intimacy to their interminable conversations, and to provide Mr. Lawrence with repeated opportunities for vivid pictorial records of chiaroscuro, plein-air, genre, and figure-painting in words. This he does to admiration as always, though the fastidious may complain that he chooses the vocabulary of the butcher's shop in preference to that of the anatomy class. It is possible to justify this choice by the effect it produces, but Mr. Lawrence has already in his own characteristic repetitive style a medium for producing certain effects. The particular atmosphere of physiological reaction to psychological experience which Mr. Lawrence aims at creating is rather destroyed than increased by a violent vocabulary in reiteration. The great scene, occurring rather too early in the book to be a complete dramatic or constructive success, shows Hermione Roddice, a wealthy patroness of Art and Artists, answering letters in her library one afternoon. She lifts her eyes and sees Birkin, a school inspector, one of her distinguished house party, sitting not far away, 'minutely attentive to his author'. Birkin is reading Thucydides. Hermione is highly strung, and the half-interruption of her leisure caused by this quietly reading guest annoys her. But annoyance to a character in this book is no mild emotion, and the repetitions hail down on the page in which it is recorded. Hermione feels there is nothing for it but to kill Birkin:

[Quotes from Chap. 8, 'The terrible tension grew stronger and stronger . . . remained motionless and unconscious.' (Penguin ed., 116-17.)]

You see 'unconscious' does for the delirium of the murderess and for the unawareness of her victim, not because Mr. Lawrence couldn't have put it differently, but because he has chosen to convey the blindness of murderous irritation in terms which shall embrace as well the security of innocence. The trick is effective here; but this attempted murder in an early chapter makes of the drowning of a bridesmaid at a water picnic, the death of an industrial magnate, and the intense unmatrimonial experiences of the two sisters with whom the story, if story it can be called, is principally occupied, events in the nature of anti-climaxes, so that Mr. Lawrence is obliged to enforce them by a wilder and ever wilder flinging about of heavy words, and closer and thickening closeness of reiterated phrase.

Then, to return to the illustration with which this notice began, even as Mr. and Mrs. Smith baited their offer with the enigmatical phrase, 'Distance no object', so does Mr. Lawrence adorn his tale with unpremeditated incident. In the midst of a perfectly peaceful wedding party, for instance, while Gerald is talking to Birkin as wedding-guest to wedding-guest, Mr. Lawrence suddenly observes, 'Gerald as a boy had accidentally killed his brother. What then!' It is shocking: but then, some shocks make you giggle.

Not that Mr. Lawrence makes you giggle much. He falls too often into long and shallow pseudo-philosophical discussion, sometimes in the form of terribly boring dinner-table talk and sometimes in direct reflection, like this:

[Quotes from Chap. 31, '"God cannot do without man." . . . It was very consoling to Birkin to think this.' (Penguin ed., 538.)]

All the characters talk and think like this except when they are feeling, and they feel a great deal. There is in particular Hermione Roddice, who didn't quite kill Birkin. She 'writhed in her soul knowing what she couldn't know' on hardly any provocation at all, and when she had a successful house-party 'she seemed in a swoon of gratification convulsed with pleasure, and yet sick like a *revenant*' because her guests wore bright-coloured dinner gowns. Clothes play parts of their own in the tale. 'Enter a purple gown, green stockings, and amber necklace' would do for a stage direction if *Women in Love* could ever be dramatized. The two heroines, Ursula and Gudrun, are almost as indistinguishable in character and conversation as they are in their amours and their clothing. They have innumerable pairs of stockings, which they change several times in a chapter. But no diversification of pink hat, blue stocking, orange jumper really distinguishes one from the other, and when towards the end of the feverish tale they both go abroad even the young men who accompany them—Birkin and Crich—lose their identities and become one and the same young man. It is, perhaps, in a last effort to reintegrate their personalities that Mr. Lawrence makes one of them die of a conversation in the high Alps: ('I couldn't love *you*,' she said, with stark cold truth. A blinding flash went over his brain, his body jolted, his heart had burst into flame). So he throws himself over the precipice. It certainly is a new and original end, and, in a novel when all the characters suffer the pangs of dissolution several times a week, possibly the only fitting one. Still . . .

49. J. M. Murry in *Nation and Athenaeum*

13 August 1921, xxix, 713–14

Mr. Lawrence is set apart from the novelists who are his contemporaries by the vehemence of his passion. In the time before the war we should have distinguished him by other qualities—a sensitive and impassioned apprehension of natural beauty, for example, or an understanding of the strange blood bonds that unite human beings, or an exquisite discrimination in the use of language, based on a power of natural vision. All these things Mr. Lawrence once had, in the time when he thrilled us with the expectation of genius: now they are dissolved in the acid of a burning and vehement passion. These qualities are in-dividual no longer; they no longer delight us; they have been pressed into the service of another power, they walk in bondage and in livery.

It is useless for us to lament their servitude; with Mr. Lawrence—and the feeling is our involuntary acknowledgment of his power and uniqueness—we feel we must

> let determined things to destiny
> Hold unbewailed their way.

Mr. Lawrence is what he is: a natural force over which we have no power of command or persuasion. He has no power of command or persuasion over himself. It was not his deliberate choice that he sacri-ficed his gifts, his vision, his delicacy, and his eloquence. If ever a writer was driven, it is he.

Not that we absolve him from responsibility for his own disaster. It is part of our creed that he must be responsible; but it is part of his creed that he is not. We stand by the consciousness and the civilization of which the literature we know is the finest flower; Mr. Lawrence is in rebellion against both. If we try him before our court, he contemp-tuously rejects the jurisdiction. The things we prize are the things he would destroy; what is triumph to him is catastrophe to us. He is the outlaw of modern English literature; and he is the most interesting figure in it. But he must be shown no mercy.

Women in Love is five hundred pages of passionate vehemence, wave after wave of turgid, exasperated writing impelled towards some distant and invisible end; the persistent underground beating of some dark and inaccessible sea in an underworld whose inhabitants are known by this alone, that they writhe continually, like the damned, in a frenzy of sexual awareness of one another. Their creator believes that he can distinguish the writhing of one from the writhing of another; he spends pages and pages in describing the contortions of the first, the second, the third, and the fourth. To him they are utterly and profoundly different; to us they are all the same. And yet Mr. Lawrence has invented a language, as we are forced to believe he has discovered a perception for them. The eyes of these creatures are 'absolved'; their bodies (or their souls: there is no difference in this world) are 'suspended'; they are 'polarized'; they 'lapse out'; they have, all of them, 'inchoate' eyes. In this language their unending contortions are described; they struggle and writhe in these terms; they emerge from dark hatred to darker beatitudes; they grope in their own slime to some final consummation, in which they are utterly 'negated' or utterly 'fulfilled'. We remain utterly indifferent to their destinies, we are weary to death of them.

At the end we know one thing and one thing alone: that Mr. Lawrence believes, with all his heart and soul, that he is revealing to us the profound and naked reality of life, that it is a matter of life and death to him that he should persuade us that it is a matter of life and death to ourselves to know that these things are so. These writhings are the only real, and these convulsive raptures, these oozy beatitudes the only end in human life. He would, if he could, put us all on the rack to make us confess his protozoic god; he is deliberately, incessantly, and passionately obscene in the exact sense of the word. He will uncover our nakedness. It is of no avail for us to protest that the things he finds are not there; a fanatical shriek arises from his pages that they are there, but we deny them.

If they are there, then it is all-important that we should not deny them. Whether we ought to expose them is another matter. The fact that European civilization has up to the advent of Mr. Lawrence ignored them can prove nothing, though it may indicate many things. It may indicate that they do not exist at all; or it may indicate that they do exist, but that it is bound up with the very nature of civilization that they should not be exposed. Mr. Lawrence vehemently believes the latter. It is the real basis of his fury against the consciousness of European civilization which he lately expounded in these pages in a paper on Whitman. He claims that his characters attain whatever they do attain by their power of going back and re-living the vital process of pre-European civilization. His hero, Rupert Birkin, after reaching the beginning of 'consummation' with his heroine, Ursula Brangwen, is thus presented:

[Quotes from Chap. 23, 'He sat still like an Egyptian Pharaoh . . . a force in darkness, like electricity.' (Penguin ed., 358.)]

Through such strange avatars his characters pass, 'awakened and potent in his deepest physical mind'. European civilization has ignored them. Was it from interested motives, or do they indeed exist?

Is Mr. Lawrence a fanatic or a prophet? That he is an artist no longer is certain, as certain as it is that he has no desire to be one; for whatever may be this 'deep physical mind' that expresses its satisfaction in 'a subtle mindless smile', whether it have a real existence or not, it is perfectly clear that it does not admit of individuality as we understand it. No doubt Mr. Lawrence intends to bring us to a new conception of individuality also; but in the interim we must use the conceptions and the senses that we have. Having these only, having, like Sam Weller in the divorce court, 'only a hordinary pair of eyes', we can discern no individuality whatever in the denizens of Mr. Lawrence's world. We should have thought that we should be able to distinguish between male and female, at least. But no! Remove the names, remove the sedulous catalogues of unnecessary clothing—a new element and a significant one, this, in our author's work—and man and woman are indistinguishable as octopods in an aquarium tank.

The essential crisis of the book occurs in a chapter called, mystically enough, 'Excurse'. In that chapter Rupert and Ursula, who are said to reach salvation at the end of the history, have a critical and indescribable experience. It is not a matter of sexual experience, though that is, of course, incidentally thrown in; but there is a very great deal to do with 'loins'. They are loins of a curious kind, and they belong to Rupert. Mr. Lawrence calls them 'his suave loins of darkness'. These Ursula 'comes to know'. It is, fortunately or unfortunately, impossible to quote these crucial pages. We cannot attempt to paraphrase them; for to us they are completely and utterly unintelligible if we assume (as we must assume if we have regard to the vehemence of Mr. Lawrence's passion) that they are not the crudest sexuality. Rupert and Ursula achieve their esoteric beatitude in a tearoom; they discover by means of 'the suave loins of darkness' the mysteries of 'the deepest physical mind'. They die, and live again. After this experience (which we must call *x*):

[Quotes from Chap. 23, 'They were glad . . . and medlars and apple-tart and tea.' (Penguin ed., 354.)]

We could not resist quoting the final paragraph, if only as evidence that 'the deepest physical mind' has no sense of humour. Why, in the name of darkness, 'a venison pasty, *of all things*?' Is a venison pasty more incongruous with this beatitude than a large ham? Does the 'deepest physical mind' take pleasure in a tart when it is filled with apples and none when it is filled with meat?

We have given, in spite of our repulsion and our weariness, our undivided attention to Mr. Lawrence's book for the space of three days; we have striven with all our power to understand what he means by the experience *x*; we have compared it with the experience *y*, which takes place between the other pair of lovers, Gudrun and Gerald; we can see no difference between them, and we are precluded from inviting our readers to pronounce. We are sure that not one person in a thousand would decide that they were anything but the crudest kind of sexuality, wrapped up in what Mr. S. K. Ratcliffe has aptly called the language of Higher Thought. We feel that the solitary person may be right; but even he, we are convinced, would be quite unable to distinguish between experience *x* and experience *y*. Yet *x* leads one pair to undreamed-of happiness, and *y* conducts the other to attempted murder and suicide.

This *x* and *y* are separate, if they are separate, on a plane of consciousness other than ours. To our consciousness they are indistinguishable; either they belong to the nothingness of unconscious sexuality, or they are utterly meaningless. For Mr. Lawrence they are the supreme realities, positive and negative, of a plane of consciousness the white race has yet to reach. Rupert Birkin has a negroid, as well as an Egyptian avatar; he sees one of those masterpieces of negro sculpture to which we have lately become accustomed. It is not the plastic idea which he admires:

[Quotes from Chap. 19, 'There is a long way we can travel . . . It would be done differently by the white races.' (Penguin ed., 286.)]

We believe Mr. Lawrence's book is an attempt to take us through the process. Unless we pass through this we shall never see the light. If the experiences which he presents to us as a part of this process mean nothing, the book means nothing; if they mean something, the book means something; and the value of the book is precisely the value of those experiences. Whatever they are, they are of ultimate and fundamental importance to Mr. Lawrence. He has sacrificed everything to achieve them; he has murdered his gifts for an acceptable offering to them. Those gifts were great; they were valuable to the civilization which he believes he has transcended. It may be that we are benighted in the old world, and that he belongs to the new; it may be that he is, like his Rupert, a 'son of God'; we certainly are the sons of men, and we must be loyal to the light we have. By that light Mr. Lawrence's consummation is a degradation, his passing beyond a passing beneath, his triumph a catastrophe. It may be superhuman, we do not know; by the knowledge that we have we can only pronounce it sub-human and bestial, a thing that our forefathers had rejected when they began to rise from the slime.

SEA AND SARDINIA

December 1921

50. Francis Hackett in *New Republic*

11 January 1922, 184–5

Beautiful is the right word for *Sea and Sardinia*. It is a book shot through with beauty. Yet it is an inept and silly exhibition, in many ways, which makes it very hard to criticize.

'I like Italian newspapers', says Mr. Lawrence, 'because they say what they mean, and not merely what is most convenient to say. We call it naïveté—I call it manliness. Italian newspapers read as if they were written by men, and not by calculating eunuchs.'

There you have Mr. Lawrence's present note. Manliness, by God, manliness. Kick your wife in the stomach. No damn nonsense about tenderness and sympathy, sweetness and light. A certain amount about sunset and evening star, and a certain amount about cow droppings and water-closet. A good deal about the maleness of the male, written with a touch of femaleness. And, yes, certainly, Sardinia. That's the subject of the book.

This, if you like, is naturalness, a willed naturalness, and it is amazingly interesting. Lawrence is not naturally natural. He is, one surmises, the kind of person who ties himself into black knots trying to decide the right and the wrong way of everything. He apparently suffers a great deal from the supposed unfriendliness and resistance of the world. He has still, in a remarkable state of preservation, the ordinary English middle-class horror of having his privacy invaded by a 'bounder'. 'His mate was a bit of a bounder. . . . He had dark eyes that seemed to ask too much. . . . We rather fought shy of him.' So he speaks about a youth in a motor bus who shouted 'awkward questions' in the centre of Sardinia. But, with this tight English conventionality and itching self-consciousness you have, inside the sufferer, one of the most hungry and inflammable and rebellious of

173

imaginations. No humour about this fact whatever, but twenty times a proof that the life of the imagination is surging inside and running out like a flame that wants to embrace and lick up the world. Hence, an exciting but not a mature personality.

Because he is everlastingly faithful to this personality of his, his Sardinia notebook gives one an excellent idea of Lawrence. We have him for a week, close-up, with a pointedly seen and swiftly changing background of Sardinia. Also we have a silhouette of his accompanying wife, a mere outlander who prices vegetables and shops for saddle-bags and wants to go to the marionette show and is rather annoyingly interested in the native. She is a German. After the English fashion, she is never really introduced to us, but Mr. Lawrence nods at her with a vague head. He calls her the q-b, queen bee. Had he come from Peoria he'd indicate her as the squaw. But in essence if not in the idiom of his facetiousness D. H. Lawrence does come from Peoria. He is the Middle Westerner athirst for beauty, aflame with imagination, and aching with ideas as with apples devoured green.

To specify those green ideas is hardly necessary, but you may observe Mr. Lawrence in the rôle of the satiated aesthete:

Life is life and things are things. I am sick of gaping *things*, even Peruginos. I have had my thrills from Carpaccio and Botticelli. But now I've had enough. But I can always look at an old, grey-bearded peasant in his earthy white drawers and his black waist-frill, wearing no coat or over-garment, but just crooking along beside his little ox-wagon. I am sick of 'things', even Perugino.

Back to the ox-wagon! Or the sound, basic sex war. Or the dear love of freedom.

[Quotes *Sea and Sardinia*, Chap. II, 'How glad to be on a ship! . . . to the opaque earth.' Heinemann ed., p. 45.]

It reads like one of the happiest flights of Gilbert and Sullivan, or like the Gimbel man trying to imitate the noble seraphic style of the Wanamaker man. But it is D. H. Lawrence when soulful:

[Picks up same quotation and carries it on from 'opaque earth' to 'the glad lonely wringing of the heart.']

It is a mood, but the 'ahs!' and the 'ohs!' and the repetitions and the sighs and the sobs and the susurrus have the ineffable ululation of the sophomore. It is true mid-Victorian gush, giving us the 'small, quiet, lonely ship' without a destination, without a cockroach. 'Oh, God,' exclaims Mr. Lawrence at Nuoro, 'what a blessed relief, to be with people who don't bother to show off.' But these purple patches, these flights to freedom and glad lonely wringings of the heart, are just as much showing-off as Victorian wax-flowers and castles in cork. They exaggerate human susceptibility. They are embarrassingly artistic.

Mr. Lawrence is not dishonest. He suffers honestly from exaggerated susceptibility. Being the kind of susceptible man to whom personal contacts present an enormous problem, and consequently the kind of man who is often thrown out of delicate adjustment into exasperation and annoyance and resentment, it is natural for him to seek recompense in the sights and scenes around him, and in erotic daydreams possibly, and in a voluptuous imagining as to history and as to the meaning of symbols and the shape and stamp and ring of lovely words themselves. So, when he leaves out or lifts us over his grinding account of his own temperament and exhibits the attunements of that temperament in wintry but coloured Sardinia, we have a superb chance to enjoy Sardinia. For D. H. Lawrence is so susceptible, so saturable, that what one receives (outside his *agacement* and his human judgments) is as keen a sense of actual experience as any traveller ever gave. And this without any of the ordinary intellectual, historical, social aids and with less than the ordinary ascertainment of the views and feelings of the primitive people who live in Sardinia.

Because what D. H. Lawrence communicates is his own feeling. He gives us the stone-damp houses, the innkeeper with a wine-dripped shirt-front, the nerve-drained bus driver who is yet such a smooth master of his machine, the priest with a long nose who spits, the young wife restless from her bridal bed, the little cabin in the ship with a panelled slide-door and no room to move, the icy dawn that is like the kiss of a corpse, the kid roasted in front of a roaring oak-root fire, the impudent peddlar packed with *aqua vitae*, the Italians sugary with sympathy and linked together in fondness, with feelings as nude as sausages. Whatever Lawrence experiences he experiences with full savour, and he has retrieved an astounding number of his experiences in this book of Sardinia.

Yet it is the book of an aesthetic *parvenu*, just as Jan Juta's striking poster-like illustrations are *parvenu* illustrations. What I feel is that Mr. Lawrence owes me a rather better understanding of himself. I am not afraid of the word posterior or rump, and I am willing he should explode into poesy or antique postures or tell me about the 'timeless glamour of those Middle Ages when men were lordly and violent and shadowed with death', and swallowed nail-parings and believed in witches and never washed their feet. But it makes me tired to read an accepted artist who doesn't accept himself, who is still occupied with the bourgeois bogey and who cannot escape into life. The impersonal *cicerone*, after all, has much to be said for him, especially in a book with a subject like this. For with the impersonal *cicerone* such as Gissing one is allowed to see the light stream through the many-coloured dome. With Lawrence the light, much of the time, streams *on* the dome. It is, I believe, a question of more and less. But with an introvert so pronounced as Lawrence it must take years before he learns to command his personality rather than dote on it.

AARON'S ROD

April 1922

51. J. M. Murry in *Nation and Athenaeum*

12 August 1922, xxxi, 655–6

A year ago, reviewing Mr. Lawrence's last novel, which seemed to us full of a noxious exasperation, we said that he was an elemental force, perhaps the only one in modern English literature. With him criticism was unavailing and irrelevant; we must 'let determined things to destiny hold unbewailed their way' [see No. 49].

Well, they have held their way for another year, with a result that we could not have prophesied. Mr. Lawrence's sun shines forth after the darkness of eclipse. The exasperation, the storm and stress are gone. He has dragged us with him through the valley of the shadow; now we sail with him in the sunlight. Mr. Lawrence's new book ripples with the consciousness of victory; he is gay, he is careless, he is persuasive. To read *Aaron's Rod* is to drink of a fountain of life.

Mr. Lawrence is like the little girl. When he is good, he is very, very good; and when he is bad, he is horrid. Now we feel that he will never be horrid again, but go on from strength to strength, until the predestined day when he puts before the world a masterpiece. For Mr. Lawrence is now, indisputably, a great creative force in English literature. We have always believed he was that potentially; even when we have crusaded against him, we have merely been paying tribute to his power. No other living writer could drive us to a frenzy of hostility as he has done; no other fill us with such delight.

Aaron's Rod is the most important thing that has happened to English literature since the war. To my mind it is much more important than *Ulysses*. Not that it is more important in and for itself than Mr. Joyce's book. No doubt it is a smaller thing. But *Ulysses* is sterile; *Aaron's Rod* is full of the sap of life. The whole of Mr. Joyce is in *Ulysses*; *Aaron's Rod* is but a fruit on the tree of Mr. Lawrence's creativeness. It marks a phase, the safe passing of the most critical phase in Mr. Lawrence's development. He has survived his own exasperation against the war. We did not doubt that if he did survive it, he would survive it splendidly; but after *Women in Love* we doubted deeply whether he would survive at all. *Women in Love* seemed to show him far sunk in the maelstrom of his sexual obsession.

Aaron's Rod shows that he has gained the one thing he lacked: serenity. Those who do not know his work may read it and wonder where the serenity is to be found. They must read all Mr. Lawrence's work to discover it fully. They must allow themselves to be man-handled and shattered by *The Rainbow* and by *Women in Love* before they can appreciate all the significance of his latest book. For the calm is but partly on the surface of *Aaron's Rod*, it lies chiefly in the depths. As before, Mr. Lawrence offers a violent challenge to conventional morality; as before, he covers us with the spume of his ungoverned eloquence. But the serenity is there. Mr. Lawrence can now laugh at himself without surrendering a jot of his belief in the truth he proclaims. It is as though he looked back whimsically at his own struggling figure in the past, saw all his violence and extravagance, and recognized that he could not have become what he is if he had not been what he was.

Not that *Aaron's Rod* is a perfect book; it is very far from that. It is, indeed, in some ways an extremely careless book. A lady who is Josephine Hay on one page becomes Josephine Ford—for no reason—in the next. At another moment the author clean forgets that Lilly, who is, with Aaron Sisson, the chief character in the book, has not been through the war. Then it has a positive carelessness, also, which is purely refreshing. Mr. Lawrence breaks off a couple of pages of splendid psychological presentation with this:

> Don't grumble at me then, gentle reader, and swear to me that this damned fellow wasn't half clever enough to think all these smart things, and realize all these fine-drawn-out subtleties. You are quite right, he wasn't, yet it all resolved itself in him as I say, and it is for you to prove that it didn't.

It takes a big man to be able to do that nowadays without breaking the spell. Mr. Lawrence's spell is not broken: he is a big man. He exults in his strength. He is so exultant that he really doesn't trouble to carry on his book—after page 200. When he has brought us to the point at which we are completely absorbed in the relation between Aaron and Lilly, he fobs us off with a passionate adventure of Aaron's, important enough in its way, but of which we know the conclusion beforehand, and three or four pages of conversation between them.

We could riddle the book with criticism, but not one of the shafts would touch its soul. It is real; it is alive. We have seen it said of *Aaron's Rod* by a well-known critic that whereas the presentation of the characters is vivid, the author's philosophizing is (as usual) esoteric and portentous. That is not true. Mr. Lawrence's philosophizing in this book is as vivid and vital as the rest. He is tackling a real problem and offering a real solution, and we think the philosophizing is, if anything, even better than the characters. Perhaps that is because we happen to agree with it. But to talk of Mr. Lawrence's philosophizing at all is misleading; he is not and never has been a philosopher; he is and always has been a moralist. Sometimes we have thought him a pernicious one. In the light of *Aaron's Rod*, we see him as a man who has experimented deeply and sincerely with human relationship in the determination to find some bedrock on which to build. Sometimes, in the torment of his search, he has wrapped up his experiences in the jargon of a mystical metaphysic. Now, having found what he sought, with the solid simplicity of conviction beneath his feet, he speaks plainly and persuasively.

That, we think, is the word for *Aaron's Rod*. With all its imperfections, all its carelessness, all the host of minor characters who refuse to become properly substantial—we judge them by Mr. Lawrence's own standards of achievement—it is persuasive. The style rings with the same clear truth as the message. Mr. Lawrence offers happiness; he points a way to security, and his words have the carelessness of confidence. No longer, as has been the case with his books of late, have we to content ourselves with sudden brief visions of shining beauty in the midst of inspissated and writhing darkness, like the shimmering rush of the bride out of the wedding carriage at the beginning of *Women in Love*. There is beauty everywhere in *Aaron's Rod*, beauty of the thing seen, beauty of the seeing spirit; and everywhere the careless riches of true creative power. *Aaron's Rod*—truly symbolic name—satisfies Arnold's test of magic of style. It is life-imparting.

After all that, it is most irrelevant to mention what the book 'is about'. It is simply the story of the effort of a man to lose the whole world and gain his own soul. Aaron Sisson leaves his wife, though he loves her and knows that he loves her, because he feels instinctively that she is engulfing him. He never returns to her in the book; neither does he ever deny the reality of the bond between them. Aaron is the

instinct to which Lilly supplies the consciousness; and we are left with
an indication that between these two men there is eventually to be a
profound and lasting friendship. Mr. Lawrence's theme is the self-
sufficiency of the human soul. The book convinces us that he at least
is within a measurable distance of having attained it.

52. Edward Shanks in *London Mercury*

October 1922, vi, 655–7

Edward Shanks (1892–1953). Poet, critic. Assistant editor *London Mercury* 1919–22.

Mr. Lawrence is, of course, the most *interesting* figure that has appeared in the seemingly decaying English novel since Mr. Conrad. Mr. Brett Young has failed so far to develop enough force, Miss Romer Wilson is still markedly immature, Mr. Joyce revolves on an eccentric orbit which is of more interest to writers than to readers. The rest, even those whose achievements are of more substantive merit than Mr. Lawrence's —for example, Mr. Beresford—are, with unimportant variations, following along beaten tracks. The catalogue I have given by no means exhausts the list of novelists who are contributing to contemporary literature; but the others are doing no more than that. They are doing nothing which can have any conceivable influence on the novel of the future. Mr. Lawrence, like Mr. Joyce, explores and experiments. Unlike Mr. Joyce, he writes novels near enough to the normal to be something more than Tom Tiddler's Grounds for other novelists.

His new book is, oddly enough, best described as 'a slice of life'. It is by no means a slice of life in the old sense, for it is not at all what used to be described as realism. Mr. Lawrence is not and never has been a realist. The creatures who inhabited his last work, *Women in Love*, were such as never existed on land or sea: their language and their actions were, in the last degree, *invraisemblable*. But throughout that book, as throughout this, there was perceptible an accent of genuineness not to be mistaken. Characters, action, and language had a real reality in the author's mind and were capable of becoming real in all minds capable of understanding his. But the characters and the language were, then as now, the main part of the achievement. The story was desultory and accidental.

Now it is fair to argue that a novelist may do himself much damage by confining himself within the rigid limits of a preconceived plot. But it is equally clear that the complete neglect of plot (which, in the last resort, means structure and proportion) tends to disperse and weaken whatever other good qualities he may have. And Mr. Lawrence's Aaron Sisson has no story. He is a person imagined and described up to a certain point. He is a miner in the Midlands. He plays the flute. He leaves his wife and children and sets out adrift in the world. He makes friends, observes life, arrives in Italy, has a love affair, and discovers that marriage is in his bones. But this exposition of character is made without inevitable events, just as the exposition of a valuable idea may be made without inevitable words. The sense of such an apothegm as

> We must endure
> Our going hence even as our coming hither:
> Ripeness is all

might be rendered in far other words with equal truth and with far less effect. Mr. Lawrence fails to get the full effect of Aaron and of his other characters because he has not stated them in terms of events which appeal to us as the sole and inevitable terms of expression. One feels that he has *imagined* the characters but that he has *invented* the actions. Aaron goes to Italy; he makes love to the Marchesa del Torre; but he might have done other things and been for us none the less the Aaron that Mr. Lawrence imagined. There is not even anything deliberately illustrative in the accidentalness of his fate. It is not so with the characters of Shakespeare or, to take an example from the novel, with those of Mr. Hardy. Here we must make a prolonged inquiry into the workings of the creative artist's mind before we come on any traces of invention. As we read, as we enjoy, we feel that the events are inevitable, are inseparable from the characters which in fact they illustrate.

This predominance of invention is a characteristic of the modern novel and, as a rule, it matters very little. But Mr. Lawrence's creations of characters are genuine and impressive, though he does so little with them. And, little though he does with them in comparison with what he might do, they are always springing up into vivid life. Lilly, a saturnine adviser, remonstrates with one of his friends woundingly:

[Quotes *Aaron's Rod*, Chap. VIII, 'Bah, love! . . . I should have to do it,' (Penguin ed., p. 102.)]

Mr. Lawrence has a leaning towards such scenes of unexpected violence. In *Women in Love* a woman suddenly upped and hit a man with a lapis-lazuli paperweight as he sat reading. That scene was grotesque and unconvincing; but this is not. It is a record not of what happens physically but of what happens mentally, the sudden uprush of the mind and will against life and even the most persuasive philosophy of it. It is in this sense that Mr. Lawrence's novels are 'slices of life': they are slices of the real life which lies under the surface of action and expression. None of us has ever met an Aaron Sisson. No Jim ever arose and hit his mentor one in the wind. When Mr. Lawrence makes Aaron say to the Marchesa, 'Shall we be lovers?' and makes her answer, 'Yes, if you wish it,' he does not intend us to understand that such a dialogue ever took place. He is stripping off the physical superfluities and revealing the spiritual essentials. And it is an extraordinary performance, one which is full of promise for the future of the novel. The novel has hitherto been weighed down by the apparent necessity for a wealth of physical realism, with which Mr. Lawrence shows us how to dispense. Let him go one step further, let him present the life he imagines in a significant inevitable form, without the wastage that attends his present accidentalness of method, and his place in English literature will be secure enough. Perhaps it is secure already, but it is in his power to make it higher.

FANTASIA OF THE UNCONSCIOUS

October 1922

53. J. M. Murry in *Algemeen Handelsblad*

31 March 1923, *Derde blad*, p. 9

The following is the English text as printed in *Reminiscences of D. H. Lawrence*. Murry also wrote a review of *Fantasia* in the *Nation and Athenaeum* (same date), but the present text reveals more fully the changes in Murry's view of Lawrence that took place between the publications of *Women in Love* and *Aaron's Rod*.

About two years ago I wrote in an essay in an English review that 'Mr. D. H. Lawrence is the outlaw of English literature, and he is the most interesting figure in it.' [See No. 49.] In substance that opinion of mine may still stand. But a nuance of modification is necessary. Mr. Lawrence during the last two years has become a little less of the outlaw, and a little more perceptibly the most interesting figure among the writers of his generation. The cultivated people who wagged their heads and called him 'mad' a year or two ago, now nod their heads and murmur 'genius'. Their real feeling is, of course, unchanged. They cannot get on with Mr. Lawrence any more now than they could then; but they feel themselves compelled to pay at least lip-service to the growing and only half conscious recognition that Mr. Lawrence is of a quite different order from his contemporaries.

Lawrence—with whom we are quickly compelled to drop the polite prefix—is primarily a novelist. As such his work falls outside the province of my criticism in the *Handelsblad*. He is also a notable poet; but it is a long while now since he published a volume of verses. In the last year, however, he has presented to the world two volumes which contain an exposition of his beliefs. Of these, the more important by far is the latter one, *Fantasia of the Unconscious*, which has just fallen into my hands.

There are many things which might be said of *Fantasia of the Un-conscious*—things most pertinent and necessary to be said, for which there will, alas, be no room in this brief article. I must content myself for the moment with pointing out the significance and indicating the context of two perfectly commonplace facts concerning this remarkable book. The first of these may seem almost puerile. The book has been published in America, and not in England. For the time being, if we desire to read it, we have to procure it from the United States. And the meaning of this is that Lawrence—an Englishman of the English, born in a Midland mining village, where the grim Black Country fades into some of the most beautiful rural scenery that England possesses—is, or has been, in a state of rebellion against his native land. By a monstrous abuse of the law in 1915 one of the most significant of his novels, *The Rainbow*, was suppressed on a fantastic charge of im-morality. Shortly after, so soon, in fact, as the material opportunity offered—the suppression of the one book made publishers fearful of accepting work from him—he shook the dust of England from his feet and began a slow and haphazard journey round the world, which has ended temporarily in the south of the United States. This was the period of his outlawry in spirit and in fact. He was anathema to English criticism. Even I myself—let me admit it freely—though I had been his intimate friend for many years, attacked him violently in the very article in which I declared that 'he was the outlaw of English literature, and the most interesting figure in it.'

I felt, and I said, that he was an enemy of civilization. It was perfectly true. He is the conscious and deliberate, yet passionate and potent, enemy of modern civilization. If our modern life, our modern civiliza-tion, is fundamentally good and true and valuable, then indeed the cry must be raised against Lawrence: *Écrasez l'infâme*! It is war to the knife between them, and two years ago the attack and the defence were alike angry and embittered. I do not wish to suggest that, at that or any other time, I was the equal antagonist of Lawrence. He has a sheer creative power that is completely beyond my range. But at that time I was the only English critic who took Lawrence with the im-passioned seriousness he deserved: the rest had washed their hands of him long ago, or, if they wrote of him at all, wrote only of his early novels and poems in a tone of mild regret that he should wilfully have forsaken such comparatively mild and flowery paths. At all events it so happened that I was the only English critic who took up his challenge with a vehemence comparable to that with which he had flung it down. After all, it was not surprising. I had known Lawrence intimately. I had realized, beyond any faint shadow of doubt, that he was the most real and powerful personality, the most naturally gifted man, among all my coevals. And perhaps I knew what Lawrence *meant* by his writing far better than other men. Therefore I cried, with vehemence and passionate sincerity, over the débris of a broken friendship: *Écrasez l'infâme!*

Well, I changed. I came to believe that Lawrence was right and I was wrong. In reviewing his next novel, *Aaron's Rod*, I published my recantation, with these words: '*Aaron's Rod* is the most important thing that has happened to English literature since the war. . . . To read it is to drink of a fountain of life.' [See No. 51.] For the bitterness had gone out of Lawrence's hostility to modern life. No less, nay, even more profoundly the enemy of modern 'civilization', he was no longer an angry and venomous enemy. He had reached the gaiety and serenity of a man who has come, through bitter struggles, into the secure possession of his truth. He had lived out life to an issue.

That brings me to the second of my simple facts, in order to explain, as briefly as I can, the nature of Lawrence's challenge to modern life. Both of Lawrence's expository or philosophical volumes start from a psycho-analytical basis. Lawrence was the first man in England, and I believe the first man in Europe, truly to realize the scope, the *envergure*, of the problems of which psycho-analysis has touched the fringe. This knowledge he had not as a student of Freud or Jung, but directly and instinctively by his own intuitive apprehension of life. The language and conceptions of the psycho-analysts were useful to him sometimes in giving expression to his own discoveries; but his discoveries were his own: they were also far in advance of anything the professional psycho-analysts had reached. For Lawrence knew, as a creative artist delving into his own depths for the life of his characters, what the professional psycho-analysts even now are only dimly aware of, that the problem they have (almost inadvertently and almost ignorantly) touched is the central problem of life—the problem to which all religions are in some sort attempted answers: 'What shall a man live by?'

The professional psycho-analysts had discovered that in modern 'civilization' some great primal urge—'Sex' for Freud, something less simple, *Libido*, for Jung—was thwarted and contorted with disastrous results to the individual. They began, clinically, to elaborate a subtle technique for liberating these suppressions. They have only just begun to see that when the suppressions are liberated, the problem of life remains, only more conscious and urgent than before. For the victim of neurosis, the man who cannot live in modern life, has at least a *modus vivendi* in the framework and among the compulsions of our industrial 'civilization'. If he becomes a machine, he also acquires some of the numbness of a machine. To make him aware of his own deep discomfiture, his lack of true satisfaction, his poverty of being, is only to increase his pain and his impotence, unless you can give him something new and true to live by. Psycho-analysis, without knowing what it is doing, has assumed the responsibilities of a religion without having religious duties to impose or religious satisfactions to offer.

This then is the cardinal issue which Lawrence has faced continuously and unflinchingly during his life as a writer, in moods that have passed through anger, embitterment, dismay, to a final serenity and insouciance. Men must enter into a new order of being. It is the conclusion of the great minds of modern times—of Dostoevsky, of Tolstoy, of Nietzsche, of Whitman. But how? In *Fantasia of the Unconscious* Lawrence gives, with a joyful spontaneity of language which is itself an augury of the newness of life he proclaims, his answer to the question. And, for my own part, I will declare my faith that it is essentially a true one; that D. H. Lawrence is the only writer of modern England who has something profoundly new to say; and finally that he must inevitably become a figure of European significance.

ENGLAND, MY ENGLAND

October 1922

54. Unsigned review in *New York Times Book Review*

19 November 1922, 13–14

Ten short stories, several of which should perhaps be classified as studies or impressions rather than short stories, have been collected in this volume, named after one of them, *England, My England*. They are tales of different types and classes of people, living under different conditions and different situations, but many of them, almost all of them, in fact, are fundamentally concerned with the struggle between the sexes, the so-called 'sex war'. For one reason or another, through one set of circumstances or another, there is a conflict, open or concealed, between the protagonists, man and woman, of nearly every tale. And in practically all of them it is the man who is the victim, the terrorized and dominated, weakly submissive, struggling or defiant. In *Tickets Please*, this sex war becomes an actual physical tussle between the philandering John Thomas Raynor, Inspector in the tramway service, and the girl conductors on his line, a single track line, which went racketing through 'the wild, gloomy country' of the Midlands. These girls to whom he had made love, one after another, locked him into the little waiting room at the depot, and there flew at him with a kind of maenad fury. 'Outside was the darkness and lawlessness of wartime', inside were the wild, reckless and enraged girls of the tramway, who turned the debonair young man into 'a strange, ragged, dazed creature'.

But usually the manifestations of this sex war are more subtle, less violent and obvious, if no less cruel. The young soldier's methods of final, desperate self-defence in the story called *Monkey Nuts*, and those used by his older friend, the Corporal, in defending him from the young woman who meant to seize her prey where she saw it, have a certain stark nakedness of intent. *The Primrose Path* ends in hatred, while the longest, most subtle story in the book, *England, My England*, the story of two who began their married life madly in love with each other, closes with a welcome to death. 'To forget! Utterly, utterly to forget, in the great forgetting of death. . . . Let the black sea of death itself solve the problem of futurity.' The characters of the pair in this tale are sharply, finely etched. There was the woman, Winifred, who had 'an almost barbaric sense of duty and of family', the man, Egbert, who evaded all duty, all responsibility, yet even while evading responsibility toward them, contrived to win his children away from her, their mother; 'he stole them from her, in emotion and spirit, and left her only to command their behaviour'. Within a few pages, Mr. Lawrence has compressed the bitterness and tragedy of those black years of spiritual conflict. And Crockham Cottage, a relic of 'the old England of hamlets and yeomen', with its small, glowing garden 'scooped out in the little hollow among the snake-infested commons', is an appropriate setting for all the fierce sense of suppression and bafflement and despair.

By far the greater number of these stories have a subtlety, an evasive quality underlying yet penetrating the texture of the exterior plot. Even when they seem simple, they are in truth intensely complex, composed of innumerable tiny fibres of thought and feeling and instinct, passing into one another by imperceptible degrees. And Mr. Lawrence seldom explains, never expounds. He tells us of the conditions, the surroundings; shows us, so far as the keenness of our own perceptions will permit us to see them, those multitudinous little fibres, so delicate, so slender and fine, yet so often strong as steel. Sometimes they are a part of the individual's consciousness; more frequently they are hidden away in the dim haze of the borderland, or belong entirely to the unconscious, so that it is we, the readers, who must divine their existence. Consider, for instance, that very peculiar story *You Touched Me*. There is the outward framework, plain enough even to the most obtuse; the young man with 'his watchful, charity-institution instinct . . . cautious, and without frankness', the two girls 'already old maids', according to the standards of the ugly industrial town which was their home; the silent pottery, where once the grey clay had spattered and the rough lasses had shouted and shrieked at one another, the dying man's sudden caprice. All of this is of the simplest, the most easily understood; but beneath, like the blood and muscles and nerves beneath the skin, is a whole throbbing, sensitive organism of desires and motives and emotions of which even their possessors are often unaware. And what is true of *You Touched Me* is true also of most of the stories in the volume.

That they are all written in a flexible style of fine shadings and swift, delicate strokes is a mere matter of course to everyone who is at all familiar with Mr. Lawrence's work. He has the ability, not merely to show us a place, but to make us feel its spiritual atmosphere. 'That silent house approached between a colonnade of tall-shafted pines' in which Isabel Pervin lived with her husband, the young, strong, sensitive man blinded in the war, is described in a very few words, yet we see and feel and know it, as we know the little town through which *The Horse Dealer's Daughter* passed so hurriedly to the churchyard on that 'grey, wintry day with saddened, dark-green fields and an atmosphere blackened by the smoke of foundries not far off,' and feel the sweeping rush of the tramcar as it went helter-skelter 'up hill and down dale . . . bouncing the loops . . . slithering round the precipitous drop under the church,' while Annie stood on the car-step, peremptorily demanding 'Tickets, please!'

They are not tales for those who wish merely to be amused, to read and enjoy without using their own brains, these tales of Mr. Lawrence's. He is one of those writers who demand more than a little co-operation from their readers. But to those able and willing to give that co-operation *England My England* will prove a fruitful and long-enduring source of pleasure.

THE LADYBIRD

March 1923

55. Unsigned review in *Times Literary Supplement*

22 March 1923, 195

The Ladybird was published in U.S.A. as *The Captain's Doll*. Both editions consist of *The Ladybird*, *The Fox* and *The Captain's Doll*.

Among our novelists there is no one who seems to be the voice of some compelling power in quite the way that Mr. D. H. Lawrence does. It is a power astonishingly rich in beauty, deep-flowing, very near the sources of life, but it can also be so darkly physical and overwhelming as to spread the oppression which he appears to feel. How good, then, to find him in a mood where he is at ease with his inspiration and not submerged by it: the stream running clear, and his own interest not flagging. Delightful, too, to see him refuting the critics by telling a story with the ease and mastery he shows here. The three stories in *The Ladybird* are each of them little novels of eighty pages or so; it is a pleasant form, and it suits Mr. Lawrence, giving him something of the range and depth he wants, and a limit too.

All three tales are studies of the unreasoned, incalculable magnetisms between men and women; and the first is almost phantasmal. For the little Bohemian Count, a wounded prisoner in England, who finds Lady Daphne again there and fascinates her, is like some dark, early god of the Underworld, and sees himself as the lord of a dim Hades. The girl is well sketched, the mental ravages of the war are subtle, and it is all told very exquisitely. But the Count, and even to some extent the English husband, seem to be ideas which the author has brought to life rather than living people; and so the story floats like a romance which is straining at its moorings in the real. The two girl-farmers in *The Fox* are intensely real, closely and humorously studied, and so is the wilful, laconic boy who breaks in on them. Again there is a touch of fantasy in the fox's spell, which merges, however, in a sense of the oneness between man and nature. The atmosphere round the farm is drawn close with a physical tenseness—the attraction is inexplicable, painful, almost terrible, and brings a tragedy; yet it is possible, and we feel that Mr. Lawrence is in control of it. At the end he simplifies freely. But the episode has been told, the future implied, and it is hard to quarrel with a passage which gathers up the meaning like this:

[Quotes from *The Fox*, 'She had to be like the seaweeds . . . And she had been so used to the very opposite.' (*Tales*, Secker 1934, p. 476.)]

There is Mr. Lawrence's prose, with its rhythmical, hypnotic seduction, like the spell of these affinities. And then the air lightens again in the third story; he shows us another manner. It would give little idea of the story to say that the protagonists are a Scottish officer in the Army of Occupation and a German Countess; just as it would not tell much to say that all the stories have an echo of the war, because Mr. Lawrence, with all his keen sense of the present, treats the war as art must treat it in the future. Again there is a magnetism, and the enigmatic captain is diverting, as seen through the German's eyes; but this time the clash of wills shapes a comedy. *The Captain's Doll* is an original and unexpected stroke of Mr. Lawrence's; his wit comes out, and he is amusing in a way he seldom allows himself for long. And he keeps the eye of a poet; wonderful, among all his scenes and settings, is the mountain walk here, and the glacier. The whole book, indeed, is steeped in imagination. The very things which give titles to the stories make, each of them, an image. And the tension in the stories, through which beat the mystery and pulse of life, is relieved and made beautiful by this imaginativeness.

56. Charles Marriott in *Manchester Guardian*

6 April 1923, 7

Charles Marriott, signed 'C.M.' (1869-1957). Novelist and art critic of *The Times* (1924-40).

Everything else in the three stories contained in this book is secondary to the effect of creative power. This effect is only intensified by occasional baddish or, at least, awkward writing, as if the author were taken at a loss by the creatures of his own imagination, by some over-elaborate description, and by a general tendency to exaggerate the discrepancies between the conscious and the unconscious in the workings of personality. These but indicate that helplessness of the artist which is the surest proof of his genius. Every now and then one feels that Mr. Lawrence may be mistaken in his reading of his characters, but never that they did not exist, speak, and behave exactly as he has presented them.

Different as they are in character, incident, and setting, all three stories, *The Ladybird, The Fox,* and *The Captain's Doll,* deal with the same inexhaustible theme—the conflict between that compromise of habit and circumstance which is conduct, and that inner meaning of the individual which is life. To call it the conflict between reason and instinct is to obscure the issue, and to a reader whose previous acquaintance with the work of Mr. Lawrence is limited to one short story this book comes as an agreeable surprise. One had gathered that Mr. Lawrence was over-obsessed with the physical side of love. In these three stories, at any rate, it is not true. If he has an obsession it is with the spiritual aspirations which disturb the physical side. Over and over again he dwells, now tenderly, now with ironic humour, upon the baulking of bodily passion by its own essence. The scene in *The Ladybird* where Major Apsley suddenly realizes that his wife is in love with Count Psanek, the Bohemian prisoner of war, and that in *The Fox* where the boy, calculating by nature, realizes that March is a woman, and accessible, are cases in point. It is true that Mr. Lawrence has a queer turn for the physical accidents of humanity; if he mentions hair on the limbs once he mentions it a dozen times; but these accidents confuse rather than stimulate his characters in their effect. His constant theme is the perplexing nature of love as an expression of life. That, as in *The Fox*, love should lead to crime does not for a moment identify it with lust.

The very nature of the theme makes the stories obscure in argument. They are for telling at length. In *The Ladybird*, Lady Daphne Apsley, not unhappily married, but with repressions, and Count Psanek belong to each other only in the dark of their natures. Their conscious selves are, if not slightly hostile, at least ironically polite. He has a philosophy of the matter, expressed with some not very convincing references to Egyptology and the 'ladybird' which is the crest of his family, but it is a commentary rather than an explanation. In *The Fox* the actual beast excites the mood which lays March open to the influence of the Canadian boy-soldier on leave to whom she and her girl friend, Banford, give lodging for the night at their poultry farm; and the conflict in her is between her conscious love for Banford and her unwilling response to the boy. *The Captain's Doll*, the scene of which is Cologne during the British occupation, is done in the comic spirit—for all that it contains a violent death. Countess Hannele zu Rassentlow and Captain Hepburn have been lovers, but her conscious regard for him is expressed in a doll in tartan trews. After the death of his wife he asks Hannele to marry him, to honour and obey but not to love. 'All this about love', he said, 'is very confusing and very complicated.' It is, and Mr. Lawrence makes you realize it while telling the external incidents of the stories with a crispness of narration and a rightness in the dialogue, expressing the surface personality and exact social status of the speaker, which one would expect only in the novel of manners. It is doubtful if anything in recent fiction combines so true an impression of life with so vivid an account of the accidents of living.

57. Unsigned review in *Spectator*

14 April 1923, 630–31

A paradox is a truism standing on its head. When Mr. Ford Madox Hueffer said that no reader ever cared what a book was about he evolved a typical paradox, though the truism which appeared if the paradox was scratched was perhaps itself a superficial one. It is not, he said, because they are about the wars of the Greeks and Trojans, or even because they are about war in general, that we admire the *Iliad* and *Troilus and Cressida*; it is the presentation, it is the artist's share in the total product that gives the story its value. If we skate lightly upon it and do not rudely break through to the fact that the *Iliad* is really about the behaviour of human beings submitted to various elaborated circumstances of stress, we shall find that this theory throws useful light. It may help us to find out what pleases us in quite a number of different sorts of narrative.

Mr. D. H. Lawrence's new book of stories is a case in point, and to summarize the actual events of the stories, which are full enough of movement, is to realize how subtle is Mr. Lawrence's art. We have probably at school had to learn from those anatomical figures made either in coloured plaster or in cardboard, in which the mannikin's full dress is his suit of superficial muscles. You pull layers of his substance off him till you come in the end to his bones, his heart and his liver. Upon the number of these layers depends the price of the mannikin. Mr. Lawrence's characters are like the very best sort of mannikin; their delicacy of structure, their elaboration is almost incredible, but, as in the case of the mannikin, it is the elaboration of setting forth and setting bare, not the elaboration of the tailor and the milliner.

In the first story the chief group are a 'Society Beauty', a Hungarian Count, who is a prisoner of war, and an English soldier of a well-known, aristocratic type; and incidentally there is a perfectly-drawn portrait of a type of Englishwoman who has seldom been portrayed save from the inside, and never before by so sympathetic and yet so detached an onlooker:

[Quotes from *The Ladybird*, 'She was a little frail, bird-like woman ... She ordered the car and went alone ...' (*Tales*, Secker 1934, pp. 357–8.)]

The story, however, really concerns the group of people we spoke of before. We wish Mr. Lawrence would make a really enduring picture of a type he has sketched here with such delicate skill. Such people were the fine flower of a civilization that has gone, and they are still here in London or in their villages, moving, breathing and easily to be observed.

The next story, *The Fox*, sounds commonplace enough in outline. Two young women who have been land girls during the war run a farm together. One night a young soldier calls by chance at the farm. He stays and finally courts the younger of the two women. Her partner is furiously jealous and tries to dissuade her from marrying him. To his despair, she almost succeeds in doing so. He returns to the farm, and half accidentally, half purposely, in felling a tree for them, he manages to kill the obstacle who stands between him and the woman he longs for. Actually the story is very strange; it moves, as does real life or as does the best sort of lyrical poetry, upon two or three planes of consciousness at once: the result is an extreme richness and intricacy of texture.

The last story is a little more ordinary in atmosphere and has a strong element of comedy in it. Again, without being poetical, it touches planes not usually found outside poetry. Here particularly the reader is conscious of a curious quality in Mr. Lawrence's writing; he uses refrains just as a poet would do. At first the reader may think the trick accidental repetition and be surprised at finding such a thing in writing so fine in texture, but he reads a little further and finds that it is nothing of the sort, but a use of repetition as deliberate as in a poetical or musical refrain. The reader will probably feel that this is not a legitimate prose device; we wonder if Mr. Lawrence feels that it is altogether satisfactory. However, till he or another has evolved another or better device, it certainly does serve to give a certain atmosphere.

Was it not Pélissier in one of his Potted Plays who said that the ordinary drama was concerned with ordinary people in extraordinary situations, while he would give a drama of extraordinary people in ordinary situations? Mr. Lawrence goes beyond this formula and shows us the extraordinariness of ordinary people in ordinary situations.

It is interesting to see that, as in *Aaron's Rod*, Mr. Lawrence is still sure of the necessity for women's submission to man's domination if their love life is to bring satisfaction to either.

These stories would not have made Mr. Lawrence's reputation, but they sustain it.

58. Edward Shanks, 'Mr. D. H. Lawrence: Some Characteristics', *London Mercury*

May 1923, viii, 64–75

Mr. D. H. Lawrence lives at the bottom of a dark pit. He is always trying to clamber out of it; and sometimes he thinks that he has succeeded. He is, however, invariably wrong when he thinks so: his fingers slip on the brink, he slides back, and the struggle begins all over again. He believes, too, that the whole of the human race is living at the bottom of the same pit. Perhaps he is right. But the question whether he is right or not is one that, sooner or later, when we consider his work, we must ask ourselves: he himself does not allow us to evade that question. The persons of his imagination are persons in ordinary circumstances, farmers, colliers, elementary school-teachers and the like, living in the unfamiliar but not specially romantic or legendary coal-district of Nottinghamshire. But in their physical experiences they are a little, and in their mental and spiritual experiences, more than a little, abnormal. The ostensible mode of all Mr. Lawrence's books, whether in prose or in verse, is what we are accustomed to call realistic. These are people who get up and go to bed, who talk, sometimes, in a recognizable dialect, who wash and eat and have holes in their socks. But

[Quotes from *Women in Love*, 'Swiftly, in a flame that drenched down her body . . . shattering his heart.' (Chap. 8, Penguin ed., pp. 117–18.)]

This scene takes place in an English country-house, in the boudoir of Hermione, who is a cultivated member of the governing classes. She strikes the blow: the recipient of it is Rupert Birkin, an inspector of schools, who is sitting there reading while she writes her letters. When it is over, he goes out, takes off all his clothes, runs about in the rain and feels better. The invention of the scene is strange enough, but one detail in it is even stranger. Why should Rupert, at a moment when one might have expected him to be startled and frightened into unsubtle normality—why should he, just then, experience horror at being reminded of Hermione's left-handedness?

Let us take another example—this time from Mr. Lawrence's verse of an earlier period, from the poem called 'Snap-Dragon':

[Quotes from 'Snap-Dragon', 'She turned her flushed face to me for the glint' . . . 'The low word "Don't!" ' . . . .' (C.P., I, 125.)]

Now such a symbolic condensation of an emotional crisis is less unexpected in verse than in prose; but it is typical of what Mr. Lawrence constantly does in both. Even where verse deals with everyday life we do not ask of it that the details shall be verisimilitudinous, we expect it to go beyond the larger surface and give us the smaller core. But in novels, more particularly where the author says: 'She wore a dress of dark-blue silky stuff, with ruches of blue and green linen lace in the neck and sleeves; and she had emerald-green stockings,' we expect all the events and details to be invented, however they may be arranged, strictly with a view to probability. It is something of a shock when we find they are not. Now Mr. Lawrence does nothing to soften this shock. He is, on the surface, neither a romantic nor a symbolist. He seemed even, to some of his early reviewers, to be a painter of the manners of the Midlands, not incomparable with Mr. Arnold Bennett. Perhaps the Nottingham colliery-district of which he wrote was so unfamiliar that London critics were at first ready to believe of it almost anything they were told. Mr. Bennett indeed had often insisted on both the incredibility and the strict truth of his pictures of the Five Towns. These pictures were not, perhaps, so amazing as he would have had us believe; but critics are impressionable creatures, or they would not be critics. They came, very likely, to think that another dispensation obtained north of the Chilterns, in which southern standards of probability must be applied with caution. But gradually it began to be obvious that if one were to take the realistic texture of Mr. Lawrence's work, whether in prose or in verse, at its face-value, one would have to conclude that it is peopled with ill-mannered, hypersensitive and hysterical lunatics, one would have to begin and end with the judgment that human beings do not talk like this, do not behave in this way.

It is a first sign of Mr. Lawrence's quality that he does not allow us, he has never allowed anyone, to come to such a conclusion. Today we are rather apt, indeed, to be over-impressed by obscurity. We cannot help remembering that an earlier generation thought not only Browning but even Tennyson to be unintelligible; and, with this recollection in our minds, we go about in modern literature a good deal too ready to buy any pig in a poke, because to us the existence of the poke connotes the superlative goodness of the pig. But Mr. Lawrence's obscurity has a different effect. Here we feel that the author is doing his best and that some of the effort towards comprehension must come from ourselves. Here is work which will perhaps appear to a later generation as lucid as most of Browning does to us, work which, like the famous Sonata of Marcel Proust's Vinteuil, must gradually create its own understanding audience. If we can take a few steps in that direction, we shall have done something on which we may congratulate ourselves. But, before we do so, we must renounce the pleasure of objecting that members of the English governing classes do not beat school inspectors over the head with lapis-lazuli paper-weights. We must remember, to begin with, that Mr. Lawrence's work has enough obvious and normal virtues to prove him not to be an idiot.

His work is considerable in extent for a career which began no longer than twelve years ago. It consists of seven substantial novels, a volume of short stories, a volume of long-short stories, two plays, four collections of verse, and two books of travel. Not all of this bulk is equally good; but none of it is trivial or even can be described as having been lightly undertaken. Mr. Lawrence sometimes writes badly: he seems never to write with anything less than the full intensity of which he is capable. And it must be remembered, in computing his total production, that between *The Rainbow* in 1915 and *The Lost Girl* in 1920, he published no novel. This was no doubt due to the unfortunate suppression of *The Rainbow*.

The important part of this work is to be found in the novels. But would Mr. Lawrence, under other conditions than those which obtain today, have chosen the medium of the novel? Has he been altogether wise in doing so? These questions are difficult to answer. One is inclined at first to maintain that neither his material nor his particular talent for expression is suited to this form, and that, but for the tyranny which rules our literature and decrees that any man who wishes to earn a living in it must be either novelist or reviewer, he would have chosen some other. And yet *The Trespasser* at least, his second novel, apart from the magnificent descriptive passages which it contains, is excellent in form, a well-told, compact and shapely story. And, of the scenes which one remembers how many could have been rendered in any other medium?

Mr. Lawrence's novels are mostly shapeless, ragged, diffuse. But for the example of *The Trespasser* one would be tempted to say that his narrative sense is incapable of standing by him for above half a dozen pages: even his short stories are generally amorphous lumps. *The Rainbow* rambles on through three generations. Each generation is elaborately painted in, only to be discarded when the next is old enough for the author to take interest in it. From the point of view of telling a story, this book contains more wasted labour than almost any other I know. Tom Brangwen might well say that if he was so soon to be done for, he wondered what he was begun for. But he leaves the book in one of the best of Mr. Lawrence's scenes. He is drowned, while a little drunk, in an unexpected flood; and the reader does not forget his death. His adopted daughter, Anna, and her husband, William Brangwen, fade out far more ignominiously, only to make belated and ghostly appearances in *Women in Love*. It is Ursula to whom the rainbow appears, Ursula on whom the full force of the book is concentrated; and Ursula is not born till more than a third of the book is done, does not develop a personality till it is half way through. When she does, Mr. Lawrence throws aside the characters on whom he has spent so many pains and whom he has not completely explained, and turns to her.

There is not, in all this, any suggestion of subtlety or premeditation: one does feel on the contrary, quite definitely, that Mr. Lawrence is making it all up as he goes on, leaving one page to suggest the next, penetrating to the hearts of his characters only one page in advance of his readers. In more demonstrable ways, he is almost insolent in his carelessness. *The White Peacock*, though it is told in the first person, contains scenes of which the narrator could not possibly have had any knowledge. In *The Rainbow*, events are huddled together or dwelt on with no regard to the symmetry or the substantiation of the story. Ursula and Skrebensky have indulged in a passionate and secret love affair for a considerable time. Then:

> He could not come again to Nottingham until the end of April. Then he persuaded her to go with him for a week-end to a friend's house near Oxford. By this time they were engaged. He had written to her father, and the thing was settled. He bought her an emerald ring, of which she was very proud.

Now to such persons as these are, as Mr. Lawrence has conceived them, the public avowal of a mutual relation must have been an important event: nothing is gained, something is lost by this brusque dismissal of it. In another writer it might have been a yawn, in Mr. Lawrence it is the hunter's eagerness; but it is not good narrative.

It is not incapacity, it is merely the author's striving after something which occupies his mind more than comely and lucid story-telling. But to say that suggests that Mr. Lawrence altogether neglects the flesh and bone of the novel, that he emaciates it to a gaunt ugliness in his search for something of the spirit. This, however, would not be true. There are few living writers more capable of clothing what they imagine in solid and beautiful flesh. To be sure, he can write badly, with his eye anywhere but on the object, as in the instance of the rabbit:

[Quotes from *Women in Love*, 'And suddenly the rabbit, which had been crouching as if it were a flower . . . the old red walls like a storm.' (Chap. 18, Penguin ed., p. 273.)]

Three similes to describe one rabbit and two of them as unsuited to the purpose as can be imagined. Indeed, in the tumult of his later work Mr. Lawrence's impressionistic power of rendering material things and scenes does appear to have lost some of its certainty. He is feverishly determined to render the half apprehended, almost wholly incommunicable mental states of his characters and, when he is describing their surroundings, distracted by this, he fumbles, he repeats himself, he blurs the image by attempting to infuse into it something he has failed to express elsewhere. Perhaps this old power is one of the things he must, or feels he must, throw over in the pursuit of his new goal. But his earlier books had extraordinarily full, rich and vivid backgrounds. As one turns over the pages of *The White Peacock*, one is astonished to find how many descriptive passages there are and how warmly they glow with life. As one reads the book, one hardly observes their profusion, for they are a true background. Mr. Lawrence is never irrelevant or self-conscious in the use of his descriptive powers. But when one looks for them they yield themselves, separable and lovely. Here is the episode of the keeper's funeral:

[Quotes from *The White Peacock*, 'Till the heralds come . . . repeating their last syllables like the broken accents of despair.' (Chap. 11, Penguin ed., pp. 207–9.)]

I wish I could continue the quotation to the end of the chapter, to the narrator's return home:

The house was quiet and complacent; it was peopled with ghosts again; but the ghosts had only come to enjoy the warm place once more, carrying sunshine in their arms and scattering it through the dusk of gloomy rooms.

The thing is perfect of its kind. It is just because among the novelists who come after Mr. Hardy and Mr. Conrad so few can do so much, so few appear even to want to do it, that the modern novel is the rather arid and unsatisfying thing which we feel it to be.

In *The Trespasser*, again, the scene blends with the story and there are unforgettably beautiful passages of description. After this the background is not so pervasive or so consistent in excellence, though Mr. Lawrence did not by any means lose at this point his impressionistic power. But already in *The Rainbow* it is directed more closely to the realization of mental states and in the volume of travel sketches, *Twilight in Italy*, published in the following year, the most impressive pages are of this order. Mr. Lawrence now begins to make the reader vividly aware of his struggle to get out of the pit, which body and soul have made between them, or at least to understand why he is in it. There is a hint of this in the remarkable first sketch, 'The Crucifix':

[Quotes from 'The Crucifix Across the Mountains', 'The body bent forward towards the earth . . . mad because he cannot escape.' (*Twilight in Italy*. Penguin ed., pp. 10–11.)]

Here already Mr. Lawrence is entering into the curious condition of torture which has produced his later books.

The earlier novels were comparatively normal. There is, in *The Trespasser*, a hint of that mysterious hatred between lover and beloved which puzzles Mr. Lawrence so much. But there is nothing very extraordinary in, for example, the keeper in *The White Peacock*, the man of 'one idea:—that all civilization was the painted fungus of rottenness.' There is nothing abnormal in the character of Paul Morel, in *Sons and Lovers*, the young man unbreakably bound to his mother, unable to give himself in love to either Miriam or Clara. In these books there is much that is good, normal and in the ordinary tradition of the novel. Mr. Lawrence can create characters, though, because he is so little concerned with story or plot, one is apt to forget in which book each occurs. George Saxton might stray from *The White Peacock* into *The Rainbow* without producing any effect of oddness. Alice Gall, in *The White Peacock*, and Beatrice Wyld, in *Sons and Lovers*, are surely the same person: at any rate the mind very easily confuses them.

This at least must be said, however, that, though Mr. Lawrence's novels are often shapeless and straggling, they do produce an effect of real life lived by real persons. Even as late as *Aaron's Rod*, this power is distinctly noticeable. The opening scenes of that book, the Christmas Tree in Aaron's home, the bar-parlour at the 'Royal Oak' are paintings at once of extraordinary vividness and extraordinary solidity. Indeed, one might go through these books for a long time, picking out such things—the splendid last fifty pages of that disappointing work, *The Lost Girl*, which describe the life of the Midland girl Alvina with her peasant through the Calabrian winter, the death of Tom Brangwen, the rabbit-hunting in *The White Peacock*, and so on. These things stay longer in the memory than the complete books from which they come: they are at all events the body of Mr. Lawrence's work, if not its soul. And to them may be added here the more simple and success-ful of his two plays, *The Widowing of Mrs. Holroyd*, with its beautiful last scene, in which the mother and the wife lay out the body of the dead miner who has given them both so much pain.

I have questioned above whether the novel is the proper medium for Mr. Lawrence, whether under other conditions than those of our day he would himself have chosen to use it. But he was at all events born in a time when, however tyrannically the novel was pointed out as his path, it was possible for him to get his verse at least taken seriously and not merely as a novelist's recreation. His first book of verse, *Love Poems and Others*, immediately followed *The Trespasser*; and it contained many beautiful things. Verse, indeed, one was in-clined to think then, was his proper medium: it seemed suitable for his impressionistic richness, for his intensity of concentration on the passionate and symbolic moment. There were poems here which equalled the grave and measured beauty of the funeral-scene I have already quoted:

[Quotes from 'Love on the Farm', 'Into the yellow, evening glow . . . Into the evening's empty hall.' (*C.P.*, I, 42—revised text.)]

There were also the dialect poems, including the queerly realistic and poignant little story of the girl whose policeman lover had been seduced by the widow he lodged with. Mr. Lawrence has since published three more collections, which contain many good pieces; but on the whole I doubt whether verse is a medium which serves him better than, or even as well as, prose. From the first there was an awkwardness in his versification, a breathless scrambling to get at the rhymes, which was characteristic enough but which he would have been better without and which, I fancy, he would have been glad to get rid of. It drove him to free verse; and in free verse he tended to become bombastic, hysterical and false. At his best he can write such a piece as this:

[Quotes the whole of '*Giomo Dei Morti*' (*C.P.*, I, 232.)]

At his worst he writes:

[Quotes from 'Mutilation', 'And if I never see her again? . . . the skies would break.' (*C.P.*, I, 213.)]

It won't do: it reminds one irresistibly, though painfully, of the man in one of Mr. Wells's books, who said: 'If she is dead, I will r-r-rend the heavens like a garment!'

These two extracts are taken from *Look! We Have Come Through!*, the book in which, as it seems to me, Mr. Lawrence made a definite attempt to discover whether verse might not be made to serve his purpose instead of the prose novel. I have always thought that in this attempt he must have been influenced by the German poet, Richard Dehmel—not so much by the *Roman in Romanzen, Zwei Menschen*, as by the lyrics in *Aber die Liebe*, which obviously tell the same story, but less deliberately. This may or may not be so: I have no means of telling. At any rate, there is a decided resemblance in more than one point between the two writers. Both concentrate, sometimes with success, on the passionate and symbolic moment. Both take an equally mystical and sensual view of life and, in particular, of love. Both are often betrayed by the turbulence of their emotions into mere violence of language which does anything but express their meaning.

Of the two extracts I have given, the first, for all Mr. Lawrence may say of the unity of his book, is distinctly detachable. It is 'the sort of poem modern poets write', an impression, an anthology piece, beautiful and valuable for its beauty, but inevitably with something of its author left out of it. Mr. Lawrence can do this and often does; but when he attempts to get more of himself into his verse, as a rule he fails. *Look! We Have Come Through!* fails by reason of both violence and obscurity. The language is often, as in my second extract, too turgid and exaggerated to convey any impressive emotion. And the meaning of the passionate moments which the book successively describes, their relations with each other and their significance for the persons who experience them are never clear. The central idea of the work never emerges so clearly as in the 'Argument' with which it begins; and even the 'Argument' helps the reader very little to fit the separate pieces together into one scheme. But this explanation is worth quoting:

[Quotes the 'Argument' of *Look! We Have Come Through!* (*C.P.*, I, 191.)]

Conflict of love and hate! Some sort of conclusion! Some condition of blessedness! The first phrase has a meaning which is real enough when we look at Mr. Lawrence's latest books. In writing the other two, he seems to have deceived himself. His world is a world of struggle, in which love is very much like hate, in which indeed one connotes the other and in which both are equally bitter. But with this endless struggle he is endlessly concerned. In *The Rainbow*, Tom Brangwen makes a speech at Anna's wedding, in these terms:

[Quotes from *The Rainbow*, '"There's very little else, on earth ... and there's no bottom to it."' (Chap. V, Penguin ed., p. 140.)]

The gnawing of the soul, its declaration that there is something it must have—these are things which are very real and very terrible to Mr. Lawrence; and his acute consciousness of them is really the force which fills his work with life. In most men this sense of longing is roused from time to time by 'someone's death, a chorus-ending from Euripides', is recognized by them as unappeasable and set aside, suffered or enjoyed, as best it may be. But Mr. Lawrence will not admit that it is unappeasable; and he is forever trying to find the proper satisfaction for it. He has sought the solution in love and marriage; but, though he finds these indispensable to man, the perfect solution is not there. Tom Brangwen is unsatisfied, Will Brangwen is unsatisfied, Ursula finds that Skrebensky cannot give her what she wants and sends him away. *Women in Love* ends with the tragedy of Gerald and Gudrun, and with Rupert and Ursula not quite happy, he because marriage does not give him all he demands, she that he should feel this. Aaron Sisson finds that he cannot be the lover of the Marchesa del Torre because he 'feels his wife somewhere inside him'; but he does not turn home to his wife. From marriage Mr. Lawrence turns to the ideal of comradeship which he finds in Whitman. In an essay on Whitman, he argues that we must not destroy marriage but surpass it and reach 'the sheer friendship, the love between comrades, the manly love which alone can create a new era of life'.

It would be absurd to attempt here to criticize the philosophical value of these ideas; but it will be something if we can disentangle the effect produced by them, and by the passionate striving whence they spring, on Mr. Lawrence's work. They have beyond all doubt increased its wildness and unreality. The attempt to appease an unappeasable desire might be expected to transcend the ordinary means of expression; and so here it has proved in several curious ways. It has led Mr. Lawrence's style towards a strange, almost childish naïvety. The author of *The White Peacock* knew all about literary English and accomplished prose. The author of *Aaron's Rod* prefers to write like this:

> They were quite a little family and it seemed quite nice . . .
> So Aaron went skipping off to his appointment, at seven o'clock. Judge of his chagrin, then . . .
> But need we say that Mr. Aaron felt very much out of it.

It is almost like a little girl telling a story in the nursery to her companions: it is not very remote from the style of Miss Daisy Ashford. Now is this the detestable deliberate naïvety of sophistication? I think it is not. I think that Mr. Lawrence, under pressure of his desire to attain to some goal, has come to the single-mindedness of childhood.

So it is, I believe, with the distortions and unrealities of his later books. *The Lost Girl*, *Women in Love* and *Aaron's Rod* are all, outwardly, ordinary realistic novels. The dress of the characters is described, their food is described, there are little satirical sketches of odd persons. But the principal characters are always and consistently abnormal both in their speech and in their actions. A novel, of course, which gave a pure reflection of normal existence would be a very dull affair. A novel must at least deal with an interesting case, must show its persons under some sort of strain: it must almost necessarily have in it some situation which is not usual. But a novel which is one long abnormality, which on almost every page diverges from daily experience, is a different business. And one remembers of what a tissue of events and conversations these novels of Mr. Lawrence's are made up. One remembers that amazing Italian touring troupe in *The Lost Girl*, the initiation ceremony by which Alvina is received into the Natcha-Kee-Tawaras, the wrestling match between Gerald Crich and Rupert Birkin, the tirade which Ursula delivers against Rupert. And one comes to the conclusion that these are not, and are not intended to be, human beings as we know them.

They are, in fact, the symbols by means of which Mr. Lawrence expresses what continually occupies his mind, the belief that somewhere there *must* exist some appeasement for the intolerable yearning which possesses the mind of man. Whether there is such an appeasement or not does not concern us here: it is enough if we have disentangled this as the chief motive force of his work. We have still to consider whether he is wise in presenting his symbols under the appearance of men and women from the coal-grimed Midlands. There are obvious disadvantages in this method. It is easy to say, as I have already said, that his world is peopled by ill-mannered, hypersensitive and hysterical lunatics. It is easy to exclaim that human beings do not speak like this, do not behave like this. It is a stronger complaint that from Aaron Sisson playing with his children and washing in the back-kitchen we are dragged with a sickening jerk to Aaron Sisson, an impossible mythological giant making love in an impossible way to an impossible Marchesa del Torre.

Against this there is a good argument. Modern myths are difficult to invent and generally unwieldy when they are invented. We do not want Mr. Lawrence to take to classical machinery or to the concoction of Jurgens. Perhaps his clinging to the framework of ordinary life as the material for his books prevents him from flying off into the confused nightmares of Strindberg, who was often little less delirious than Mr. Lawrence can sometimes be. He is in no danger of forgetting that what he has to express, and the symbols he uses for expressing it exist, after all, only for the service of ordinary life. Above all—he is a man of genius; and we must wait and see, without expressing any too dogmatic opinion, where the path he has chosen will take him.

We have seen already what the taking of this path has involved. He is the rare example of a man who, endowed with every gift for writing beautifully and movingly, has thrown them aside in order to follow the line of thought and feeling which his nature ordered him to follow. It is possible to say that the solutions he offers of the great problem oppressing him are empty and false. I think they are. I think there is no answer to this riddle. I think Mr. Lawrence would be a more prudent and a happier man if he were to abandon the hope of finding one. But then Keats would have been a more prudent and a happier man if he had not permitted himself to love Fanny Brawne. Much great literature comes out of passionate follies. Mr. Lawrence's passion may be a folly. He may be wrong in thinking that it is possible for us to climb out of the pit in which we lie. He may be wrong on looking at this life as a pit. But, if so, out of his error comes a flame of poetry, smoky, strange and disconcerting as it may be, which is at least genuine and which is hardly paralleled by any of the novelists of his generation.

STUDIES IN CLASSIC
AMERICAN LITERATURE

August 1923

59. Stuart P. Sherman, review, *New York Evening Post Literary Review*

20 October 1923, iv, 143-4

Stuart P. Sherman (1881–1926). University teacher, editor, critic. Became literary editor of *New York Herald Tribune* 1924. The review is entitled, 'America Is Discovered'.

It is with some difficulty, after reading the book which suggests the title above, that one refrains from calling its author, Mr. D. H. Lawrence, an interesting 'fellow'—as an act of reciprocity. He has been visiting us, sojourning physically, I believe, in New Mexico, and mentally, I am sure, among our raciest exponents of *belles-lettres*. He is a good guest: he studies his host and makes extraordinary efforts to adapt himself to the habits and manners of the family. One surmises that he is now wearing a sombrero, driving a Ford, drinking iced water qualified perhaps with white mule, reading the Albuquerque *American*, and smoking Camel cigarettes. The internal evidence for this surmise lies in the style which 'the greatest of living English writers' employs to address his American audience. For the nonce, Mr. Lawrence is resolved to be a genuine *Americano*. Something of a linguist, he has attempted to master the idiom and actually to write his book in the vernacular. A critic to the manner born, like Mr. Mencken, may justly complain that his idiom is by no means flawless; yet to the uncensorious native there is a subtle flattery in hearing the loved accents of the mother tongue slipping so nonchalantly from the lips of a gifted alien. Here are examples:

(1) Marie Antoinette got her head off for playing dairymaid, and nobody dusted the seats of your pants till now for all the lies you put over us. [Apostrophe to Rousseau and other advocates of a return to Nature.]

(2) You bet, Robinson Crusoe was a highbrow of highbrows.

(3) The law we broke, indeed. You bet!

(4) Poe has no truck with Indians or Nature. He makes no bones about Red Brothers and Wigwams.

(5) Oh, Benjamin! [B. Franklin.] Oh, Binjum! You do not suck me in any longer.

I will admit that my first impression, after a hasty dip into these studies, was that Mr. Lawrence was rather vaingloriously engaged in demonstrating how much more expeditiously and perfectly than Mr. Francis Hackett, late of the *New Republic*, he had become an *Americano*. I did him an injustice. Mr. Lawrence has a more serious purpose than that. He has even what certain of our own critics would call a 'messianic' purpose. He has borrowed our language and discussed our classics in order to deliver, in a style intelligible to us and with illustrations suited to our comprehensions, his own message. This book, like his novels and his philosophical works, has a thesis. I think that he may now congratulate himself on having put his thesis 'across' in a fashion to engage sympathetic attention from many readers who have been unable to penetrate through the dense underbrush of his fiction to the philosophic cave-man, Mr. Lawrence himself, glaring fuliginous from his cavern, and far more interested in winning male converts to his philosophy than silly women to hear his story.

Mr. Lawrence is a philosophic cave-man—but let us pause long enough to see what that means. A caveman hunts and fights and mates and scratches on the walls of his cavern rude images of the beasts which cross the *camera obscura* of his mind. When hunting in his own neighbourhood becomes poor, he explores new forests. The male purpose and conscience dominate the scene in a vivid awareness that livelihood and life depend upon the male's exerting, like a thunderbolt, his own will at every critical turn of his affairs. He unquestioningly obeys the passional instincts of his 'blood', which courses through its channels uncooled and uncorrupted by 'ideals', untrammelled by conventions. He admits no equalities which he can resist. His woman is his woman for her proper hour at eventide; but the day is his. He knows her tendency to use her sex 'as a she-devil for the endless hurt of her man. She doesn't know it. She will never believe it if you tell her. And if you give her a slap in the face for her fiendishness, she will rush to the first magistrate in indignation. . . . Give her the great slap just the same, just when she is being most angelic.' Now, when a cave-man begins to justify his instincts we call him a philosophic cave-man.

In the book before us Mr. Lawrence attempts to justify his instincts by demonstrating the presence of a latent, suppressed, and disguised cave-man philosophy in all the vital part of American literature. That may appear to be an easy task, if you assert, as some critics do, that vital literature in America began with Mr. Dreiser or with Mr. Anderson. But Mr. Lawrence is not so naïve as that, and he scorns an easy victory.

Brushing Mr. Anderson and his contemporaries aside, he pushes boldly into the little, quiet, decorous, classical past of our letters, and, clapping that sturdy storekeeper, Benjamin Franklin, on the back and twirling him around with many a shrewd punch in the midriff, explains just why he doesn't care for the 'old scout'; no artist, too much of a storekeeper, too much cold calculation of profit and loss, a utilitarian—he *'used* venery'; in short, he was no cave-man. 'Oh Benjamin! Oh Binjum! You do not suck me in any longer.'

Next, he seizes upon Hector St. John de Crèvecœur, and explains why, with all his faults, he takes to 'Hector'. The good fellow prated, to be sure, about Nature and the Noble Savage in the perfumed terms of eighteenth-century sentimental illusion; but if you follow 'Hector' closely you discover that he knows a sight more about Nature than he quite dares to admit. He knows that Nature is red in tooth and claw; and he secretly hankers for her fierce wilderness; he deeply, instinctively responds to the 'beauty' of her rending claws and the bright flash of blood on her talons. 'Hector' was a cave-man, all right—a cave-man with one foot in a French *salon*.

In Fenimore Cooper, two men: outside, a simulacrum of a man, a white man, an American citizen, a democrat and equalitarian, inflated by a hobnobbing with European aristocracy, a faithful American husband, the uxorious author of the 'white novels'; inside, a real man, a cave-man, hungry for the untamed wilderness, scornful of the molly-coddledom of domestic ties, projecting the unfulfilled passion of his innermost self into the feigned adventures of the Leatherstocking novels—poetic escape from the vast unendurable humbug of the Founders of the Republic.

Poe—poor Poe! He was not a cave-man; but he was the next best thing to it. He was a dissolvent of the rotting old European ideals by the fierce excess of his attachment to one of them. At the extreme of nervous development away from the large healthy sanity of the cave-man, poor Poe embraced, as his ideal, dissolution in the ecstasy of spiritual union—with a woman. Bah! In *Ligeia*, in *Eleanora*, in *The*

Fall of the House of Usher, Poe unconsciously proved the necessity for the return and revival of cave-man philosophy by demonstrating the ghastly stench of decaying personality which results from the abandonment of it.

'Hawthorne, you little *blue-eyed darling*,' says Mr. Lawrence in effect —the epithet is his—'you were a cave-man; but you fooled them. Your *Scarlet Letter* was conceived in irony, in deep satirical irony, which passed over the heads of your commentators, leaving them blandly unscathed. The *Scarlet Letter* is not a tract on behalf of irretrievable marriage. It is a strange, symbolical, yearning plea of the blue-eyed darling's suppressed hunger for passion, voluptuousness, Oriental richness and colour. "Nathaniel," you were a starved, demure, enigmatic, hypocritical little cave-man, but a cave-man just the same, and an artist by the same token, and among the fantastic arabesques of your cozy little New England cavern you scratched, in spite of yourself and in spite of your cozy little wife, images of the cave-woman that your "blood" desired, tentative sketches of Pearls to come in later years, Pearls who now constitute the necklace of American women of the younger generation, hanging about the arrived young cave-man's neck.'

Dana and Melville Mr. Lawrence clasps to his heart in fraternal embrace. Brothers, they were of his 'blood'. In their youth, at any rate, the heavy chains of intellectualizing, conventionalizing, idealizing New England could not hold them. With wild young lustihood they rushed from the sugary palaver of democracy into the savage tyranny of life before the mast. They recovered the hunter's elemental joy in a 'naked fighting experience' with the deep. They mixed with savage islanders of the southern seas. They cruised under a fanatical captain (i.e., Puritanism) in quest of Moby Dick, the White Whale —here interpreted as 'the deepest *blood-being* of the white race'. But they could not kill it. The White Whale 'got' them; and with a flick of his fantastic omnipotent tail he scattered them in a gorgeous truancy from 'Puritanism' among the dusky, scarlet-hibiscus-garlanded daughters of the South Pacific foam. What though they returned at length to Home and Mother, they were cave-men—in their day.

Finally, Whitman. In him again, two men, one detestable, the other a captain to follow into the unknown. The detestable Whitman is the enamoured democrat, the intoxicated equalitarian, the decadent lustre for the ecstasy of dissolution into union with anything and everything. 'I am he that aches with amorous love', quotes Mr. Lawrence. This, as a popular conception of the ideal state of being, Mr. Lawrence attacks by a critical method, of which this is a characteristic specimen:

[Quotes from *Studies*, Chap. XII, 'What do you make of that? . . . Walter, leave off.' (Heinemann ed., 154.)]

The Whitman that Mr. Lawrence admires as 'the first white aboriginal' is the Whitman that obeys the deep masculine prompting of his blood to the open road, to fresh hunting grounds, to unending expansion of his own self-contained inviolable personality. What he regards as fundamental, as vital, in Whitman is the aristocratic-barbarian, the well-integrated, colossal cave-man, which Whitman, in spite of himself, projected as his suppressed desire into the democratic smoke of the *Leaves of Grass*.

Mr. Lawrence is, as I have almost permitted myself to say, an 'interesting' fellow, perceptive, receptive, inquisitive, sincere, violent, and vengeful. But he is far less of a cave-man than he would have his feminine readers believe. His violence and vengefulness are acquired, deliberately assumed, characteristics. The barbaric harness of the inviolable male personality is not his native integument. It is a coat of thin armour with which he is attempting to protect his excessive sensibility. Throughout those recent novels in which he strives so successfully to make women seem demons, and romantic love a horrible mania, and the entire matter of 'sex-relationships' an abomination— throughout these novels one detects the stridulous note of a sufferer who is recovering by an extravagant emancipation from an equally extravagant subjection to 'the influence of fair persons'.

It may be safely assumed also that his attack upon American intellectualism and idealism proceeds from a reaction for the recovery of his own balance. Indeed, he himself declares flatly against any real reversion to the cave. One of his mystical certainties is that the destiny of the white man points him ever forward into a larger and larger *conscious* self-realization. The actual savage and primitive man is not a model. What we are to rediscover and make room for and respect is the residual but irreducible ultimate savage within the civilized man. Without the deep reminiscent boom of barbaric drums and the wild tinkling of barbaric cymbals our finest orchestral music becomes thin and unsatisfying and disquiets the soul with poignant nostalgia and an ache of inanition.

Out there in New Mexico under sombrero our Americano *pro tempore* has come in the present year of grace to conclusions which

Emerson, Thoreau, and Whitman reached seventy-five or a hundred years ago. The discovery that he has been so long anticipated naturally fills Mr. Lawrence with a lively sense of the high modernity and immense sophistication of our ancient classics. His own special need for cave-man philosophy as a remedy for his surfeit of European romanticism makes him peculiarly keen in his quest of the suppressed cave-man in New England literature. His appreciation of the fine wild things in the American genius is perhaps unequalled by any our native writers except Whitman. His book will doubtless stimulate other explorers to a fresh psychoanalysis of the national spirit. It will probably be welcomed by all our critics of the Party of Nature and condemned by most of our critics of the Party of Culture. As for myself, I have found its curiosity and its sincerity invigorating.

As a critical exhortation to our men of letters, it appears to me to have one rather serious defect: it does not stop to inquire whether at the present moment our novelists are suffering from excessive intellectuality and ideality. Has Mr. Lawrence considered the consequences of that precocity in our 'old folks' which he so eagerly points out? Doesn't it occur to him that while over in England, don't you know, they are recovering from an excess of Tennysonian sweetness and idealism, here in America perhaps we begin to feel the need of recovering from an excess of Whitmanian robustness and realism? Is there any present lack of the coarse full flow of animal life in the channels of our literature to justify his entering 'Macedonia' with his English dredge— as an apostolic measure? I am in some doubt on that point. And as to Mr. Lawrence's latest stylistic vesture, I suspect that our younger *literati* will tell him that this coal-heaver style was quite the thing ten years ago, but that it is now regarded as rather out of date.

KANGAROO

September 1923

60. Unsigned review in
Times Literary Supplement

20 September 1923, 617

We are to presume that Mr. Lawrence has visited Australia, like Richard Somers, through whose eyes he sees in this novel; and he has found a spell and inspiration there. He says that its beauty seems to lurk always just beyond the range of vision; yet the greyness of the bush, the deep fern-world, the radiant sea-shells and unafraid birds are clear in his pages. He has drawn pictures exquisite in colour and suggestion, with words which seem to be a vision-language even more than to be chosen for their own beauty; and when he puts his whole impression in a phrase it has a subtle passionateness:

[Gives two quotations from *Kangaroo*: (1) 'The flimsy hills of Australia . . . bungalows, shacks, corrugated iron and all.' (Penguin ed., Chap. XVIII, p. 381.) (2) '. . . the soft, blue, humanless scene . . . And on the new leaf, nothing'. (Penguin ed., Chap. XVII, p. 365.)]

These are morsels of one permeating atmosphere. You remember the humanless scene almost more than the humans; but Mr. Lawrence comes to us with a tale—the tale of a very few people in Sydney and the country. Somers and his wife are Europeans; William James, the Cornishman, is but half assimilated. But Jack, the young ex-soldier, is wholly Australian—easy, tranquil, indifferent, yet with a dark fire in him that blazes out into instinctive, reckless action. His wife Victoria is instinctive in a more wistful way. Willie Struthers, the Labour leader, is seen twice at crucial instants and often heard of; and then, dominating the action of the book, there is his rival Mr. Cooley, nicknamed 'Kangaroo', the leader of the Diggers; a strange mixture of culture and will, intellect and a deep essential tenderness, whose love of his fellow-men consumes him as a victim in the end, and singes Somers.

But while Mr. Lawrence paints the scene as we should fancy it can never have been painted, and dives deep, it would seem, into the Australian temper—though that must be judged by the Australians— Australia is scarcely the subject of his novel. It is, you must say, about Australia, which supplies the curiously right embodiment; but the essence, if that can be torn from the body, is a drama of thoughts and minds. Man is a thought-adventurer, in Mr. Lawrence's words, and so it is with this novel. It might be called an inquisition into love, not so much the love of man and woman as the love which would save nations and solve evils; and again, the love men trust in as a rhythm of the universe. Must we say that love is always relative to something deeper than itself, as well as to the apartness of individuals? Again, there is the strife between ideals of the spirit, which time has made mechanical, figments of the head, and an unknown force which wells up from below, half-savage, half-creative. The dark God whom Somers feels for in his heart seems now and then remarkably like Moby Dick's white whale. He is a God of fear and aloneness, unrevealed and un-revealable; yet it is love, when love ignores this opposite, that Somers turns from as a strangling white octopus.

To exhibit the two sides of the novel, outer and inner, we have sundered it; but its artistic interest lies in the way they are united. This depends to a great extent on Somers, in whose thoughts, per-ceptions and stray touches we seem to recognize the thinly disguised 'I' of Mr. Lawrence. But he is vividly objectified. Were it not for the consistency with which we see it all through his eyes, the long retro-spect of his war-time experiences would be more distracting than it is, and the odd, whimsical apologues on love and life more interrupting. Mr. Lawrence can be as unscrupulous as Balzac, but he is much wittier; and then he knows when he digresses. Kangaroo is perhaps the weak spot in the book; both in the inner man and in his outer likeness to the national animal he is something of a chimera, though a generous one. But the tense climax of his end and the whole Australian scene fit close to the design. And for that scope and design one may feel gratitude; it shows once more that a novel need not be a mere love-story, but can blend a deep interest of thought with astonishing vividness in externals.

Somers's reflections are by turns dark, illuminating, and dismaying; and they may seem to lead to an inhuman blankness. But the book does not make you angry or leave you, as *Aaron's Rod* did, with a sense of empty desiccation; it is clearly written out of plenitude. The point has its importance when we remember that this is the fourth book of Mr. Lawrence's which has been published this year; if there were less quality in them, such a rate of production would be alarming. But, while his prose is deliberately brusque, he has never been more of an artist in vision and word; he has released his wit and humour, and he seems to be escaping from his obsessions into confidence, if not sereneness. At the same time he is being drawn beyond art into prophecy. Will the ways part, or will he, as in this novel, intriguingly combine them? Here at any rate, in spite of flaws, is a fine book: experimental, masterful, challenging the rules and his readers, yet compelling us to recognize that the form of the novel has been used with strength, diversity and beauty.

Alyse Gregory (Mrs. Isobel Powys-Marks, 1884–1967). Novelist, essayist and critic.

This is a composite review of *Kangaroo, Psychoanalysis and the Unconscious, Fantasia of the Unconscious* and *Studies in Classic American Literature*.

At last Mr. D. H. Lawrence is being acclaimed by critics and public alike as the most significant fiction writer of his generation. And yet in those days when the drugging rhapsody of his words sounded to ears too angry or too insensible to heed he wrote, we believe, his most moving and important prose. Stalking always through his pages with wild intractable glance was the tiger of lust, the tiger of lust that the Anglo-Saxon race had beaten back and back, until it crouched down cowering with only its two unconquerable eyes glimmering out of the darkness. Not, indeed, that sex has not been a theme for poets and philosophers since time immemorial, but Mr. Lawrence, it would appear, was the first writer to embody in artistic form the intimations of psycho-analysis with his own singular and authentic vision. Suddenly those vague conflicts and enmities, those tense wary advances, cold withdrawals, and entombed intimacies between the sexes were revealed and amplified. Henry James could expose with the delicate scalpel of his intellect the nerves of thought underlying complex situations, but Mr. Lawrence ignored thought altogether, hardly acknowledged its existence, and like a man under the spell of some mystical admonition in himself, slipped past every artistic warning down and down until he reached the subsoil of creation itself. In *Sons and Lovers*, in *The Rainbow*, in *Twilight in Italy*, and in a few of his poems Mr. Lawrence is, we believe, at his best. Here his febrile and tortured genius flows richly and turbulently. Every passing stir upon his sensitiveness is passionately or beautifully recorded. The mother-complex in *Sons and*

Lovers is artistically convincing without being obtrusive, the picture of the old miner, his father, done with sharp and restrained veracity, and even if the author himself as the hero seems a trifle priggish, no one could read this book through without feeling in its pages something wholly new and vital in the literature of our day. Perhaps *The Rainbow* is less integrated as a work of art, but it also contains passages of greater beauty, passages in which every seed and flower in the English landscape seem to share that same vibration of life which moves so inscrutably in the frames of men. As animals prey on each other in order to sustain life to which every passing hour is a recurrent threat, so Mr. Lawrence showed us men and women in their obscure destructive combats for empire, in their isolations and irremediable woes and curative returns to the soil.

Not until the appearance of *Women in Love* did we begin to detect the real trend of his developing philosophy. And then what a sorry— what a very pitiful and unexpected spectacle met our startled eyes! The very tiger that he had loosed so magically with his own hands, the tiger of sex was slowly turning and driving him back, inch by inch, into the hermetic cell of dogma. Birkin and Gerald are but two aspects of Mr. Lawrence himself, just as Gudrun and Ursula are animated dolls set up to play off his theories one against the other. Gerald must be destroyed by Gudrun because he has sunk all his capital in sex and thereby lost his power to dominate her. Birkin struggles to find his necessary *manly* connection with the outside world while Ursula seeks to imprison him for ever in the stultifying circle of their intimacy. Only the feverish Hermione in spite of artistic distortion has reality; and perhaps Mr. and Mrs. Crich, who are presented with that narrowed percipient power of Lawrence's for probing straight through to the essential and mute differences between certain associated couples.

If *Women in Love* left us with a residue of doubt in our minds *The Lost Girl* corroborated our worst fears and in spite of some lovely passages toward the end of the book it is as a whole boring and unconvincing, a shell of the Lawrence we have honoured. And *Aaron's Rod* continues the disillusion. Here Birkin and Gerald are replaced by Aaron and Lilly. It is Lawrence hypnotizing himself, ceding his ground step by step to the avenging tiger, scattering his messages through the pages as would a prisoner about to be entombed and already beginning to lose direct communication with the outside world. Always the *dénouement* is the same. It recurs in *The Ladybird*, in *The Captain's Doll*, in *The Fox*. 'Away, oh women, out of the world of disturbing ideas, of politics, of men's activities! Seek your salvation and ours in the dark caverns of *willing* obedience! Up, men, and assert your power. The only way you can keep your women docile is by seeking out some male purpose greater than sex.' It is as absurd to think of a clever English girl like Alvina Houghton submerging herself for ever in her Italian husband as for March in *The Fox*, an eager, intelligent, modern young woman, once clear of the fog of sensuous desire, submitting her soul to the limited, murdering bully she married.

It is not, however, until Mr. Lawrence steps clean out of the field of fiction into that of metaphysics that he delivers himself over completely into our hands. But perhaps if, as Mr. Bertrand Russell says, 'Metaphysics is the attempt to conceive the world as a whole by means of thought', Mr. Lawrence cannot even be termed a metaphysician; for it is rather with the 'brutish sting' of his inflamed sensibilities than with the pen of reflection that he traces his manifestos and slips with them into that exalted area where are usually assembled the most profound and imaginative minds of the day—scientists, poets, philosophers. Yet it is hardly a case of slipping, either. For not reverently, with no deprecatory bow, no indeed, but with one great whirling leap in hobnailed boots Mr. Lawrence lands squarely on his two feet in the midst of this grave and eclectic company, apparently oblivious to the fact that he is not alone in the universe. It is hardly necessary to say that from the pens of mystics have come truths beautiful and eternal, and science is forever resolving the world for us into new and liberating shapes and sequences. But it is, we feel, when these two aspects of insight are artistically fused that the greatest literature is written. In Mr. Lawrence's *Psychoanalysis and the Unconscious*, and *Fantasia of the Unconscious* there is neither the exquisite intimate discovery of a poet like Blake nor the passionless appeal to intellect that one demands from a scientific statement. There is only Mr. Lawrence looking about him with slightly dilated and belligerent eyes. And really what a comic picture he presents in his new rôle of spiritual leader to mankind: this bearded, fox-eyed, irascible prophet with a thundering Jehovah-complex turning suddenly full blast upon the rapt and fluttering procession of women who have flocked with such unprotesting reverence at his temperamental and erratic heels and in stentorian tones crying out, 'And so, men, drive your wives, beat them out of their self-consciousness and their soft smarminess and good, lovely ideas of themselves.' To try to understand the divagations and recoils of Mr. Lawrence's logic in its eccentric movements is as difficult as to follow the zig-zag flight of a snipe disturbed on a frosty morning. He is one of those very familiar writers on the complexities of sex, who, starting with the assertion that men and women are forever and ever *ad infinitum* different—mentally, morally, biologically different—and can never therefore hope by the barest possibility to understand each other, forthwith proceeds to devote endless pages to instructing this mysterious other sex as to its own secret desires.

He cries out pugnaciously that man is alone, alone, alone, forever isolate and adrift upon this planet and then hems him in on all sides with dangerous currents, 'dynamic flows', 'blood polarities', each with subtle and puissant commands upon his balance.

He disposes of Freud's *Interpretation of Dreams* as 'insulting to the integrity of the human soul' and in its place sets up another of his own which may be pleasing to the soul, but certainly pays small attention to the reason.

Of course, it would be impossible for Mr. Lawrence to write a book without saying many shrewd and illuminating things, but in this case they are vitiated at the root by his obsession to attain security and control in the sexual relation. 'Ah, how good it is to come home to your wife when she believes in you and submits to your purpose that is beyond her', he writes. Is his sarcastic disdain when alluding to American women either to be deplored or wondered at under the circumstances? Nobody, least of all Mr. Lawrence, likes his most tender and intimate desires to be greeted with airy laughter.

In *Studies in Classic American Literature* we see this versatile Englishman in still another attire, that of interpretive critic of literature. Like some of the scientists he takes such pleasure in deriding he has always a new thesis up his sleeve, or rather the old thesis in some new form. America is, as it were, suffering from a father complex. She ran away, bolted, in fact, from the domination of Europe, only to find herself unable to establish a separate life of her own. Her strident assertions of a new freedom are but hysterical cries with which she seeks to quiet her unassuageable tension and fear, for underneath smoulders always a secret rebellion against her ancient masters. Slaves on the one hand—slaves perishing for the need of a despot—and on the other a few self-tortured and deluded idealists, idealists driven up into the arid air of false sentiment, denying the deep voice of their own subconscious knowledge and predilections—here we have the great New World according to our distinguished visitor. The very concept of democracy is created for the sole purpose of undermining the European spirit, of breaking the spell of the old mastery, and once this is accomplished American democracy will evaporate into thin air and American life will begin; the old fear will be replaced by a new mastery, the mastery of a deep native, *individual* soul. Such is Mr. Lawrence's main theme which he buffets from page to page as an excited school boy might bat at an evasive and recalcitrant baseball, emitting strange guttural noises the while which we are, it is supposed, to understand as the 'real, right' American vernacular. A veritable Babe Ruth of literature, indeed, in the matter of vigour and 'bully' hits, dashing muscularly forward and returning with swinging strides to his home base.

Benjamin Franklin was the arch rationalizer. It was he who set up 'the first dummy American', invented a list of virtues 'which he trotted inside like a grey nag in a paddock'. He is the *practical* type of American, while Crèvecoeur, on the other hand, is the emotional, the first of his countrymen to transcribe with veracity the savagery and strangeness of the animal life about him, a savagery which the upper levels of his mind refused to accept and so subverted into spurious idealism. Here according to Mr. Lawrence is the typical American artist whose real insights are forever being betrayed by the falseness of existing ethics. But perhaps this dualism remarked by the author is even more clearly illustrated in the case of Fenimore Cooper's *Deerslayer*, where the hunter says 'Hurt nothing unless you are forced to' and yet exults in the hunt and exists only by killing. For, says Mr. Lawrence, 'Idealism in America is a sort of by-play. The essential American soul is hard, isolate, stoic, and a killer. It has never yet melted.' And so with a chance cunning he thrusts his finger straight through the flimsy draperies of our public pretences and touches the sharp and jagged blade beneath. For can any one deny that this is not true of America? Do we not see it exemplified in the figure of Woodrow Wilson, also alluded to by the author? What other country could have raised to such absolute power a person so rational, sanctimonious, and soft-spoken on the surface, and so impenetrable, so secretly implacable at the centre? And is not the same division to be found in our institutions? In our administration of justice, in business, even in our theatres? A callous unassailable hardness beneath, and on the surface a thousand assurances of justice and goodwill.

In writing of Edgar Allan Poe Mr. Lawrence connects his lively theories about sex with his no less active interpretation of America to the great detriment of the author of *Ligeia*. But what a light one gets on his own limitations when he tells us that *The Fall of the House of Usher* is 'an overdone vulgar fantasy' and that Poe's 'so-called' style is false and meretricious.

Perhaps in the end what emerges from this book as most interesting, most significant, is the indestructibility of man's craving for worship. Tear his illusions from him one by one; show him the very earth upon which he exists as insignificant in the whole scheme of the universe; attack his gods as mere distortions of his own obscure instincts calling up to him through strange labyrinthian passages; then lead him stealthily down, step by step, until he is brought face to face with the origin of these instincts which rise like poisonous vapours from his own imperishable egoism. And what does he do? He falls down upon his knees and worships! From a subman he raises up a superman and unweary of the old game puts into his mouth an entire new morality, a new morality with which once more to ensnare the human race, or at least that unfortunate half of the human race who because of their sex have been long accustomed to the manipulation of such adroit and artful traps.

One wishes that one might close here and cancel forever from one's mind the memory of Mr. Lawrence's latest novel, *Kangaroo*. Would that he himself had remained uncorrupted by the disease of ideology which so exasperates him in others and in the throes of which he likewise now lies prostrate. When we read sentences such as the following we find it hardly possible to believe that their author is one of the most established in the Anglo-Saxon world of letters and has already, if we remember correctly, published sixteen or more books including plays, novels, essays, short stories, and poems.

'His presence was so warm. You felt you were cuddled cosily, like a child in his breast—that your feet were nestling on his ample, beautiful "tummy".' [Or] 'I am sorry to have to stand, a sorry sight, preening my wings on the brink of the ointment pot, thought Richard. But from this vantage point let me preach to myself. He preached and the record was taken down for this gramophone of a novel.'

Surely such expressions as these, and there are many of them, are unpardonable when coming from an artist who expects serious consideration from even the most lenient critics. In bartering with the little tin gods which perform so nimbly and obediently for Mr. H. G. Wells Mr. Lawrence's eyes have become glazed and his ears dulled. In spite of his vigorous honesty and his insight he has not the kind of background or information that could justify even so fragmentary a venture into the fields of sociology, economics, or psychology. Nor has he those temperamental qualities of reverence and detachment which are necessary if a fact, most delicate and evasive of all things in life, is to be convincingly established and lucidly interpreted. But though the construction of *Kangaroo* is bad, the characters unreal, the dialogue and reflections vulgar and wearying beyond belief, we are every now and then reminded by a passing phrase that Mr. Lawrence is still living and still potential. And even if he should never write a sentence again penetrated with that quality of mobile response to the savage and destructive beauty of life at its foundation which has been so uniquely his gift to our literature, but should turn gradually into an inflammable and churlish fanatic whom everyone hastens for the sake of peace to placate, we shall still continue to revere and respect him. For have we not, to balance against his worst literary indecorums, certain other transcendently revealing pages; and to have written even two books and a few poems that contain flashes of pure genius, that most sacred of all gifts which life has to offer, is to have done more than enough to justify the acclaim he has received in a disoriented age with many bogies and few gods.

BIRDS, BEASTS AND FLOWERS

October 1923

62. Unsigned review in *Times Literary Supplement*

13 December 1923, 864

This review also discusses *Love Poems*.

There often seem to be two people in Mr. Lawrence the writer, individual as he is upon the whole. One is a subtly creative artist of vision who makes us see things by his fine and deep perceptions; the other is a subject of vehement, instinctive feelings, for which he is trying to shape a coherent expression and even—however he dislikes the word—a philosophy. The two sides are definite and arresting in his prose, while his verse, as might be expected, shows more oneness of emotion. To read *Love Poems and Others*, written ten years ago and now reprinted, is to feel this impression confirmed. But until the new book, *Birds, Beasts and Flowers*, we have had no verse from him since his prose struck out new lines; and the point may be worth noticing because his changes have been more than changes of technique. All Mr. Lawrence's qualities seem to be in movement, even if they do not move as one.

The name of this book and the laconic titles of its poems—'Fig', 'Mosquito', 'Elephant', and so on—seem to announce very simply a record of visible things. The blank, free verse in which it is all written suggests an enumeration of what he happens to find. It has a fairly definite and persisting cadence, as well as changes of tone, and it might be called an effective poetic equivalent of Mr. Lawrence's prose rhythms. At times it drops into what is not so much prose as talk, but each poem has its clear ring at the beginning and the close. Attracted, however, by the substance rather than the form, we have at first the entirely pleasing sensation of straying in a demi-Paradise, a subtly chosen and contrasted little 'wonder-Zoo' of plants and animals which have been fascinating to Mr. Lawrence. He can write of a small tortoise as tenderly as Clare does of the 'jetty snail', if more inquisitively. The trapping and death of a beautiful wild creature in a lonely canyon moves him to say:

[Quotes from 'Mountain Lion', 'And I think in this empty world . . . that slim yellow mountain lion!' (*C.P.*, I, 402.)]

This poetry, like all, is very soon found to go far beyond simple perceptions. It is not a question of feelings merely, but of the kind of vision. Everything seen has called up an emotion which images it. The special vividness of these poems lies just in the transforming change which each flower or animal has suffered; reborn in the mind, it emerges a new creature. But each is lively with character. So it is with the living candelabrum of the fig-tree, the almond-blossom spraying out of iron; and so with the cyclamens:

[Quotes from 'Sicilian Cyclamens', 'Dawn-rose . . . Yet sub-delighted.' (*C.P.*, I, 311.)]

Whether that has more of intuition or of fantasy, it shows Mr. Lawrence's power of giving back the visible in an image. And the poems draw on other strains. The wit and humour which have appeared in his prose are indulged freely; he is amusing, mocking, and at times decidedly sardonic—at the expense of men rather than nature. Besides his vision of the living things there is a less convincing mixture of the feelings and ideas which sway his interest. All these strains come out with his tortoises, which have so much engaged Mr. Lawrence's attention that he devotes a little cycle of poems to them, making such a portrait of the lonely reptiles as can never have been given in verse before. '*Lui et Elle*', a singular glimpse of the conjugal relations of the parents, huge female and lesser male, ends thus:

[Quotes from '*Lui et Elle*', 'She seems earthily apathetic . . . rows her dull mound along.' (*C.P.*, I, 361–2.)]

Mr. Lawrence's championship of the male and his reading of the sexual moment in the poem which follows are both characteristic. He has lit up in this book the deeps and the sharp edge of instinct: the strangeness of nature, and yet the commensalism of men and things.

But then there are also stresses of his own, more subjective than imaginative: comments, arguments, assertions which belong to opinion rather than to poetry. The form is not united because his spirit wavers, denying us complete refreshment and the full satisfaction of beauty. But we fancy Mr. Lawrence has done what he meant to do, which was less than this. He has made something which has an exhilarating fascination, without quitting the level where he can give racy utterance to his thoughts and without attempting the heights of emotion. One poem, however, does stand out from all the others because it has taken a higher pitch and kept it on the whole. By a pleasing extension of the natural he has inserted four poems on the Evangelistic Beasts or emblems. The one from which we quote is of 'Matthew the man', drawn to the Uplifted:

[Quotes from 'St. Matthew', 'So I will be lifted up, Saviour . . . life horizontal and ceaseless', and 'I am Matthew, the Man . . . So be it.' (*C.P.*, I, 321 and 323.)]

Mr. Lawrence falls a victim once to a jarring triviality:

> And at evening I must leave off my wings of the spirit
> As I leave off my braces.

Yet in this curious poem, the movement of which can hardly be conveyed in extracts, he does exercise that more intense and penetrative vision which frees the mind besides rejoicing it.

Coming back to *Love Poems and Others*, we find that this intenser kind of music sweeps us along. Mr. Lawrence conceals neither the stings of love nor the bewildering smarts of life, but he makes them beautiful. That is not merely because he shows himself a melodist in rhyme and metre, although compared with the free verse of the other book this verse has its music of precision. It is rather because in almost every poem he has gone to the heart of some emotion and rendered it with a deep and clear sincerity. The tone is comprehensive, ranging from a physical intensity of passion and the poignant mixture of sensation, pity and emotion in 'Cruelty and Love' to the airy magic of 'Kisses in a Train' and the pure melody of 'Song-Day in Autumn'. The dialect poems and his 'Schoolmaster' show versatility without loss of power. Throughout the book that deep-drawn sense which Mr. Lawrence has of the vital rhythm in man and nature is at the core of his poetry. He can show men instinctively as fragments of nature:

[Quotes the following passages: 'Transformations: III Men', 'You who are twisted in grief . . . what are you, oh multiform?' (*C.P.*, I, 73); 'Renascence',

'And now I see the valley . . . she's the giver.' (*C.P.*, I, 38); 'Corot', 'The subtle, steady rush of the whole . . . On all for us to scan.' (unrevised text as in *C.P.*, II, 914–15).]

The spirit and achievement of this book gave it a place of its own among contemporary verse; and noting the sure touch of one piece after another one can hardly doubt that it marks Mr. Lawrence's highest attainment as a poet. Yet if his new book, by comparison, is verse at a lower pressure, it shows, like his later novels, the trace of new and fertile capacities in feeling and thought. They are confused as yet in his verse and they can distract his prose; but if he controls the host of fresh impressions, external and mental, which he is visibly receiving, we should not be surprised to find him writing greater poetry than any he has written.

63. Edwin Muir in *Freeman*

2 January 1924, viii, 404-5

Edwin Muir (1887-1959). Poet, critic, translator.

Mr. Lawrence's genius still burns on wastefully. He has as little command over his resources as he had at the beginning, but his resources,
on the other hand, seem to be inexhaustible. They are richer now
after a decade spent in squandering them than they were when he
started fresh. He goes on like a house on fire, or rather like a conflagration which spreads, and gets brighter—and more unmanageable—
the longer it burns. For a long time now the fire-brigade have stood
in an aesthetic trance, admiring the flames, their water-hoses quite
forgotten in their hands. All the winds of the earth fan the flame: the
sirocco of Italy, balmy breezes from India, a cold wind off the Rockies.
Mr. Lawrence, at the centre of the conflagration, keeps on puffing
lustily and shouting hoarsely to encourage the fire. And it does leap
higher and casts up more smoke and ashes than ever.

There are in this volume more astonishing strokes of natural genius,
and in greater number, than in any other volume of contemporary
poetry; there is not a single good poem. Images come one after another,
newly smelted out of Mr. Lawrence's brain, in their original splendour
and without ornament. Otherwise everything is molten, everything is
in a state of eruption; and when the definite image is shot out it still
has in it some of the heat of the chaos where it was shaped. It has the
violence of a newly-forged thing in which one can still see traces of
the brutal power which clamped it together. It has not decisively *become* something; one still feels in it the torment of becoming. But how
splendid is the power which throws up these flying images in comparison with the effect which they produce! What an uncritical thing a
conflagration is! How wasteful! Mr. Lawrence is one of the most
expensive writers we are likely to see for a long time. He has got into
a state—to change the metaphor—in which he does not seem to care
whether he hits the nail on the head or not as long as he is allowed to

swing the hammer more and more lustily. People admire the curve of his two-handed hammer in the sky, but his work suffers, the aesthetic nail is not driven in. And after a while one can no longer continue to admire uncritically a vast amount of force directed to no definite end.

It is hard to understand how a writer with as much genius as Mr. Lawrence has should be artistically so casual. About life he is not at all casual; he has enough sincerity in the ordinary sense to serve ten writers; but of artistic sincerity he seems to have hardly a trace. I mean the kind of sincerity which makes an artist wait until the object has become completely clear to him, yielding up every outline in what seems perfect rest, and he feels he has passed beyond the possibility of error and can at last set down what he has seen. It is this sincerity, in which the mists between the poet and the object are cleared away and both have unsullied light around them, which translates intuition into art. This makes great poetry of simple lines like

> O they rade on, and farther on,
> And they waded rivers abune the knee,
> And they saw neither sun nor mune,
> But they heard the roaring of the sea,

and Wordsworth's

> My apprehensions come in crowds;
> I dread the rustling of the grass;
> The very shadows of the clouds
> Have power to shake me as they pass.

But set Mr. Lawrence's poetry beside these passages: they hardly seem to be in the same world. That is because, in spite of the intensity of Mr. Lawrence's genius, in some very important direction he is not nearly intense enough. Artistically he is disingenuous; he does not get his effect—he carries it off; hence his arrogance—not really one of his virtues, but the cloak of a mind which is uncritical and is too wide-awake not to know it. But this disingenuousness is precisely what ruins a complete aesthetic enjoyment of his work. It leads him into unaccountable, almost frenzied repetitions. One takes up his poem on the almond tree, and reads:

> Wet almond trees, in the rain
> Like iron sticking grimly out of the earth,

a vivid and satisfying picture. But he has not achieved his effect, and two lines farther on he beats against the unconquered object again, with a variation not at all happy:

Like iron implements, twisted, hideous, out of the earth.

Then a little later he returns to the attack with

Almond trunks curving blackly, iron-dark, climbing the slopes,

then

Black, rusted, iron trunk,

finally

With iron branching blackly, rusted like old, twisting implements.

These lines look more like notes for a poem not begun than passages from a poem completed. A writer with a more complete literary conscience would have waited until all these images had come to rest in his mind, and then discovered the expression that was right. But Mr. Lawrence blindly plunges into his theme, and can not disentangle himself again; finally he relies upon his genius to get him out of the scrape. Often it does, but at an excessive cost. And frequently it does not. Take this passage, and decide if repetition could be more frenzied or more impotent:

[Quotes from 'Figs', 'Folded upon itself, enclosed like any Mohammedan woman . . . and you burst to give up the ghost.' (*C.P.*, I, 283.)]

It is simply one thing, said over and over again, and always with less point, and always without knowing that it has already been said. This is the penalty which Mr. Lawrence must pay for his lack of artistic sincerity.

Or rather it is one of the penalties, for his lack of conscience lays him open to other artistic vices, unsuspected by himself. To sentimentality:

When the tired flower of Florence is in gloom beneath the glowing Brown hills surrounding.

To mere cleverness in the description of bats with

Wings like bits of umbrella.

To raw, prosaic statement in the poem on fishes:

[Quotes from 'Fish', 'No fingers, no hands and feet . . . None.' (*C.P.*, I, 335.)]

which is a mere catalogue of what is not there. To the purely farcical:

> Women I loved and cherished, like my mother.
> Yet I had to tell them to die.

To an unsuitable provincialism, monstrous, incredible, in the poem on St. John:

> Ah, Phœnix, Phœnix,
> John's Eagle!
> You are only known to us now as the badge of an insurance company.

Reading that, one asks in amazement what conceivable concern it can be to anyone what Mr. Lawrence thinks of St. John.

Faults so great as these would be of no importance in a bad book; they are significant only because the book is very good, showing genius in eruption on almost every page. It is true, men will always prefer genius at rest rather than in violent commotion, just as necessarily they prefer form to chaos; but genius in any form whatever is eventually salutary, and even should Mr. Lawrence lose himself—one sincerely hopes he will not—he will not be lost to mankind. His philosophizing, his declamations against Matthew, Mark, Luke, and John are not of much value, for one cannot conceal from oneself that these writers— or whoever it was—had a much surer grasp upon life than Mr. Lawrence has, and that it is a platitude to say that they were almost inconceivably more profound. Mr. Lawrence is, of course, a powerful thinker; he is generally right in what he says; but he is terribly one-sided: he is not merely pleased to see one aspect of the truth; he becomes the personal enemy of all the other aspects. Where he is really great is in the power of his imagination. There are passages of splendid beauty in this volume, even if there is hardly one with rightness of form. These passages confront us with the savage magnificence of nature and give us a sense, vivid as personal experience, of the abundance and roughness of natural life. The description of the lion is glorious:

[Quotes from 'Mountain Lion', 'So, she will never leap up that way again . . . the Lobo dark valley-mouth!' (*C.P.*, I, 402.)]

That would be hard to beat, and Mr. Lawrence equals it very often in this volume.

THE BOY IN THE BUSH

August 1924

64. L. P. Hartley in *Spectator*

13 September 1924, cxxxiii, 364–6

L. P. Hartley (b. 1895). Novelist and critic.
The Boy in the Bush was written in collaboration with M. L. Skinner.

Whether one enjoys reading Mr. Lawrence or not, it is impossible to take him lying down. He sets out to disturb one's complacency, confound one's sense of values, to depress the conscious and exalt the subconscious mind. He has no irony and very little humour; his characters, being always in deadly earnest, are touchy, angry, suspicious, prone to take offence at a word. They would rather be injured than insulted, hated than tolerated, feared than loved. Even to express their habitual state of mind by the passive voice misrepresents them; they cannot compromise, or come to terms, or give ground, or yield, because they feel they would corrupt and betray their essential personality if they made the smallest concession. They are, in fact, in a state of nature towards each other, in a state of war; and their lives which, to the fireside reader, look solitary, poor, nasty, brutish, and short, to them are coldly illumined by a remote glory and pride, the glory and pride of keeping their will intact, of never for a moment doing what they feel they ought, instead of what they know they want, to do. This selfishness has nothing hedonistic or self-seeking about it; it is incomparably above and beyond the tame and squalid desires which centuries of civilization and communal life have grafted upon man; it has to make what it can of these desires, using them for its own purpose, but never letting them get the upper hand. It is a selfishness to be fostered through thick and thin with religious intensity and regardless of appearances.

And yet, paradoxically, no writer makes one feel the force of appearance more keenly than Mr. Lawrence. Jack Grant, afterwards to be the Boy in the Bush, has been sent to Australia to make his way because certain high-spirited pranks at school, and afterwards, have got him into ill-odour and convinced his parents that the Antipodes is the best place for him. We can, if we will, regard him as already a martyr to his ideal of the higher selfishness; but it is much simpler to regard him as a rather tiresome adolescent who had never been properly put in his place as a child. This is the impression his behaviour gives us, an impression in no way altered by Mr. Lawrence's interpretation of that behaviour. The facts of his career show him to be a handsome, self-willed young scapegrace, with a physical attractiveness to women of which he is determined to make the most and which he justifies by identifying it with the law and lord of his being. Mr. Lawrence, more didactic in this novel than ever before, will have it that his hero is in the right, is the one hopeful phenomenon in a generation which never clearly feels or strongly wills because it is corrupted by ease and sympathy and kindliness. He is desirable because he is wild; they are undesirable because they are tame. Wild animals are pure, but tame animals are vicious.

'Forward to the animals!' then, appears to be Mr. Lawrence's slogan. At one point it looked as though the whole of his hero's troubles would have been solved by his becoming a naturalized Turk. He wanted two or more wives and he wanted unquestioning obedience. 'You won't oppose me when there's anything I want to do, will you?' he almost plaintively demands of Monica, who, already the mistress of two men, might be expected to be complaisant to a third. 'What's the good of keeping your virginity!' later he urges Mary. 'It's really mine ... You will come with me to the North West and be my other wife.' Mary declines, and charges Jack with want of feeling in thus pressing his suit. 'I don't care about feelings,' he characteristically replies. 'They're what people have because they feel they ought to have them. But I know my own real feeling. I don't care about your feelings.' Following this rebuff Mr. Lawrence gives a page of Jack's indignant musings. 'Why, Mary ought to go down on her knees before the honour, if I want to take her,' he assures himself. But this mood passes too, and like Whitman, he sighs for the companionship and outlook of animals. 'Vision is no good. It is no good seeing any more. And words are no good. It is useless to talk. We must communicate with the arrows of sightless, wordless knowledge, as Jack communicated with his horse, by a pressure of the thigh and knees.'

But the greater part of *The Boy in the Bush* is articulated clearly enough, and what do Mr. Lawrence and Miss Skinner mean by it? In none of his earlier novels has Mr. Lawrence come out into the open as he has in this. Once the subconscious peered darkly forth from a jungle of metaphor; it was a beast in the jungle, always prowling but always screened by metaphor. Now it has been taken out, stuffed, and set up to be worshipped. It has a likeness to the God of the Old Testament, Jack says, and he will be an Abraham to this god, migratory, polygamous and patriarchal. This is the practical outcome of Mr. Lawrence's theories, the kind of life that, if applied, they would result in. And we cannot shirk the practical issue, because his unremitting didacticism forces it upon us. In his earlier books, in *Women in Love*, for instance, chaotic and difficult as it was, the persistent anger and sense of isolation under which the characters laboured was unformulated and inseparable from them. One could interpret their inward uneasiness the way one chose, as mysticism or as extreme individualism. It was the rich, sombre accompaniment to a theme that dealt with real relationships: Gudrun and Ursula, Gerald and Birkin were stars of the first magnitude, influencing and influenced by each other. But Jack Grant is the study of a man whose essential self-sufficiency allowed of no such reactions. He is real; the rest are puppets. Women have a prescriptive right to nonentity. 'All women were only parts of some whole, when they were by themselves.' One must live one's own life. 'Ay, if one could wash off one's associations! If one could be alone in the world!' But how is life conceivable apart from its associations? The weakness of *The Boy in the Bush* lies in the fact that Grant's sensory perceptions, being dulled and preoccupied, no longer record impressions with Mr. Lawrence's old vividness; and the impressions are constantly devitalized by the application of moral judgments. And, after Bishop Berkeley's verdict upon the nature of reality has been so heartily endorsed, we feel there is a cynicism in allowing Jack to take in pure observation any interest at all. Lovers of Mr. Lawrence's peculiar quality will find much to delight and to stimulate them, but on the whole the book is disappointing. Hasty, ragged, over-emphatic writing spoils the beauty of the details, and the imposed, rigid philosophical system crushes out the substance.

65. John Franklin in *New Statesman*

27 September 1924, xxiii, 706–7

But surely, if he is a 'genius', he wouldn't go on drowning his gift in these turbid floods of semi-mystical nonsense? After all, he has been writing for some time, and, if his power is an authentic power, some serenity ought to have emerged by now out of this lava-flow of dark gods, red earth, lumbar ganglia and dangerous thighs. The good bits of description are mere islands in the mess, unconnected. We are tired of listening for the ring of true achievement. Now and then comes a note we love, but it dies into nothing more significant than the hiss of the lava-stream or the maddening thud of tom-toms in a tropical night.

So might a sympathetic but baffled admirer of Mr. Lawrence speak. Let him go on; there is some sense in this, if not the final truth of criticism.

Disappointment again; and not because *The Boy in the Bush* is in collaboration. Probably it is a case of writing over, as the Elizabethans wrote over old plays, the original being a framework of facts and incidents, some story of the settling of Western Australia in the '80s. Perhaps indeed the framework helped to keep Mr. Lawrence straight, for he does keep relatively straight until the Skinner element peters out towards the end and he goes off on his hippogriff into the inane. Anyhow, there is much here of Mr. Lawrence at his best, especially towards the beginning—descriptions of raw primitive scenery and colonial life in the early days, queer provincial folk and the monotonous beauty of the bush, and all bathed in that freer, emptier air that he loves so deeply and reproduces so vividly. Admirable is the impression he conveys of looseness, freedom, irresponsibility, with a wonderful harmony between the emotional setting and the details. There is no one like him for giving you the feeling of a family at breakfast, a crowd of rough colonials dancing in a barn, or the smell and colour of gum trees felled and burning. A strange vibration connects him and all living things, manifesting at its best in his dealings with trees and flowers, the whole vegetable kingdom. With men and women disturbing factors enter, so that he cannot create an individual, though he can excite, so that you almost smell it, the sense of male or female. What he knows he knows, but mostly with a knowledge that seems wholly of the senses, with the minimum admixture of the intellect. Yet, when he is relying honestly on this knowledge, it is surprising how wide its range can be and how deep its penetration.

But what remains when this warm quality of descriptive truth, coming and going in patches, has been savoured? Something which, even more here than in earlier books, is unconvincing, whether as a created action existing in its own right or as a set of symbols to translate a vision of the soul's progress. Jack is an English lad, public-school educated, but over-fond of pugilists and horsey men, who is shipped into the rough-and-tumble of Australia. He is put with a family up-country, and soon shows himself as good a man as the colonials. But he can never really mix. Loathing England as dead, a spiritual prison, he comes alive in the virgin bareness of the Antipodean world; yet his proud old English blood cannot liquefy into colonial commonness. Out of this dilemma the real man is born, relying on nothing in heaven or earth but the proud, lonely spark of self deep within him. The family includes two girls, and the spark within him knows that he must possess them both. After a series of exploits—the taming of a dangerous horse, a fight with a kangaroo and a fight with a bully—he is sent up to the never-never land to make good. Two years there harden him into a 'red earth' man, a 'lord of death'. He returns to find his first-choice girl (Monica) seduced by the bully and about to be married off to someone else. He shoots the bully, losing a finger in the fight, marries the girl and takes her off to the gold diggings. Having made his pile he rides back

[Quotes from *The Boy in the Bush*, '. . . with two pistols in his belt . . . and a bandit chief.' (Chap. 24, Penguin ed., 350.)]

In this rig he invites his second-choice girl (Mary), who has relapsed into Aunt Matilda and respectability, to join him and Monica as second wife. He feels 'hard and mischievous' towards 'the dead-certain people of this world':

[Quotes from *The Boy in the Bush*, 'I thought they would know the Lord was with me . . . to drive Him out again.' (Chap. 25, Penguin ed., 379.)]

That is because Mary refuses. Over the manner of his offer to her and over his encounter with a third girl, who thinks there is a lot in the idea of two wives and will join him and Monica later—he riding away on a red stallion, she thundering after on a grey mare—it will be best to draw a veil.

Le Byron de nos jours! Jack is not a created character. His inner growth and the things that happen to him are phantasms, an emanation to which the real Mr. Lawrence stands in much the same relation as the real Lord Byron stands to the pilgrim of eternity. If only he would soberly cultivate his turn for description and leave these cloudy problems of life and death alone!

Thus far the sympathetic doubter, rightly from his standpoint. But the standpoint is inadequate. Let us test rather more closely the two sides of Mr. Lawrence's work; first, the pure manifestation of his power in description, and then its impurer manifestations in reflection and mystico-philosophical exposition.

Take some isolated descriptive passage—the domestic scenes at the beginning of *Aaron's Rod* will do—and consider its emotional quality. It has a peculiarity which may be described as getting inside the skin of the subject. This is felt whenever Mr. Lawrence is speaking with his own authentic voice, and it is felt with such intensity and perfection that to recognize it is to see that a true poetic mind is committing itself simply and completely to the task of interpreting its vision. You may see no significance in the task, but you must admit that the mind engaged in it is one that has burnt its ships, with complete courage and complete honesty. This is the integrity that goes to the very quick of life. And it is no small matter; no other work of this and many preceding days shows it in the same degree. Of what other writer of this generation can we be sure, from the mere sound of his voice, as we are sure of the greatest in the past, and as we are sure here, that what is urgent for expression in him, what he will make words express come what may, is something that satisfies his whole being? To feel this certainty is to know that Mr. Lawrence's power is of the same kind as that of the greatest, that it belongs to the highest order.

But, save for brief snatches (I think, for instance, of the poem called 'Matthew'), it never comes to fruition. There are two angles from which we may approach this question of the nature of first-order work. First, from the point of view of that of the creative mind itself; here what is relevant is, first and foremost, the question, on which I have already touched, as to the degree of integrity. Secondly, there is what may be called the objective side, although in the last analysis the two will be found to coincide; I mean the point of view from which the relevant question is what is the degree of significance, what is the scope and measure of the validity for others, that the work possesses. Now in the case of a first-order work this significance is universal; there is no limit to its validity for others, or only the practical limits imposed by their ability to comprehend it. Thus, the Bible or a first-order Shakespeare play are valid on every level, ranging from that of the aesthete, through that of the plain man who, not merely enjoys, but lives by the surface of the work, to that of the man who comprehends the whole work and lives by it. And in every smallest part of such a work this degree of validity, this universality of significance, is implicit, as the flower is implicit in the seed. The poet's task is, by organizing his isolated acts of power (which are not acts of intellect or of sense alone, but of an experience including and transcending both) to develop an apparatus which will be the final and perfect expression of this significance. What is then expressed will be strictly unstateable in words; the work itself is the only possible expression of that individual experience, and the work is not a statement. But the work has the mysterious power of communicating the experience, which, when comprehended, is received by the reader or listener as a living enlargement of his consciousness. This over-condensed analysis is offered, not as a complete answer to the question what constitutes first-order creative power, but in the hope of indicating what I mean by my claim for Mr. Lawrence; which is that the difference between him and the greatest poets is not that his power is of a different and lower kind from theirs, and that this would be evident when he speaks out of his integrity—if the full pregnancy of his utterance could be brought to fruition. For it would then be clear that he had effected a vital enlargement of our consciousness.

What, then, if I am right, is the difference? It is that, although embarked on the same adventure as the greatest, he does not fully trust his poetic vision. The command on the poet is to master his experience by complete submission to it, and it is as if some flaw deep in Mr. Lawrence forbade him to submit, compelling him, instead of working in faith and humility at the task of building symbols for the shadowing forth of the inexpressible, to argue hotly about that which is outside argument. Personally I find the argument of absorbing interest. That knowledge is not of the head but is sightless and wordless; that we have reached a dead end of human consciousness, where there is no health in us; that the future of humanity depends on our recovering, on our level, the wholeness of the savage or the beast: I am held by Mr. Lawrence's gyrations round this theme because he seems to me to be fumbling with a mass of truth that is urgent and vital for us. Our impatience should properly be directed, not towards the particular terms chosen to express the truth he fumbles after, the darkness, the blood, the sex (in point of fact they often minister to splendid discoveries both of beauty and of truth), but, more generally, to the ever-repeated attempt to express by statement what cannot be stated. It is a perpetual return to a vomit. In short, the point which criticism of Mr. Lawrence must elucidate if it is to be helpful, is not how far his theme is metaphysically or intellectually negligible, but that, just because he is a poet of the first order, he is doing himself and us bitter wrong in straining to express by this method what can only be conveyed by poetic creation. There is even a sort of dishonesty in the wrong, as if this obstinacy were a refusal to face something in himself, which yet would be faced if he had the full confidence in himself and his vision, which he ought to have and which he so arrogantly professes. Out of what manner of weakness does this denial come? That is the question which criticism, recognizing Mr. Lawrence's power for what it is, must try to answer. Meanwhile the symptoms of the weakness are unmistakable; in style, in the endless repetitions hammering at the same point; in matter, in the determination to convince by violence—'I am a dark lord of death, you are carrion'; and these continual excursions into the *outré*, with every extreme of experience no sooner conceived than it is hastily grasped and unnaturally simulated. Clearly, what the psychologists call a compensation process is at work, stunting the growth of the true poetic mind and feverishly protecting the existence of a semi-real personality. Can Mr. Lawrence stop the process? There is every hope, because in the very process it is plain that he knows, as few do, what loyalty, reverence and respect are. He is not merely talking about them. He knows them already, only something prevents the full admission and surrender. 'But, lo, thou requirest truth in the inward parts, and shalt make me to understand wisdom secretly.' His acts are a denial, but something in him knows, in his sense of knowing, what is required of him.

66. Lloyd Morris in
New York Times Book Review

26 October 1924, 9 and 17

Lloyd Morris (1893–1954). Author and critic.

It is extremely unlikely that the two groups of Mr. Lawrence's admirers will find themselves in agreement respecting his latest book, a
novel of Australian life written in collaboration with an Australian
authoress. Those who have found his recent work deficient in the
beauty, power and significance which they discovered in his earlier
stories will probably praise *The Boy in the Bush*. Those of his admirers,
however, who prefer his recent to his earlier stories may perhaps regret
that the novelist in Mr. Lawrence has once again all but silenced the
social theorist. Judged solely in terms of its total effect upon the reader,
The Boy in the Bush is easily the most distinguished piece of fiction
which Mr. Lawrence has given us since *Sons and Lovers*. In it he offers
us a picture, not a clinical diagnosis, of life. And the effect of his picture
is to make us live through the common experiences of which he writes
with a deeper perception of their intensity and intelligibility than life
itself habitually affords us. To say this is merely to imply that Mr.
Lawrence, in his latest novel, has abandoned argument and dogma for
art.

    The Boy in the Bush tells the story of a few years in the life of an
English lad who, sent out by his people to the Western Australia of
forty years ago, joins a family of settlers on the land and lives, works and
grows up among them. Reduced to a bare sentence, the subject would
not seem to promise a novel remarkable for its imaginative scope. Yet
it is precisely this for which *The Boy in the Bush* is remarkable. Like
the settlers about whom he writes, Mr. Lawrence has staked out a claim
to far-reaching spaces and wide tracts of life and he has permitted no
least margin of his extensive territory to escape cultivation. The result
is a novel in which the imagination of distance is everywhere; as in

certain novels of Tolstoy, not only are the horizons illimitable, but the march of time seems of infinite duration, even the richly varied population that passes through the book seems free to wander in a wide and virgin world. It is through this impression of space and distance, of an action constantly extending to far horizons, that Mr. Lawrence has succeeded in suggesting the life of an entire continent. The story which he tells actually involves only a relatively small number of characters, each sharply individualized, but so convincing in their typical truth, so clearly representative of the mass dimly perceived beyond them, that their fortunes and careers seem to illustrate the general fortunes of life.

The experiences with which the novel is concerned are the familar ones of pioneer life on the frontiers of civilization; the conquest of a recalcitrant environment, the necessity for subduing primitive nature to the needs of the race, the gradual evolution of a complicated communal life with its ultimate oppressions upon individual freedom. Against this background of the settlement of the land looms the cycle of common experience as it is exemplified in the fortunes of the central character; youth and its adventures, labour and its discipline, the conflict between the individual and the mass, the struggle for existence, friendships, the passing of the old generation, love, marriage and the birth of children. By its very familiarity and its infinite repetition in the life of the race this common cycle seems to express the very march of life itself, the procession of the generations in their order. When Jack Grant comes out as a youth of eighteen he listens to the tales of the old generation of pioneers, the men and women who arrived in Australia in the early years of the last century. We follow him through his gradual adaptation to the primitive environment of the farmers and ranchers and woodsmen of the interior, through his adventures in the sparsely settled bush where all contact with civilization is lost, and after five years we leave him mature, married and with a growing family, a successful miner in the wilderness of the north.

The theme of the story, in so far as it is explicit in the fortunes of the central character, is the perpetual conflict of which individual life is compact, a conflict viewed by Mr. Lawrence in its three aspects of conflict with environment, with God and with one's self. To make this theme effective, Mr. Lawrence has wisely chosen a central character in certain ways somewhat superior to the general average of his environment. Jack Grant, bred as a child in England, comes out to West Australia with the hope of freedom in a new land, but with the determination not to relax his grasp upon the essentials of a civilized life. He exceeds the people among whom his lot is cast in keenness of intelligence, in sensitiveness of feeling, even in hardihood of body and strength of spirit. His struggle with his environment begins when he discovers that even in a new land, in primitive surroundings, the community tends to subject the individual to constraints, and his reluctance to capitulate pushes him constantly out beyond the settlement into the diminishing frontier. The forces with which Jack Grant finds himself in conflict—environment, God and his own soul—have all the large impersonality of purely natural forces. The God conceived by Jack Grant is the mysterious beckoning spell of the bush which incites the individual on to adventure, to conquest and to freedom. The self with which he struggles is the force of physical desire, which, in conjunction with the claims of the community, operates to restrict his freedom of action, to impede his primitive strength, to bring him into subjection and conformity. The general fact of sex and its influence enters the story in this fashion as a permanent force of nature operating either for good or for evil in the life of the individual. It is not, as it has been too frequently in Mr. Lawrence's recent novels, a hypothesis supporting a study in abnormal psychology.

Mr. Lawrence has been particularly successful in projecting this life of the frontier in all its aspects. Scene after scene brings home the relentless struggle with the soil and the wilderness. Around the character of Jack Grant he has created a group of clearly defined vital figures, each with an individual life extending beyond the immediate circumstances of the story. The whole Ellis family, from the superbly etched old grandmother to the smallest baby, stands out in this fashion. So do the two women who so profoundly affect Jack's existence. So, too, do the innumerable minor characters of whom we have a single glimpse as they are tossed up by the stream of life only to disappear again into the vast spaces of the unconquered continent. Each is a complete portrait, though each is achieved with the greatest economy of means. In his novel Mr. Lawrence has not only re-created an epoch: he has populated a continent. And in the last analysis his great accomplishment has been to give elbow-room to our imaginations in an intensely vital world.

67. Edwin Muir, 'D. H. Lawrence', *Nation*

New York, 11 February 1925, cxx, 148–50

This article was also printed as the second in a series on 'Contemporary Writers' in *Nation and Athenaeum*, 4 July 1925. For Lawrence's reaction see Introduction, pp. 17–18.

Mr. Lawrence's most obviously striking quality as a writer is a kind of splendour, not of the spirit, nor of the mind, but of the senses and the instincts. His spirit is exalted only when it takes fire from his senses; his mind follows the fluctuations of his desires, intellectualizing them, not operating in its own right. But his senses can be set alight by anything natural. They reach far, downwards and upwards, and they drink joy from everything they touch. The sun and moon, the sea, trees, and flowers, animals, sex, instinctive love and hatred—of all these he has written in a new way, and as if he were not their observer but a mystical sharer in their being. They absorb him into themselves while he writes, but having absorbed him they give him all their riches, suffusing his senses, and through them his mind and soul, with a confused magic which is purely of the earth. So it is often difficult in reading him to tell whether his magic is a satisfaction of his being or a bondage; whether he is exercising it or is in its power. His novels produce always a double impression—of a breaking through, and of an imprisonment in the strange and beautiful, but subterranean, realm to which he has broken through. From this subterranean place he sees a far richer world than others do who are content with the light of day. His trees and flowers he seems to see almost from the inside; they have an interior glow and a violence of being which could only be rendered by one who by an unconditional act of imagination entered into their life. Mr. Lawrence's imagination has done this so completely that it has never entirely come out again. There seems nothing natural which it cannot enter into, either in nature or in the instinctive life of men and women. It recoils solely before the things in which the imagination has till now found its chief inspiration: the conscious life of mankind, ordinary relations and problems, the tragedy and comedy of life as we know it. Mr. Lawrence has deepened these for us, but he has also dived beneath them so far that in effect he ignores them. And that is because he is on the side of the instincts, and against all the forms, emasculated or deformed, in which they can be manifested in a civilized society. His view of life is one-sided in a magnificent and obvious way, like the instincts, or like nature.

This one-sidedness, however, is the chief source of his strength as well as of his weakness. It is his identification of himself with nature which gives him that extraordinary knowledge of natural potencies which seems occult to more rational minds. This identification is so close that in describing nature he cannot write merely like one who sees with his eyes and his imagination but rather like one whose whole being, whose blood, lusts, instincts, and senses are ecstatically sharing in the life of the thing described. We smell and touch the objects he describes, and he makes us feel such things as heat and cold, growth and decay, more vividly than any other writer has ever done. His landscapes are vivid not because they are visually clear but because they are intensely apprehended by all the senses together, as if there were between Mr. Lawrence and nature an unspoken masonic understanding. They are peculiarly radiant and full, yet dreamlike, as if they were reflected not in the mind but in the blood.

Even his most rapid descriptions have this dreamlike quality. When in *The Boy in the Bush* Jack Grant rides after the kangaroo we do not see the grey scrub, the grey-white sand, the yellow light as vividly as Mr. Masefield would have made us see them, and Mr. Forster would have given us a clearer impression of movement and flying trees. With Mr. Lawrence, on the other hand, we pass through a very vivid but rather vague experience in which we seem to see something in Jack Grant passing into the landscape, and something in the landscape passing into him. This out and in-flowing communicates to everything a heightened life; the substance of experience is changed as if by alchemy. A communication has been established, a number of potencies have been released, and these alter everything. The horses which follow Ursula Brangwen over the wet field in *The Rainbow* give us the same feeling. They were not visual entities merely, nor are they psychological ideas in Ursula's mind. They are rather instincts which have suddenly become articulate, and which communicate with Ursula through the unconscious language of identification and repulsion—the two great forces which in their many forms Mr. Lawrence has described again

and again in his novels and poems. For this unconscious communication all his characters strive; it is their ecstasy and fulfilment, and the
intellect has hardly any part in it. On this field everything in his novels
happens. He has not deliberately sought it out for description. On the
contrary, it is plainly the realm of consciousness which he can best
describe.

Nature he comprehends mainly through identification: mankind
he comprehends almost as much by repulsion. What he understands in
his characters is not the qualities which make up their personalities
but rather the thing which arouses this unconscious attraction or
repulsion: their natural foundation, healthy or the reverse. He apprehends this exactly and subtly, with an unconscious knowledge which
men in cultivating their intellects have almost lost, and the remaining
remnants of which they distrust. But he trusts this unconscious knowledge more than anything else. The responses of his instincts are not
to him merely phenomena to be judged by the mind; they are truths
whose force is conclusive. What he tells us about his characters is
simply what these responses tell him.

It is difficult to define what that is. But if we were to grant
that the instinctive body of man had an outline of its own, forming a
large and fluctuating envelope surrounding his actual body, then that
would be what Mr. Lawrence habitually describes. Action arises in his
novels when the instinctive field of one character impinges on that of
another, producing something like an electric shock. Two vital
principles are enraged, violated, or glorified by each other, while the
mind looks on and knows its irrelevance. Thus fate in Mr. Lawrence's
novels is woven not by character but by instincts which colour character and sometimes seem independent of it. He has described these as
they have never been described before. He shows them in all their
states: in their insatiability, their almost mystical peace when they are
at rest, their cunning which makes them move crookedly to their goal,
their acrid surrender when they are finally defeated, their wisdom
which is like that of a being of vast experience.

His problem as an artist was to present clearly this drama of the
instincts. In reckoning up his success and failure one must take account
not only of his achievement but of the difficulties of his task. These
were enormous. He had to translate into a conscious thing, language,
states which are fluid and unconscious, and cannot be directly denoted.

He tried to do this by employing a peculiarly telepathic style, a
style which does not render things so much as the feeling of things.

Sometimes merely an unavailing struggle with language, a senselessly repeated assault which does not break through, this style has splendid moments when it sets the object before us in the full glow of its aura. His dialogue is a graph of the movements of the instincts: it does not depict character nor define situation. Like his narrative style, it has an underlying content, suggested by the words but not contained in them; and that is the most important thing. So his characters sometimes say things which as conscious statement are absurd, while as delineation of the unconscious they are true. In *The Rainbow*, for example, Skrebensky's 'heart grew smaller, it began to fuse like a bead. He knew he would die.' But he does not die, he is not even at a supreme crisis in his life; Mr. Lawrence takes him through many more crises of the same kind. Again, in *The Boy in the Bush* Jack Grant

could feel his body, the English cool body of his being, slowly melting down and being invaded by a new tropical quality. Sometimes he said to himself, he was sweating his soul away. That was how it felt: as if he were sweating his soul away. And he let his soul go, let it melt away out of his wet hot body.

Yet in the next sentence there is no sign of this tremendous change. Things like these happen constantly in Mr. Lawrence's novels, and they are bad: they show that he has not found the indisputable form for his thought. But there is a justification in imagination for them; they are true to the workings of the instincts. For the instincts are concerned only, so far as we know, with absolutes. They recognize only things like life and its opposite. For a frustration or an insurmountable obstacle they have only a word like death. And so, in delineating the instincts, it was a fine stroke of imagination to omit the conditional, which only belongs to conscious life, and to set absolute against absolute, life against death, stating both opposites in their full power, and indicating in the fluctuating line through which they flow into each other the line of life. The outline which emerges is not that of life as we know it, but it is something which deeply corresponds to that.

Mr. Lawrence, then, secures his effect thus far, though in a manner which commits him to an almost habitual exaggeration. He shows us the life of the instincts. But he has never shown us an instinct coloured by the personality which it occupies: he has never drawn a complete character. We remember the scenes in his novels; we forget the names of his men and women. We should not know any of them if we were to meet them in the street, as we should know Anna Karenina, or Crevel, or even Soames Forsyte. We never ask ourselves whether they would have done this or that; we have never met people like them, or rather everybody we have met is, at a certain unpredictable level, like them. They are not men and women; they are male and female. They all love in the same way, or at most in two or three ways. Any of them can become one of the others at one of those crises in Mr. Lawrence's novels when everything is dissolved in instinct. Jack Grant is the good, natural man in *The Boy in the Bush*, Easu, the bad; yet Jack is often given Easu's emotions, and becomes Easu when he is directly opposed to him, reaching identification through hatred.

Thus character in Mr. Lawrence's novels is always melting into instinct, and human nature into nature pure and simple. He does outline a struggle, vague and obsessed, between the humanly acquired characteristics of his characters and instinct, but that struggle would be infinitely more moving if the two sides were more equally balanced. He was right in making the struggle vague, for it is vague; it has not the clarity which moralists and theologians have given it. But he was wrong in not stating more impressively the second factor, as essential as the first. In that he shows most clearly his chief limitation: his necessity to be always on one side, and to realize it so intensely that he becomes blind to the other. So he is unfair to everything conscious— to civilization, the mind, character, in all of which art finds so much of its subject-matter. He has written about these in his essays, but he has never brought them into his art. He desires, one sometimes feels, to build up again on the basis of the instincts all that has already been built up, partly on them and partly on other things. He hates the intellect when it is free and working by its own laws, for he wishes it to be an extension, perhaps a sublimation, of the instincts, and to say over again in a different language what they say. So he has little appreciation of the mind, the soul and character, in themselves. He shows us one marvellous province of life, but not, like the great artists, life itself.

The tragedy in his novels is a tragedy not of outward misfortune, nor of personality, but rather of subterranean defeat. The agonized breaking of an instinct against an obstacle too strong for it is a recurring motive. In *England, My England*, the young wife

prayed beside the bed of her child. And like the mother with the seven swords in her breast, slowly her heart of pride and passion died in her breast, bleeding away. Slowly it died, bleeding away, and she turned to the church for comfort, to Jesus, to the Mother of God, but most of all to that great and enduring institution, the Roman Catholic Church. She withdrew into the shadow of the church. She was a mother with three children. But in her soul she died, her heart of pride and passion and desire bled to death, her soul belonged to the church, her body belonged to her duties as a mother.

That is not Mr. Lawrence at his best. I have quoted it because it is rather a melodious echo of a score of other scenes where his extraordinary powers are most clearly shown. It is clear that the tragedy described in it is not fully human for the simple reason that when the unconscious powers of the character are exhausted there is no conscious power left to carry on the struggle. The will is not merely weak and inarticulate, it is in abeyance; it does not come into action. To this tremendous extent the tragedy in Mr. Lawrence's novels fails in significance. It is a tragedy almost purely of nature rather than of human nature; it might befall a lion caged or a tree mutilated as easily as a human being thwarted in his unconscious desires. It is new in literature, it is sometimes very beautiful, but it has not the full significance of human tragedy.

The revolt against the forms of conscious life was in Mr. Lawrence's work at the beginning. It was only formulated intellectually in his later works. But the formulation did not mark a true development; it did not enrich and clarify his art, but rather made it didactic. His vision is not more lucid now than it was in *The Rainbow*; his philosophy is only more set and clear. That philosophy, in other words, has not been fused with his art, it has been arbitrarily imposed upon it. So we have a novel like *Kangaroo*, which is mostly loose discussion, and a tale like *The Captain's Doll*, which is falsified to point a moral. More and more Mr. Lawrence's theories are encroaching on his art, and pushing it out. And this misfortune was bound to happen, simply because his art has never attained clarity in itself, and therefore something possessing clarity had to be set alongside it to illumine it. Through an inner weakness, or that negligence which he dignifies into arrogance, Mr. Lawrence has not brought his art to its perfection; and he theorizes because there is something which he cannot see clearly enough to describe.

There remain his gifts, splendid in their imperfection, thrown recklessly into a dozen books, fulfilling themselves in none. His chief title to greatness is that he has brought a new mode of seeing into literature, a new beauty which is also one of the oldest things in the world. It is the beauty of the ancient instinctive life which civilized man has almost forgotten. Mr. Lawrence has picked up a thread of life left behind by mankind; and at some time it will be woven in with the others, making human life more complete, as all art tends to do. He has written of what he has rediscovered as only a great writer could. Life has come to him fresh from the minting at a time when it seemed to every one either soiled or banal. He has many faults, and many of these are wilful. He has not fulfilled the promise shown in *Sons and Lovers* and *The Rainbow*. He has not submitted himself to any discipline. But if he has not written any completely satisfying work, he has written in almost all his books more greatly than any other English writer of his time. And, what is perhaps most important, he has awakened our minds to the existence of a new realm of consciousness, in which his successors may find riches of supreme value.

ST. MAWR

May 1925

68. Stuart P. Sherman, review, *New York Herald Tribune Books*

14 June 1925, 1–3

The title of this review was 'Lawrence Cultivates His Beard'. It was reprinted in *Critical Woodcuts*, 1926. (The Dr. Collins referred to on p. 251 was the author of *The Doctor Looks at Literature*, London, 1923.)

D. H. Lawrence has been rushing through an evolution. When he first faced the public he was open-faced, clean-shaven and looked at one squarely from big, glowing eyes. Now he resembles a moujik, now he makes himself up to resemble a moujik as much as the heir of all the ages can—a shag of hair across the forehead, eyes alert, defiant, glinting like a squirrel's, snubby nose sniffing the air and a big bush of a beard.

The beard is sacred. It is worn out of respect for the impulses from our 'lower' natures, out of reverence for the Dark Gods which inhabit the Dark Forest of one's own being. As Mr. Lawrence wears the beard it is intended also to suggest and symbolize his isolate and inviolable 'otherness', 'separateness', 'maleness'. He does not insist upon an exclusively male aristocracy. He respects also the isolate 'otherness' of women who attain that form of self-realization. But for himself, he is a conscientious barbarian, a revolutionist in favour of a cultivated, individualistic, aristocratic barbarism. He wants to bring back the beard, and to rebuild the ancient barriers between the naturally and the artificially smooth-faced sexes. I am not sure when he first restored the beard to fiction, but there is a sacred beard in *Kangaroo* and a still more sacred beard in *St. Mawr*—a rather fascinating book, which can be read easily enough but can hardly be taken in, with its full import, unless one has in mind everything that led up to it.

'Who is D. H. Lawrence, who, you think, would interest me?' So, sitting on the lid of cultivated English fiction, wrote Henry James to that able look-out for young talents, Mr. Hugh Walpole, in 1913, on the appearance of Mr. Lawrence's third novel, *Sons and Lovers*. 'Send him and his book along'—he continued, 'by which I simply mean inoculate me, at your convenience . . . so far as I can *be* inoculated.' Next year, in his much-quoted essay on 'The New Novel', James warily circled around Mr. Lawrence three or four times, without actually boarding him, with, I suspect, a dim septuagenarian presentiment that Mr. Lawrence was a power, and, potentially, an intensely hostile power. As he was. As he is. Mr. Lawrence admired *William* James: he wore a beard. Henry James was a smooth master of *bienséances*—smooth-faced and bland as a Roman prelate.

In 1922 Mr. John Macy, who, with characteristic generous enthusiasm, had flung up his cap for *Sons and Lovers*, ranked Mr. Lawrence with Meredith and Hardy, and declared that he knew of no other writer of his generation 'endowed with his great variety of gifts'. In 1923 Dr. Joseph Collins, psychologist and alienist, allured to the task by Mr. Lawrence's obvious interest for the psychoanalyst, avowed that he once had had high hopes of this man, but he added sternly that Lawrence had 'sown in glory and raised in corruption', that his instincts were perverted and that it was a pity the British did not 'annihilate every trace of him'.

In 1924 Mr. Herbert Seligmann carried on the defence in a little monograph, *D. H. Lawrence, An American Interpretation*, of which the main contention, couched in very mixed metaphors, is that Mr. Lawrence is a great genius who is striving to do our Western world good. Mr. Seligmann's expression of this thought is memorable: 'D.H. Lawrence, like a well-tempered chisel or some sharp boring instrument, goes to America's vitals, not to destroy but to strip off the lies and duality and subterfuges that prevent its voice singing out.' One doesn't ordinarily use a 'boring instrument' as a stripping instrument, but when by such an operation one can get 'singing' out of a nation's 'vitals' one shouldn't be too particular.

Something there is discussable and even exciting in Mr. Lawrence. There is much of England and Europe in him, and quite a bit now of Australia and the United States. The World War is in him and a violent individualistic reaction against war and the pressure of mobs and the crush of democracies upon the 'isolate' self; see *Kangaroo*. There is much current emotion and contemporary psychological interpretation of it in him. He appears to possess abundant energy and drive and more and more definiteness of purpose and direction. It is surmised in some quarters that the future is going his way and that he is leading it. Of the little group with the 'bloom' on them, which James discussed a dozen years ago, he seems still as well worth watching as any. If what he will do next cannot be surely predicted, that is a considerable element in our interest.

This much can be said with assurance: his novels do not leave you where they found you. They have designs upon you. They quicken your consciousness, enlarge your capacity for feeling. They invade you, pluck at you, pervade you, stir the centres of emotion, as Mr. Seligmann suggests—or else they produce a reaction of repugnance and send you out slamming the door after you, as Dr. Collins has done. Mr. Lawrence has this token of genius, that he affects readers as Whitman, Hardy and Dostoievsky affect them: He makes flaming disciples, on the one hand, and on the other hand he allures a certain number of temporary devotees, who subsequently shudder away from him as from the brink of a precipice and the roar of chaos. I suspect this second group is composed of those who were first charmed by the luxuriance of natural beauty in his earlier novels and then shocked by the frank insistent association of beauty in his poetry and elsewhere—in *Amores*, 'Tortoises' and *Birds, Beasts and Flowers*—with Alma Venus, the generative and reproductive forces in nature.

For my own part, I came to him in his strenuous and somewhat yeasty middle period, between *The Rainbow*, 1915, and *Kangaroo*, 1923, when he was troubling our censors with things which they were probably incapable of understanding, such as *Women in Love* and *Aaron's Rod*. Though I felt immediately the power and the seriousness of intention in these books and their unfitness for children and censors, I was—by reason of an antecedent inoculation—nearly immune to them, very little stimulated by them till *Studies in Classic American Literature* struck me by its original critical force and interested me in the course of Mr. Lawrence's development. The two books in which I felt most his captivating charm and his substantial power as a novelist were *The White Peacock* and *Sons and Lovers*.

The undebatably potent and enthralling virtue in Mr. Lawrence and the central source, I think, of his power as a writer is his marvellous awareness of life in nature. To a limited extent he responds to the life in people, particularly in deep, vital, inarticulate people. The articulate life of people in society he regards as mainly tedious. But he responds as if there were no barrier between him and the life which pulses in beasts, birds, flowers, clouds, the sea and the spumy star clusters of the Milky Way. Arnold called Wordsworth 'a priest of the wonder and bloom of the world'. It is a beautiful phrase, but it should have been reserved for D. H. Lawrence. Wordsworth was an interpreter of the contemplative *mind*. Wordsworth saturated nature with purely human emotion, he filled the woods with the 'still sad music of humanity', he tinted the skies with a divine benevolence not their own. Mr. Lawrence does not taint the air with human preconceptions or 'pathetic fallacies'. And to reward him for his disinterested adoration of the multitudinous spirit of life, the 'thing in itself', it seems as if life had let him penetrate into intimacies unknown even to those who have made most boast of her confidences.

One might illustrate the point by quoting innumerable lovely things from his record of the bright intoxicating passage of the seasons over the English land. But the question here is not primarily a question of beauty, and not at all a question of conventionally recognized beauties. It is a question of life and the adorableness of life. It is a question of life discovered afresh by a sixth sense, magically rendered, rippling and quivering under the impulse of the *élan vital*. To illustrate Mr. Lawrence's incessant captures of moving life I could ask nothing more conclusive than this:

[Quotes from *The White Peacock*, 'I met George trampling across the yard . . . wrath into the evening sky.' (Pt. 2, Chap. VI. Penguin ed., p. 260.)]

If the reader will pause now and thoughtfully consider the *point of view* from which the phrase 'with a luscious gurgle' was written he will be close to one secret of Mr. Lawrence's incomparably vital interpretations of nature. He sees nature with a vision more intuitive than was possessed by even those 'clear Greek eyes' which Heine envied Goethe for possessing. He looks at nature for nature's sake, acknowledging nothing superior, nothing equal. Nature through the eyes of the old god Pan—fecund, fair and flecked with blood, without sentiment, but passionately urgent. Nature, with humanity standing back, fearful of interruption, holding its breath, not to stir the down, not to hurry the drifting mist, not to mar the pale bloom on blue plums, not to drown the whisper of the grass, not to alarm the thrush moulding the mud of her nest with her breast, not to quicken the little heart of the rabbit palpitating under the brown fur, not to lose the faint tinkle of stubble, not to dim the light in the moth's eye.

The second conspicuous interest of Mr. Lawrence's work he believes is intimately and profoundly related to the first. I refer, in general, to the erotic interest and, in particular, to his searching, exhaustive and exhausting exploration of certain phases of sexual attraction and sexual repulsion, and the bearings of these violent and excessive emotions upon human conduct. Where and how he acquired the psychopathic lore which fills the pages of *The Rainbow*, *Women in Love*, *The Lost Girl*, *Aaron's Rod* and *The Captain's Doll* I shall not here inquire. It is clear that for a dozen years he has been a 'specialist' in that form of violent 'love', which, as he says, is to be regarded rather as a 'duel' than as a 'duet', as a bitter and shattering clash of contending egotism —'wildcats in a red-hot iron cage'. This tract of Mr. Lawrence's labours is before us. It appears to me important to take an intelligent attitude toward it. Whether we wish it or not, Mr. Lawrence's remorseless studies in sex psychology will no more be annihilated by wishing than sex will be annihilated by wishing. These studies are dangerous to the young; sex is dangerous to the young. The men and women in these novels, exclaims Dr. Collins, can be referred to definite abnormal types, easily recognized and named by the psychopathologist. But that supplies no principle for annihilating Mr. Lawrence's novels. Doubtless Dr. Collins has often seen in hospitals or insane asylums men easily recognizable as the type of Orestes or King Lear or Othello. We don't dispose of Othello by saying 'epilepsy', or of King Lear by saying 'senile dementia', or of Orestes by murmuring 'paranoia'. The critical attitude, commendable for young and old, is to recognize Mr. Lawrence's studies of excessive and perverse passion for *what they are*. Classify them, name them, see them clearly, and then these books may be as safe and useful on the shelf as a labelled bottle of carbolic acid.

To adult readers moderately acquainted with European literature, with Tolstoy and Dostoievsky, with Zola and Flaubert and the Goncourts, with Ibsen and Strindberg and with D'Annunzio, there is little that is novel in Mr. Lawrence's representation of the various erotic furies. In *The Triumph of Death*, for example, D'Annunzio worked out for middle-aged people, a generation ago, the entire course of exactly such passions as rage through *The Rainbow* and *Women in Love*. D'Annunzio's sophisticated and megalomaniac poet-hero aspires through sexual excess to a state of the 'soul' which shall 'surpass carnal sensibility and communicate itself to an ultra-sensible element of the inner being'. He is an aristocrat, his mistress is of the peasantry,

STUART P. SHERMAN IN *New York Herald Tribune Books*

and, through her lower animal nature, he hopes to enter into communication with every form of natural life. In a short time, however, he discovers that the central ingredient of his relation to his mistress is hatred—'the mortal hatred of the sexes which is at the bottom of love.' He recites to himself the words of the Preacher: '*Non des mulieri potestatem animae tuae*' ('Give not power over thy soul into the hands of a woman'). He begins to frame for himself a 'male' ideal of physical force, robust health and savage joy. He struggles to assert himself against the woman, and has a premonition that he will never attain complete 'self-realization' except by killing her. And the book ends with the appropriate mortal consummation of sex-antagonism: the two of them roll fighting over a precipice in a last embrace.

Mr. Lawrence's *Women in Love* is, psychologically, identical in most important respects. He introduces this variation in his Alpine scene: Gerald Crich releases the throat of Gudrun, when he has her nearly choked, with this reflection: 'As if he cared about her enough to kill her, to have her life on his hands.'

The story of violent and egotistical loves faithfully, remorselessly told is always, I am inclined to believe, as 'moral' as hell fire or Holy Writ. 'Her guests are in the depths of hell.' And Mr. Lawrence impresses me as a far more austere 'moralist' than D'Annunzio. As I have said elsewhere, my abiding impression from these books of his middle period is a sense of his

studious, remorseless revelation of what a horrible, devouring mania sexual passion may be: how involved with mortal fear, and with cold, probing curiosity, and with murderous hatred. . . . He is coming to the conclusion that —for men, at any rate—passional surrender is not the greatest thing in the world . . . and that the romanticists have all been on the wrong tack in representing as the height of human experience that ecstasy in which one individuality is merged and absorbed in another. This is an aspiration toward death and disintegration, from which the inevitable reaction is disgust. The virtue of a man is to preserve his own integrity and to resist the dissolution of union. 'When he makes the sexual consummation the supreme consummation, even in his secret soul,' says Mr. Lawrence in his *Fantasia of the Unconscious*, 'he falls into the beginnings of despair.'

St Mawr carries on, from there, Mr. Lawrence's 'criticism of life'. It carries on his moving representation of the soul's fiery struggle for independent self-hood, for individuality. In this case the chief protagonists are women. From the first Mr. Lawrence has been a feminist— of a sort. Far back in *The White Peacock* he had spoken with profound insight of Lettie's despairing determination to ignore her own self and to empty her own potentialities into the vessel of another:

[Quotes from *The White Peacock*, 'This peculiar abnegation of self . . . progress of one's life is terrifying.' (Pt. 3, Chap. V. Penguin ed., p. 365.)]

St. Mawr is a shorter novel than Mr. Lawrence is accustomed to write —only 222 pages, unencumbered by dissertations or digressions. Its tempo is much brisker. The narrative moves at a swift canter. The characters are sharply and brilliantly drawn, *so far as is needful for their function, and only so far*. The novel is not a contribution to contemporary 'realism', and should not be so approached. It is a piece of symbolism, which is, however, so well written that, if you are a child, you are at liberty to read it as if it were the story of a horse, of a superb golden stallion, who rears and throws his rider.

But St. Mawr is a symbolical horse as Melville's Moby Dick is a symbolical whale. It is Mr. Lawrence's hobbyhorse. Readers of his *Studies in Classic American Literature* will remember that he interpreted the whale as the subconscious seven-eighths of man's life, what goes on beneath the twinkling surface of intelligence, 'the deepest blood-being of the white race'. The golden stallion has exactly the same significance: he is the deepest instinctive 'blood-consciousness'. It may be noted in passing that the big bay stallion in *Sons and Lovers*, the red Arab mare in *Women in Love* and the horses which thunder ominously through two or three pages of *The Rainbow* are steeds of the same stable. See also Plato's horses.

The characters arrange themselves in a scale beginning with the horse, and *descending*, according to their degrees of 'blood'-potency, to Flora, who is an ordinary woman of the social world. Next to the horse is his own groom, Lewis, who is a dark, silent, shaggy mystical Welshman with a sacred beard; he understands the horse, speaks to him in Welsh and is in perfect sympathy with him. There is a second groom of mixed Mexican and Indian blood; he is almost as sympathetic. Then comes the mother, Mrs. Witt, from Louisiana, inheriting a strain of dark Welsh blood through her grandmother: having exhausted society, despising most of the human animals, including her son-in-law, she admires the horse and shares his spirit. Next comes Lou, the daughter, an American girl, much Europeanized, very sophisticated. At twenty-five she marries an artist, the best thing in sight, handsome, healthy, with a desire for a fashionable success in London. Lou buys St. Mawr for her husband, hoping that he will ride him with effect. The husband,

Rico, has outgrown horses, doesn't like St. Mawr, and the golden stallion has an instinctive repugnance for him. Ill-managed, St. Mawr throws his rider and breaks several of his bones. The last character in the scale is Flora, who after the accident seizes upon Rico, and proposes to buy, castrate and tame the horse. The immediate upshot of the affair is that mother and daughter fall in love with the horse and with the grooms and carry them off to America.

A superb creature, St. Mawr, if one knows how to ride him.

If one has but the merest rudiments of symbol-reading, the main meanings of all this and subsequent developments will be clear enough. The story is excitingly told, independently of its meanings. But it is obvious that this symbolical novel is intended to be mordantly satirical, as well. Mr. Lawrence's first theme is the emancipation of the two American women from the perfunctory type of men, and their adventure in quest of an independent self-hood. His second theme, pervading his entire conception of the tale, is his own profound revulsion from polite tea-table literature, his sense that the English scene is exhausted, his quest for a newer, younger land in which, as George Moore would say, to 'enwomb' a vital art.

The last chapter, in a slackened tempo, pictures the last refuge of Lou and her mother: an abandoned, rat-pestered, goat-ruined ranch in the mountains of the American Southwest. I know what Mr. Lawrence means by that, but I believe in leaving something to the imagination of his readers. To mine, I recommend reading *St. Mawr*, and thinking it over for some time before deciding.

REFLECTIONS ON THE DEATH OF A PORCUPINE
December 1925

69. Edward Sackville West in *New Statesman*
10 July 1926, xxvii, 360–1

Edward Sackville West (1901–65). 5th Baron Sackville. Novelist, musician, literary and music critic.

This is a composite review of *Reflections* and *David*.

The first essay, *The Crown*, in Mr. Lawrence's new book of fantasia, dates from 1915. It was written in the shadow of the author's detestation of the war, which gives it its curious intensity. It was written before Mr. Lawrence had evolved the 'yelling' style that so unfortunately characterizes his later commentaries on Life, Men and Manners. It is long. It is repetitive. It is over-emphatic. These are the qualities which make it so difficult for the reader to listen to Mr. Lawrence; but it is of great importance to try to understand him, for he is one of the few contemporary men of genius.

His physiological mysticism runs straight up against scientific fact, but Mr. Lawrence is a poet and succeeds, on the whole, in 'coming out on the other side' of his blatantly mendacious assertions. His 'Idea', if looked at when the light of our imagination is turned off, appears the merest rubbish; but, the moment we allow our minds to admit and deal in the images he so vividly and poetically provides, communication is made and we understand with our hearts. What this Idea is it is risky to describe in words other than Mr. Lawrence's own; the following quotation gives it as clearly and concisely as any single passage can:

[Quotes from *The Crown*, 'There are the two eternities fighting the fight of Creation . . . are the Crown, the Absolute.' (*Phoenix II*, p. 371.)]

Now, two opposite attitudes are possible in face of such a passage as this. Either we may regard it as pure nonsense, Neanderthal; or else the whole elaborate simile grips our minds and makes us *feel* the relation that the writer is striving to explain. He has done it better for us else-where—in a story called *The Ladybird*, where the agonies of the characters carry this idea over to us more or less implicitly. But it is no good, as Mr. Lawrence says, arguing about it and intellectualizing his imaginative appeal. We must let ourselves understand him, as one understands poetry, and let him 'incite us to an attitude', as Mr. I. A. Richards would say. For the important point, and one with which we feel entirely in sympathy, is that *the religious state of mind is disappearing from Western Europe*, as a result (by no means necessary) of the progress of scientific knowledge:

Without God, without some sort of immortality, not necessarily life-everlasting, but without *something* absolute, we are nothing. Yet now, in our spitefulness of self-frustration, we would rather be nothing than listen to our own being.

Again, Mr. Lawrence writes, 'Your spirit will be like a dead bee in a cell', if you 'set up as absolutes' scientific facts. So, for lack of this religious spirit, this smokeless flame that should burn in every man, modern civilization is decaying *inside its own shell*, wherein it seeks to reform itself, turning and turning upon itself in a vain effort to bring good out of evil. It is only when we have broken the shell that the new shoots of life will spring up and we shall be born again. As Zarathustra, Mr. Lawrence's spiritual father, beautifully said: 'One must still have chaos in one, to be able to bring forth a dancing star.' Christianity has exhausted itself and has died a natural death; it is time that the old gods of Power came back to us—of Power that is not the same as Will, but the force that made Sardanapalus, and Saul, and Cæsar. The sense of values, all but destroyed by (1) Scientific Materialism, (2) the War, must once again be cultivated. The Heroic Idea will reappear.

The first criticism that must leap to the mind on reading this is that such a new world does not, on the present showing, contain much to recompense us for the loss of (1) the Intellect and its pleasures, (2) the affections; though no doubt Mr. Lawrence would retort that neither of these is worth having, both being implicit in what he calls the 'Flux of Corruption'. In for a penny, in for a pound!

The remaining essays in the book, all much shorter, belong to more recent years and exhibit the inequalities already referred to. We cannot but admire the intensity of the writer's conviction and the occasional brilliance of the language in which he expresses it, but he too frequently takes the step which lies between the sublime and the ridiculous. On the subject of the novel he has much to say that is both interesting and original; but, unfortunately, here as elsewhere, strength of feeling leads him, as it often led Swinburne, into vociferation, and our prejudice is aroused at the outset by having our ears assaulted by prose resembling the back-chat of a guttersnipe. A good case can be made out against Tolstoy *the man*, on the ground that his philosophy was unconscious humbug. We may agree that his novels succeed triumphantly in spite of their author's otiose pietism. But there are ways and ways of expressing the attack. This is Mr. Lawrence's way:

[Quotes from *The Novel*, 'And old Leo tries to make out it was all because of the phallic sin . . . a castrated Father!' (*Phoenix II*, p. 417.)]

This is sad stuff, which forfeits the reader's serious attention. What is meant is true enough and worth saying, but this sort of vulgar slang weakens the writer's attack immeasurably. All through these later essays we have the deplorable spectacle of Mr. Lawrence trying to get force by violent methods—screaming and yelling into ears that close instinctively in self-protection. Thus, *Him With His Tail in His Mouth* is rendered mere gibberish, and *Love was once a Little Boy* is not much better, though it contains one purely descriptive passage about a cow that is worth all the commentary that succeeds it. The essay that gives its name to the volume begins with an account of the writer trying to extract porcupine quills from a dog's nose and of his subsequent killing of the porcupine—a magnificent piece of narrative such as only Mr. Lawrence could have written. Perhaps the best thing in the whole volume—indeed, one of the best things its author has ever done, is the description in *The Crown* of a wounded soldier on a pier at the seaside. Here the 'purpose' has become one with the vision and the result is pathetically, terribly beautiful.

Where Mr. Lawrence is at his best, he is the equal of Blake in his finest prophetic mood; at his worst, we seem to hear a street-arab shrieking abuse at someone who has not given him a large enough tip. But—I repeat it—he is one of the few writers of genius now alive and he has almost all the qualities of a great novelist—lyricism, the power of communicating atmosphere, a gift of dialogue, humour (harsh and exultant), ability to portray character. But he has little or no sense of construction and no restraint whatever. This last fault, grave as it is, only vitiates a page or two at a time of his novels; but it frequently renders an entire essay nugatory.

Mr. Lawrence the playwright is a very different subject. It would be hard to beat *David* for sobriety, for the deliberate and well-managed archaism of its diction, for clarity of thought and beauty of detail. The theory on which the play is based is to be found scattered through the pages of the book of essays discussed above. For Mr. Lawrence Saul is a better man than David. He sees in Saul the possessor of that Power, which we of the modern world have lost; but in David he sees the incarnation of Will, as opposed to the blind Power—the cunning, cautious, foxy ability that is the curse of contemporary civilization. Mr. Lawrence would say, with Zarathustra: 'I love all who are like heavy drops falling one by one out of the dark cloud that lowereth over man; they herald the coming of the lightning, and succumb as heralds.' Such was Saul: such is Mr. Lawrence's true aristocrat—the embodiment of the Heroic Idea.

It is interesting to compare this play with another on the same subject, André Gide's *Saül*. M. Gide's conception of the story and its protagonists is a totally different one; he also has his theory, but it is a far more 'literary' one. He makes of Saul a sort of feeble Baron de Charlus, assailed by the demons of neurosis (brought on to the stage), and the interest of the play is frankly erotic. Mr. Lawrence's Jonathan is rather a strong character, a 'lithe stripling', and in his relations with David he takes the ascendant. M. Gide, on the other hand, sees him as a beautiful, fainting, effeminate creature, in a state of hysterical rapture over David's physical strength. The rivalry between Saul and Jonathan for David's affection makes the central theme of the play. There is a shade of affectation in this point of view, which is conspicuously lacking in Mr. Lawrence's austere drama. Sensuously beautiful as are the David-and-Jonathan scenes in *Saül*, yet they do not compare, in subtlety and depth of restrained feeling, with Scenes V and VIII of *David*. Yet we can scarcely imagine the latter play on the stage, whereas *Saül* should be effective enough, with its strange, quasi-modern diction.

Perhaps the best of Mr. Lawrence's play lies in the last two scenes— the abnegation of Saul at the hill of sacrifice, and the scene of the shooting of the arrows and the parting of David and Jonathan. Here the author has cast some of the images, in which he habitually bodies forth his own philosophy, in the biblical mould, and the result is superbly moving. The chorus of prophets and the gradual declension of Saul before the strong voice of the soldier has all the quality of a complex musical crescendo, in which one phrase eventually dominates the whole in a sombre climax.

The final scene is one of great emotional solemnity. To give an idea of the strength and beauty of the prose, one cannot do better than quote a few lines of the last speech of Jonathan:

[Quotes from *David*, 'Thou goest, David! . . . whelp of the lion of Judah!' (Sc. XVI. *Complete Plays*, p. 153.)]

THE PLUMED SERPENT

January 1926

70. Charles Marriott in *Manchester Guardian*

29 January 1926, 9

Signed 'C.M.'

All through Mr. Lawrence's later fiction *Kangaroo, The Ladybird, St. Mawr,* and now this novel of contemporary Mexico, we have the odd feeling that he is looking behind him for something that is really ahead. That the complete unity which he, through his principal characters, desires may have existed at an earlier stage of man's development, and that it has been disturbed by the cultivation of rational or, as he might say, 'monkey-like' faculties, is reasonable enough to believe; but that is only a parallel to the often-observed growth of a foal: fore and hindquarters alternately. When the forequarters are too much in evidence one hopes that the hindquarters will catch up. But whether Mr. Lawrence, or rather Kate, the Irishwoman of forty who represents him in this novel, is right or wrong in holding that 'We must go back to pick up old threads. We must take up the old, broken impulse that will connect us with the mystery of the cosmos again, now we are at the end of our tether', there can be no question that the desired connection with the mystery of the cosmos is the most interesting theme in the world, the dream of every poet, and the effort of every religious person; and when a writer of Mr. Lawrence's imagination and abilities pursues it we have no reason to complain. Particularly when he pursues it through such absorbingly interesting surroundings as in this present novel.

Quite apart from the circumstance that it deals with the attempted revival of an old religion, that of ancient Mexico, this is an intensely religious book. Indeed, it might be compared to the confession of faith of a man who had never heard of any of the orthodox creeds, confirming them in essence while differing from them in statement. What Don Ramón and Cipriano are after is not in any sense a 'new religion', but only an adjustment of the old to capacity. 'So if I want Mexicans to learn the name of Quetzalcoatl,' says Ramón, 'it is because I want them to speak with the tongues of their own blood.' That this involves the banishment of Christianity implies no hostility to Christianity itself; and the chapter in which the figures of Christ and the Virgin are removed from the church to be burnt on an island, a young Catholic priest assisting, in order to leave the church free to Quetzalcoatl, is as sympathetic—one might almost say as reverent—as it is exciting. The idea is that God, as Christ, has ceased to function for the Mexicans and must go back to heaven to be renewed; while His 'brother', Quetzalcoatl, who has been 'resting' since the introduction of Christianity, returns to earth to take up His burden. All the passages treating of the relationship between the two religions are touched with extreme beauty of feeling.

This, however, is anything but a 'novel of ideas'. The people and their surroundings are made extraordinarily real. Kate, who has been twice married, was driven to Mexico by sheer disgust at the mechanical civilization of Europe. Intelligent, courageous, and impatient, but warm-hearted and humorous, she is taken for granted—felt rather than seen—all through the book. Her most unexpected actions or remarks are felt to be in character. By casual meeting she becomes acquainted with Ramón, who is a moral rather than a political reformer, and his less idealistic but passionately loyal supporter Cipriano, General Viedma, who is pure Indian. Half attracted, half repelled by them and their movement, Kate is drawn into it, incidentally saving Ramón's life when he is attacked by assassins, and her union with Cipriano, as a sort of subsidiary deity, fantastic as it is in the telling, seems perfectly natural. From the point of view of characterization the triumph of the book is Juana, Kate's servant, whose groping, undeveloped mind, more animal than human, is presented in its own accents—as if a monkey spoke. The actual writing suffers somewhat from Mr. Lawrence's habit of repetition, as if he were trying to lift prose to the special potency of verse, but the effects produced are remarkably vivid and full of colour. How far the atmosphere is 'like' that of the real Mexico it is impossible to say, but, like that of *Kangaroo*, it produces the effect of truth. The best proof of Mr. Lawrence's genius is that though he returns again and again to the same central idea we have not yet had enough of it, and there is always the exciting feeling that he will presently come face to face with what he has been seeking in the recesses of human nature.

71. L. P. Hartley in *Saturday Review*

30 January 1926, cxli, 129–30

Pity the poor reviewer, confronted by Mr. Lawrence's latest book. Nearly five hundred pages of close print describing how, in Mexico, the Christian religion was ousted by the cult of Quetzalcoatl, the Plumed Serpent to whom the Indians had said their prayers in remote times before the Spanish conquest; how the Irishwoman, Kate Leslie, disgusted with the United States and the 'half-dead' countries of Europe, also suffered a change of heart and married the General, the secular arm of the new religion; and how she and he, under the names of Malintzi and Huitzilopochtli were publicly worshipped, and with Ramón, the high priest of the cult, the reincarnated Quetzalcoatl, formed a species of Christianity and established the worship of the Plumed Serpent as the state religion of Mexico. The cult Quetzalcoatl is highly symbolic, but the narrative is told neither romantically, allegorically nor symbolically; it is a plain realistic account of a supposed contemporary religious revolution, as seen through the eyes of a competent, hard, independent, twice-married widow of forty; a woman, like so many of Mr. Lawrence's characters, without real ties, intensely interested in herself and the attainment of her own happiness. And, again like the majority of Mr. Lawrence's characters, she was very hard to please.

[Quotes from *The Plumed Serpent*, 'She had a strong life-flow of her own . . . until one has flung *oneself* down.' (Chap. XVII. Penguin ed., 264.)]

Kate would have had a short way with her relations, and had they visited her in Mexico she might have found them an oubliette. As it is, she takes a hand in a ferocious stabbing and shooting affray organized by the Catholics to rid themselves of Don Ramón. She is good in a tight corner but without charm, we think, in ordinary life. Her husband, Don Cipriano, a bearded 'almost cocky' little man whom we have met before in Mr. Lawrence's books, has a quality of vitality which does not recommend itself to us as it did to Kate; it is aggressive rather than magnetic. He kills prisoners in cold blood after giving them a lecture couched in prose poetry. Don Ramón, the leader of the movement, is too solemn, feels his godhead too acutely to move easily among human beings; we can respect but cannot like him. The personal issues of the book are dependent on these three characters; and we do not care, except intellectually, what becomes of them. This is a great handicap in reading a long book. Moreover, Mr. Lawrence is no longer interested in the ordinary workaday relations between people. He is obsessed, and his characters are obsessed, by the idea of fusion; they cannot bear to be themselves, yet they cannot bear that anyone else should tamper with or encroach upon them; they forever preserve and lament a kind of spiritual virginity. '*Nec mecum nec sine me vivere possum*' is their cry. And therefore, emotionally, each has a defeatist attitude towards the rest: it is like a game of blind man's buff played by confirmed solipsists. From each emotional contact they try to extract more than it will yield; they strive to approach an absolute approximation, one with the other; and a breath of disagreement is like a blow. The middle register of emotion is almost left out of them; they swing to and fro between ecstasy and hate, getting no solace from the routine work of existence, the daily round, the common task with which the lives of most people are bolstered and kept warm. They are *dépaysés* and *désoeuvrés* even in their own country and at their own work. It is hard to have patience with them and fatiguing to follow relationships which terminate automatically in an impasse.

[Hartley continues by quoting from Lawrence on the need to 'bow and submit in reverence to the gulf' which must always exist between a man and a woman. But novels, says Hartley, are made out of contacts, not separation, and the continual illustration of the failure to hit, even though characters miss each other at the shortest possible range, is monotonous.]

It is a great pity that Mr. Lawrence has tied his characters to this convention (or truth, it may be) of mutual inaccessibility. For his imaginative powers are as great as they ever were, his sensory perceptions are as keen: thanks to the richness of his language and the flexibility of his style he can reach shades of meaning which no one else can. He tears the heart out of Mexico as he tore it out of Australia; his observation never sickens, it can assimilate anything. And the directness of his attack, the bold sure flight of his imagination, is a thing to marvel at. When he deals with people he seems to divide his mind; when he writes of things he multiplies it, as though he had the consciousness of a dozen men at his command. He could describe with equal vividness a volcanic eruption or the fall of a leaf. And he revives

an entire religion, with rites, ethics and beliefs, a tremendous apparatus
of mysticism, and makes it almost credible, in order to prove to himself the possibility of a relationship which he might stumble upon any
time he met two lovers in a lane.

72. Katherine Anne Porter in *New York Herald Tribune Books*

7 March 1926, 1–2

Katherine Anne Porter (b. 1890). Novelist and short-story writer. This review is reprinted in *The Days Before* (New York, 1952).

This book is a confession of faith, a summing up of the mystical philosophy of D. H. Lawrence. Mexico, the Indians, the cult of the Aztec god Quetzalcoatl—the Plumed Serpent—all these are pretexts, symbols made to the measure of his preoccupations. It seems only incidentally a novel, in spite of the perfection of its form; it is a record of a pilgrimage that was, that must have been, a devastating experience. Lawrence went to Mexico in the hope of finding there, among alien people and their mysterious cult, what he had failed to find in his own race or within himself: a centre and a meaning to life. He went to the Indians with the hope of clinching once for all his argument that blood-nodality is the source of communion between man and man, and between man and the implacable gods. He desired to share this nodality, to wring from it the secret of the 'second strength' which gives magic powers to a man. But blood itself stood between him and his desire.

'She had noticed that usually, when an Indian looked at a white man, both stood back from actual contact, from actual meeting of each other's eyes. They left a wide space of neutral territory between them.' . . . This acute flash of insight he gives to Kate Leslie, the Irish woman, the only white person among his chief characters. She carries all the burden of doubt and fear for the author, and is the most valid human being in the book. With all his will, his psycho-analytic equipment, and his curiosity, which is like a steel probe, Lawrence could not cross this neutral territory. These, and his poetic imagination touched to wonder, drive him resistlessly within touching distance. His mind sniffs out delicately, the filaments of his thought are like living nerve-ends, they shudder and are repelled at the nearness of a secret steeped,

268

for him, in cosmic possibilities. He remains a stranger gazing at a mystery he cannot share, and his fancy dilates it to monstrous proportions.

He has confessed somewhere that he was in a raging temper from the moment he passed over the line from the United States to Mexico. He blames this on the vibrations of cruelty and bloodshed in the country, the dark hopelessness that rises from the peasants and the very soil in an almost palpable vapour. He felt that the Mexican motive of existence is hatred. Lawrence is a good hater; he should know hate when he sees it. But it was not altogether an occult effluvium from the earth. His terror came half-way to meet it. A serpent lies coiled in the Indian vitals; their eyes are centreless. He cannot acknowledge blood-kin with them. He gives them a soul and takes it away again; they are dragon worshippers, only half-created; he surmises reptilian ichor in their veins. Yet he loves their beauty, and with all his soul be adores their phallic god; and so he remains a stranger, but makes his obeisance.

The genius of Lawrence lies in his power to create out of his own inner experience, his own sensitized fibres, a personal world which is also our world, peopled with human beings recognizably of our own time and place. His world is a place of complex despair, his tragedies are of the individual temperament in double conflict, against the inner nightmare and the outer unendurable fact. Terror of death and nausea of life, sexual egotism and fear, a bitter will-to-power and an aspiration after mystical apartness, an impotent desire for the act of faith, combine into a senseless widdershins; they spin dizzily on their own centres of sensation, with a sick void at the core.

Lawrence has turned away from this world, these persons, exhausted by their futility. 'Give me the mystery and let the world live again for me,' Kate cried in her own soul. 'And deliver me from man's auto-matism!' This woman is a perfect study of that last upsurge of romantic sex-hunger, disguised as a quest of the spirit, that comes with the grand climacteric. Lawrence identifies her purpose with his own, she repre-sents his effort to touch the darkly burning Indian mystery. It could not happen: he is too involved in preconceptions and simple human pre-judice. His artificial Western mysticism came in collision with the truly occult mind of the Indian, and he suffered an extraordinary shock. He turned soothsayer, and began to interpret by a formula: the result is a fresh myth of the Indian, a deeply emotional conception, but a myth none the less.

For sheer magnificence of writing, Lawrence has surpassed himself.

His style has ripened, softened, there is a melancholy hint of the over-richness of autumn. Who looks for mere phrases from him? He writes by the passage, by the chapter, a prose flexible as a whiplash, uneven and harmonious as breakers rolling upon a beach, and the sound is music. His language rises from the page not in words but in a series of images before the eye: human beings move in vivid landscapes, wrapped in a physical remoteness, yet speaking with a ghostly intimacy, as if you were listening to the secret pulse of their veins.

All of Mexico is here, evoked clearly with the fervour of things remembered out of impressions that filled the mind to bursting. There is no laborious building up of local colour, but an immense and prodigal feeling for the background, for every minute detail seen with the eyes of a poet. He makes you a radiant gift of the place. It is no Rousseau-like jungle of patterned leaves and fruits half concealing impersonally savage beasts. The skies change, the lights and colours, the smells, and feel of the air change with the time of day; the masses of the Indians move with purpose against this shifting landscape; the five chief characters live out a romantic drama of emotions, accompanied by all the commonplaces of every day, of dress, of food, of weather. A nation-wide political and religious movement provides the framework for a picture that does not omit a leaf, a hanging fruit, an animal, a cloud, a mood, of the visible Mexico. Lawrence puts in beside all his own accumulated protests against the things he hates. His grudge against women as opposed to his concept of woman, his loathing of the machine. His contempt for revolution and the poor is arrogant, not aristocratic: but he is plainly proud of his attitude. It is a part of his curiously feline disgust of human contact.

The triumph of this book as a work of art lies in this: that out of his confusions, the divisions of his mind, he has gained by sheer poetic power to a fine order, a mystical truth above his obsessions and debased occult dogma.

[Quotes from *The Plumed Serpent*, 'Mexico pulls you down . . . the roots that reach down, beyond all destruction.' (Chap. IV, Penguin ed., pp. 87-8.) Then follows a paragraph explaining the revival of the Quetzalcoatl religion and 'the old phallic cult'. The review continues:]

And what, in fact, is the conclusion after all this grandiose preparation? The Indians must still be saved by a superior expert tribal Messiah and by means of the same worn-out devices. The living Quetzalcoatl works through the cumbrous machinery of drums, erotic-mystic ritual, ceremonial bloodshed. He is a marvellous study of the priestly pedagogue fired with a fanatic vision of a world saved and standing at his right hand praising his name forever. This is the answer we are given to a great quest for the meaning of life: man is not a god, and he must die. But he may hypnotize himself into momentary forgetfulness by means of ceremonial robes and a chorus of mystic mumblings accompanied by synthesized gesture in praise of his own virility.

The hymns of Quetzalcoatl form a broken cycle through the story, curious interruptions to the muscular power of the prose. There are many beautiful lines: 'And say to thy sorrow, "Ax, thou art cutting me down. Yet did a spark fly out of thy edge and my wound".' Mostly they are booming, hollow phrases, involved as the high sounding nonsense of a sixteenth-century Spanish mystic; their ecstasy follows the pattern of artificial raptures, self-conscious as a group of Gurdjieff's American disciples revolving in a dervish dance.

Altogether Lawrence cannot be freed from the charge of pretentiousness in having invaded a mystery that remained a mystery to him, and in having set down his own personal reactions to a whole race as if they were the inspired truth. His Indians are merely what the Indians might be if they were all D. H. Lawrences. The three characters who act as his mouthpieces are simply good Europeans at bottom—further variations of Lawrence's arch-type, the flayed and suffering human being in full flight from the horrors of a realistic mechanical society, and from the frustrations of sex.

When you have read this book read *Sons and Lovers* again. You will realize the catastrophe that has overtaken Lawrence.

73. Richard Aldington, 'D. H. Lawrence as Poet', *Saturday Review of Literature*

1 May 1926, ii, 749–50

Richard Aldington (1892–1962). Poet and novelist. First met Lawrence in 1914 and remained a life-long friend. Author of several articles and books on Lawrence, the most important of which is *Portrait of A Genius But . . .* (1950).

If a difficult problem were being set for what Mr. Bennett calls the 'young aspirant' in criticism, there could scarcely be found a better topic than Mr. D. H. Lawrence. He is not the sort of man who becomes master of Balliol or an Oracle to thoughtful, cautious *rentiers*. His personality is abrupt, independent, and unreliable. His writings are full of faults and also of possible qualities. You can dislike him irrelevantly, because you have the Anglo-Saxon complex about sexual matters or because you share the pedant's follies about correctness and 'models' or because you hate a man with a red beard. You may like him equally irrelevantly, because you share his lust for metaphysics, or because you think he has a working hypothesis of Love and Hate, or because he was stupidly persecuted during the war. But the point I wish to make about Mr. Lawrence's work in general, and his poetry in particular, is simply this; he is a great artist in words. And he is an artist almost unconsciously, certainly without troubling about it. To me it is a matter of indifference whether Mr. Lawrence's philosophical and psychological notions are accurate and original or not. (Who wants to argue Dante's theology or Tasso's history?) What I seek in poetry is poetry. In some of Mr. Lawrence's free verse I seem to find it.

Like many writers of wayward and independent genius, Mr. Lawrence has been more influenced by contemporaries—often far less gifted—than he or his professed admirers would admit. Take his three salient books of poetry, *Amores, Look! We Have Come Through!* and *Birds, Beasts, and Flowers.* The first is not a little Georgian; the second shows the influence of the Imagists; the third of the modern Americans. A tendency to redundant and merely decorative language in the first book is purged away in the next, which shows a tight discipline, and this is abandoned in turn for a reckless liberty and colloquialism in the last. But, in a larger sense, these are mere accidents of form, and are more interesting to other poets than to the public. The permanent interest of Mr. Lawrence's poetry lies in his essentially poetical way of seeing and feeling. That poetic mind is startlingly present in his novels. Even the preface to the 'M. M.' book contains that marvellous evocation of the Italian hill monastery; even the *Dial* articles gave us the vivid and penetrating dance of the Indians. These things live in one's mind with a special vitality of impression given us only by great poetry. And the wonderful thing is that this is given us, not by some long dead and consecrated master, but by a living man who has passed through the same great events as ourselves, whose work, therefore, has a peculiar poignancy and meaning for us, such as it will never have for the future which can only make up in reverence for prestige what we gain from intimacy and sympathy.

In judging poetry, remember Schlegel's 'Internal excellence is alone decisive', and 'there is no monopoly of poetry for particular ages and nations'. What is it one admires in Mr. Lawrence's poetry? It seems to me he is one of the small number of men who think, feel, and live for themselves, a man intensely alert to the life of the senses and the mind, whose great purpose and pleasure are the explanation of himself and the universe. Add to this the talent for conveying these discoveries in poetic symbols. Mr. Lawrence lives poetically. I don't mean that he dresses a part or is languishing or literary or any of the stock libels of the ignorant; I mean that he apprehends the world directly by images. How useless is the discussion about Mr. Lawrence's 'attitudes', and whether he has taken the wrong or the right philosophical path! *D'abord il faut être poète.* And a poet is the antithesis of the English gentleman, educated or the reverse. In our society, and in all over-organized societies, poetry either droops heavily and wearily or dances and giggles politely, or the poet becomes an outcast. Even Voltaire was an outcast in an unpoetical society. For it is the glory of a poet like Mr. Lawrence that he does not accept a ready-made existence, that he scorns futile social laws, amusements, behaviour, all herd-suggestions, and tastes the dangerous voluptuousness of living.

Take Mr. Lawrence's poems and observe how absolutely free his mind and body are; his revolt against stale, tame lives is perhaps too vehement and scornful, but how comprehensible! See the pallid senses, the cautious, confined spiritual and mental life of our tame intellectuals and *arrivistes*, and then observe the sensual richness, the emotional variety, of Mr. Lawrence. 'Better to see straight on a pound a week, than squint on a million,' said Mr. G. B. Shaw; and better, how much better, to starve and suffer and endure pangs of intolerable pleasure and bitter disappointment and ecstasies for the love of beauty with Lawrence, an outcast, a wanderer, than to live in the dull monotony of comfort. 'The world's good word, the Institute!' All that a man like Lawrence asks of the world is to be left alone; it is all the world can do for him.

Now that ecstasy for life and beauty blows through Mr. Lawrence, as he says, 'like a fine wind', and he has an almost mystic sense of loyalty to his talent:

[Quotes from 'The Song of a Man Who Has Come Through', 'If only I let it bear me, carry me . . . spoil no expression.' (*C.P.*, I, 250.)]

'Sensitive, subtle, delicate', these Mr. Lawrence is indeed in his poetry, though he has other and uglier moods, the worst of which is the poetical equivalent to that little mocking titter of his—a useful thing, though, to keep him hard and unsentimental. Perhaps that sense of mockery has been as valuable as his fearlessness in exploring and expressing a whole country of emotions into which nearly all contemporary English poets are afraid to penetrate. They are eaten up with the disease of self-love and respectability. Mr. Lawrence is a poet as untrammelled as an Elizabethan. To me he seems one of the last authentic voices of the great but decaying English people. Angry revolt against the grey, servile, querulous, futile, base personalities of the world, stabs Mr. Lawrence to almost hysterical denunciation:

[Quotes from 'Hibiscus and Salvia Flowers', 'I long to see its chock-full crowdedness . . . real souls spring up.' (*C.P.*, I, 315.)]

I do not think that Mr. Lawrence is at his best in such passages, but they have a sinister significance for those who understand the meaning of poetry in human life. It should be sinister, at least for modern society to know that its best poets despair of it utterly, as they do. Life, said Marcus Aurelius, may be lived well even in a palace; but in a ruthless, mechanistic commercialism—? If the poetry of D. H. Lawrence is largely a revolt, it is a revolt against a non-human scale of values.

74. T. S. Eliot, from 'The Contemporary Novel' (original English text of 'Le Roman Anglais Contemporain', *La Nouvelle Revue Française*)

1 May 1927, 14ᵉ Année, 669–75

T. S. Eliot (1888–1965). Poet and critic. This is the first of Eliot's published comments on Lawrence. An entry in Virginia Woolf's *A Writer's Diary* (London, 1953, p. 51) for 26 September 1922 summarizes remarks on Lawrence made by 'Tom', who may be T. S. Eliot. Other comments include a letter to the *Nation and Athenaeum*, xlvii, 5 April 1930, p. 11; a review of J. M. Murry's *Son of Woman*, 1931 (see No. 97); passages in *After Strange Gods*, 1934; Foreword to *D. H. Lawrence and Human Existence* by Father William Tiverton, 1951; a reference to *Studies in Classic American Literature* in 'American Literature and the American Language', an address given at Washington University in 1953; and comments in 'To Criticize the Critic' (1961), printed in *To Criticize the Critic and Other Writings*, London, Faber and Faber, 1965, pp. 24–5. Nottingham University also possesses the unpublished MS of a deposition which Eliot was prepared to make, but was never called upon to give, at the *Lady Chatterley's Lover* trial of 1960. The deposition was drawn up by a lawyer, but certain annotations and corrections are in Eliot's own handwriting.

'The Contemporary Novel' was first printed in French under the title, 'Le Roman Anglais Contemporain'. The following passage is an excerpt from Eliot's original English text, recently discovered by Mrs. Valerie Eliot, by whose kind permission it is reprinted here.

[In this article Eliot cites Henry James as the supremely moral novelist, and, using him as a criterion, argues that contemporary novelists in England and

America are devoid of moral concern. In Eliot's view the influence of psycho-analysis has further contributed to a loss of seriousness and of the right, Jamesian, sort of profundity. Lawrence is an example of contemporary false seriousness and of the limited sense of reality to which the novelist may be brought by psychology.]

. . . Mr. Lawrence who, it would seem, is serious if anybody is, is intently occupied with the most 'fundamental' problems. No one, at any rate, would seem to have probed deeper into the problem of sex—the one problem which our contemporaries unanimously agree to be serious. No line of humour, mirth or flippancy ever invades Mr. Lawrence's work; no distraction of politics, theology or art is allowed to entertain us. In the series of splendid and extremely ill-written novels—each one hurled from the press before we have finished reading the last—nothing relieves the monotony of the 'dark passions' which make his Males and Females rend themselves and each other; nothing sustains us except the convincing sincerity of the author. Mr. Lawrence is a demoniac, a natural and unsophisticated demoniac with a gospel. When his characters make love—or perform Mr. Lawrence's equivalent for love-making—and they do nothing else—they not only lose all the amenities, refinements and graces which many centuries have built up in order to make love-making tolerable; they seem to re-ascend the metamorphoses of evolution, passing backward beyond ape and fish to some hideous coition of protoplasm. This search for an explanation of the civilized by the primitive, of the advanced by the retrograde, of the surface by the 'depths' is a modern phenomenon. (I am assuming that Mr. Lawrence's studies are correct, and not merely a projection of Mr. Lawrence's own peculiar form of self-conscious-ness.) But it remains questionable whether the order of genesis, either psychological or biological, is necessarily, for the civilized man, the order of truth. Mr. Lawrence, it is true, has neither faith nor interest in the civilized man, you do not have him there; he has proceeded many paces beyond Rousseau. But even if one is not antagonized by the appalling monotony of Mr. Lawrence's theme, under all its splendid variations, one still turns away with the judgment: 'this is not *my* world, either as it is, or as I should wish it to be'.

Indeed, from the point of view which I have indicated, Mr. Law-rence's series of novels mark, from the early (and I think the best) *Sons and Lovers*, a progressive degeneration in humanity. This degeneration is masked, and to some extent relieved, by Mr. Lawrence's extra-ordinary gifts of sensibility. Mr. Lawrence has a descriptive genius second to no writer living; he can reproduce for you not only the sound, the colour and form, the light and shade, the smell, but all the finer thrills of sensation. What is more, of *detached* and unrelated feelings, in themselves and so far as they go feelings of importance, he has often the most amazing insight. In *Aaron's Rod* there is a passage in which an Italian marquis explains the difficulty of his relations with his wife. You hear the marquis speaking English perfectly, but with a slightly foreign intonation; you follow every rise and fall; it is a living voice. And the situation he describes is one which might occur to anybody, not necessarily a very complex or very highly cultivated person, but which has never been set forth with such accuracy or completeness before. It is revealed. And yet, when you read on, you feel that Mr. Lawrence has not grasped the meaning, that indeed its *meaning*, whatever it might mean for us, is meaningless for Mr. Lawrence. And this is one of the directions in which psychology—not psychology for the psychologists, for that is a science with the right to go where it likes, but psychology in its popular inferences—may have misled the novelist: in suggesting that momentary or partial experience is the standard of reality, that *intensity* is the *only* criterion.

LADY CHATTERLEY'S LOVER

July 1928

75. Unsigned comment, 'Famous Novelist's Shameful Book', *John Bull*

20 October 1928, xliv, 11

There has been brought to our notice within the last few weeks a book which we have no hesitation in describing as the most evil outpouring that has ever besmirched the literature of our country.

The sewers of French pornography would be dragged in vain to find a parallel in beastliness. The creations of muddy-minded perverts, peddled in the back-street bookstalls of Paris are prudish by comparison.

The book is by one of the best known of modern English novelists, Mr. D. H. Lawrence. It is entitled *Lady Chatterley's Lover*.

Mr. Lawrence is a man of genius. As a psychologist he is in the front rank of living writers; as a stylist he stands supreme.

Unfortunately for literature as for himself, Mr. Lawrence has a diseased mind. He is obsessed by sex. We are not aware that he has written any book during his career that has not over-emphasized this side of life.

Now, since he has failed to conquer his obsession, the obsession has conquered him. He can write about nothing else, apparently.

That his works have hitherto contained little that could fairly be called offensive to a broad-minded public is obviously due to certain police powers which enforce a standard of decency on publishers and booksellers.

Mr. Lawrence has surmounted that difficulty by having his latest novel printed and published abroad.

There is no law to prevent a man shutting himself up in an English study and creating a literary cesspool with an English pen on English paper.

Therefore, we do not suggest that Mr. Lawrence slunk out of the country with his shameful inspiration for the more congenial air of, say, Port Said.

He may have written *Lady Chatterley's Lover* in Chelsea. The policeman on his beat would have been powerless to stop him, even had he known what this bearded satyr was up to.

That is by the way. Some months ago Mr. Lawrence found a kindred soul in Florence—the home of Dante—one L. Franceschini, master of a printing shop called the 'Tipografia Giuntina.'

What Lawrence had written Franceschini was prepared to print, Dante or no Dante.

The edition was limited to a thousand copies, and priced in English at two guineas. It was then broadcast to the capitals of the Continent, where it has been snapped up eagerly by degenerate booksellers.

We are informed that the thousand copies of *Lady Chatterley's Lover* have sold like hot cakes, particularly in Paris, and that they are now changing hands at from five to twenty guineas among British decadents.

We would not mind that. If Lawrence-lovers choose to steep their evil minds in the fetid masterpiece of this sex-sodden genius we are indifferent—so long as they don't come near us.

But some of them have seen an opportunity of making a handsome profit out of the obscenity and have succeeded in smuggling considerable numbers over to London.

These are not openly on sale, but may be had at a price, and in secret, from certain booksellers.

One Oxford Street shop which was approached last week denied with a show of indignation that it stocked the novel, but when the customer was leaving he was approached by a salesman who whispered to him that he could get a copy privately and purely as a personal favour if twelve guineas were paid on the spot and no receipt was asked for!

It is not our custom to publish an attack on a man without detailing, more or less explicitly, the offence to which we, as a public newspaper, take exception. This course is impossible in the present instance.

Lady Chatterley's Lover defies reproduction in any manner whatever that would convey to our readers the abysm of filth into which Mr. D. H. Lawrence has descended.

We have said that it is the foulest book in English literature. Though our knowledge of excursions in the lascivious by Oriental writers is limited, we do not hesitate to say that if a search were made through all the literatures of all the ages, as foul a book might be found, but certainly not a fouler.

Mr. Lawrence is a great artist. It is because of this that his book excels in filth. A merely nasty-minded novelist of limited talent could not have written it.

It was created, and created only, out of the turgid vigour of a poisoned genius. We leave it at that.

The circulation in this country of *Lady Chatterley's Lover* must be stopped.

As for Mr. D. H. Lawrence, we have no doubt that he will be ostracized by all except the most degenerate côteries in the literary world.

That there is no law at present under which he may be ostracized more completely and for a good stiff spell, we much regret.

76. J. M. Murry in *Adelphi*

June 1929, ii, 367–70

One thing is certain. No one who reads *Lady Chatterley's Lover* to the end with the responsiveness without which the book is not merely obscene but nonsense as well, will be troubled by its obscenity. He will end by finding quite natural the repetition on a printed page of words which give him a turn when he finds them on the wall of a privy. No ordinary alchemy is demanded for such a transmutation.

Mr. Lawrence, as all the world knows, happens to believe in Sex. He really does believe in it, and now he has reached a point where, on the surface at least, he believes in little else. There are, *apparently*, for him, about two ultimate realities in human life: one, the absolute and utter isolation of the individual, the other, the sole real emergence from that isolation in the perfect sexual fulfilment. When a man feels about sex with that degree of vehemence and conviction, it is quite impossible for him to be obscene in any but the Bow Street meaning.

The story of the book is quite simple; it tells of the discovery of each other by the wife of an aristocratic coal-owner, and her husband's gamekeeper—a man who (like others of Mr. Lawrence's heroes) has passed beyond class-distinction to an individual self-awareness—and of their progress towards the complete sexual fulfilment, which, Mr. Lawrence holds, contains the sole possibility of a new beginning for this worn-out world. As a narrative it is perfectly convincing: the two people are real, and most real precisely where Mr. Lawrence would have them appear most real, namely, in their sexual mating. But in such a narrative a philosophy is implicit; and the philosophy makes us pause. Not that we necessarily disagree with it. It leaves us with a feeling less of its untruth than of its incompleteness.

For the moment we will say that Mr. Lawrence's novel absolutely justifies itself. Rather paradoxically (if its philosophy were taken literally) it is the work of a very conscious man. Mr. Lawrence knows precisely what he is after in using the novel in this way.

[Quotes from *Lady Chatterley's Lover*, 'It is the way our sympathy flows and recoils . . . ostensibly on the side of the angels.' (Chap. 9, Penguin ed., pp. 104–5.)]

That is Mr. Lawrence's defence of himself; and it seems to us unanswerable. In so far as *Lady Chatterley's Lover* causes the tide of our sensitive awareness to flow about the secret places of life—and it does this abundantly—it is not merely justified, but positively good. It is a cleansing book, the bringer of a new 'katharsis'.

But Mr. Lawrence does more than this: and it is the more which gives us pause. He is not content to say that it is right and necessary that men and women should come to a sensitive awareness of the sexual mystery; he goes on to say something much more questionable. He says, in effect, that the only sensitive awareness we need, the only one indeed that is real, is the awareness of and in the sexual mystery. The effect of this insistence is one of monotony, and finally, of almost suffocation. For all its fiery purity *Lady Chatterley's Lover* is a deeply depressing book. Were it not for a few words of unconscious wisdom from Lady Connie towards the end, we could scarcely breathe at all. Her words provoke a reluctant admission from Mellors, which is crucial. We will quote the passage in full. Lady Chatterley has been demanding that they should make a new life together. Mellors has been withdrawing into his old mistrust and aloofness. 'What *is* the point of your existence?' she suddenly asks.

[Quotes from *Lady Chatterley's Lover*, 'I tell you, it's invisible. I don't believe in the world . . . It's our crying need.' (Chap. 18, Penguin ed., p. 290.)]

The Mellors of this dialogue is not far from Mr. Lawrence himself. For all practical purposes they are identical. It shows he must sometimes be asking himself whether he really has 'the courage of his own tenderness'. That tenderness is very great—unique in our generation. Why should it always (as it is in this book) 'be mixed up with a lot of rage'?

And the answer, we think, is this. Mr. Lawrence has the tenderness; but he has *not* got the courage of it. When it comes to having the courage of it, he will have it only where his courage is shocking. When the courage of his tenderness runs together with the current of his rage, then the flood-gates are opened; but not otherwise. What would the world think of him, if he were really to have the courage of his tenderness? God knows, but it might even love him. And that would be terrible. 'Hate me,' he implores, 'and for God's sake let me hate you.'

Probably there is no danger. If Mr. Lawrence really did have the full courage of his tenderness, it is not likely he would be loved. He would be hated rather more. He would become really dangerous, as he ought to be. He would become a leader, which he is not. As it is, he can be disregarded with ease, by those who wish to disregard him. He has chosen to be the prophet of a half-truth. It is the seed of a whole one, but why should they look for the seed? They take Mr. Lawrence at his own declared face value, and they do not trouble even to hate him.

'Sex is the closest of all touch.' True. It is the deepest and most primary touch: to be recognized, to become aware of, and to be obeyed. But is it the only touch? Do I not touch Mr. Lawrence at this moment through his book, even though he hides himself within? Veritably touch him, and closer than by laying my hand upon his arm? And do I not touch other men, long dead, and do they not touch me? Why should I deny them? Mr. Lawrence may, if he wills it so, but why should I? Organic contact is in many modes. In the name of one to deny the others is to impoverish life. Our duty is to see to it that the contact in every mode is organic indeed. We shall not reach a future by cutting ourselves off from the past; we shall only die. The tenderness of which we humans are capable has been painfully learned. Great men have shown us the way, sometimes they have given up their lives to shield the birth of a new tenderness in and through themselves. Mr. Lawrence wants to cheat himself, and us, into believing it was all there at the beginning. But even the sex relation which he would have us learn is not an old one; it is very new. A thousand other touches than the sexual in Mr. Lawrence have shaped it to what it is. To deny the obligation is ungrateful and untrue: worse still, it will prevent his ideal from being realized save in a false and perverted form.

Perhaps a word should be said on the question whether or not this book should be circulated. Certainly it is a book of the utmost value: for all its incompleteness and its still smouldering rage, a positive, living, and creative book. It glows with its own dynamic force, and in it is the courage of a new awareness. But it is no use pretending that all the world is fit to read it. If it were, Mr. Lawrence would have no excuse at all for his still smouldering rage. In a sense, therefore, the point of the book is that the world is not fit for it. If it could be circulated it would not be quite what it is. And it would be quite foolish to work up indignation because it has to creep into England. The necessity is implicit in the book itself.

After all, it is yet another nucleus, among the many which Mr. Lawrence has flung into the world, of a new kind of consciousness, which we believe must some day come. This consciousness will be conscious of many things besides those on which Mr. Lawrence insists; but of those on which he insists it must be conscious. Without this deep 'passional' awareness of which he chiefly has lit and guards the tender flame, the new consciousness can only be a sterile and intellectual thing—a mere combination of new words without vision, without meaning, without life, and without simplicity. In those who know in their depths what Mr. Lawrence is after, the seed he lets fall will grow. Like a growing thing it will push its way even through the denials which Mr. Lawrence himself would still impose upon it. There is no living element in life which it will not incorporate into its own tissue, if it is once received into good ground where it can bring forth thirty, or sixty, or a hundredfold.

That Mr. Lawrence shrinks from completing his own doctrine, and still rejects deliberately what some of us will not and cannot reject, is ultimately of small importance. It takes from his perfection, but not from his significance. On the level of this awareness, our criticism here is largely beside the mark. What Mr. Lawrence has to give is of a kind that completes itself: it is organic. And if our criticism should be used as an excuse for glancing aside the full impact of his latest, his calmest, and his most 'appalling' book, it had better not have been written. Assuredly it was not written for anyone who would abuse it thus.

77. Unsigned review in
Times Literary Supplement
25 February 1932, 130

This review and Nos. 78 and 79 are reviews of the authorized expurgated edition of *Lady Chatterley's Lover* published in England, February 1932, and in U.S.A., September 1932.

It would be idle to pretend that D. H. Lawrence's novel *Lady Chatterley's Lover* has not been emasculated by the omissions that have been made in what is called the 'authorized abridged' edition. That the omissions were inevitable so that the book could be placed on sale in this country without rendering its publisher liable to prosecution is equally undeniable. And, without entering into the difficult general question of art and morals of which this book is an instance, it must be agreed both that it is better to have the bulk of this work available than none of it, and that, in its present form, it does not represent its author's intention. Those who have read Mr. Middleton Murry's *Son of Woman* will remember what he says of this book and of its place in the story of Lawrence's development. No novel by this great writer was simply conceived as a work of art: all were expressions of a stage in that incessant and unfulfilled search for a view, or a manner, of life that should purge it of what seemed to him its deadness. In *Lady Chatterley's Lover* he thought he had found a solution in a mystic of sex-communion which he deliberately expressed in scenes and language which were, literally and intentionally, shameless. Like all Lawrence's solutions, it was imperfect: the very shamelessness was an imperfection, and yet the removal of that imperfection takes half the life out of the work. The asterisks which replace the scenes in question certainly purge these pages of much that might be injurious to immature minds, for which they were never intended; but they sadly weaken the contrast that throughout Lawrence was concerned to draw between the warm fruitfulness of a sexual union in which nothing of feeling or emotion is held back on either side and the cold, selfish unions between men and women that breed bitterness and death in the soul.

Nevertheless, even in this form, whether it strikes the reader as ugly or beautiful, it remains unmistakably the work of a genius. In a sense it is almost wholly painful, for it is inspired with so intense a rage against the unhuman, unloving, sordid and unheroic life of our day. Lawrence observed not only a chill in the relations between men and women, a numbness in their cores which superficial pleasures and money-making could not heal, but also the overlaying of an England robust and whole—aristocratic England—by an industrial growth that was purely mechanical, producing no happiness, nothing but money, pleasure-seeking and discontent.

The plot of this novel is simply that Constance Chatterley, who had married her husband without any strong physical inclination, and who, after the War, continued to live with him although he was half-paralysed, thus gradually drying up in the springs of her life, suddenly fell in love with her husband's keeper, Oliver Mellors, and with him came to realize that 'the old Adam and the old Eve' were the most important things in human life. Mellors, as is well known, stands for Lawrence himself. His is not only a reflection of Lawrence's own sexual life, but his views are Lawrence's. Constance Chatterley, though the dry, contemptuous narration of her married life gives her a kind of individuality, is little more than a complement of Mellors, the ideal female complement which such a man could not resist, however greatly he feared the 'outside Thing' that would make life bitter for them. Clifford Chatterley, on the other hand, is a brilliantly drawn character. He is one of the 'tin people', and at the same time he is the only character that develops as the book proceeds. The changes that take place in him—a man irremediably bruised in body and soul by the War—under the influence of his nurse, Mrs. Bolton, are enough by themselves to illustrate Lawrence's greatness as a novelist, just as certain scenes in the keeper's hut reveal the poetic genius. There is no very marked drama, and the story stops rather than ends; and yet the long letter from Mellors to his love which closes it seems to sum up all that Lawrence then had to say. What he has to say, even at its crudest and harshest, is arresting in expression and noble in intent. Like the Ancient Mariner, he cannot be eluded.

78. V. S. Pritchett in *Fortnightly Review*

1 April 1932, cxxxi, 536–7

V. S. Pritchett (b. 1900). Novelist and critic.

The evils of suppression, as the publication of this 'first authorized British edition' of *Lady Chatterley's Lover* shows, are visited upon the third and fourth generation. Ban a book and the smugglers, pirates and expurgators get to work and become the strange and uninvited allies of those who regard themselves ordained to prevent 'the corruption of public morals'. (One does not know what the phrase means but one remembers that the charge of corrupting the morals of the youth of Athens was the pretext of the murder of Socrates.) And this state of affairs is likely to continue as long as the law is in the hands of a generation far too old to understand the changes in morality, custom and speech which took place in England just before the Great War and are now deeply established; and as long as our demagogues have their natural spiritual allies in the popular press. This press can survive only by the exploitation of news: to clamour for the banning of a book makes a better story by titillating prurient hopes—which the press intends to defraud—than would merely reviewing the book without prejudice or ignoring it on principle. The result is that until this press acquires a moral sense, it will be almost impossible to expect or desire the ban on writers like Lawrence to be lifted.

The popular press, was, however, defrauded of its 'rake off' on *Lady Chatterley's Lover*. Officialdom had already seized the book, had no doubt winked and sniggered over words which are part of every man's vocabulary—without noticeable 'corruption to public morals'—and which shock him when he sees them in black and white as part of the proud heritage of the English tongue. We used not to be so squeamish nor so genteel. D. H. Lawrence may have been mistaken: 'prophetic' writers, as Mr. E. M. Forster reminded us, suspend their sense of humour. His fault, which the future may conceivably hold a virtue in him, was that he tried to rescue these colloquialisms from the dirt into which hatred of life had thrown them, before he was not free of that hatred himself. In straining after the sublime, he overstrained and dropped into the ridiculous. What he and ourselves needed was the humane. The ranting of Lawrence is so frequently indistinguishable, alas, from the ranting of his censors; but his anger is the anger of life against the living dead.

Because of its irrelevant issues censorship has not only made it difficult to see Lawrence whole and to put all these silly charges of pornography in their place, but it has artfully succeeded in making this question seem the most important one. His doctrine is not censored: it is his dramatization of it in his prophetic art which is made to suffer.

This expurgated edition is the final crime against him. One felt a note of regret in the popular press when—the new edition of *Lady Chatterley's Lover* being expurgated—there was nothing to exploit. It was not mentioned that Lawrence's trustees for some reason felt justified in making cuts in the book which he himself refused to make during his lifetime. The result is that what was in the original not very good Lawrence has been deprived of half its point and much of its poetry. A rather ludicrous scene has gone too—sublime and ridiculous together—and what remains is a commonplace story, naïve in characterization, pointless yet flooded with his curious slovenly vitality. It is this vitality which over and over again redeems the preacher in Lawrence, as it redeemed Dickens. The original had bursts of lyrical prose which, in a great degree, transformed the book—but the most important of these have had to go. Beyond this one can say no more for it would be unfair to discuss the book in detail. It is not *Lady Chatterley's Lover* as Lawrence wrote it and it would have been better to have left it unpublished until such time as our guardians recover their sense of proportion. There is a good case to be made, in view of our national temperament, for the suppression of the obvious pornography which is displayed in our chemists' shops; but there is no case for the suppression of serious works and works of art.

79. Henry Hazlitt in *Nation*

New York, 7 September 1932, cxxxv, 214–15

Henry Hazlitt (b. 1894). Editor and author. At the time of this review Hazlitt was literary editor of *Nation* (1930–3).

A few weeks ago, in these pages, Mr. Morris Ernst reviewed impressively the unbroken chain of legal defeats to which the vice-snoopers have been subjected in recent years, and he summed up by remarking:

> Since 1915 the leading vice agency of the United States, the New York Society for the Suppression of Vice, has failed to gain a conviction in a single case where a book was published with an established publisher's imprint, or where the book had been openly sold by the retailers and reviewed by the press.

Against that encouraging record we must set the present edition of *Lady Chatterley's Lover*. It is called, on the paper jacket and on the title page, the 'authorized abridged edition'. And on the jacket there is also printed a statement by Frieda Lawrence, the author's widow, which I quote in full:

> It is a relief to know that you are bringing out the only authorized edition of *Lady Chatterley's Lover* in the United States, after all the expurgated pirated editions. Lawrence considered it his greatest work, and I feel that even in this revised form it has all the beauty of the original edition, and that it suggests to the greatest possible extent the original's strength and vigour.

And that is all. There is no preface, no publisher's note.

When we read the book, what do we find? It is abridged indeed, but the deletions are of only one thing. With complete thoroughness, and with surgical accuracy, the editor has removed every description of the physical act of sex. He has removed every four-letter word to which a censor could possibly object. Even this might be forgivable, if the reader had still been permitted to know at just what points his chastity was being protected from the depraving influence of the original volume. But though the editor occasionally inserts a row of asterisks where whole pages of matter are missing, the reader unfamiliar with the original edition is left to conjecture that these are the editor's asterisks and not the author's. And there is no consistency even in the use of asterisks: whole pages are dropped with no hint of the fact whatever.

It is misleading, then, to call this an 'abridged' edition. The honest word is 'expurgated'. It is doubly misleading for the publishers to print Mrs. Lawrence's statement that this is the only 'authorized' edition 'after all the expurgated pirated editions'. The implication of such a statement is that the present edition is *not* expurgated. And even to call the present volume expurgated would not be enough. It is expurgated and bowdlerized.

Let us see some of the things that have happened to it. The first omission, I believe, is that of the passage describing Connie's first intimacy with Michaelis. The omission of this, and of descriptions of succeeding intimacies, makes Connie's later aversion to Michaelis unintelligible. The omission of every passage describing any of her physical relations with the game-keeper, or her emotions during them, leaves her love for him largely unaccounted for. As the whole story turns upon her love for him, the omission is rather important; this becomes, indeed, a clear case of *Hamlet* with the Prince left out. As for the bowdlerization, one becomes aware of it before the end of Chapter IV. One character remarks:

Me? Oh, intellectually I believe in having a good heart, a lively intelligence, and the courage to say things in front of a lady.

In the real book, the character believed in having another organ in addition to a good heart. And he did not say 'things'.

It cannot be denied that for the most part the euphemistic substitutes are orthodox. Connie's 'heart' is made to do constant service for another part of her; and 'love', ambiguous and all-embracing, takes the place of a more specific verb. But this substitution often makes Lawrence's words seem meaningless. What does the gamekeeper mean by 'cold-hearted loving'? What does he mean when he tells Connie: 'You like loving all right: but you want it to be called something grand and mysterious, just to flatter your own self-importance'? And surely the editor is sometimes much too timid. Has 'body' itself become an obscene word? When Lady Chatterley tells her lover, 'I liked your body', the present editor changes it, meaninglessly in the context,

to 'I liked you'. And why a sentence like 'The Italians are not passionate: passion has deep reserves' is omitted in Chapter XVII I cannot even
imagine, unless Mussolini's dictatorship is wider than I thought it was.

Let us admit that there is a relative justification for the present book.
The authorities will not permit the original edition to be sent to this
country; it is certain that, if it were openly published here just as it was
written, the publisher would be prosecuted. What has actually happened, therefore, is that several pirated editions have been brought out
here, and sold through underground and bootleg channels. And
recently one particularly unscrupulous publisher brought the book out
openly, bowdlerized to get by the censors, but with no acknowledgment either of the theft or of the bowdlerization. It was sold in many
of the so-called respectable bookstores, whose owners, presumably,
would have indignantly refused to handle a book in which the organs
of the human body, and the act by which children are conceived, were
described in good plain English, but who thought it quite all right to
act as receivers of stolen goods.

Under these circumstances, the regular publisher of Lawrence was
certainly justified in at least partly protecting himself and Lawrence's
widow by bringing out an expurgated edition of his own. But would
it not have been better to tell the reader, in a publisher's note, candidly
and plainly just what the limitations of the present volume were, and
why it was being published? Would it not have been fairer, both to
the reader and to Lawrence's reputation, to let the reader know precisely how much and where something was being held back from him?
Would it not have been better, instead of bowdlerizing, to have used
dashes—to have printed, for example, one of the lines quoted here,
like this:

Me? Oh, intellectually I believe in having a good heart, a chirpy ——, a
lively intelligence, and the courage to say —— in front of a lady.

Would it not have been better to print it so throughout, letting
the reader know that the dashes were not Lawrence's, or even blacking
out the words, as in the recent *Censored Mother Goose*, to emphasize
what a nasty and ridiculous thing censorship at bottom is? It might
even be possible, now, to print the book in its original form. With
the imposing list of court decisions already built up, with the liberties
permitted to novelists like Hemingway and Dos Passos on the one
hand and to sex writers like Mary Ware Dennett, Marie Stopes, Van
de Velde, Dickinson, and Beam, and all the psycho-analysts on

the other, it would seem to be impossible for the courts to rule, with any consistency, at least, against *Lady Chatterley's Lover*.

I do not wish to be understood as accusing Mr. Knopf of lack of courage in this matter. That sort of accusation is too easy for perfectly safe people to make. Anyone who makes that charge should be prepared either to buy the rights himself or to offer to defray the expenses of the inevitable legal prosecution. I am merely saying that this emasculated edition should at least have been presented for exactly what it was. It is not enough to reply that half a loaf is better than none, or that many fine passages remain. The simple truth is that the editor has taken out precisely the passages and the words for the sake of which Lawrence really wrote the book. There is no need to ask what Lawrence himself would have thought of this edition. He has already told us in this little pamphlet on *Pornography and Obscenity*:

> The whole question of pornography seems to me a question of secrecy. . . The insult to the human body, the insult to a vital human relationship! . . . Away with the secret! . . . The only way to stop the terrible mental itch about sex is to come out quite simply and naturally into the open with it.

The editor of the present volume, as I have hinted, has been a skilful surgeon. Out of *Lady Chatterley's Lover* he has carved nothing but the heart. The heart? I find I am using the language of the editor himself. Lawrence would have been more accurate.

80. André Malraux, Preface to *L'Amant de Lady Chatterley*

(translation)

Paris, Librairie Gallimard, 1932, 7–11

André Malraux (b. 1901). Novelist, critic, politician, man of action.

The following translation of Malraux's text is by Charles K. Colhoun, and first appeared in the *Criterion*, January 1933, xii, 215–19.

Once that he had finished his manuscript, Lawrence left the work of cutting out what public opinion could not stomach either to his editor or to his collaborators, for no one is the leading novelist in his country without the knowledge that he must settle accounts with mankind and its stupidity. The insistent voice of physical pain, and the constant forebodings of death were to make Lawrence throw himself heart and soul into his determination to write and publish his book before dying. And perhaps nowhere else more than in France does this book lend itself to misinterpretation for the simple reason that it is founded on eroticism. With us, eroticism is in opposition to other passions, above all to vanity (whence the subtle sadism of *Les Liaisons Dangereuses*). The fact that a hero of Nerciat can control his emotions, or that a Valmont can dominate those of his associates, makes these people hateful to Lawrence, for whom the febrile consciousness of sensuality is alone capable of fighting against human loneliness. The fact that Restif, so clever and so voluptuous when faced with the rape of Mme. Parangon in a novel, can become *so* stupid in his clandestine publications, may indeed seem curious. The explanation of this is, that for him (Restif), as indeed is the case with all our second-class writers, the erotic book is a means of which emotion is the end. These means change with writers, but, when all is said and done, the years carry them all away in the same narrow stream.

Above all, there is in the first place the Renaissance, where we have what can be termed the physical technique of eroticism, then towards the eighteenth century, there appears what we may call the psychological technique; men belonging to the white race discover that an idea can be more exciting to them than an instrument, or even the beauty of a body. Next we have an eroticism that has become individualized, and for this, the perfect end-of-the-nineteenth-century book would have been a supplement to *Rouge et Noir*, where Stendhal would have told us how Julien would have gone to bed with Mme. de Rénal and with Mathilde, and would have given us an idea of the sexual enjoyment of all three concerned. Each of these phases increases the growth of eroticism, and gives it a wider place in men's lives. Little by little, eroticism is coming nearer to the individual; formerly it was the devil, now it has become one with man, and we shall see it outstrip man and become his purpose in life. That is the core of the book, and also its historic significance, for there eroticism ceases to be the expression of the individual, and becomes a state of the soul, a state of life, in the same way that opium became part of the life of the Chinese of the later dynasties; it is the individual now who is only a means.

There is in France a psychological and an ethical individualism. The first of these bases its system of values on differentiation, on the character of the individual, while the second has an absolute right to action demanded by the individual. Let us take the Rousseau-Gide school as an example of the first, and the Nietzsche-Balzac following as an example of the second type. Lawrence knew nothing of the first of these two persuasions, and, inasmuch as the second is concerned, the most important point for him was not the defence of his freedom, but the knowledge of what could be made of that freedom. As he sees it, it is not by the consciousness of what he has peculiar to himself that the individual is affected, rather is it by the most complete consciousness of what he has in common with others, namely his sex. It was in this aspect, above all others, that the English critics read pagan teaching, and a few forget-me-nots whose misfortune it was that they came from Oxford, gave these critics a right to uphold their views. And yet there exists no more [translator's mistake—*moins hédoniste*—no *less* hedonistic] hedonistic book than this one. It is not a question here of escaping from sin, but of making eroticism a part of life, without its losing that force which was its debt to sin. It is a question of giving it all that hitherto was given to love, of making it the means of our own revelation. Lawrence has no wish to be either happy or great; he is only concerned with being. And he thinks that it is more important for him to be a man than to be an individual. This passion for differentiating is now replaced by another whose strength can be determined: it is a question of being a man to the fullest possibility, that is to say, of making our erotic consciousness in all that it has that is most virile, the scale of values of our own life.

What, then, is the fate of woman? The moral sense with which man endows her is always the key to the ruling mystery of love. For the Hindu, woman can be the instrument of a contact with the infinite, but after the fashion of a landscape. Lawrence, whose wish it is that woman alone should be held responsible, attacks the traces of the Hindu which he finds in each one of us, and his first enemy is eternal woman. The Christian has never seen an absolute human being in woman.

Woman's sexuality eludes Lawrence, because sexual experience is not transmittable from one sex to another (it is always the eroticism of the other sex that is a mystery). Fundamentally different from us, and avid of that unity in which rather has she possession of herself than is she possessed, woman becomes [translator's mistake—should be *in The Plumed Serpent*] *The Plumed Serpent*, the indispensable instrument of world-possession. Her restored eternity is no more in her eyes, but in her sex, which is itself eternal. As the sole means by which a man may attain his deepest life through eroticism, and as the sole means of escaping from the human condition of the men of his time, Lawrence wants to possess woman spiritually as well as carnally, and he questions her in the voice of all his characters, and it is to her that he devotes that book he is writing when he is already fascinated by death.

How then is it possible for Lawrence to pass from this haunting meditation of the flesh into the lives of the beings that he has created? The whole technique of the novel lies in the means of which the author makes use for the purpose of substituting the living person of Mellors for sexuality, or vice versa. The desire of motherhood which makes Constance cry when she sees the chickens, and which leads her to share the gamekeeper's hut for the first time, is an artifice. The relations between herself and her new lover had to be impersonal, she had to become his mistress before knowing who he was, before even having spoken to him. What does she want? To reveal herself to herself with the help of her own sexuality. The means by which this awakening is effected matter little. Mellors must first reduce himself to a cunning nameless sex, he must not on any account play the part of the seducer, for the real dialogue is between Lady Chatterley and herself. Mellors will never radically withstand her, for he is not a person of extremes, he is individualized, *but he is not independent*. A gamekeeper is not necessarily either a retired officer or a perspicacious lover, a man of sterling worth. Mellors talks in dialect, but this is premeditated, and his sense of human destiny dominates Sir Clifford's; Lady Chatterley was lucky. Rooted to her sex through her horror of death, she might have found a phantasm in her lover, or an enemy. For a man who is searching so frantically for his purpose in life, I distrust pledges whose roots strike into the very depths of flesh and blood; I fear both their nature and their duration. For a great longing for solitude accompanies these characters of Lawrence, in fact it may be said that for this 'couple-advocate', the 'other party' scarcely seems to count at all. The conflict or the communion is set up between the being and its emotions. Lawrence's art consists in preserving through the convincing portrayal of an emotion that is as primitive as it is profound—the desire to become a mother, for instance—the passing from fiction to ethical affirmation. And the doctrine is inseparable from this art, from the breathless feverishness with which he tries to paint the darker side of life in dazzling colours. It will be by this art, above all else, that the importance of the 'partner's' personality will be minimized, a partner who is now no longer a lover, and whose only significance lies in the fact that he is conscious of a particular condition which it is in his power to attain and to impart. It is not in the least necessary that such a partner should be possessed of any 'individuality'. But then our love-passion is founded on this 'individuality' of the lover, of the mistress. We are concerned with destroying the myth and with the creation of a new sexuality-myth, with making a norm of eroticism.

What then can we expect in this country of myths? Perhaps an increase in our capacity for perception. We think that our attitude towards life is normal, is universally accepted, is human, and yet we have only to go as far as India to find that this attitude of ours surprises Asiatics, for when we tell them that it is a rational attitude, they reply, somewhat mystified, that our music and our painting are based on eroticism, and that our literature deals almost entirely with love. What do we know ourselves of this eroticizing of the universe which Asiatics thus attribute to us?

A myth admits of no discussion; either it lives or it does not live. It appeals not to our reason but to our complicity. It is by our desires, by our experiences in embryo, that the myth gets hold of us, and this is the reason why ethical science has for the last hundred years used the language of myths. Any prophecy on this score would mean that we should let ourselves in for prophesying about the world, for myths do not develop in the way that they control emotions, but only in so far as they justify them.

81. Yeats on *Lady Chatterley's Lover*

Extracts from *The Letters of W. B. Yeats*, ed. Allan Wade,
London, Rupert Hart-Davis, 1954, 810

W. B. Yeats (1865–1939). Poet and playwright.

---

22 May 1933, to Olivia Shakespear: . . . 'My two sensations at the
moment are Hulme's *Speculations* and *Lady Chatterley's Lover*. The first
in an essay called *Modern Art* relates such opposites as *The Apes of God*
and *Lady Chatterley*. Get somebody to lend you the last if you have not
read it. Frank Harris's *Memoirs* are vulgar and immoral—the sexual
passages were like holes burnt with a match in a piece of old newspaper;
their appeal to physical sensation was hateful; but *Lady Chatterley* is
noble. Its description of the sexual act is more detailed than in Harris,
the language is sometimes that of cabmen and yet the book is all fire.
Those two lovers, the gamekeeper and his employer's wife, each
separated from their class by their love, and by fate, are poignant in
their loneliness, and the coarse language of the one, accepted by both,
becomes a forlorn poetry uniting their solitudes, something ancient,
humble and terrible.'

25 May 1933, to Olivia Shakespear: '. . . Of course Lawrence is an
emphasis directed against modern abstraction. I find the whole book
interesting and not merely the sexual parts. They are something that
he sets up as against the abstraction of an age that he thinks dead from
the waist downward. Of course happiness is not where he seems to
place it. We are happy when for everything inside us there is an equivalent something outside us. I think it was Goethe said this . . .'

COLLECTED POEMS

September 1928

---

82. J. C. Squire in *Observer*

7 October 1928, 6

At a very reasonable price in a very pleasant binding, Mr. Secker has now collected Mr. D. H. Lawrence's poems in two volumes. The enterprise is to be applauded. Mr. Lawrence is not always a poet, but he is always himself. Good or bad, he is himself, and symptomatic of his time. Three-quarters of his poems must irritate either the man who is fastidious about expression and form or the man who dislikes crude generalizations about life as a whole or indiscreet revelations of the life of an individual. The fact remains that Mr. Lawrence, passionate, brooding, glowering, worshipping man, is undoubtedly a man of genius and big and fiery enough to eat a dozen of his merely clever contemporaries.

The two volumes are headed, one *Rhyming Poems* and the other *Unrhyming Poems*. It well exemplifies Mr. Lawrence's logic that the second volume contains a considerable number of the poems in rhyme. He did not arrange this as a feeble, practical joke, probably; he merely did not notice. He is too febrile, hectic, full of blood and haunted by dreams to be precise about title-pages and the arrangement of books. That is the defect of his qualities. We may be, as we are, fairly certain that his work will not be logically arranged, or even arranged as he says it will be; but we know he will never be dull, and we know, before we open his volumes, that even his preface will not be perfunctory. The ordinary Englishman, great or small, great as Lord Tennyson or small as Mr. Snooks, when he publishes his collected poems, is moved to write in the most impersonal way, suggesting that he has preserved what was least incompetent from among his compositions, and that he is prepared to stand or fall by his readers' judgment of him as an artist. There is none of this reticence about Mr. Lawrence. He does not, like

299

most poets, wear his heart on his sleeve in his poetry, and almost refuse to tell the time to an unintroduced stranger when poetry is not being written. All his vitals are on exhibition, and he doesn't mind who knows it. Not for him one of these bowing and smirking introductions in which 'I have to thank' and 'my thanks are due to'; Mr. Lawrence thanks nobody and he curses only himself. He contrives (which is a very unusual thing) to write a thoroughly interesting and candid introduction. He has, he says, tried to arrange the poems in chronological order:

[Quotes from Preface, 'The first poems I ever wrote . . . written them and been pleased with them.' (*C.P.*, I, 27.)]

'*Nous avons changé tout cela!*' No respectable young lady could, or at any rate should, be pleased with a good deal that Mr. Lawrence has written since that day. What precisely were the defects of these poems we are not allowed to see: Mr. Lawrence does not print them in his collected edition. But he does say 'I never "liked" my real poems as I liked "To Guelder-Roses".' It is a strange confession. He writes his poems on theory, and he judges them on theory. 'How beautiful' he thinks of something that he has written; then, pulling himself up, he says, 'Tear it up, I like it.'

This is revelatory; so is another statement.

[Quotes from Preface, 'It seems to me that no poetry . . . the place, the time, the circumstance.' (*C.P.*, I, 28.)]

He is afraid of what he likes; and he is anxious that what he writes should be interpreted in the light of his life. He has no idea of letting himself go without reserve; and he does not suppose himself to be setting down generalizations which would be valid, as those of the great epic and lyric poets will be valid, even if all record of his individual biography were lost.

Mr. Lawrence must be read in the light of these statements; and of his other statement that 'the things the young man says are very rarely poetry. So I have tried to let the demon say his say, and to remove the passages where the young man intruded.' He is, in other words, a limited, a writhing, a bewildered poet: honest, muscular, out of touch with ordinary mankind, afraid of himself and afraid of others, at one moment surrendering to beauty, at the next tortured by the thought that the surrender may have been too easy. A philosophy nobody but a solemn ass will ever get out of Mr. Lawrence: he is a poet, a brooder, an introspective sensualist: a man capable of violent flights towards the ideal and violent revulsions against it: but quite incapable of philosophic generalization, or any such understanding of other people as would make him feel that his experiences were universal. His form is not usually lyric: but for what he is worth he is in the category of Heine, Burns, and Catullus, though these were all better artists than he: the interest goes out of his work if there is no interest in himself.

There will be, I think. Nobody up to the present (though one knows not what the future may hold) has called Mr. D. H. Lawrence lovable. He confides enough, in all conscience: if concordats could be made on the basis of confessions about fleshly weaknesses, we should all feel that Mr. Lawrence had sounded the 'All Clear'. He is not, however, one of those who speaks for the rest of us: he is a self-willed, obstinate, shrinking, sometimes snarling, outlaw who speaks for himself and suggests that he is speaking more for us than we are willing to admit. We do not admit it; he reiterates what he has said. The supernatural does not interest him, and he has no views about it. But he sees forces at work in the world, sexual forces and egoistical forces, which do interest him. Mr. Lawrence might almost have been possessed by Pan. On the very first page of these volumes we come across this:—

[Quotes from 'The Wild Common', 'Rabbits, handfuls of brown earth . . . their spurting kick.' (*C.P.*, I, 33.)]

The urge of life: the pullulation: the violence; these are always present to him. So also that other pagan thing, the conflict of sex. He was a very young man when he wrote:—

[Quotes from 'Discord in Childhood', 'Within the house two voices arose . . . 'neath the voice of the ash.' (*C.P.*, I, 36.)]

The poems he has written since then, whether good or bad, are mostly on the lines of these early ones. Mr. Lawrence is acutely aware of the physical which leads to ordinary violence, and the physical that leads to sexual violence. He once, in a prose book, expressed a wish that he could be a whale, a great ten-thousand-gallon sac of blood with hardly any brain at all. He cannot get away from blood, and he cannot get away from sexual attraction: on occasion he mixes the two, a killer-man proceeding from the slaughter of rabbits to the conquest of a woman. 'Flesh', 'Slinking', 'Procreant', 'Fecund': Those, and many other such words, appear frequently in these poems. There is a long series of poems, extraordinarily good, so far as they go, on tortoises;

culminating in verses on the sexual ecstasies of tortoises. The tortoises get to the point of screaming with love: 'the voice of the turtle is heard in the land.' Nothing could be more skilful, journalistically, than the descriptions of the lumbering tortoises under their hard shells, the peering heads, the wrinkled necks, the crinkled trousers, the flat paws, the stumpy tails. Nothing could be more sympathetic than Mr. Lawrence's attitude towards the tortoises when love-stricken: and he enters, with equal eagerness, into the feelings of the turkey-cock, the fish, the snake, and the kangaroo. With regard to the last two he is especially good: anybody who admires Mr. Ralph Hodgson's 'The Bull' may be recommended to peruse Mr. Lawrence's poems on other vigorous, if unrefined animals. Yet, after all his contortions, all his desperate efforts to escape the normal, all his admirations of cruel physical manifestations, coils and springs, fangs and yellow eyes, it is probable that the most admiration of his readers will return at last to those few simple poems in which he does not bother to express his differences from other people, or to justify his sexual career: such poems as, for example, Giorno dei Morti, which begins, in a quite unsophisticated manner:—

[Quotes the first four lines. (*C.P.*, I, 232.)]

Here there is something that affects everybody; there is also musical sound. When Mr. Lawrence 'kicks' he tends not merely to say things which do not universally appeal, but to say them unmusically. Form does count, in spite of what he says about the supplementary information that may be given by biography: the greatest works would be very little impaired were nothing known about the authors. Mr. Lawrence is a very modern product: a man who protests violently against everything that has been proposed to him, a man excited, humourless, unorthodox at every point. But he is at least a man of genius and not a mere exhibitionist or wit. Even his weakest novels embody the struggles of a soul; and his poems are better than his novels.

83. Unsigned review in
Times Literary Supplement
15 November 1928, 852

The poet has always been discernible in Mr. Lawrence's prose, illumin-
ing the novelist's characterizations and his darker prophesyings. But
when a poet is writing prose fiction there is some degree of metaphor
in speaking of his quality. It only appears in substance, and with a
subtle change, when he is using his own medium. Mr. Lawrence's
powers have been revealed intermittently in half-a-dozen small
volumes of verse during the last fifteen years, but this collected edition
offers a much better means of appreciating their value.

In a short preface with several points of interest, biographical and
critical, Mr. Lawrence says that he has arranged his first volume as far
as possible in chronological order, 'because many of the poems are so
personal that, in their fragmentary fashion, they make up a biography
of an emotional and inner life.' This leads him presently to an opinion
that no poetry should be judged as if it were quite detached, in the
absolute. 'Even the best poetry, when it is at all personal, needs the
penumbra of its own time and place and circumstance to make it full
and whole.' It might be tempting to discuss that dictum, and to urge,
perhaps, that what shows the best poetry to be the best is just its power
of appearing as something absolute. However, there is Mr. Lawrence's
proviso, 'when it is at all personal'; and for the rest, though his clues
are of illuminating interest, his verse scarcely needs them for a consideration of its poetry. Its outstanding quality, and a mark of genuinely
poetic truth, is its power to convey the whole of an experience. This
is visible in an early poem like 'The Little Town at Evening':—

[Quotes the whole of this poem. (*C.P.*, I, 48.)]

But Mr. Lawrence tells us that the earlier poems have been often recast,
because 'the things the young man says are very rarely poetry.' It is
characteristic of him to say that the authentic voice is the voice of his
demon; but it shows, at least, that what the artist's control makes
explicit is a compelling experience.

While this is often an inner experience, in the fullest sense, it is linked hardly less often with the sights and sounds of Nature. And these, definite as they are, are not invoked merely as a background or for the creation of an image; for with Mr. Lawrence Nature tends to be a partner in the emotion. His verse, without losing precision, has a fluid quality that shapes itself pliantly to a mood; and on the visual side he has at times a curious, Shelley-like magic of transmuting objects through atmosphere. In one or two poems, where suburban ugliness is transfigured in this way, the dull brick streets volatilized by haze or sunshine, or the gaunt school-building emerging as a refuge amid snow —'a red rock silent and shadowless'—have an effect like a painter's impressionism. But the delicately beautiful verses called 'Corot', where Mr. Lawrence is defining some such effect, turn in the end behind the visible:—

[Quotes from 'Corot', 'For what can all sharp-rimmed substance . . . before we can scan.' (*C.P.*, I, 68-9.)]

And the sight of a rising moon leads him in the same way to muse on the ubiquitous seed of life:

[Quotes from 'Red Moon-Rise', 'And even in the watery shells . . . an unknown fire.' (*C.P.*, I, 89.)]

It is in this sense of a universal rhythm in things that Mr. Lawrence is most at one with life and persuasive in his vision. But the most poignant of his poems are those which seem to be the most personal. The poems on the death of a mother, and the 'long haunting' which follows it, have a passionate and often exquisite tenderness, with an assurance that underlies and finally triumphs over anguish; and the other poems of love and passion picture the flux and reflux of moods no less intimately. In both there are the visible marks of conflict between one self and another. But, perhaps because poetry is more concise than prose, while Mr. Lawrence's control is certainly firmer, the outcome is much more definite in form than it is apt to be in his fiction. There is something assured, for instance, that gives peace to the retrospect of 'History':—

[Quotes the whole of this poem. (*C.P.*, I, 248-9.)]

Not all, by any means, of the series *Look! We Have Come Through!* have this kind of finality. They were written, we are reminded, in a dark time of the War, and their own theme reflects pungent alternations of joy and recoil, oneness and difference. There is a passionate and confined rebelliousness to which Mr. Lawrence has accustomed us that would rob them, one might think, of universal value; yet in their unshrinking statement they are a haunting, perhaps a unique, mirror of the experience of modern lovers. What is physical in them is vitalized by passion. It is the obsession of the conflict of selves and sex that inevitably gives them a distortion. But one cannot question the sincerity which has tried to find words for unattempted things, or the intrinsic purity of the flame which can dart thus into a lyric:

[Quotes the whole of 'Valentine's Night'. (*C.P.*, I, 239.)]

These two volumes end with the unrhymed poems of *Birds, Beasts, and Flowers*, which were a lighter harvest of travel. Compared with the rest they are a diversion, and their attitude of imaginative observation, with the cool or sardonic humour that plays about it, carries us nearer to prose. But they are original, amusing and often enchanting; and almost any fragment will show their precision of eye and image:

[Quotes from 'Cypresses', 'Yet more I see you darkly concentrate . . . And tombs.' (*C.P.*, I, 297.)]

Dexterously as the free verse fits these last moods, one cannot help feeling some regret that Mr. Lawrence should have exchanged the rhymed verse in which he found so often a simple and perfect form, for the unrhymed poems of his last volume. The reason, no doubt, is that he has more complex things to say; but the result is less pure in poetry. There are obviously perils in free verse for a writer like Mr. Lawrence—chief of them, perhaps, the temptation to argue—and a didactic note does creep in here and there at the end of his more serious poems, although he has succeeded in giving it the accent of discovery. What one would regret most would be that he should confuse his poetry, or forsake it. There is evidence in these volumes that he is a more natural artist, and a finer one, in verse than in prose. What, however, chiefly proves his power is a jet of inspiration such as is rare in our contemporary poetry. A richer and sharper emotion than is common has been awakened by life and taken the substance of poetry.

THE PAINTINGS OF
D. H. LAWRENCE

June 1929

---

84. T. W. Earp in *New Statesman*

17 August 1929, xxxiii, 578

T. W. Earp (1892–1958). Art critic and translator.

Lawrence's paintings were exhibited at the Warren Gallery, Maddox Street, London from 14 June 1929. On 5 July the exhibition was raided by the police who took away thirteen of the pictures that were considered to be obscene. At the subsequent court hearing, presided over by Mr. Mead, the Marlborough Street Magistrate (8 August, reported *The Times*, 9 August 1929, 9), the pictures were ordered to be returned to their owner on condition that they would not be re-exhibited. *The Paintings of D. H. Lawrence* is a volume of reproductions of these paintings which was put on sale at the exhibition. It includes an Introduction by Lawrence.

As the result of a recent hearing in the magistrate's court, several of the pictures shown in Mr. D. H. Lawrence's exhibition at the Warren Gallery have been withdrawn from public view, and copies of the book of reproductions issued by the Mandrake Press were ordered to be destroyed. This book contained an introduction in which Mr. Lawrence stated his views on painting, and they, apart from the censored pictures, are worthy of consideration. As a phase of his general outlook, expressed in the prose which is his real medium, they form an important section of his philosophy. Yet, as in all his writing, with the exception of the poems and novels, what is of value in his pronouncement is embedded in a large amount of dross.

Mr. Lawrence's bonnet, like those of many geniuses, is not without its bees. When he is engaged with matters of theory, he is apt to write so vociferously as to shout down his own arguments. He tells us in this essay that, although he attended revivalists' meetings in his youth, he remained unaffected by their doctrines. He has, however, in controversy, been considerably influenced by their style; and while it is refreshing to find a writer expressing himself as if he really did care passionately about his subject, Mr. Lawrence occasionally lashes himself into an hysterical, exacerbated violence which not only detracts from the force of his argument, but gives an impression of merely fevered excitability rather than forceful reason. The fact that his words were to be privately printed was too easy a temptation to be shocking and needlessly violent.

The English, says Mr. Lawrence, have produced few good painters because the national spirit became atrophied with fear at the time of the Renaissance. This fear· was caused by the wave of venereal disease which then swept over Europe. High and low alike were tainted—Mr. Lawrence gives a lurid account of the Tudor and Stuart dynasties—and the result was a shuddering, universal attack of sex-repression, which obliterated 'Merry England' and has continued with gathered strength to the present time. It was reflected in literature by the morbidity of the Elizabethans, the emasculated intellectualism of the cavalier poets, and the coarseness of Restoration comedy. Thus a mental attitude towards life took the place of an intuitional one. By the time English painting really got started with Gainsborough and Reynolds we had lost our imagination and freedom of expression. France, because it had affected some sort of rational compromise with sexual necessity, was a little better off. But gradually everything has gone from bad to worse. This sex-repression, caused by the fear of disease, has by now robbed us of the power both of artistic creation and appreciation. 'We, dear reader, you and I, we were born corpses and we are corpses.' Such is Mr. Lawrence's general thesis, and such his general nonsense.

In order to make our poor dead flesh creep, he turns history into a dirt-track and rides round it on a hobby-horse. Yet all is not really for the worst in the worst of all possible worlds. In calmer mood he himself admits a few happy features, and the list of his preferences and reservations is much the more interesting part of his introduction.

Blake, as we can well understand, he appreciates, for much of his own work is an embroidery on *The Marriage of Heaven and Hell*. He praises the classic English landscape-painters, too, though he blames them for not being figure-painters instead. And the French Impressionists painted light admirably—though why paint light? In fact, Mr. Lawrence really wishes to get from painting such satisfaction as we get from his own novels. It is the relationship of men and women that most interests him, and he is incapable of attaching much value to any work not somehow bearing on this relationship.

But when he consents to enlarge a little the implications of his theme, he is pertinent and illuminating. It is hard not to agree that painters have been too much influenced by social vogues and fashions; and that too many pictures have been done from painting into painting, instead of from life into painting. The purely technical aspect obtained such dominance that it needed a Cézanne to restore to art the reality that had been lost.

In Cézanne's apples Mr. Lawrence finds the first and only successful attempt for centuries to portray actual matter. The *cliché*—the way others had painted them, and preconceived bourgeois notions about them—prevented Cézanne from doing as well with figure and landscape, though the portrait of Mme. Cézanne almost succeeds. Mr. Lawrence's eulogy of the Master of Aix is noble and moving; though obviously his conception of Cézanne himself as an heroic character—a literary figure—has much to do with it, and makes a strong appeal to Mr. Lawrence the romantic novelist. And because he is so good a novelist we are interested in his views on painting. His own pictures, alas! do not give him interest as a painter.

For painting to Mr. Lawrence is simply what his violin was to Ingres. It may be a delightful hobby, but the exhibition as a whole showed no signs of a vocation. There was imagination and there was passable draughtsmanship; but the alternate muddiness and garishness of colour, and the clumsiness with which the pigment was laid upon the canvas, revealed a basic inability in mere picture-making. The honesty of Mr. Lawrence's effort is not questioned, yet the pictures, although there were no desire to shock, were really shocking from the point of view of art. The magistrate remarked that the most beautiful picture in the universe might be obscene, but if Mr. Lawrence's pictures had been beautiful it is doubtful whether they would have been prosecuted. The offensiveness lay in the bad painting.

PANSIES

July 1929

85. Unsigned review in
Times Literary Supplement

4 July 1929, 532

With the same fascinated loathing with which Swift railed at man's animal nature and animal actions, and with a no less passionate hatred, Mr. Lawrence attacks everything in modern life which deprives man of his animal delights and checks the noble and beautiful savage. And yet we hesitate to say that it is the noble savage whom Mr. Lawrence exalts. We hesitate to describe what Mr. Lawrence likes in any other terms but those which he himself uses. For he writes from a fixed point of prejudice, a small island in a sea of disgust; and if we do not mark the point with precision, or by a false turn of phrase evade it, we are likely to be swept into the sea. And Mr. Lawrence's disgust is easily aroused, since even to put a baby into the wrong kind of perambulator is to incur his loathing:

> But then you need only look at the modern perambulator
> To see that a child, as soon as it is born,
> Is put by its parents into its coffin.

With a comprehensive hatred he is nauseated by all rarefied civilization and by every refinement of sublimation. 'Man', as he says, 'is lop-sided on the side of the angels':

[Quotes from 'Fate and the Younger Generation', 'Anyhow, the Tolstoyan lot simply asked for extinction . . . so very much, either.' (*C.P.*, I, 533-4.)]

But Mr. Lawrence's hatred becomes uncontrollable when he thinks of money:

[Quotes from 'Fight! O My Young Men', 'Old money-worms . . . and god, how they stink!' (*C.P.*, I, 456-7.)]

Mr. Lawrence calls money muck, and he actually feels the same sharply physical and lingering disgust of it that Swift felt of real muck. But real muck Mr. Lawrence would probably not abhor, and it seems to be only the disguises of it that he cannot abide. Money, machines, the middle classes and industrial amusements stink alike in Mr. Lawrence's nostrils. But there are some women who seem to epitomize all that Mr. Lawrence dislikes:

> Will no one say hush! to thee,
> poor lass, poor bit of a wench?
> Will never a man say: Come, my pigeon,
> come an' be still wi' me, my own bit of a wench!

Mr. Lawrence is a master of the pathetic, and the lines are written, one might almost say, in the little language of Swift. But the last line has not yet been quoted; and the revulsion of hatred is the more violent since it comes with so crushing an emphasis immediately after a tender appeal:

> And would you peck out his eyes if he did?

These pansies and passions of hatred directed against the lilies and languors of virtue are called pansies because, as Mr. Lawrence tells us, 'they are rather *pensées* than anything else', and he wishes them to be taken as 'casual thoughts that are true while they are true, and irrelevant when the mood and circumstance changes'. They are not written in prose because 'there is a didactic element about prose thoughts which makes them repellent, slightly bullying'. Certainly Mr. Lawrence's thoughts are not bullying, for there are few things so consolatory in some moods as a comprehensive dislike of most things; but neither are they, as he wishes them to be, exactly like flowers, 'merely the breath of the moment and one eternal moment easily contradicting the next eternal moment'. On the contrary, they fix with an unusual precision a particular set of opinions and memorialize disgust of our civilization as few treatises by social reformers could hope to do.

> We climbed the steep ascent to heaven,
> Through peril, toil and pain,
> Oh God, to us may strength be given
> To scramble back again.

So Mr. Lawrence sings, and sums up the purport of his poems. But to what are we to scramble back? It is in describing this desired territory that Mr. Lawrence becomes most a poet and can best exercise his concrete and physical metaphors.

[Quotes from 'Poverty', 'I don't want to be poor . . . a natural abundance.' (*C.P.*, I, 498.)]

Mr. Lawrence uses with great sensibility a metre which is perhaps derived from translations of Chinese poems, and has been of much use to gnomic poets. He is naturally most ambitious as a poet when his ideas are most subtle, though his thought, when it is intricate, seldom gathers itself up into a single and quotable line, perhaps because he does not seem to polish his poems with any assiduous care. Even Mr. Lawrence's neatest epigrams seem to spring like happy turns of conversation; when he plunges into remoter recesses of thought and feeling, and would express by recondite metaphors the borderland of sense, he is often impressive, but not often so precise. Yet in the use of a rare image he sometimes gives the appearance of precision to that which can never be really precise, and this is certainly one of the aims and effects of poetry. And, while there is much modern poetry which does not seem to express anything that the poet greatly wished to say, there is scarcely a line of Mr. Lawrence's verses which does not sound like a piece of the author's mind, in both the obvious and the idiomatic sense of the phrase.

86. Mark Van Doren in
New York Herald Tribune Books

15 December 1929, 15

Mark Van Doren (b. 1894). Poet, critic, university teacher, editor.

Mr. Lawrence's title is his way of saying that here at last he has set down his opinions, his bare opinions, nakedly in verse. For *Pansies* means 'Pensées'—these are the straight thoughts of Mr. Lawrence concerning subjects which he has hitherto treated either in novels or in psycho-analytical discourse or in long and relatively indirect poems. All these other methods, indeed, were indirect; now he pursues the quite simple method of epigram and image, of statement and idea. Not that he claims completeness for the present result or expects to stand by these particular propositions forever. They are only pansies after all, not immortelles.

[Quotes from Foreword to *Pansies*, 'I don't want everlasting flowers . . . you won't keep it any better if you do.' (*C.P.*, I, 424.)]

So I shall not nail Mr. Lawrence down, though it is worth pointing out that the things he says here are recognizable as his personal things; there is a consistency between this book and all his other books; and indeed the interest of the volume lies partly in the fact that it reminds one how closely Mr. Lawrence has stuck to an attitude from first to last. Here is the same old fury against civilization, the same old unutterable contempt for ideas—unutterable yet endlessly uttered—the same old hatred of certain brands of weakness, the same angry insistence that just so much of sex and no more is tolerable, the same impetuous, hard-breathing style, the same loud irony and the same mad wit. Here, one is tempted to say in spite of Mr. Lawrence, is the index to his opinions, the articulated skeleton of his thought.

Many of the poems, if such they may be called, are distressingly flat. We could have gone anywhere else, for instance, and been told that

> There is no point in work
> unless it absorbs you
> like an absorbing game.

or

> That society must establish itself
> upon a different principle
> from the one we've got now.

But it is not in such passages that Mr. Lawrence speaks characteristically. When he has all his faculties about him, his wit as well as his anger, his sense of absurdity as well as his conviction of the truth, he makes such significant observations as the following:

> Elephants in the circus
> have aeons of weariness round their eyes.
> Yet they sit up
> and show vast bellies to the children.

Or he breaks out in this really noble and at the same time humorous way against professional pacifism:

[Quotes 'Peace and War', (*C.P.*, I, 495–6).]

Now whether or not that amounts to much as a poem, I am sure that it was worth saying in this way—not, perhaps, in some other way. Which is another manner of admitting that it is a poem, and a successful one. The book has many such pieces in it; one remembers them, if only to read them with amusement to one's friends. Mr. Lawrence is quite right in saying that *Pansies* should not be taken too seriously, for if it is not so taken it turns out to be one of the sincerest books which this strangely interesting man has published.

PORNOGRAPHY AND OBSCENITY

November 1929

---

87. Unsigned review, *New Statesman*

23 November 1929, xxxiv, 219–20

Both the following reviews consider Lawrence's pamphlet in con-junction with *Do We Need a Censor?* by Viscount Brentford, which was also published in 1929. Sir William Joynson-Hicks, Viscount Brentford (known as 'Jix'), was Home Secretary, 1924–29. It was he who answered Pethick-Lawrence's question about the seizure of the MS of *Pansies*. (Nehls, iii, 308–12.)

Messrs. Faber and Faber have just published a remarkable pair of pamphlets. One is called *Pornography and Obscenity* and is written by Mr. D. H. Lawrence; the other is called *Do We Need a Censor?* and is written by the late Home Secretary, Lord Brentford, who is still rather better known as 'Jix'. Each pamphlet costs a shilling. We cannot remember ever to have seen the two sides of an important public controversy set forth with so much vigour or such unimpeachable sincerity.

Mr. Lawrence's pamphlet is profound and original in a very high degree. Lord Brentford's contains an exceedingly competent and com-plete exposition of the attitude of those who cultivate the very common human desire to enforce their own ideas of morality upon their fellow-men. With his point of view we have a sort of sneaking sympathy. 'Jix' undoubtedly wants to do the right thing. He is not temperament-ally a tyrant. His views are merely those of his father and his grand-father before him; he does like things to be decent; and he is not perhaps acquainted with the probably broader views of his great-grandfather or of any of his pre-Victorian ancestors. At any rate he states the Victorian case admirably, and were it not for the devastating force of Mr. Lawrence's argument he might perhaps be considered to hold the field.

[The reviewer discusses Lord Brentford's claim that the Home Office is 'a censor of indecency' and questions the right of the Home Secretary to give his 'considered opinion' of doubtful books. While agreeing that a book which is likely to have a corrupting influence on the young should not be favourably treated because it is a work of art, the reviewer thinks that he might disagree with Lord Brentford 'as to the precise character of the sort of book which is really likely to debauch the young.' He then continues:]

But, to come to the other side of the question, Mr. Lawrence's pamphlet is far more interesting and important. It is, as we have already suggested, a genuinely profound study of the very elements of the problem. It is a real masterpiece of fundamental analysis written by a man of genius from the very bottom of his heart. Mr. Lawrence in our opinion is abnormally obsessed with all those questions which centre round the crude facts of sex. But his very obsession makes him in some respects clearer-sighted than most of us are on these subjects. He writes with a freedom which very few of us would venture, as well as with a veracious insight which very few of us possess. His definition of 'pornography', though not comprehensive, is admirably simple and convincing. He says in effect that pornography is that sort of writing or painting which tends to stimulate or encourage the practice by either sex of private masturbation. Plain words are necessary in such a discussion, and Mr. Lawrence has the courage to use them. We must certainly confess that his definition seems to us the most accurate and the most practically useful definition that has hitherto been formulated. He enlarges upon it with a verbal exuberance which we might not be inclined to imitate, but what serious student of the psychological aspects of the question can deny that he is right? He has hit the nail exactly on the head. His definition explains succinctly what has puzzled many people, namely, why Rabelais and Boccaccio and Ovid and all the other great 'indecent' writers are somehow *not* pornographic. Their works are calculated to produce perhaps a certain amount of sexual excitement, but it is of the right sort, not of the wrong sort; such books, frank as they are, could not injure the mind of a child. What does injure the minds both of children and of adults is the secrecy with which Victorian manners have sought to surround the whole subject of sex—the 'dirty little secret'. Nineteenth-century manners is what Mr. Lawrence calls them, and he does not believe that they ever existed before the nineteenth century. Very probably he is right. He finds in the twentieth century two important reactions. One is represented by the 'scientific' attitude of Dr. Marie Stopes and her supporters, and the other by the very young generation which, having learned to have no respect for sex, treats it as a sort of joke which should not be taken seriously at all. Both these attitudes Mr. Lawrence regards as essentially pernicious because they destroy the enormous emotional meanings and possibilities of sex. They are not so bad in his view as the onanistic secrecy of the Victorians, but they are highly pernicious all the same.

On the immediate subject of discussion—the existing or threatened censorship—Mr. Lawrence is we think entirely in the right. Pornography should be suppressed. But what is too commonly called 'indecency' should not be suppressed. Every month, without any hint of risk of Home Office interference, there are published dozens of novels—largely written by young women—which are fundamentally pornographic, that is to say, which present the intimacies of sex not as a perfectly natural activity of the human species (or even as a solemn Stopesian scientific ritual), but as something which is inevitably furtive. In most of such writings there is a sense both of secrecy and of futility. Vera or Dorine, as the case may be, suddenly takes off all her clothes in the presence of one or more young men—but nothing follows except a painstaking analysis of her sensations and of those of her equally ineffective and equally narcissistic demi-paramour. If only the result were twins one might forgive her, but there is no such result. The multitudinous demi-vierges in all ranks of society today are not to be forgiven; they can hope only for the demi-absolution of the blind eye cast by elderly Victorians.

We must say again that in this pamphlet Mr. Lawrence has hit the nail on the head. His analysis of the factors of the sexual problem might well be suppressed by any Home Secretary of what he calls the 'grey' type; but for all its vehemence and extravagances it is one of the most powerful and sane and penetrating pieces of writing that we have read for very many years. We were about to say that it ought to be very widely read, but perhaps that is not quite the right thing to say. It ought certainly however to be read by all those who understand the ultimate importance of the problem with which it deals. The question of the Censorship does not really matter very much, for in practice it can always be so easily evaded; but the questions which lie behind are concerned with the underlying factors of twentieth-century virility.

This pamphlet is the work of a profound thinker. It is not necessary to agree with all that he says, but it is certainly necessary to know and to ponder what he has said. He may be normally too much concerned in his mind about sex, but on this occasion he has got hold of the right end of the stick. His pamphlet is a pamphlet which, if it wins understanding, may well mark an epoch in the history not only of censorship but of the reasonable appreciation of the realities of sexual morality and sexual honesty and decency. Perhaps Mr. Lawrence has never before written anything quite so powerful or so effective. We all know his passionate sincerity, but here there is real understanding as well. He has probed to the very heart of the problem, and if his language is not always that which is employed in polite society that is merely because the almost pathological prudery of the nineteenth century cannot be adequately discussed in polite language. 'The whole question', he says, 'of pornography seems to me a question of secrecy. Without secrecy there would be no pornography.' And again: 'Sentimentality is a sure sign of pornography.'

My love is like a red, red rose only when she is *not* like a pure, pure lily. And nowadays the pure, pure lilies are mostly festering anyhow. Away with them and their lyrics. Away with the pure, pure lily lyric, along with the smoking-room story. They are counterparts, and the one is as pornographic as the other. . . . If only Robert Burns had been accepted for what he is, then love might still have been like a red, red rose.

The reader must of course take his choice. He may prefer 'Jix' to Lawrence—the pure or demi-pure lily to the red rose. But in our view at any rate Lawrence wins hands down. His frank and startling pamphlet is one of the most vigorous and effective pieces of polemical writing that have appeared in recent times. It might be answered perhaps, but certainly a 'Jix' would have been wiser to suppress it than to attempt to answer it. 'Jix' talks in the language of the temporary jack-in-office—honest but without thought—Lawrence in the language of a man who can survey the centuries. The two pamphlets should be read together. Pamphleteering is an art which has fallen almost into disuse, but here is a very interesting and important revival of it.

88. E. M. Forster in *Nation and Athenaeum*

11 January 1930, xlvi, 508–9

E. M. Forster, signed 'E.M.F.' (b. 1879). Novelist. Met Lawrence in 1915, when, according to Lawrence, 'He was very angry with me for telling him about himself'—understandably if the comments were at all like those which Lawrence made on Forster in his letters of 12 February and 24 February 1915 (to Bertrand Russell and Mary Cannan respectively). To Lady Ottoline Morrell, 5 February 1929, Lawrence wrote that he had received a letter from Forster 'telling me a propos of nothing that he admires me but doesn't read me'. Other comments by Forster on Lawrence: *Aspects of the Novel*, 1927; letters to *Nation and Athenaeum* deploring the tone of the Lawrence obituaries, 29 March, 12 and 26 April 1930; B.B.C talk, 16 April 1930 (see No. 95).

It was a happy and indeed a witty thought of the publishers to induce the most remarkable of our novelists and our most notorious Home Secretary to write pamphlets on the subject of indecency. Needless to say, Mr. Lawrence and Lord Brentford disagree. Yet they have two characteristics in common, and it is well to observe what these are before passing on to their differences.

The first common characteristic is an emotional uncertainty which threatens them whenever they generalize about the public. Most men and women have, to put it bluntly, no opinions at all about indecency, sex, pornography, the censorship, etc. They have habits, but no opinions. The expert cannot realize this. Definite himself, he ascribes opinions where they do not exist, and if he is a reformer as well as an expert he tends to divide the public into friends and foes, and to ask himself which section predominates. Unable to discover, he loses his aloofness, and feels that he is surrounded now by friends, now by foes, now he cries, 'He that is not against us is for us', and now, 'He that is not with me is against me'. Lord Brentford, for instance, complains that there is an enormous demand for improper postcards in England,

and then says that if the trade was suppressed not more than a hundred people would object. Both statements cannot be true. And Mr. Lawrence, though he understands his own reactions and so steers a straighter course, is likewise swayed when he thinks of the mob, hates and loves it alternately, regards it as a villain, a dupe, a comrade, rolled into one. This instability is natural. When they think of the general public, both writers echo an emotional uncertainty which was voiced long ago on the shores of the lake of Galilee.

Their second common characteristic is that each of them detests indecency, and desires to suppress it. Lord Brentford's opinion is familiar, but it is Mr. Lawrence, not he, who writes, 'I would censor genuine pornography, rigorously.' Of course, as soon as we try to define 'genuine pornography' the battle opens; still, both disputants feel that there is something in sex which ought to be prohibited. 'It would not be very difficult', adds Mr. Lawrence, but he has not yet been Home Secretary. Lord Brentford, who has, did not find it very easy.

What is this accursed and illegal thing?

['Lord Brentford', says Forster, 'dare not tell us, because from his point of view to define filth is to advertise it.' His case for censorship is based on the twin premises 'that everything in sex except marriage is evil, and that children must always be protected, whatever the cost to adults'. He is good-tempered, but confused. Forster then continues:]

To turn from him to Mr. Lawrence is to turn from darkness into light.

Into what sort of light? Many will say that it beats through the bars of hell. But even those who detest him most must admit that they can see what he is talking about, whereas with Lord Brentford they could not see, they could only infer. He can tell us straight out what he finds evil in sex, because from his point of view to define filth is to sterilize it. To him the one evil is 'self-enclosure', and under this definition he includes not merely the physical act of masturbation, but any emotional counterpart of it, any turning-inward upon itself of the spirit, any furtiveness and secrecy, any tendency to live in little private circles of excitement, rather than in the passionate outer life of personal inter-change. Man has his solitary side, but if he embraces this kind of solitude, he is damned. 'Today, practically everyone is self-conscious, and imprisoned in self-consciousness. It is the joyful result of the dirty little secret.' Here (he argues) is the only real indecency, here is the genuine pornography which he would rigorously censor, here is the harvest which men like Lord Brentford have sown.

Some readers will be shocked by his brutality, others deterred by his occasional mysticism, others again will feel that he is only inviting us to exchange one type of supervision for another, and that it is safer to be judged by Sir Chartres Biron than to fall into the hands of a writer of genius. But of the importance and novelty of his attack there is no question. He has dealt a blow at reformers who are obsessed by purity and cannot see that their obsession is impure. He arraigns civilization, because it is smeary and grey and degrades passion by pretending to safeguard it, and confuses purity with modesty, and lifts up pious eyes to heaven and cherishes dirt elsewhere. And lest this should sound like vague denunciation, he quotes a couple of poems, with devastating effect. They are famous poems. One of them is, 'My love is like a red, red rose'. Is this a pure poem? No; 'my love is like a red, red rose only when she's *not* like a pure, pure lily'. The second poem is 'Du bist wie eine Blume'—a pure poem and also an indecent one; the elderly gentleman is mumbling over the child and praying God to keep her pure, pure for ever, pure for the dreary little circle of his own thoughts. For Burns sends his emotions outwards to mingle with human beings and become passions, Heine shuts his up in the circle of self-enclosure, where they fester. And Heine, not Burns, is the modern man. He is a typical product of repression, and when he tires of mumbling, 'So hold und schön und rein', he will go to the smoking-room, and tell, also in low tones, an improper story.

What, then, is our remedy? Free speech? Not altogether. To say, as has been said above, that by defining filth Mr. Lawrence hopes to sterilize it, is not quite to express his attitude. He does not wholly believe in free speech, for the reason that it never leads further than Dr. Marie Stopes. However much we speak out and denounce our repressors, we shall still be imprisoned in the circles of self-consciousness, we shall merely be the grey denouncing the grey. To escape into salvation and colour, something further is needed: freedom of feeling, and how is that to be attained? He does not tell us, except by mystic hints which only the mystic can utilize, and in this direction his pamphlet comes to a standstill. But as a polemic it is remarkable. He has brought a definite accusation against Puritanism, and it will be interesting to see whether Puritanism will reply.

One might sum up the conflict by saying that Lord Brentford wants to suppress everything except marriage, and Mr. Lawrence to suppress nothing except suppression; that the one sounds the trumpet of duty, the other the trumpet of passion, and that in the valley between them

lie the inert forces of the general public. If a battle develops, we shall
all of us have to get up and take sides; but need a battle develop? There
has never been one in France. Is not a more reasonable issue possible?
Is not the solution to be found not in the ringing clarion calls of either
camp, but in the dull drone of tolerance, tolerance, tolerance? I hope
so. Nor is tolerance quite as dull as its worthy followers suggest.
Tolerance has its appropriate dangers, just as much as duty or passion.
It, too, can lead to disaster and death. It can do harm, like everything
else. It can, in the subject under discussion, sometimes injure the young,
precisely as Lord Brentford contends. But it does less harm than anything else. It blights isolated individuals, it will never poison a nation.
It is on the whole best. It is the principle which causes society the
minimum of damage, because it admits that the people who constitute
society are different. Unlike Mr. Lawrence, I would tolerate everybody,
even Nosey Parker and Peeping Tom. Let them peep and nose until
they are sick—always providing that in the course of their investiga-
tions they do not invoke the support of the law.

89. The theme of decline, *The Times*

4 March 1930, 11

David Herbert Lawrence, whose death is announced on another page, was born at Eastwood, near Nottingham, on 11 September 1885. His novel *Sons and Lovers* and his play *The Widowing of Mrs. Holroyd* are at least so far biographical as to tell the world that his father was a coal-miner and his mother a woman of finer grain. At the age of twelve the boy won a county council scholarship; but the sum was scarcely enough to pay the fees at the Nottingham High School and the fares to and fro. At sixteen he began to earn his living as a clerk. When his ill-health put an end to that, he taught in a school for miners' boys.

At nineteen he won another scholarship, of which he could not avail himself, as he had no money to pay the necessary entrance fee; but at twenty-one he went to Nottingham University College, and after two years there he came to London and took up teaching again. It was in these years that he wrote, under the name of Lawrence H. Davidson, some books on history. He had begun also the writing of fiction, and his first novel, *The White Peacock*, was published about a month after his mother's death had robbed him of his best and dearest friend.

Sons and Lovers, published when he was twenty-eight, brought him fame. Many years of poverty were to pass before his work began to make him financially comfortable; and even then the collapse of a publishing firm in America deprived him of some of the fruits of his labours. But the revolt against society which fills his books had its counterpart in his life, in his travels, and especially in his attempt to found, in 1923, an intellectual and community settlement in New Mexico.

Undoubtedly he had genius. He could create characters which are even obtrusively real. His ruthless interpretation of certain sides of the nature of women was recognized by some women to be just. Every one of his novels, as well as his books of travel, contains passages of description so fine that they command the admiration of people whom much of his work disgusts. His powers range from a rich simplicity, a delicacy almost like that of Mr. W. H. Davies, to turbulent clangour, and from tenderness to savage irony and gross brutality. There was that in his intellect which might have made him one of England's greatest writers, and did indeed make him the writer of some things worthy of the best of English literature. But as time went on and his disease took firmer hold, his rage and his fear grew upon him. He confused decency with hypocrisy, and honesty with the free and public use of vulgar words. At once fascinated and horrified by physical passion, he paraded his disgust and fear in the trappings of a showy masculinity. And, not content with words, he turned to painting in order to exhibit more clearly still his contempt for all reticence.

It was inevitable (though it was regrettable) that such a man should come into conflict with the law over his novel *The Rainbow*; over some manuscripts sent through the post to his agent in London; and over an exhibition of his paintings. But a graver cause for regret is that the author of *Sons and Lovers*, of *Amores*, and the other books of poems, of *Aaron's Rod*, the short stories published as *The Prussian Officer*, *Ladybird*, and *Kangaroo* should have missed the place among the very best which his genius might have won.

In 1914 Lawrence married Frieda von Richthofen, who survives him. He left no children.

90. 'A Genius pain-obsessed', *Manchester Guardian*

4 March 1930, 12

We regret to announce the death of Mr. David Herbert Lawrence, the novelist, which occurred in a sanatorium at Vence, near Nice.

Mr. Lawrence was a writer who has exercised a more potent influence, perhaps, over his generation than any of his contemporaries. Born (on 11 September 1885) and reared in a mining village near Nottingham, he was early exposed to the life-killing conditions in which a mechanistic industrialism has entangled mankind. He was educated at Nottingham High School and University, and, after a short period as a teacher, went to Germany. He had already written some poetry, but it was not until 1913 that he published a novel, *Sons and Lovers*, which at once marked him as a writer of unusual power. The war intensified his loathing of the 'huge, obscene machine', to the effects of which his childhood and youth had been prematurely exposed. It made him a rebel against all the accepted values of modern Western civilization, one who challenged the disintegration not only of those who were actually caught in the blind mechanism of industry but of all who reflected a stultifying materialism either in a hard possessiveness, a soft emotionalism, or a sterile intellectualism.

He could not have assailed and portrayed this disintegration with such magnetic force and insight, if he had not experienced it to an abnormal degree in himself. Endowed with an intense physical and mental sensitiveness, he personified, as only a genius pain-obsessed beyond the possibility of humour or tolerance could, the suffering of a self-conscious mind exasperated by the soulless clangour of machinery, stifled by the fumes of all its waste products, and seeking fanatically to recover unity and health by a return to the primitive. It was this which drove him eventually to Italy, Sicily, Sardinia, and Mexico. He sought the unity of an instinctive life, untainted by self-conscious thought, among the Indians, in beasts and birds, reptiles, fish, and even mosquitoes. He sought it in trees and flowers and fruits. And the finest of his writings, whether in poetry or prose, are those which evoke the hot, bright, throbbing life of unconscious things, of the primitive dance, the sleek stallion, or the fireflies in the corn.

Gifted with extraordinary powers of sensuous divination, few writers have so intimately realized in words the electric force in the form and movements of animal life or the burning beauty of nature's colours. In contact with such life his self-conscious mind found transient appeasement from its hysteria and tortured bitterness. But these were at best only moments of respite. For Lawrence's writings are one long cry of agony and protest against a conflict in himself which can never be resolved. The cry is a cry of sex. For the sexual relation epitomized for him the mystery of life and, through his failure to find satisfaction in it, the disease of modern life, its divided being, its mental and physical sterility.

Through all his novels and short stories, from the early *Sons and Lovers*, perhaps his finest, through *Women in Love*, *Aaron's Rod*, and *The Rainbow*, down to his last privately printed *Lady Chatterley's Lover* this conflict of love and hate goes on between man and woman, each seeking appeasement in the other, yet failing to find it because, tied to the physical, they are tied also to its recurring cycle of desire and revulsion, which they are too self-conscious either to enjoy or inform with spiritual meaning.

Sons and Lovers is distinguished from its successors not only by the fact that Lawrence's ideas are more implicitly embodied in the action and characters than in his later novels, but by its recognition of some aspects of love other than that of a sex battle, and particularly in his analysis of the crippling love of a son for his dead mother. Apart, however, from this novel and parts of *The Rainbow*, he was always too obsessed by sexual fever and frustration to admit, still less to analyse, such spiritual potentialities of love as self-sacrifice or human devotion. Indeed, he never ceased to denounce such qualities as springing from a weakness which was the negation of that instinctive wholeness to which he so hopelessly aspired. And because he could attain to the heaven neither of spirituality nor of pure naturalism his writing is full of the cruelty of a personal hell in which was no pity or understanding, and laughter was never heard. Nor could a writer, so obsessed by the physical and so hostile to the conscious mind which he could not silence, create varied or subtle characters. His characters are always the same protagonists. On different battlegrounds they are always a man and a woman engaged in fighting each other out of self-consciousness.

It is a grim and endless contest. As Lawrence wrote in one of his poems,

> This love so full
> Of hate has hurt us so.

Yet there is a dark, convulsed beauty in his repeated rendering of it. For he was a magnificently equipped craftsman, and he was a man possessed. In such travel-books as *Twilight in Italy* and *Sea and Sardinia*, in *David*, the best of his plays, and in the best of his poems and short stories he drew upon the primitive sources of his being with remarkable effect. And even where the struggle between tortured flesh and mind is most convulsed and relentless, or he becomes, as in *Fantasia of the Unconscious*, the fanatical preacher and theorist, a flame of agonized sincerity burns through the style. It may be, for the most part, a destructive flame, but no writer since Tolstoy has wrestled more fiercely or significantly than Lawrence with the death in life from which he could never break free.

91. The theme of decline again, *Glasgow Herald*

4 March 1930, 5

The saying that 'the age produces the man' is one that does not apply to D. H. Lawrence. He did not belong to his age nor indeed to any age; he was a phenomenon that might appear in any century and be equally unexpected in each. A poet who poured forth some of the most beautiful and impassioned verse of his generation, a novelist who according to one great critic, 'has written in almost all his books more greatly than any other English writer of his time', a short-story writer who produced gems of incomparable lustre, a dramatist who created daringly and brilliantly, and still the one great tragic failure of his time, because he never succeeded in his self-appointed task of expressing the inexpressible.

There was little in Lawrence's paternity or in his upbringing to foreshadow the dark, passionate, self-tortured genius of the man. He was born at Eastwood, Nottingham, on 11 November [*sic*] 1885, the son of a collier and a collier's wife with very little, according to their frank son to distinguish them from other colliers and other colliers' wives. With a scholarship young David Herbert Lawrence went to Nottingham High School and later on to Nottingham University. Already impaired in health by an acute attack of pneumonia, he became an elementary school teacher in Croydon.

Ironically enough, Lawrence, whose life was tragic, met with none of the discouragement that is almost invariably the lot of writers with a new message to deliver. His earliest poems were accepted immediately by Ford Madox Hueffer for the *English Review*, and his first novel, *The White Peacock*, was published by Messrs. Heinemann as soon as offered.

At twenty-six years of age Lawrence gave up teaching to live by his pen. He never became a popular author, although every critic of recent years has practically taken for granted his position as one of the half-dozen greatest novelists of our time. He never became wealthy, although he lived in comfort in England, in Mexico, in Italy, or wherever his health and his restless spirit drove him. He did not seek popularity. He had a bitter contempt for easy emotions, for sentimentalism, for gregariousness. He had, in fact, a suspicion of human contacts that was the reflex of his passionate yearning for communion with the whole animate universe. He realized this pitiable isolation. In one autobiographic fragment he tried to trace it to its source. 'I don't feel', he confessed, 'there is any very cordial or fundamental contact between me and society, or me and other people. There is a breach. And my contact is with something that is non-human, non-vocal.'

It is indeed that superlative awareness of the very soul of Nature that distinguishes Lawrence's work, that gives it its startling beauty, that isolates him as a writer, and that shut him off as a man from the majority of his kind. Like Van Gogh, and the greatest of the Impressionists, he felt the pulsating life of the world and strove to symbolize it in his work. He put scientific materialism contemptuously behind him, and strove to achieve a new and completer synthesis through the instincts.

For the conscious intelligence Lawrence had little respect. His heroes are seldom men of more than moderate intellect, but they have a feral fascination that arises from the strength of their instincts. Too often they are obsessed by the physical demands of sex, which for Lawrence was no tame amusement for poetic youth but a terrible driving force, grand, ruthless, and devastating as lightning. One touch of humour might have humanized his outlook; but he went throughout life, seeing to the very core of every passion in human nature except what was most obvious. The result was that, while he wrote more splendidly in each succeeding volume, he wrote less truly. As a novelist he attained his peak in *The Lost Girl* or even in *Sons and Lovers*. During the years that followed he became more and more theory-ridden, more and more enamoured of the abnormal.

What was at first his most striking recommendation became an obsession, an incubus. From the beginning there was in his works a hint that he was imbued with a sense of the duality of the universe. One feels the presence of the very principle of evil in the character of the Italian lover in *The Lost Girl*, in the hardness of Aaron Sisson. But year by year this primeval malignancy hovers more and more darkly over Lawrence; he sees it in the lithe beauty of the snake at the water hole, hears it in the screech of the parrot, 'that strange, penetrating, antediluvian malevolence that seems to make even the trees prick their ears, and penetrates one straight at the diaphragm, belonging to the ages before brains were invented.' Over Lawrence this steely, cold evil exerts a fascination. He cannot get away from it. Like *The Woman Who Rode Away* he surrenders himself to it with a fearful ecstasy.

Negatively and powerfully charged, he had little liking for society, but retired wherever he expected to find Nature least spoiled by Western intellectualism, there to express himself in bursts of passionate, fiery writing. His greatest tragedy was not that he was, as he says himself, 'one of those who have a horror of serving in a mass of men, or even of being mixed up with a mass', but that his own philosophy made him recognize his duality and shrink alternately from contact with different sides of himself.

92. J. C. Squire, the 'precious residuum', *Observer*

9 March 1930, 6

D. H. Lawrence is dead. The reference-book facts about him have appeared in the daily newspapers. It is enough, here, to say that he was forty-four when he died; that he left school young to become a coal-miner as his father was before him; that he had a little 'higher education' later; that he then was a schoolmaster; and that, in the years immediately before the war, he became a professional writer, and attracted 'the few' with *The White Peacock*, *Sons and Lovers*, the play *The Widowing of Mrs. Holroyd*, and the novel *The Rainbow*, which was suppressed then but certainly would not have been suppressed now.

The mention of suppression naturally leads one to think of his latest books: a pamphlet urging that the artist should be allowed to use any words he may want to use, a novel prohibited by the Customs Authorities, and a book of poems, *Pansies*, which was first of all seized in typescript by the Customs and then issued, in a limited edition, from another manuscript. These books, I think, may be rapidly passed over. Ruling out, for the moment, all questions of morals and taste, it was perfectly obvious to admirers of Lawrence's genius that these works were unworthy of him. They showed a lack of grip and intensity—*Pansies* might almost be called Whitman and Water—and they also showed that the pathological traits which had always been noticeable in Lawrence's work had become much more marked than before. It has for long been obvious (the proverb *'de mortuis'* is the most preposterous of all proverbs, for only of the dead can we speak the whole truth) that Lawrence for years was suffering from some kind of galloping disease, whether consumption or another. Diagnosis along these lines can be overdone: witness Max Nordau's *Degeneration*, which contains an immense amount of sense, but pushes things so far that scarcely an artist could pass through his net. Yet the fact remains: certain diseases do make the senses more acute and the tongue more rhapsodical. 'The lunatic, the lover, and the poet Are of imagination all compact';

330

and certain germs will give them partners. But even germs can work only upon the material they find already in existence. A Flecker or a Keats or a Stevenson, in the grip of consumption, being generous and affectionate, may become feverishly eager and vivid, but will only become his own generous self intensified. A vain, self-centred, grudging, morose man will be similarly 'screwed up', but the results will not be so agreeable. Lawrence from the very beginning was suspicious of mankind and preoccupied with sex and sexual conflict. Critics, later on, may try to explain him in terms of complexes arising from circumstances, saying (*inter alia*) that he was over-conscious of having been a working man, and that, when he was struggling to obtain his due recognition as an artist, the iron entered into his soul. Some allowances may be made for these factors; when Lawrence denounces 'respectability', and 'English ladies and gentlemen', we can make allowances. Yet it must be remembered that other men, with other temperaments, have gone through as much as he and died younger than he without thinking it necessary to denounce all the rest of the world or even to 'react' against their surroundings at all, retaining, indeed, in their misfortunes, faith, hope, and charity.

Disease, in Lawrence, was working upon a very passionate, humourless, and self-centred man. Even in the early days of *Sons and Lovers* and *The Rainbow* it was difficult for him to imagine two people coming down to breakfast without depicting them as hating each other, really hating, beneath the surface of the silence or the small-talk. He never sympathized with anybody else: it never even occurred to him that they also were pent up in imperfect bodies, struggling with an intractable world, hankering for perfection and peace. He was really telling the truth about himself when, in *Kangaroo*, he wrote:

[Quotes *Kangaroo*, '"No," said Richard to himself, thinking of Kangaroo . . . a kick in the guts like Kangaroo.' (Chap. XVII, Penguin ed., p. 373.)]

More tolerant and understanding men, even when racked by pain, do not come to that: when Lawence had to take to his bed, he took to a bed of thorns made by himself. He seemed to enjoy the self-torture: and, exacerbated by it, he flung out streams of gall against all mankind. And particularly against all womankind. He loathed women for being not entirely comprehensible: in his fury, bred of frustrated desire and baffled reason, he came at last to the view that the two sexes could only be satisfied if they returned to the animal relation, the creative male dominating the submissive cow-woman—who, to do him justice, he thought would be happier were she to forgo any aspiration after intellectual or spiritual development. In his search for a solution of his problem, which is the problem of all humanity in an inordinately accentuated form, he went back to the pagan, and even back to the beast. He fled from institutions, from the speculations, discoveries, and revelations of the past only to repose his trust doubtfully on a 'first, dark, ithyphallic god', who was simply 'Nature red in tooth and claw'; and his revulsion against the complications and frustrations begotten of the necessary relations of men and women living for a few decades on this planet of working, sleeping, and breeding, led him to this:

The highest form of vertebral telepathy seems to exist in the great sperm whales . . . Grand, phallic beasts! Bullocks! Geldings! Men! R. L. wished he could take to the sea and be a whale, a great surge of living blood, away from these all-too-white people.

It is Romanticism and Rousseauism, in its phase of revulsion, gone to seed. The diseased Nietzsche, with his convulsive dreams of the Superman, went far enough in the way of refusal: but Lawrence, with his Whale, went farther still. He regretted the human race and all the later stages of Evolution. In a milder form his reaction had been expressed before: there are complimentary remarks about animals in Walt Whitman. But where Whitman conversed, without any great discomfort to himself, Lawrence screamed at the top of his voice.

Some souls, when in pain, are content to fall back upon the bosom of humanity as they know it: there are as many pleasant as unpleasant surprises in life, and what you ask from people you usually get: the rest may await revelation. Others, living more in the world of ideas, must find a faith: they take on some ancient system which provisionally explains life, death, and eternity, and in that they find content. Lawrence was of those who refuse to reconcile themselves unless they can, in their short span of life, work things out for themselves. Of course it cannot be done: least of all by an exasperated man who is very self-centred. Lawrence discarded all other philosophies and worked out the tiniest fragment of one for himself, which was of no use socially and could never have made a convert. On the strength of his awareness of his own independence and sincerity he became as self-righteous and pontifical as the narrowest Puritan of them all. The notion that, after all, somebody else might be partly right never seemed to cross his mind: it was this self-sufficiency that enabled him to lam-

poon in novels people who had thought him their friend but had not
realized that they had established no contact with him. He was as
haggard and burning as John the Baptist: but he did not know what he
was prophesying.

Why all this about his limitations? Well, simply because he was an
artist whose best things will probably live, not because of his vague and
violent doctrines, but in spite of them. Some of his admirers, I think,
overrate him. In every generation (if one ignores the few quiet vigilant
people who live in all ages at once) certain qualities in literature are
singled out as the stigmata of greatness at the expense of all others.
Twenty years ago 'magic' was all the vogue: 'Kubla-Khan' was exalted,
and works which had the elusive quality of that fragment were
fastened on as the true gold. At the moment, I think, the qualities most
in vogue are reckless explosiveness (which may be due either to
temperament or to calculation), audacity of thought about social
institutions (and particularly as regards sex), and an intense vision of
the physical surface of things. In all these respects Lawrence appealed
to his generation, though he was a poor craftsman. He never 'saw life
steadily and saw it whole', though he was without commonsense,
humour, tenderness or understanding of human character. Yet,
ultimately, a man's works survive by virtue of what he can do: though
what he cannot do may help to define him. At the climax of his powers,
Lawrence, both in prose and verse, achieved things that no other writer
has achieved. Even in the absurdest passages of his novels he is sometimes, through sheer tensity of feeling, very powerful. All the novels
have descriptive passages, records of colour, line, and the urge of life
expressed in surface, which impress one's imagination more forcibly
than the actual things described—Mexican or Italian skies, mountains
or hippopotamuses—would have done. And when he escaped from
the human conflict which tortured him, and ceased to bother about
Pharisaism, Philistinism, Socialism, and all other delusions, pretences,
ideas and schemes of struggling mankind, he wrote poems and sketches
as vivid and illuminating as any that ever were written. Some were
grim: he tended to seek, especially in later years, landscapes—barren
deserts sown with cactuses—which ironically reflected his own despair.

But sometimes his eyes dwelt on pleasanter things—the colours of
the Mediterranean and the flowers of Sicily—and did not darken them.
Twilight in Italy and *Sea and Sardinia* are to my mind better than any
of his novels, for they make their effects perfectly and provoke no
indignant response and no untimely laughter. And superior even to

these is his book of poems, *Birds, Beasts and Flowers* (to be found with much other work that is good and some that is bad, in his *Collected Poems*), in which he seems to have penetrated to the essence (at least the essence so far as human experience is concerned) of Snakes, Bats, Kangaroos, Rabbits, Fish, Tortoises, as no man ever did before. It is as though he were saying, 'I will not let thee go': looking at the growths, animal and vegetable, of fecund nature with eyes cleared from all traditional scales: attempting to wrest from them, as though no one had ever looked at them before, their essential characteristics. Here is the end of 'Kangaroo':

[Quotes from 'Kangaroo', 'How full her eyes are . . . to the earth's deep, heavy centre.' (*C.P.*, I, 394.)]

Free verse, no doubt—as Whitman's was. But sonorous writing, not quite prose; and done by a man who long ago demonstrated that he had an ear for traditional music. Much of Lawrence's writing, a generation hence, may be regarded as preposterous and even boring: but there is a precious residuum which is unique, and will be treasured, and which might never have come out of another kind of man. 'One nation making worth a nation's pain', as the poet complacently (though that is harsh) wrote of Greece. One man making worth one man's pain. Lawrence's frenzies and strange heresies will give place to others and be regarded with humorous compassion by those who, had they been his contemporaries, would have sworn by him. But he saw, he thought, he suffered, and he cared: the best of him will live and the rest of him will easily be forgiven and even forgotten.

93. Paul Rosenfeld, an assessment of Lawrence's work, *New Republic*

26 March 1930, lxii, 155-6

Paul Rosenfeld (1890-1946). Author and music critic. Associate editor of *Seven Arts* 1916-17. Music critic of *Dial* 1920-7.

Taken as a body, the books of the late D. H. Lawrence constitute a literary work more universal, an image of creation more broad and truthful, than that of any poet or proseman strictly contemporaneous with us. He was a mystic realist, better, a realistic mystic. The ablest of his fellows, Joyce, Proust, Eliot, and Pound, more impeccable workmen than himself, are to be classed among the great romantic idealists, always to an extent at odds with a world refusing to conform to their preconceived patterns of loftiness and liberality. Lawrence, however, was content that the world should be there, quite as it was. He faced it directly and found it good. Tragic or harmonious, his work was almost uniquely glad, warm, and soaring. Something must have bloomed flowerlike for him amid the chaotic surge of things, the sickening aftermath of war, permeating them with compensatory colour and scent. Perhaps it was some 'sacred fount', source of unfailing spiritual nourishment and consummation, rendering the matter that bore and held it wonderful even in painfulness. Whatever it was, Lawrence's writing, through its fire, elevation and pressing pace, communicates a feeling of sympathy with things the best of his fellows seem never quite to have known.

It is not to be denied that, intense though they are, the man's inimitable novels individually fall somewhat short of complete reality. His representative fictions are *The Rainbow* and *Women in Love*. The subject of both is the sexual relation, a matter which Lawrence drew to the light of day, and plumbed and formulated, with an almost heroic daring, subtlety, and effectiveness. Rich, new, central, and excitingly grasped as the subject is, the two representations none the less want some broadest relativity and proportionateness. The protagonists, no Tristans and Isoldes, but English farm folk, are conceived existing in a reality which is not quite workable. Momentarily, indeed, it approaches an erotic vacuum. The social forces, effective in the life of even so isolated a farm and independent a family as the one Lawrence imagines, are never sufficiently taken into account. However romantic the lovers might have been, however unconscious of the world, the world would nevertheless have surrounded their torments and ecstasies; and a Balzac would have managed to keep it persistently in the picture.

In later novels, Lawrence did contrive, it is true, to relate the sexual play to other aspects of reality. *Aaron's Rod* associates it subtly with the communistic upheaval in post-war Italy; *Kangaroo* brilliantly with fascist tendencies in Australia; *The Plumed Serpent* audaciously with the struggle between Catholicism and the radical peasantry in Mexico; *Lady Chatterley's Lover* amusingly with industrial conditions in the English midlands. But the fierce fine white glow which played on the central sexual subject in *The Rainbow* and *Women in Love*, giving these two works a place in English fiction entirely their own, is not so strong in these later, still strenuous, but none the less secondary examples of Lawrence's art.

Besides, few of Lawrence's novels and stories bring a material quite evenly formulated. The single exception to this rule is the early, deeply moving *Sons and Lovers*, more completely realized than any of its possibly more singular and 'advanced' successors. These frequently leave their characters, principally the male protagonists, in a state of half-definition; without the aura of a complete individuality. It is actually a trifle difficult to distinguish Will Brangwen and Anton Skrebensky in *The Rainbow*, divergent as their fates are; or Birkin and Gerald in *Women in Love*; or Ramón and Cipriano in *The Plumed Serpent*; and any and all of them, including the mysterious gamekeeper in *Lady Chatterley's Lover*, from the little novelist in *Kangaroo*. And while the women characters are somewhat more definite and in-dividualized, they, too, have a strange family likeness. Indeed, it can be said of D. H. Lawrence, more justly than of Wagner even, that his work was the picture of the relationship of a pair of people, serially continued.

Hence, taken singly, these bold, often glorious fictions will be found bare of some final persuasiveness, some complete co-extension with reality. Despite his wide experience of life and sympathy with it, there is no doubt that Lawrence, possibly because of his comparative youthfulness and the pulmonary disease which sapped his final years, never transcended a certain fixity of vision, a certain obduracy of interest. His portraits of the sexual relation have a tendency to linger over the initial stages. Towards the end of his career, his writing sometimes communicated a feeling of strain, as of a harsh insistence, a wilfulness in making a point and rounding a conception. Yet these fixations and inhibitions were by no means fatal.

To focus his entire work, his thirty-odd volumes of fiction, drama, travel, criticism, poetry, and translation, not individually but inclusively, is to grow strongly aware of a broad, generous approach to the world. It is to see the figure of a veritable *grand écrivain* define itself above them. While the man–woman relation invariably figures in the centre of any picture of things Lawrence drew, the number of subjects, scenes and storm centres he experienced and collated with it was after all healthily large. Mention has been made of the inclusion of the English, Italian, Mexican and Australian scenes in his novels. The range is grandly increased by his work in the extra-fictional forms. The collection of poems entitled *Birds, Beasts and Flowers* is a Mediterranean book, exquisitely comprehensive; also an experience of the American Southwest. *Studies in Classic American Literature* is a revelation, based on readings in Hawthorne, Poe, Melville, Whitman, and others, of the gradual mergence of 'soul' with 'matter' in the American character, and the first inarticulate, dreamlike appearance of a radical and American world-vision. *Twilight in Italy, Sea and Sardinia*, parallel in the form of travel books the spiritual adventures of the novels. The poems sing a whole Noah's Ark of 'birds, beasts, and flowers'. The essays called *The Crown* and *Fantasia of the Unconscious* are characteristic forays into metaphysics. The translations are from the Russian and the Italian. Nor are these extra-fictional works of less moment than the romances. Lawrence nowhere wrote with more mysterious sharpness than in *Twilight in Italy*, nowhere more powerfully and humorously than in *Studies in Classic American Literature*, more nakedly than in the play called *David*.

Nor is the broad approach ever superficial. It invariably is incisive. Lawrence moves with the greatest swiftness and power from the concrete to the heart of things. That is the high merit of all his writing. Whatever he touches becomes rich with the feeling of the profound impulses of life. He is subtle in his perceptions of their many shy, indirect manifestations; daring in his juxtapositions of these secret, dissociated, sometimes grotesque but never unreasonable expressions;

and unflagging in the sweep with which he keeps collating, organizing and developing his perceptions and carrying them to conclusions. Not always completely formalized and worked out, *Women in Love* and *Kangaroo* and *The Plumed Serpent* are, nevertheless, broad frescoes building up with telling, vigorous strokes, new pictures of the working of things; revelations of the form and coherency of our anarchic time.

The words themselves, the mould into which his thought fell, communicate direct feeling of life. Prose or poetry, narrative or critical, writing with Lawrence was an organic action, not the expression of any single or separate faculty: reason or emotion. It was the whole D. H. Lawrence 'feeling', from the root upward; speaking, uttering, sometimes almost beyond pleasure and pain, at the pitch of intensity. He would have it an unpremeditated, unarranged, faithful response to the incandescent moment which life was perpetually engendering and extinguishing in him and about him; 'the clash and foam of two meeting waves'; of two things instantaneously, miraculously at one. Live books and poems were a series and progress of such responses. Well, there is no question that at times the writing so undertaken verges on stammering, as we feel his effort to lay hold on some sensation, some intuition, too swift and impalpable for him. Still, for each of these failures, there are many instances of re-creations of the evanescent, the shadowy, in the form of an exceptional symbol. And the great moments of his art, the scenes in *The Rainbow* among the sheaves and on the dunes, those in *Women in Love* at the lakeside and in the high Alps, have an immediacy, a seething intensity, an almost physical summary of things, making the equally representative, highly finished passages in Joyce comparatively oblique and cold.

What it brings makes us in touch with the world in an all but universal experience. More consciously than any novelist before him, Lawrence was the poet of the Whole Man; he knew how directly the line ran from Whitman to himself. The agony of that Whole Man, that flame in the human being, that spirit, in its capacity for self-determination and absorption in material, is hideously characteristic of the day. Whether the oppressive conditions be called communistic or mechanistic, fascist or industrial; whether they be thought of as external or internal, the world is full of a war on the spirit; and its subterranean defiance. Lawrence's feeling was always of this strife. It was what he sensed in the intersexual tension. It was what he felt in Sardinia, and Australia, and Mexico, in the industrial English midlands. Throughout the world, he saw, something in the human being was seeking to withdraw from contact with other beings and materials; and passivity in the male, the masculine protest in the woman, mechanization and egalitarianism and rationalism, were but so many aspects of the recoil. And throughout the world, something was blindly striving to find the way to a new unity. This is, finally, what Lawrence recorded; and the resolution toward which every piece of his presses is the resolution of this conflict, either in death, or in some new leasehold of the whole man, some new assurance and integrity.

It was himself. The Whole Man was in this irritating, passionate, strangely narrow and still piercingly sighted bearded son of the Nottinghamshire coal-side; beyond any degree attained by any writer of his time, least by those who make a shibboleth of wholeness and exclude the world. It was the spirit in him that made his approach to the universe independent; enabled him to know for himself. It was the flame that made him write as he did, trust his senses and his feelings, touch and pierce the world at so many points, and create what in the last analysis is a universal body of work. Sympathy with present creation, sense of the whole man's battle in this pitifully hateful world, direct, uncompromising expression of what he saw and felt, no matter what the world might do, were but spirit's way of breathing in an artist. Novels, poems, and essays were but spirit's expansions to its own natural circumference in ever renewed embraces of a universe with which it was ideally, potentially coextensive; renewal of itself in the animation and development of wholeness wherever it lies in germ. As such, his writings speak to us. (To the devil with rationalism! Long live true humanism!) And as such, they go flaring down the halls of time.

94. Arnold Bennett, a tribute of admiration, *Evening Standard*

10 April 1930, 9

Arnold Bennett (1867–1931). Novelist. Notwithstanding what he says here, it seems that Bennett did lend Lawrence some money; and with Galsworthy he was apparently willing to have helped with the publication of *Women in Love* (*L* 18 November 1917). For Bennett's comments on *The Rainbow* and *The Lost Girl* see Introduction, pp. 10 and 14. Bennett also wrote a brief review of *The Woman Who Rode Away* (*Evening Standard*, 7 June 1928) in which he said that Lawrence 'can be formidably unreadable; nearly all his books have long passages of tiresomeness. But he is the strongest novelist writing today'.

The late D. H. Lawrence's recent volume of verse, *Nettles* [March 1930], gave me no pleasure. And when I beheld his posthumous collection of journalistic 'fugitive pieces', with the obnoxious title, *Assorted Articles* [April 1930], I decided before I opened it that I should not like it. Which just shows how wrong one can be. For I like it very much. Twenty-three articles, some short and none long. Despite a certain occasional disdainful roughness in the writing of them, these articles might well serve as models for young journalists—also for old journalists.

Lawrence was a novelist, a dramatist, a poet, a critic, a descriptive writer, and often first-rate in every branch. And he was a first-rate journalist too. He chose his subjects well. He handled them well— clearly, succinctly, picturesquely, beautifully. He didn't flourish his pen before beginning, and when he had finished he knew he had finished, and stopped. Not a word wasted. The subjects chosen were important, elemental, fundamental, and he struck at once deep down into the core of them. Nothing could be more fundamental than 'The "jeune fille" wants to know', or 'Sex versus Loveliness', or his 'Autobiographical Sketch'.

His remarks on sex are in the nature of an apologia. He is supposed to have been obsessed by sex. The fact is that at his best he was no more obsessed by sex than any normal human being. But he wrote more frankly and more cleanly about it than most. He tried to fish up sex from the mud into which it has been sunk for several hypocritical and timid English generations past. He had a philosophy of sex, which is more or less illustrated in all his novels. But also he had a philosophy of friendship, quite as profound and revealing as his philosophy of sex. As I have no space to discuss them I will not try even to state them.

I am a tremendous admirer of Lawrence. I should hesitate to go as far in admiration as that very distinguished critic E. M. Forster, who believes that he was 'the greatest imaginative novelist of our time'. In my opinion Lawrence lacked one quality—the power to discipline and control his faculties. Especially in his earlier books he let those superlative faculties—for instance his descriptive faculty—get the bit between their teeth and gallop around with a thunder of hoofs and a lightning of glances very exciting to hear and to see; but extravagant. Lawrence seemed to me sometimes to suffer from a delusion similar to the delusion of a sick man who thinks that if a given quantity of medicine will do him good, twice the quantity will do him twice the good. I wonder how Lawrence's description of sea-sickness, had he done one, would have compared with the classic description of that malady in the 107th Psalm! I think that David would have come out on top.

Still, I would say that no finer work has been done in our time than Lawrence's finest. He is not yet understood, even by the majority of his admirers. But he will be; and meanwhile his work must accept injustice. In the future no first editions of present-day writers will be more passionately and expensively sought for than Lawrence's, unless perhaps Joyce's. I regard this as certain.

I never met Lawrence; nor heard from him, nor wrote to him, though more than once I was tempted to do so. Accounts of his individuality vary greatly. I know well some of his intimate friends. They differ, not about his brilliance as a companion, but about the benevolence of his character. Once, many years ago, our paths crossed. My friend and business agent, the late James Brand Pinker, who was then also Lawrence's friend and business agent, came to me and said that Lawrence had said to him that my duty was to support such a writer as he was during the process of establishing himself. I thought there was something in this idea. Having reflected upon it, I told Pinker that I would give Lawrence three pounds a week if H. G. Wells and John Galsworthy would do the same. Pinker informed Lawrence and returned with the report that Lawrence regarded the offer as an insult. So I confined my assistance to the preaching of Lawrence's dazzling merits.

[Bennett continues with a favourable mention of Stephen Potter's *D. H. Lawrence. A First Study*, which, he says, deals mainly with Lawrence's philosophy, and ought to be complemented with a book on Lawrence the creative artist. He concludes:]

. . . The man's philosophy will go the way of all philosophies. It will be outmoded. But his creative work cannot be outmoded. The creations of first-class emotional power never are.

95. E. M. Forster on Lawrence's art and ideas, *The Listener*

30 April 1930, iii, 753-4

This is the text of a broadcast talk first given on the B.B.C., 16 April 1930.

In one of his recent talks, Mr. Desmond MacCarthy remarked that D. H. Lawrence is a difficult writer. It is a just remark, and I wish that Mr. MacCarthy and not I were speaking of him now. With his subtle insight, mature judgment and charming delivery, he would help you to understand Lawrence, and also he would persuade you to read him. You cannot understand a writer without reading him—an obvious and painful truth, and one that is often forgotten. And the only real reward a writer can have is to be read. At present Lawrence is not being read enough or in the right way. He has two publics, neither of them quite satisfactory. There is the general public, who think of him as improper and scarcely read him at all, and there is a special public, who read him, but in too narrow and fanatical a way, and think of him as a sort of god, who has come to change human nature and society. His own public—a real public—he has scarcely found that yet, and it is in the hope of persuading you to form part of it that I am speaking. I regard him myself as one of the great writers of our time. But how am I to persuade you to share this opinion? I wish I were Mr. MacCarthy.

Lawrence belonged to the working classes. He grew up in a collier's cottage on the border of Notts and Derby, and he describes that country and the life there in his two early novels *The White Peacock* and *Sons and Lovers*, and in his play, *The Widowing of Mrs Holroyd*. He never worked down the mine himself, but was trained as a teacher—probably owing to the influence of his mother: he was devoted to his mother; she had great character and intelligence and her death was one of the most terrible things he had to bear. For a time he was a schoolmaster near London—and perhaps this accounts both for his mistrust

343

of education and for the didactic way in which that dislike is expressed. Then he took to literature, and it was then or about then—that is to say, in the spring of 1915—that I met him three or four times. I did not know him well, or meet him again subsequently, but he leaves a vivid impression—so quick with his fingers and alive in his spirit, so radiant and sensitive, so sure that if we all set out at once for one of the South Sea Islands we should found a perfect community there which would regenerate the world. Shelley must have been a little like that, but Lawrence was a rougher, tougher proposition than Shelley; there is a vein of cruelty in him, and though he did beat his wings against society in vain, he was ineffectual as a bird of prey rather than as an angel. He came to no South Sea Island. The war developed. His health was already very bad, and exempted him from military service, but not from the terrors of the imagination. He suffered acutely; moreover his wife, to whom he was devoted, was German, and they were persecuted by stay-at-home patriots and driven from place to place. He has left a description of this in *Kangaroo*, and now that war books are fashionable, perhaps this description will be read again; it is the most heartrending account of non-fighting conditions that I have yet come across. He escaped from England at last, and never settled down in it again. For the rest of his life he moved from country to country—Germany, Italy, Australia, Mexico, etc.—pursued by good advice from the admirers of his earlier work, and, greatly to his credit, never taking the least notice of it. His later work is less admired, and certainly he becomes more mannered and didactic. But his essential qualities—the poetry that broods and flashes, the power to convey to the reader the colour and the weight of objects—all that remains. Indeed to my mind his finest novel is a late one—*The Plumed Serpent*—and anyone who is under the illusion that he went to pieces at the end of his life would do well to read it. He died a couple of months ago, in the South of France.

Lawrence felt himself to be a teacher with a message to us to follow our instincts. Whether the message is sound, I do not know: it certainly is not new. But he is also a poet, and it is the relation between the teacher and the poet that I find difficult. I believe they are inseparable, and if he had not a message his poetry would not have developed. It was his philosophy that liberated his imagination, and that is why it is so idle to blame him for not keeping strictly to literature. Much of his work is tedious, and some of it shocks people, so that we are inclined to say: 'What a pity! What a pity to go on about the subconscious and the solar plexus and maleness and femaleness and African darkness and the cosmic beetle when you can write so touchingly about men and women, and so beautifully about flowers.' But we must realize that, in his queer make-up, things were connected, and that if he did not preach and prophesy he could not see and feel. We must—though it is sometimes difficult—realize that he cannot be improved. His treatment of sex, for instance, which has raised such protests—I am not going to speak of it here, this is not the place. But it does connect up with things of which I am going to speak, and to pretend it does not would be to insult his memory. Although he is a creature of moods— you seldom know what is coming next—he is not a creature of compartments. You cannot say, 'Let us drop his theories and enjoy his art', because the two are one. Disbelieve his theories, if you like, but never brush them aside. And do not scold him, even when he scolds you. He resembles a natural process much more nearly than do most writers, he writes from his instincts as well as preaching instinct, so that one might as well scold a flower for growing on a manure heap, or a manure heap for producing a flower.

His dislike of civilization was not a pose, as it is with many writers. He hated it fundamentally, because it has made human beings conscious, and society mechanical. Like Blake and other mystics, he condemns the intellect with its barren chains of reasoning and its dead weights of information; he even hates self-sacrifice and love. What does he approve of? Well, the very word 'approve' would make him hiss with rage, it is so smooth and smug, but he is certainly seeking the forgotten wisdom, as he has called it; he would like instinct to re-arise and con- nect men by ways now disused. He thinks humanity has taken a wrong turning. Book after book, he hammers away at this, and strikes many coloured sparks of poetry from it, until the whole fabric of his mind catches fire, and we get pages and chapters of splendour. He does be- lieve in individuality—his mysticism is not of the Buddhistic, annihilistic sort—and, illogical as it sounds, he even believes in tenderness. I think here that the memory of his mother counts. Theirs was an attachment which cut across all theories, and glorified other relationships when she died. Tenderness is waiting behind the pseudo-scientific jargon of his solar plexuses and the savagery of his blood-tests. It is his conces- sion to the civilization he would destroy and the flaw in the primitive myths he would re-create. It is the Morning Star, the Lord of Both Ways, the star between day and the dark.

It is obvious, from what I have said, that his novels are bound to be unusual. We usually ask of a novel, firstly, that its characters shall live; secondly, that it shall have some sort of unity, and if we apply either of these tests to his books they fail. In the earlier books, some of the people are alive because he was drawing more on his surroundings than he did later: George Saxton in *The White Peacock* was modelled on a young farmer he knew, and the mother in *Sons and Lovers* is his own mother. And all through his career he was capable of clever, malicious thumbnail sketches—the short story entitled *Jimmy and the Desperate Woman* contains one of them. But he was not a true creator of character. He was too irritable and too theoretical for that. His people have to illustrate something, he cannot allow them to wander freely or to indulge in the disinterested humorous by-play that is so characteristic of English fiction. He is in deadly earnest himself, and they have to be the same, and it is curious that with these restrictions they should be as interesting as they are. They are not alive, yet they are filled with living stuff. The quaint quartet in *Women in Love*—have you ever met young men and women like that? And one of them is supposed to be in the Board of Education. Yet do not they keep signalling to you, despite their arguments and adventures? You cannot class them as dummies or relegate them to the valley of dry bones. And a similar doubt will beset you when you apply the second of the tests suggested above—the test of artistic unity. The plots are not well made, the books are not aesthetic wholes, yet there is a satisfied feeling at the close. The sense of life has again swooped in, poetry has taken place of construction. I have already compared Lawrence to a bird, and when reading his novels I seem to follow a series of short exquisite flights, beginning and ending for no special reason, yet linking together all the spots on which the bird has perched.

One novel, though, does survive the normal construction tests, and that is *The Plumed Serpent*. It is, on the face of it, a preposterous work about three people who dress up and pretend that the ancient gods of Mexico have returned to earth. But it is beautifully put together, the atmosphere increases with the story, both culminate. We begin in the filth and meanness of Mexico City, which seems to represent the whole country; then there is the hint of something else, of an inland lake of sweet waters, where the filth and meanness are not so much washed away as recomposed; and behind the lake, above thunderclouds of horror and splendour, rise the shapes of the returning religion. As the tension grows, hymns are introduced—the finest of Lawrence's unrhymed poems—and bind the narrative emotionally until we can accept what would otherwise seem grotesque. The returning gods hold dialogue with Christianity. The images of Christ and the Virgin and the Saints are carried with reverence from the village church. They have failed, they are weary, their kingdom of love never came, they must repose. The sweet waters of the lake receive them, they go up to their peace in fire. And the ancient gods of Mexico enter the church in their place, and receive the worship of men. After that the book concludes rather vaguely, but the general effect has been superb, we have assisted at a great mystical ceremony, and all the Mexican landscape has come alive.

I will end with one of his poems: it will illustrate some of the points I have been making. It is an early poem on the death of his mother, and it looks forward to the day when he will become famous and be able to honour her—a day that is perhaps not far off:

[Quotes the whole of 'On That Day'. (*C.P.*, I, 176.)].

96. A plain man's view, Alan Reynolds Thompson on Lawrence, *Bookman* (N.Y.)

July 1931, lxxiii, 492–9

Alan Reynolds Thompson (b. 1897). Critic. Author of books on public speaking and drama.

'To me and to many thousands,' writes Mr. Stephen Potter, his most recent admirer, 'D. H. Lawrence is the greatest living writer of this generation, who has had the power, in a sense which separates him from all his contemporaries, to create a world.'

Though the admiration of the critics seems to have been somewhat damped by the posthumous publication of *The Virgin and the Gipsy*, this judgment is probably too moderately enthusiastic for some. Others would consider it wildly excessive. After his death Lawrence remains, as before, an object of controversy. But the time has come to attempt objective appraisal of his work.

Obviously much of it, particularly the later books, is such as to make one either accept him prayerfully as a prophet or dismiss him as a crank. The usual academic judgment makes him a man of one book— *Sons and Lovers*—and a few short stories. Fine as that novel is, it is written in the naturalist tradition of the nineties; and such a judgment implies that Lawrence was great when most derivative but absurd when most individual. On the other hand many literary persons, like the author of our opening quotation, admire him for his later work. It is possible to take middle ground; in such a book as *The Plumed Serpent*, which Mr. Potter considers the culmination of Lawrence's thought, to recognize extravagances of pseudo-mysticism, and at the same time to appreciate the intensity of emotion and imagination behind them.

Even those who like him least will admit his intensity. It becomes strikingly manifest when we compare Lawrence with other novelists.

Galsworthy is admirable for objectivity, for urbane and graceful irony; but we feel that he can hold himself judicially aloof perhaps because he has never been immersed in life. (I state this not as a biographical fact, of course, but as an impression.) Wells can play with panaceas like a schoolboy because he never faces the stubbornness of reality. He seems, in comparison with Lawrence, the perennial adolescent. Lawrence writes from the bitterness of suffering and struggle; his concern is not the vicarious pain of a kindly nature at the sufferings of others, or the delight of an ingenious mind in mechanisms and speculation; it is the direct expression of experience. Such a writer, let his ideas be never so foolish, will always impress readers, and speak with unrivalled immediacy to some whose emotional attitudes coincide with his.

But intensity alone is merely the energy of a mind; its value must be judged by the ends towards which that energy is directed. 'For the property of passion', said Coleridge in one of those *aperçus* which makes his greatness as a critic, 'is not to create, but to set in increased activity.' And primarily we must judge Lawrence, as undoubtedly the world will finally judge him, by the ends he sought.

Mr. Potter helps us here with an emphatic if expressionistic statement of Lawrence's philosophy.

It is an old way to divide the universe, [he writes.] Body and spirit. Below and above.

In the *Phaedrus* Plato speaks of the two halves as a team of two horses driven by a charioteer:

'The right-hand horse is upright and cleanly made, and has a lofty neck and an aquiline nose: his colour is white . . . he is a lover of honesty and modesty and temperance, and the follower of true glory. . . .

'Whereas the other is a crooked animal . . . he is flat faced and of a dark colour. . . .'

The same two worlds, but the difference lies in which way the sympathy goes. . . . Sublime: lofty: exalted: enlightenment: climbing ever higher: *higher mammals*: *higher education.* . . . To Lawrence this imagery is the language of everything in the world he most hates.

He reverses it, therefore. *Dark* comes in instead. Dark, dark, *endarkenment*, he would say. . . . He reverses Plato.

'He reverses Plato.' That is positive enough, surely, and though like all generalizations it over-simplifies, it may be accepted. In general tendency Lawrence is a dualist like Plato, to the extent that he sees in our nature a clear division, the abstracting powers of reason on the one hand, together with the voluntary effort to bring those abstractions into actuality through conduct; and on the other hand the instinctive urges that are our heritage from our animal ancestry, and that rise in us from beneath the conscious level. He sees these two halves of our nature not as parts of a normally unified whole but as naturally and even properly antagonistic. He is no naïve naturalist, fancying the reconcilement of the two an easy matter; rather he is at one with the great religious seers of the past in realizing the depths and the bitterness of their conflict.

He is at one with them so far, but no farther! His values are inverted, Plato upside-down. He becomes an advocate, as it were, for the devil; he ranges himself with Nietzsche, who divided Greek thought into Dionysian and Apollonian, and espoused the former, cursing Socrates for blighting the flower of Nature with cold reason. We know where Lawrence stands: among the most violent of the rebels who for the past hundred and fifty years have been fighting to enthrone the subrational. And we understand his popularity with literary Bohemia.

This popularity leads, by the way, to interesting reflections on human inconsistency. The literary Bohemian, as a general rule, is either hostile or contemptuous towards writers who accept traditional ethics. Art, he says loftily, when talking of the traditionalist, has nothing to do with morals. Or he attacks the man with suggestions of nasty complexes, the result of 'Puritanical' suppressions. Or, fortified by the pragmatists, he dismisses the traditional moral code as outworn anyway. At all events traditional morals, he feels, have no business in serious modern novels. But, curiously, this same Bohemian will praise Lawrence, whereas if there is anything obvious about Lawrence it is that he is strictly in the old English tradition—a consistent and persistent moralizer, a preacher, a writer who thinks so little of 'art' and so much of his doctrines that he sacrifices the one to the others continuously and carelessly. But since his doctrines find favour with the literary Bohemian, the latter finds them perfectly consistent with genius!

The sensible attitude, it would seem, is to admit that since human nature is inevitably moral—in some fashion—and that since novels inevitably reflect the characters of their authors, a consideration of their principles is necessary to a rounded judgment. Even the studied objectivity of Flaubert or George Moore is a revelation, but with Lawrence the revelation is intentional. His puppets are his mouthpieces and his plots the but slightly altered song of himself. In a book like *Kangaroo*, for example, he scarcely attempts to conceal his identity with the hero; and in all the books the characters exist less in their own right than as parts of Lawrence or objects of his aversion. So obvious is this that Mr. Potter, who admires him, writes a psychic biography solely by means of quotations and synopses drawn chronologically from Lawrence's works. The resulting account is probably as accurate as the majority of our smart modern 'lives'.

We cannot, then, even if we would, evade Lawrence's principles. But I have no wish to leave them as an abstract generalization such as that he reverses Plato. Though he made attempts on occasion to theorize, his doctrines are significant only as part of his nature, manifested suggestively in his fictions. Their consistency is that of character rather than logic, and must be deduced from general impressions. From general impressions, in what special ways does his intensity most strikingly appear? Some would say, in an obsession with sex. The comment is certainly inevitable, as Mr. Potter, who would like to avoid it, admits. But as I review Lawrence's work another trait seems possibly more noticeable, at least more significant. It is rebellion.

People who knew him praise his generosity and friendliness, but what stands out in his writing is his animosity. He was fond of the word *love* but more of the feeling *hate*. Even his lovers love with much of hatred and little of kindliness; their amorousness is mixed with fear. He nursed his aversions through all his volumes. They were evidently the product of some deep-seated psychic malaise. They set him apart from ordinary men, among both cranks and prophets. Richard Aldington inclines to place Lawrence among the latter, and pleasantly calls him a great example of the English Heretic, a 'true Anarchist, living outside human society, rejecting all its values, fiercely concentrated on his own values'.

Let us note some of the 'values' which he more particularly rejects. For one thing, he dislikes our modern industrial civilization, with its mechanized ugliness and repression of native spontaneity. He can never forget the hideous collieries of his childhood. In this aversion he is of course like most poetically-minded people, but it is his peculiarity that he devotes only passing attention to general economic or political problems, and has no interest in social programmes. It is his distinction indeed that in our day of mass reforms he looks for salvation only in individuals. (This is doubtless what Aldington means by his anarchism.) But in seeking his saviours he rejects the rest.

In particular he rejects the strong complacent blond Saxon, the hero of ordinary tales. Sham! cries Lawrence; he has given himself over to

false gods—such as Mammon—and denied his instincts! That denial
is in fact the denial of the 'Holy Ghost' within him; and it shall not be
forgiven him by Lawrence. In contrast the Lawrence-hero is small,
self-centred, and dark; a man who wants to be let alone and who obeys
his lusts. He is, as Mr. Potter admits, 'Lawrentiomorphic'; he is not
happy, but he 'lives'.

What seems to Lawrence the mental perversion of sex is indeed the
chief object of his hatred. As a result he attacks not only those who
degrade sex by sniggering and uncleanness, but even the idealizers of
love. These latter pervert the business of the body by meddling with
their minds. Love, he feels, should be subliminal, animal-like:

> You must know sex in order to save it, your
> deepest self, from the rape
> of the itching mind and the mental self,
> with its pruriency always agape.

Male intellectualists are bad enough, but female bluestockings are to
him, as they were to Strindberg, as a red rag to a bull. The reason is
probably that Lawrence, like Strindberg, knew and feared their
power over him. Hermione Roddice in *Women in Love* is a particularly
unpleasant example. She starved her instincts by attempting to intel-
lectualize them; she lusts less for sexual satisfaction, of which she is
incapable, than for power over men; she wants to know, not to feel.
On one occasion, to be sure, she does follow her instincts, and in a
sadistic fury brought about by amorous frustration nearly brains her
lover. But of course her instincts were perverted.

As has been suggested, this hatred of Lawrence's seems the result of
fear—a continual fear of anything that might encroach upon his ego.
Such a suggestion is speculative, but the hatred is so extraordinary that
speculations are inevitable. Indeed the melodramatic methods of
psycho-analysis are in Lawrence's case so tempting that we may safely
prophesy their use soon in at least one 'modern' biography. We need
to remind ourselves that all such methods are unscientific and subjective.
But one or two further suggestions seem justified by the intensely
autobiographical nature of Lawrence's work.

Lawrence feared above all the loss of spiritual integrity. Probably the
story in *Sons and Lovers* and the early poems is accurate: his emotional
development in adolescence was nearly frustrated by the love of a
clinging mother. One need not, however, call this the 'Oedipus
complex' or swallow Freud entire to understand how such an experi-

ence might lead to the fierce assertion of 'maleness' and touchy egotism. If, as seems likely, Lawrence's later experiences with women reinforced his original bias, the dominant trend in his writing is comprehensible.

In this connection the parallel with Strindberg seems so striking as to deserve further extension. Both men had literary genius; both had extraordinary emotional and imaginative sensibility. Both idolized their mothers, idealized women and were disillusioned, rebelled against their own bondage to love, and vociferated masculinity. In their books both sought to objectify and universalize personal difficulties. Strindberg, struggling against his desperate need of the impossible dream woman, turned general misogynist. Lawrence, with greater sanity and less violence, was content to hate only the intellectual.

Lawrence's personal aversions as a result became rationalized as parts of a doctrine, mixed with eccentric prejudice. His preference for dark men is either symbol or whimsy. His attack on the intellectual perversions of sex, on the other hand, contains much that is sound and subtle. His rationalizing activity, like that of the paranoiac, was immense and often admirable but never objective and impersonal. His ideas were not on this account wrong, of course, for one can be very far from agreement with him generally and yet applaud some of his prejudices. Certainly he was not sentimental like Sherwood Anderson, and always spoke his mind like a man.

But no one can rest happy in hatred, least of all a poet with a sensitive soul. One must have also his admirations. Of all Lawrence's books *Lady Chatterley's Lover* is, I suppose, most abhorrent to the conservative, considering its frequent use of indecent monosyllables, its celebration of adultery, and excessive delight in carnality. Yet here we find perhaps his nearest approach to normal love. In this late story he seemed to have worked free from that fear-born savagery that characterizes most of his lovers, for here there is something like tenderness as well as lust, and the lovers find that integration of body and spirit which should be the criterion of a normal life. But though Lawrence idealizes the result, doubts obtrude themselves.

These doubts do not concern themselves with the question of obscenity and pornography. Lawrence himself, in a pamphlet on the subject, indicates in characteristic excited style that he had a high moral aim in *Lady Chatterley's Lover*. Since the question is not fundamental we may take his word for it. What shocks one age may not shock another; and it may be a healthy thing for grown men to scribble in books what small boys scribble on walls. It is not such things, but a writer's general influence and tendency which are ethically important.

Again, we may well forego the charge that Lawrence's animality was perverse. Doctor Joseph Collins, who looked at literature a few years ago, had something to say on the subject. The doctor's glance at literature was amateurish enough, but he may well be an expert in psychiatry. The question is best left to the experts.

Our doubts concern Lawrence's objects of admiration. To the majority of men a successful sexual union, desirable as it may be, is not the end of a good life; it must by liberating the powers lead on to other ends. When Mr. Potter quotes Lawrence to the effect that sex should be 'a consummation in darkness preparatory to a new journey towards consummation in spirit', we may heartily agree; but though of physical consummations there are a great plenty, the spiritual consummation is notable for its absence. Physical ecstasy is a door like Dunsany's Glittering Gate: it opens, not on heaven, but on emptiness.

But let us do Lawrence justice in the matter. Naturalist though he was, his naturalism was not the usual soft disintegration of the human into the animal, not the familiar sentimental disguising of animality by a pretended spirituality or art-worship. Lawrence cast scorn on the romantic dream of 'going native' in the South Seas; and he had a virile delight in conflict which makes life vivid as well as hard, insisting on distinguishing civilized from savage, human from animal, as well as male from female. He is distinguished from the ordinary naturalistic primitivist, romantic or scientific, who without knowing it uses his head to worship his loins.

Lawrence knew what he was doing. He would have no truck with the sentimental idealists; he would away with mealy-mouthed hypocrisy, call things by their Anglo-Saxon names, and be true to his lower nature. His fierce assertion shows both energy and a clear mind. Yet since he could not rest in negations and hates, but had abjured the spirit of light, his need for affirmation led him inevitably to fantastic pseudomysticism. He had forsworn Apollo. The only course left was to prostrate himself before the dark god. But the dark god in his stark nakedness could not be worshipped comfortably by a poet, even though Lawrence attempted it; and he began to dress his idol. He was careful not to borrow plumes from the bright spirit, but gave the idol a sinister and lustrous coat pleasing to the aesthetic if not the moral sense—symbolically, the skin of a snake. His god could then appear fearful and strange and mystical. It is not surprising that he should find final embodiment in the bloody religion of a barbaric race. *The Plumed Serpent*, with its conversion of a civilized woman to love of a Mexican Indian and worship of Quetzalcoatl, is the result. The dualism of our nature is abandoned at length by extinction of light in darkness.

But deny the light of reason and control, and you deny humanity. As Lawrence admits, you cannot revert to savagery, or to the beasts. You are shut out of the sentient universe. The physical world is there, waiting. . . . The doctrine leads to death. One is reminded of another naturalist poet, similarly obsessed with sexuality and inclined to hate mankind—Robinson Jeffers. The almost insane violence of the latter's themes finds its recoil in a longing for the tomb. The expression of such a longing is familiar, but usually sentimental. With Jeffers it seems sincere, and it is certainly logical, the inevitable outcome of his pessimistic naturalism. Lawrence is less ruthless and consistent, for by mysticizing physical fulfilment into a religion he preserved his optimism.

So much for general principles. Important as these are, we must not overlook other literary qualities.

Lawrence was not a stylist. Artistry did not interest him, and although he had obvious powers of expression, he did not attempt to prune and polish. On the contrary he was content to get an effect simply by 'harping'. 'She was there so small and light and accepting in his arms, like a child, and yet with such an insinuation of embrace, of infinite embrace, that he could not bear it, he could not stand. . . . Then for a few seconds he went utterly to sleep, asleep and sealed in the darkest sleep, utter, extreme oblivion.' Yes indeed, he went to sleep; there is no doubt about it! But what of it? We might reasonably assume from so much shouting that the fact was of some importance, but we would be wrong. It is simply Lawrence's usual way of emphasizing the erotic excitement of his characters. He continually cries his characters' emotions at us; the general effect is of tension without adequate cause, and for less incandescent spirits than his, tiresome.

His narrative style tends to be either brutally abrupt and bald, or garrulous. At times, when his heaped repetitions develop a really crucial situation, he has power. But he repeats too often, exclaims too much; his fervour becomes as monotonous as the 'final clinches' of screen lovers. In his rimed verse his versification is perfunctory and rough, his phrasing seldom memorable. Naturally he preferred free verse, in which negligence seems appropriate and spontaneity is less hampered. With Wordsworth's definition of poetry in mind, we may consider Lawrence's a good example of what might be called the *overflow* theory in practice. Lawrence, like Wordsworth, shows its faults, but he lacks Wordsworth's occasional sublimity.

His plots, like his style, are rambling and careless. He introduces characters only to drop them; he builds up situations of extreme emotionality, and they come to nothing; and at any time he engages in *longueurs* of discussion, as freely as Aldous Huxley but without the latter's wit or range, letting the story go hang. The plots are unimportant for him. In this, to be sure, he is like some great novelists, who are valued for their parts, not their wholes, and are great in spite of their lack of construction. But Lawrence offers us no such compensations.

He is praised for his description, and indeed he has a remarkable power of *Einfühlung, feeling* himself *into* surrounding nature, or reconstructing the alien life of a fish or a tortoise in its own terms. What distinguishes the descriptive passages in the novels seems to be chiefly his faculty for seeing nature as symbol or background for men's erotic needs. 'The wood was silent, still and secret in the evening drizzle of rain, full of the mystery of eggs and half-open buds, half-unsheathed flowers. In the dimness of it all trees glistened naked and dark as if they had unclothed themselves, and the green things on earth seemed to hum with greenness.' His fondness for repetition applies to certain words, as in this passage *secret*, *mystery*, and particularly *dark*. The effect is an emotional heightening that comes from suggestion and symbol, not the logical sense of the words; at times indeed his prose verges on unacknowledged free verse. The mystery of sex was doubtless to him incommunicable except by suggestion; but to the critical reader his practice at times seems merely uncontrolled emotionality.

The people of his books are seen little on the surface as 'characters', and are usually, as has been said, projections of himself and his dislikes. It is rather in his analyses of emotional relationships of men and women —of what Mr. Potter calls the flow beneath the surface of social intercourse—that he manifests his power. We are constantly bidden look at the anatomy of impulse, or rather, its physiology. In support of his central belief in the instinctive Lawrence elaborated a physiology of nerve-centres, to correspond to the 'polarities' of the 'unconscious'. The subliminal region, surprisingly enough, is not all sexual as Freud assumed; its centres are four nerve ganglia, front and back, abdomen and chest, each with its specific tendency towards acceptance or repulsion of the outer world. Here again we gladly leave Lawrence to the experts, merely recording our unscientific feeling that all this is either symbolism or twaddle. But at all events the scheme of bodily 'polarities' serves him continually in his books: his men and women communicate, as Mr. Potter says, praising him for a new thing, with their whole body; they affect each other less by faces than by thighs and buttocks.

The result is undoubtedly, whether we like it or not, an important cause for his fame and his difficulty. His people do not act after the conventional patterns of fiction, or of life as we ordinary folk see it. They obey impulses not explained; they respond to mysterious magnetisms in each other's bodies that reason does not recognize; they take us out of the normal world into a distorted, elemental, savage region where we cannot make the accustomed emotional responses and are kept perplexed and frustrated. Yes, say the disciples. Lawrence has created a new world. It is an achievement of genius. But we may perhaps still be sceptical. Granting the novelty of the creation, we may still doubt its value. The dark god is by definition irrational and indefinable; his doings, as recorded by Lawrence, are not therefore necessarily the product of a higher insight. The subliminal uprushes of Lawrence's characters may be the intuitions of a seer; they may also be the phantasies of a romantic dreamer with a psychosis. They may indeed throw light less on the character than on Lawrence. Shakespeare, in the sleep-walking scene, wrote a masterpiece of objective insight into other minds. In Lawrence's works can we find a single similar scene? Do we ever really look into the mind of anybody but Lawrence?

The narrowness of Lawrence's interests is noteworthy. Even his treatment of sex is narrow. Love between parents and children is seldom described and usually perverse. Of course that idealizing of the loved object which is the age-old activity of normal poetic spirits is to him anathema. For one who talks so much of living the instinctive life Lawrence shows a surprising lack of interest in those instincts connected with sex which lead a man to desire a family, to cherish as well as lust after a woman, to adore his children. And for one who seeks 'fulfilment' so ardently, he seems totally to overlook the fact that normal women feel their lives unfulfilled unless they have had, not lovers, but babies.

And in certain general qualities usual in great writers he is deficient. In the travel books and free-verse poems he seems more at ease and objective than in the novels, and at times is even whimsical. But the whimsical mood is not characteristic, and in the major works his intense preoccupation shuts out more of humour than occasional bitter sarcasm. And he is of course not interested in the world of the intellect. He can report the chatter of 'intellectuals' about the latest things in art and science; but his attitude toward all such chatter is contemptuous. The talk of serious thinkers he seems not to know at all. To him, as to Ursula Brangwen at college, the world of books and speculation is unreal, and its inhabitants not quite alive. Incapable of impersonal thought, he could not understand it. We are reminded of a comment of Santayana on Browning. 'Browning's hero,' he writes, 'because he has loved intensely, says that he has lived; he would be right, if the significance of life were to be measured by the intensity of the feeling it contained, and if intelligence were not the highest form of vitality.' To Lawrence intelligence, instead of being the highest form of vitality, is its enemy.

But let us close by recalling Lawrence's achievements. He was by nature passionate, sensitive, imaginative. Early experience seemingly fixed in him a permanent dread of being absorbed by 'smother love'. He rebelled therefore against all apparent causes of frustration, and desperately sought manhood and integrity, hitting right and left against what seemed to him their enemies. He thought he found salvation in abandonment to sexual instinct. This abandonment led him to subtle psychological analyses of himself and to a pseudo-mystical worship of the dark god of primitive instinct. It enabled him to throw over his wordy and otherwise tiresome tales an atmosphere of feverish passion. And it made him a prophet for those of our time who, as W. C. Brownell has put it, think themselves emancipated but are only unbuttoned.

97. 'The victim and the sacrificial knife', T. S. Eliot on Lawrence, a review of *Son of Woman* by J. M. Murry

Criterion, July 1931, x, 768–74

Mr. Murry has written a brilliant book. It seems to me the best piece of sustained writing that Mr. Murry has done. At any rate, I think that I understand it better than most of his recent writings. It is a definitive work of critical biography or biographical criticism. It is so well done that it gives me the creeps: probably these matters matter no longer to Lawrence himself; but any author still living might shudder to think of the possibility of such a book of destructive criticism being written about him after he is dead. But no one but Mr. Murry could have done it; and I doubt whether Mr. Murry himself could do it about anyone but Lawrence. The victim and the sacrificial knife are perfectly adapted to each other.

Near the beginning Mr. Murry says:

> If Lawrence is to be judged as the 'pure artist', then it is true that he never surpassed, and barely equalled, this rich and moving record of a life (*Sons and Lovers*). But Lawrence is not to be judged as a pure artist; if ever a writer had 'an axe to grind', it was he. Set in the perspective—the only relevant perspective —of his own revealed intentions, *Sons and Lovers* appears as the gesture of a man who makes the heroic effort to liberate himself from the matrix of his own past.

This is true. But I am doubtful what the term 'pure artist' means to Mr. Murry; and I am doubtful whether this criticism is praise or condemnation. I agree that Lawrence was not a 'pure artist', in that he never succeeded in making a work of art; but then, that is just relative failure, that is all. And if he was not trying to make a work of art, then he should have been: the less artist, the less prophet; Isaiah succeeded in being both. And to be a 'pure artist' is by no means incompatible with having 'an axe to grind'; Virgil and Dante had plenty of axes on the grindstone; Dickens and George Eliot are often at their best as artists when they are grinding axes; and Flaubert is no exception. Unless there was grinding of axes, there would be very little to write about. Mr. Murry quotes a sentence of Gourmont which I have quoted myself: *ériger en lois ses impressions personelles, c'est le grand effort d'un homme s'il est sincère*. Well, Lawrence tried to do that, certainly, but to my mind he failed completely, and this book is the history of his failure. Lawrence simply did not know how. He had plenty of sensations, undoubtedly; no man of his time was more sensitive; but he could neither leave his sensations alone and accept them simply as they came, nor could he generalize them correctly. The false prophet kills the true artist.

Lawrence had the making of an artist, more than one might suppose from reading this book. Mr. Murry quotes with astonishing accuracy and justice—I do not believe that there is a single quotation in the book which is mutilated or unfair to the subject, and such justice is very rare in criticism—but it is not part of his intention to insist upon Lawrence's successes as a writer at those moments when Lawrence was not occupied with the fatal task of self-justification. Not only are there magnificent descriptions here and there, everywhere, throughout Lawrence's work, but there are marvellous passages—in nearly every book, I believe—of dialogue or narrative, in which Lawrence really gets out of himself and inside other people. There is a fine episode in the life of an elementary schoolmistress in *The Rainbow*; there are one or two remarkable dialogues in *Aaron's Rod*; and there is a short story called *Two Blue Birds* which has no relation to Lawrence's own emotional disease, and in which he states a situation which no one else has ever put. Mr. Murry is fully able to appreciate these achievements, but he is fairly enough not concerned with them in this book. But to me they indicate that Lawrence ought to have been a 'pure artist', but was impure. And I wonder also whether, had Lawrence been a success in this sense instead of a failure, Mr. Murry would have been so interested in him.

What Mr. Murry shows, and demonstrates with a terrible pertinacity throughout Lawrence's work, is the emotional dislocation of a 'mother-complex'. (It should show also how inappropriate is the common designation of 'Œdipus complex'.) And he makes clear that Lawrence was pretty well aware of what was wrong; and that Lawrence, throughout the rest of his life, was a strange mixture of sincerity or *clairvoyance* with self-deception—or rather with the effort towards self-deception. Lawrence's subsequent history, and the history of his novels, is accordingly a record of his various attempts to kid himself into believing that he was right to be as he was, and that the rest of the world was wrong. It is an appalling narrative of spiritual pride, nourished by ignorance, and possibly also by the consciousness of great powers and humble birth. Now, the 'mother-complex' of Lawrence does not seem to me in itself a sign of the times. I find it difficult to believe that a family life like that of Lawrence's parents is peculiar either to a particular class or to a particular age. Such family life, with such consequences to a sensitive child, can hardly have taken place only in the latter part of the nineteenth century. What is peculiar to the time is the way in which Lawrence tried to deal with his peculiarity. That is what is modern, and it seems to me to spring from ignorance.

When I use the word ignorance I am not contrasting it with something which is popularly called 'education'. Had Lawrence been sent to a public school and taken honours at a university he would not have been a jot the less ignorant; had he become a don at Cambridge his ignorance might have had frightful consequences for himself and for the world, 'rotten and rotting others'. What true education should do —and true education would include the suitable education for every class of society—is to develop a wise and large capacity for orthodoxy, to preserve the individual from the solely centrifugal impulse of heresy, to make him capable of judging for himself and at the same time capable of judging and understanding the judgments of the experience of the race. I do not think that the unfortunate initial experience of Lawrence's life led *necessarily* to the consequences that came. He would probably have been always an unhappy man in this world; there is nothing unusual about that; many people have to be unhappy in this world, to do without things which seem essential and a matter of course to the majority; and some learn not to make a fuss about it, and to gain, or at least to strive towards, a kind of peace which Lawrence never knew. He is to be grieved over and his faults are to be extenuated; but we can hardly praise a man for his failure. It is by the adoption of a crazy theory to deal with the facts, that Lawrence seems modern, and what I mean by 'ignorant'.

I may make this clearer by instancing a peculiarity which to me is both objectionable and unintelligible. It is using the terminology of Christian faith to set forth some philosophy or religion which is fundamentally non-Christian or anti-Christian. It is a habit towards which Mr. Lawrence has inclined his two principal disciples, Mr. Murry himself and Mr. Aldous Huxley. The variety of costumes into which these three talented artists have huddled the Father, the Son, and the Holy Ghost, in their various charades, is curious and to me offensive. Perhaps if I had been brought up in the shadowy Protestant under-world within which they all seem gracefully to move, I might have more sympathy and understanding; I was brought up outside the Christian Fold, in Unitarianism; and in the form of Unitarianism in which I was instructed, things were either black or white. The Son and the Holy Ghost were not believed in, certainly; but they were entitled to respect as entities in which many other people believed, and they were not to be employed as convenient phrases to embody any cloudy private religion. I mention this autobiographical detail simply to indicate that it is possible for unbelievers as well as believers to consider this sort of loose talk to be, at the best, in bad taste. The Holy Ghost does not figure in Mr. Murry's index of fictitious personages at the end of the book, but that surely is an oversight.

A better illustration of Lawrence's 'ignorance', and a fault which corrupts his whole philosophy of human relations—which is hardly anything *but* a philosophy of human relations and unrelations—is his hopeless attempt to find some mode in which two persons—of the opposite sex, and then as a venture of despair, of the same sex—may be spiritually united. As Mr. Murry spares no pains to show, the whole history of Lawrence's life and of Lawrence's writings (Mr. Murry tells us that it is the same history) is the history of his craving for greater intimacy than is possible between human beings, a craving irritated to the point of frenzy by his unusual incapacity for being intimate at all. His struggle against over-intellectualized life is the history of his own over-intellectualized nature. Even in his travels to more primitive lands, he could never take the crude peoples simply for what they are; he must needs always be expecting something of them that they could not give, something peculiarly medicinal for himself. He was looking for it there, just as he looked within the men and women he knew, without finding it. Other men and women have needs of their own. There is a passage from *Lady Chatterley's Lover* (one of the novels which I have not read) which Mr. Murry quotes very much to the point.

I held forth with rapture to her, positively with rapture. I simply went up in smoke. And she adored me. The serpent in the grass was sex. She somehow didn't have any; at least, not where it's supposed to be. I got thinner and thinner. Then I said we'd got to be lovers. I talked her into it. So she let me. I was excited, and she never wanted it. She adored me, she loved me to talk to her and kiss her: in that way she had a passion for me. But the other she just didn't want. And there are lots of women like her. And it was just the other that I *did* want. So there we split. I was cruel and left her.

Mr. Murry has analysed this passage so shrewdly that it is an impertinence to say much more; but I should like to be sure that it shocked Mr. Murry, as a confession, as deeply as it shocks me. Such complacent egotism can come only from a very sick soul, and, I should say, from a man who was totally incapable of intimacy. The girl was obviously in love with him, in the way appropriate to her youth and inexperience; and it was not good enough for Lawrence. What a pity that he did not understand the simple truth that of any two human beings each has privacies which the other cannot penetrate, and boundaries which the other must not transgress, and that yet human intimacy can be wonderful and life-giving: a truth well known to Christian thought, though we do not need to be Christians to understand it. And that the love of two human beings is only made perfect in the love of God.[1] These are very old and simple truths indeed. But Lawrence, as I believe Mr. Murry says, remembered the second injunction of the Summary of the Law and hoped to practise it without recognizing the first. And is not this same sad burden of the unsatisfactoriness of human relations wailed thinly by the corrupt characters in Mr. Murry's novels, as well as some of Mr. Huxley's? It is the old story that you cannot get a quart out of a pint pot; and the astonishing fact that you cannot even get a pint out of it unless you fill it. As if human love could possibly be an end in itself! And all these sad young men try to believe in a spectral abstraction called Life; yet the occasional whiffs of sepulchral high spirits wafted from their limbo are chillier than the gloom.

There remains, however, one book, which I have not read, but which I judge from Mr. Murry's account to be worthy of the importance which Mr. Murry assigns to it: *Fantasia of the Unconscious*. It would appear that in this book Lawrence reached his culmination, and that his subsequent work marks chiefly decline and collapse.

As Lawrence says, there is a great fascination in a completely effected 'idealism', that is, a completely achieved mental consciousness of our own natures. To this fascination the modern world is succumbing; this is, indeed, the distinguishing mark of the modern world—that which makes it modern.

Lawrence was more deeply involved in this process than any other man. It is

[1] To many human pairs, of course, common tastes, or a common interest, as in Tariff Reform or the enfranchisement of African natives, may appear an excellent substitute.

quite wrong, totally mistaken, to conceive of him as a sort of primitive emergence. He belonged, completely, to the modern world and its 'idealism'; the intensity of his revulsion against it is the index of the completeness of his identification with it. Where he differed from the vast majority of intellectuals and 'idealists' was that his ultra-sensitive organism was early aware of the fearful perils that lay along this seemingly inevitable road of complete mentality.

This seems to me important, sound and well put. Yet it would seem that Lawrence only differed from the 'vast majority of intellectuals' in his greater intellectual vision; in a fluctuating ability of diagnosis, without the further and total ability of prescription and régime. That, in my view, is only to be found—and only in our time with great difficulty if at all—in Christian discipline and asceticism. To this Lawrence could not and would not come; hence his relapse into pride and hatred.

One must, in considering a writer like Lawrence, confess what will be called one's prejudices, and leave the rest to the reader. I agree with Mr. Murry that there must have been a great deformed capacity for love in the man; he hungered and thirsted for love though he could not give it and could not take it. Mr. Murry's comparison and contrast of Lawrence with Jesus strikes cold upon my imagination, though I could have understood a comparison with Rousseau. Unwillingly in part, I admit that this is a great tragic figure, a waste of great powers of understanding and tenderness. We may feel poisoned by the atmosphere of his world, and quit it with relief; but we cannot deny our homage as we retire. A fateful influence he must have been upon those who experienced his power; I cannot help wondering whether Mr. Murry was not compelled to write his book in order to expel the demon from himself; and if so, I wonder whether Mr. Murry has succeeded.

Bibliography

ARNOLD, ARMIN, *D. H. Lawrence in America*, London, Linden Press, 1958. Includes an Appendix on the history of Lawrence's reputation in America and Europe, which briefly surveys criticism up to 1925; gives a year-by-year account of comment, 1926–53; and briefly summarizes 1954–8.

BEAL, ANTHONY, *D. H. Lawrence*, Edinburgh, Oliver and Boyd, 1961. Last chapter briefly surveys development of Lawrence's reputation, 1914–59.

BEEBE, MAURICE and TOMMASI, ANTHONY, 'Criticism of D. H. Lawrence: a Selected Checklist with an Index to Studies of Separate Works'. *Modern Fiction Studies*, v, No. 1, Spring 1959. An extensive list of items, concentrating mainly on 1950–8 as a supplement to Edward McDonald and William White (q.v.). (Further supplementation to Beebe and Tommasi will be found in Keith Sagar—q.v.)

DRAPER, R. P., *D. H. Lawrence*, New York, Twayne, 1964. Last chapter discusses the reputation and influence of Lawrence up to 1964.

DRAPER, R. P. 'A Short Guide to D. H. Lawrence Studies.' *Critical Survey*, ii, No. 4, Summer 1966. Surveys Lawrence criticism and scholarship, concentrating on recent work.

GREEN, MARTIN BURGESS, *The Reputation of D. H. Lawrence in America*, Ph.D. dissertation, University of Michigan, 1957. (University Microfilms, Ann Arbor, Michigan, 1966.) Summarizes the more important reviews and discussions of Lawrence in America, 1911–56.

MANLY, J. M. and RICKERT, E., *Contemporary British Literature*, London, Harrap, 1928. Lists studies and reviews, 1914–27.

MCDONALD, EDWARD D., *A Bibliography of the Writings of D. H. Lawrence*, Philadelphia, The Centaur Bookshop, 1925. Section on studies and reviews of Lawrence lists, in alphabetical order, contributions in books, 1914–25, and in periodicals, 1911–25.

MCDONALD, EDWARD D., *The Writings of D. H. Lawrence, 1925–1930: A Bibliographical Supplement*, Philadelphia, The Centaur Bookshop, 1931. As above, books and periodicals, 1925–31.

MOORE, HARRY T., *The Life and Works of D. H. Lawrence*, London, Allen and Unwin, 1951. Appendix A, 'Books About D. H. Lawrence', surveys very rapidly the history of Lawrence's reputation, 1914–51.

MOORE, HARRY T., *The Intelligent Heart*, New York, Farrar, Straus and

Young, 1955; revised ed., London, Penguin Books, 1960. Standard biography of Lawrence, including incidental references to the development of his reputation during his life-time.

MOORE, HARRY T., *The Achievement of D. H. Lawrence*, Edited in collaboration with F. J. Hoffman. Norman, University of Oklahoma Press, 1953. The Introduction surveys criticism and memoirs up to 1953.

NEHLS, EDWARD, *D. H. Lawrence, A Composite Biography*, 3 vols. Madison, University of Wisconsin Press, 1957–9. Collection of reminiscences by many different people who had contact with Lawrence at various stages of his life, interwoven with extracts from Lawrence's own writings and letters. Contains several incidental comments on his work, and is especially useful for material relating to the controversies over *The Rainbow*, *Lady Chatterley's Lover*, *Pansies* and the paintings.

POWELL, LAWRENCE CLARK, 'D. H. Lawrence and His Critics. A Chronological Excursion in Bio-bibliography', *Colophon*, 1940. Annotated annual list of some of the Lawrence criticism and biographical comment, 1925–39.

ROBERTS, WARREN, *A Bibliography of D. H. Lawrence*, Soho Bibliographies, London, Rupert Hart-Davis, 1963. Standard bibliography of Lawrence. Section A gives details of the editions of Lawrence's work, each entry concluding with a list of reviews (which is not, however, comprehensive). Section D, devoted to translations, gives some impression of the spread of Lawrence's reputation abroad. Section F lists books and pamphlets about Lawrence, 1924–61.

SAGAR, KEITH, *The Art of D. H. Lawrence*, Cambridge University Press, 1966. Useful bibliography which supplements Beebe and Tommasi (q.v.).

WHITE, WILLIAM, *D. H. Lawrence: A Checklist. Writings About D. H. Lawrence, 1931–1950*. Detroit, Wayne State University Press, 1950. Title self-explanatory.

WORTHEN, T. J., *The Reception in England of the Novels of D. H. Lawrence from* The White Peacock *to* Women in Love, Unpublished thesis, University of Kent, 1967. Detailed discussion, with ample quotation, of the development of Lawrence's reputation as a novelist up to *Women in Love*.

Index